THE
NEAR WEST

Medieval North Africa,
Latin Europe and the Mediterranean
in the Second Axial Age

Allen James Fromherz

EDINBURGH
University Press

Edinburgh University Press is one of the leading university presses in the UK. We publish academic books and journals in our selected subject areas across the humanities and social sciences, combining cutting-edge scholarship with high editorial and production values to produce academic works of lasting importance. For more information visit our website: www.edinburghuniversitypress.com

Edinburgh University Press Ltd
The Tun – Holyrood Road
12 (2f) Jackson's Entry
Edinburgh EH8 8PJ

First Published in hardback by Edinburgh University Press 2016

Typeset in 11/15 Adobe Garamond by
Servis Filmsetting Ltd, Stockport, Cheshire,
printed and bound in Great Britain by CPI
Group (UK) Ltd, Croydon CR0 4YY

A CIP record for this book is available from the British Library

ISBN 978 0 7486 4294 6 (hardback)
ISBN 978 1 4744 2640 4 (paperback)
ISBN 978 1 4744 1007 6 (webready PDF)
ISBN 978 1 4744 1008 3 (epub)

CONTENTS

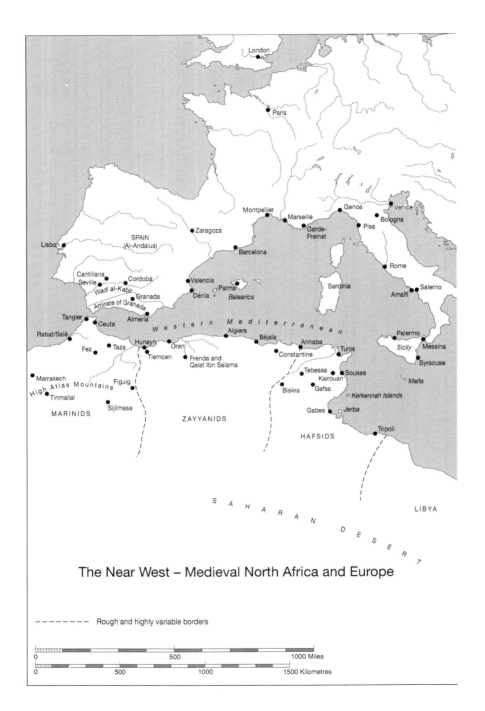

The Near West – Medieval North Africa and Europe

– – – – – – – Rough and highly variable borders

0	500	1000 Miles	
0	500	1000	1500 Kilometres

Constantinople

Ottoman Empire
(1359)

T U R K S

Konya

Athens

Crete

Cyprus

Baghdad

E a s t e r n   M e d i t e r r a n e a n

MAMLUKS
Damascus

Jerusalem

Alexandria

Gaza

Cairo

Siwa

MAMLUKS

River Nile

R e d   S e a

Madina

Yanbu al-Bahr

Jeddah
Mecca

PERSONAL NOTE AND
ACKNOWLEDGMENTS

This is a book that will tell stories about individuals who lived in the past; it seems only fair to briefly mention my own individual reasons for writing this book, beyond the simple pursuit of knowledge for its own sake. The reader should feel free to skip immediately to the introduction should this personal story not be of interest.

I was not born with any particular proclivity to study the Middle East or North Africa. I grew up in Polk County in the 1980s and 90s, a small place in rural Oregon. I am a descendant of German Catholics who came searching for a new promised land on wagon trains in the nineteenth century. My family went to the Episcopal Church, something that had to do with my parents and the 1960s and not feeling welcome with the mother church of my Dad's side of the family. There were stained-glass windows of log trucks. I was almost as far away as one could get from North Africa. As a college student interested in the Middle East, I was the first of the millennial generation, I was 21 during 9/11 and its aftermath.

I was part of a new wave of Middle Eastern and North African studies specialists and historians, a wave that has yet to fully crest. Although 9/11 looms in our collective past, it is not the focus of most of our work. In my position now as President of the American Institute of Maghrib (North African) Studies, an organization dedicated to the study of North Africa, I chair a grants committee that has seen almost a doubling in the number of applicants over the past several years. In fact, I had started college thinking I was mostly interested in a different subject. I used to view myself, despite the hopelessness of the pursuit in the academic job market, as a budding classicist, enthralled by Rome and interested in the histories of the Latin West. Through both the excellent mentoring of my professors (Gene Garthwaite and Dale Eickelman must be thanked here) and a desire for adventure in under-explored corners of history, I shifted to North Africa and found a home. I wrote a Dartmouth Honors Thesis on Ibn Khaldun (d. 1406), whose writings were, at the time, only known among specialists. Although now the likes of Mark Zuckerberg are recommending his writings, their depths continue to fascinate me and, I believe, continue to remain woefully underexplored by scholars everywhere.

My very first trip to the Middle East was to a historical birthplace of Arab civilization, Yemen, in 2002. I could already see the sad warnings of the end of stability in that magnificent country of astounding cultural diversity. My first long-term journey, however, was to Morocco where I lived for several years. I was there on a Fulbright Scholarship and then with support from various sources including the Royal Historical Society, which supported my research at St. Andrews. The American Institute for Maghrib Studies also assisted me. I also spent many months in Tunisia and lived there for a summer two years before the Jasmine Revolution. I also spent time teaching in Qatar, witnessing, with astonishment, the sheer pace of social, cultural and economic change in that part of the world and deciding, along with North Africa, to focus my research on that part of the world as well. Finally, I have visited and lived on the European side of the Mediterranean, leading study abroads to both Spain and Italy, overwhelmed on each visit by the magnificent beauty of the arts and architectural expressions shared between different faiths.

Since I began my journey into the world of the Western Mediterranean, I have felt both hope and despair, fear and belonging, both deep friendship, hospitality and, although hard to admit, some feelings of estrangement. These complex feelings, I soon learned, were not at all atypical. In fact, there was a whole genre of them, epitomized by the writings of Paul Bowles' *Sheltering Sky*, a book as much about America as about Morocco. At one time Bowles regularly visited the American school where I studied Arabic in Tangier, teasing the American students in the Arabic program. Although he was gone when I lived there for a summer in those 1970s dorms in 2004, it seemed he had only recently left us. Bowles died only five years before in 1999. He seemed to haunt corners of Tangier, a city of so many beginnings and endings, both geographically and emotionally. There are many reminders of a past before 9/11 and before the Casablanca Bombings and the interventions of George Bush, a past in which Tangier, ruled for a time by an international tribunal of different consulates, was the heart of an apparent age of cosmopolitanism and freedom. Throughout North Africa I vaguely "sensed" that romanticized, cosmopolitan era of relative freedom and self-exploration.

Ghosts of other Americans, expatriates who had found themselves here, before me, seemed to follow me through the suqs and into the stunning landscapes of Atlas Mountains and endless, wild beaches on Atlantic shores. Americans such as Tennessee Williams, Ginsberg, and Kerouac were both self-destroyed and self-enriched by terrible freedom in a "strange" land and the Moroccans such as Mohamed Choukri who worked with them, living and writing into this now-romantic past of both self-discovery and self-estrangement. I was not, however, satisfied to simply give in to the *anomie* and estrangement that, from Camus to Bowles, is regrettably at the heart of so much modern literature of Europeans and Americans in North Africa. Using my historical training, I wanted to understand the historical roots of this society. I knew that where there is seemingly inescapable contradiction, there is also, often, the secret, "hatch-door" of context. Sometimes this door is only seen when you move to a sufficient chronological distance.

Instead of looking only at recent ghosts of cosmopolitanism, cultural conflict and searchings for the soul, I saw evidence for common roots buried much deeper than I could have ever imagined. In the medieval walls and qasbahs and half-completed, Almohad monumental mosques of Rabat, deeper still in the manuscripts, the poetry, chronicles, the mellahs (Jewish quarters), madinas (medieval cities) and even the religious texts, was an era that is long-gone. This was also a time when Europe was in the midst of the Twelfth-Century Renaissance. England had a population that was growing to as much as 6 million in 1215. Italian cities were growing in wealth and independence. North Africa was very much a part of and a major cause of the Commercial Revolution and the Twelfth-Century Renaissance: eras coined by most medieval scholars to describe Europe almost exclusively. North Africa was point-edly left out. The point of this book, however, is not to suggest that we return to this era of shared North African and European history to solve the problems of the modern world.

Instead, if any contemporary lesson could be gained from this book, it is tentative. Perhaps if we can understand a period when both Europe and North Africa shared in a Golden Age in the midst of both conflict and sharing there may be an opening to reconsider the differences height-ened by colonialism, nationalism and modernity. The Almohad period and the twelfth century was an era that still forms the proud, Golden Age for Algerians, Tunisians and Moroccans, of Arabic and Berber speakers alike. This "Golden Age" of the medieval North African past, under the great Almoravid and Almohad empires, although as familiar to my Maghribi friends as the American Revolution is to us, has been neglected in most west-ern scholarship, especially scholarship in English. Yet that so-called Golden Age was also far more complex than the nationalist vision. Like the Golden Age of my own American invention, of Bowles and Burroughs and Choukri thriving in a tolerant Tangier, the realities of the medieval period, were far more interesting than I could have ever imagined.

I want to thank my mentors and teachers and my family. My colleagues at GSU, Hugh Hudson, MaryAnn Romski, Gayle Nelson, Michelle Brattain, Isa Blumi, Ghulam Nadri, Ian Campbell and many others, have been sup-portive. Vince Cornell, Rkia Cornell, Scott Kugle, Benny Hary and Roxani Margariti at Emory have been a great encouragement to me during my time in Atlanta. I want to thank the NEH Mediterranean Seminar and NYUAD Humanities Institute. Nicola Ramsey at EUP is one of the best editors in the field and I appreciate her patience, as well as that of Eddie Clark in the production department and James Dale, the editor who first proposed the project to me while I was completing *Ibn Khaldun, Life and Times*. Thanks also to Sue Dalgleish for her patient copy-editing. Although about a more recent era, Julia Clancy-Smith's volume, *Mediterraneans: North Africa and Europe in the Age of Migration*, was an inspiration. I owe a great deal to her guidance and support. I also want to thank Mary Rolison, Nelly van Doorn, Miriam Cooke, Gene Garthwaite, Dale Eickelman, Emily Gottreich, Philp Naylor, Louisa Burnham, Justin Stearns, Mike Ryan, Sharon Kinoshita, Ron

Messier, Kenneth Perkins, Brian Catlos and others for their support. I thank my graduate student Leah Kleinberger for assisting me. I am very grateful to Amira Bennison for her supportive and helpful comments on a draft of the text. I am completely responsible for any exisiting mistakes. I received support along the way by the American Institute for Maghrib Studies, Gerda Henkel Stiftung and internal grants from Georgia State University, including the Provost's research grant. I want to thank my mother Robin, father Allen and sisters Rebecca and Amy for their support. I write this in memory of Grandma Wright who traveled and explored so much. I thank William Tomlin, Glenn Faulk, Bill Crawley, Hugh Latta and Joe Maxwell for being wonderful friends.

INTRODUCTION:
NORTH AFRICA AND THE
MEDITERRANEAN PARADOX

This book tells a story of interaction between Berbers, Arabs, Latins, Muslims, Christians and Jews in North Africa and Latin Europe and across the Western Mediterranean. The book proposes medieval Western European and North African history were part of a common Western Mediterranean culture. It tells the history of North Africa and Europe through the eyes of Christian kings and Muslim merchants, emirs and popes, Sufis, friars and rabbis. It argues North Africa and Europe together experienced the Twelfth-Century Renaissance and the Commercial Revolution. When Europe was highly divided during the twelfth century, North Africa was enjoying the peak of its power, united under the Berber, Almohad Empire. In the midst of a commercial growth throughout the medieval period, North Africa and Europe also shared in a burst of spirituality and mysticism. Indeed, parallel developments in intellectual, religious and economic history in North Africa and Europe were so common, they cannot be considered purely accidental. This growth of spirituality occurred as representatives of Judaism, Christianity and Islam debated and defended their faiths, dreaming of conversion even as they shared the same rational methods. Growth of organized mysticism instigated a Second Axial Age in the history of religion. Sufis and Franciscans, followers of voluntary poverty, rubbed shoulders in the bustling markets of Tunis, Marrakech and Bèjaïa. Challenging the idea of a Mediterranean split between Islam and Christianity, the book shows how the

Maghrib (North Africa) was not a Muslim-Arab monolith, nor an extension of an exotic Orient. North Africa, not the Holy Land to the Far East, was the first place where Latin Europeans encountered the Muslim other and vice versa. At the same time, medieval North Africa was as diverse and complex as Latin Europe. North Africa was, in fact, an integral part of Western history.

Paradox of Sources

A mystery within a paradox is written into this book. It is a paradox of the book's sources. Due to the nature of our evidence, two very different, but parallel, histories of the relationship between medieval North Africa and Latin Europe could be written. One history, based on a superficial reading of some of the writings of Jewish, Christian and Muslim chroniclers and legists, monks and religious scholars, would tell a story of conquest, a story of conflict. It would tell the story in apocalyptic proportions of the dream of conversion. It would cast reason and rational thought, inherited from the classical past, as a mere means to an end: the transformation of the Western Mediterranean into a Sea of Christ or a Sea of Islam. For Jews, this story would be primarily about desperate attempts to avoid assimilation and conversion under majority rule. For Berbers and other ethnic minorities, it would be a history of assimilation into more dominant cultures. Focused only on a select number of sources, one could easily write a history focused on violence, pogrom, crusade, *jihad*, and of great religious wars. To say the least, gender minorities and homosexuality in this history would be extinguished from the scene or relegated to the role of distinguishing the clean and the unclean. Yet, as the title of the book "The Near West" suggests, North Africa, much of which is actually situated to the west of Western Europe, was an integral part of a common Mediterranean. Its inclusion also pulled the Mediterranean both to the Sahara and towards the Atlantic coast. North Africa was part of a cultural legacy that developed over the medieval period and peaked during a shared, Twelfth-Century Renaissance in commerce and spirituality. Contrary to most medieval scholarship that concentrates on the Twelfth-Century Renaissance in Europe, this Renaissance was also experienced in the lands of the Maghrib. This story remains highly relevant. A long, shared history between North Africa and Europe should give pause to current pronouncements of the "failure of multiculturalism" in Europe today.[1]

A different set of sources or a different look at the same sources can often yield a different story. There is, for instance, a history of poetic sources, of composite Muslim-Judeo-Christian or Arab-Latin-Berber art and architecture, a history of music, medicine and, to some extent, commerce; the religious or linguistic other is not so much an enemy to be annihilated as a co-conspirator in profit, a source of desire, and a partner in complex tragedy. Transmission and sharing of ideas, cultures, rational systems and artistic influences happened in the midst of conflict. Indeed, looking beyond battles and wars in isolation, such sharing often happens *because* of conflict and competition. Scholars of the artistic and poetic imagination in the medieval Mediterranean have remarked on a stubborn feature of the form and nature of their sources: even in the midst of bloody wars, reprisals and conflict between different faiths or groups, there was simultaneously an easy mixing of the cultures and cultural influences between those faiths.[2] The paradox of exchange in the midst of conflict was not limited to architecture and art.

Even historical writing itself, our main source for the political history of the period, was not immune to the mixing of cultures. The Mediterranean, that great corrupting sea, has also mixed up and amalgamated our sources, making them far more than simple chronologies of events. The sources, both written and artistic, that make up the basis for our knowledge of the medieval Mediterranean past contain within them paradoxes that would make a modern polemicist blush. At the same time, these sources should cause scholars to rethink the marginalized role of North Africa, the Berbers and Islam in the medieval histories of the Mediterranean.

The paradox in our evidence is not limited to some rare instances. The difference between poetry and art on one side and chronicle and religious writing on the other cannot be explained easily as simply a medieval fantasy of pure coexistence or violence. If it could, our ability to describe the nature of cross-cultural interactions in medieval Mediterranean history as a whole would still be very difficult, but far easier. One could argue there was a division, perhaps, between educated elite, wanting to maintain religious and cultural distinctions, and a common mass of sub-alterns, mixing more freely and pushing this into the public through art and taste and culture. Another option may be that art was seen differently from religion, that cosmopolitanism in art and poetry was allowed only figuratively, even in the midst of more strident religious conflict.³ One might also make a primarily economic argument, explaining religious fervor and conflict as simply a zero sum game of commercial dominance, a pragmatic means of securing scarce resources. Yet, as this book will show, the Commercial Revolution sparked a spiritual revolution, which benefited both Muslim and Christian, both European and North African shores. Again, one could easily divide between "classes" of clerics, merchants, and artists or poets, all with very different motivations but fundamentally driven by economic realities. Instead, the sources do not make it that easy.

There is an intriguing reason for this lack of ease: the paradox of a cross-cultural Western Mediterranean in the midst of conflict exists not only between the sources but also within them. One example of this inner conflict in the sources was the geographer Al-Idrisi, a twelfth-century Muslim scholar born to an elite Ceuta family from northern Morocco; he explored the world, wrote about Iceland and Lake Victoria, and deep voyages by Berber and Arab navies in the Atlantic. Although he claimed Arab blood, he descended from the Hammudids, the great Berber dynasty that controlled traffic between Tangier, Ceuta and Algecerias across the Straits of Gibraltar.

The prince of an exiled and defeated Berber dynasty, Al-Idrisi worked for the court of the Norman King Roger II of Sicily, building the Christian King a massive silver planetary sphere and a map that was copied by Europeans for centuries. The map described the cities and ports of North Africa and much of the known world. He detailed especially their suitability as ports and their economic resources. Even as Al-Idrisi spoke of his patron, the "Great King" Roger, his works seemed full of praise for what were once the great cities of the Muslim Zirid, and Hammadid Berber rulers in the North African cities that his Christian king was determined to conquer. The glories of the Zirid court, the magnificent defenses and the gold colored arches of the city of Al-Mahdiyya, according to Al-Idrisi, dumbfounded his Christian patron when he entered the city in conquest. This pride existed despite the fact it was the Zirids who defeated Al-Idrisi's family, the Hammudids, and exiled them to Ceuta on the northern Moroccan coast.⁴ There was also Ibn Khaldun (d. 1406), who, although he claimed pure Arab ancestry, wrote perhaps the most important history of the Berber peoples. He worked for Berber rulers in the cities to appease both Arab and Berber tribes in the countryside.

Sometimes, the very same chronicler or monk or Muslim judge who wrote of the religious other, of the apocalypse, of the glories of crusade and *jihad*, was also the poet who wrote love triangles between Muslim, Christian and Jew, between Berbers and Arabs. The anti-Berber, anti-Muslim or anti-Christian polemicist who railed against the "other" could just as easily have a mixture of Berber, Arab, Christian, Muslim and Jewish blood.[5] The Muslim Berber king (such as Tamim bin Badis) who fights against the infidel could often be the very same poet who wrote freely in verse, describing his desire for a young Christian maiden parading through the streets of Tunis. Likewise, a Christian, Castilian king who just conquered Muslim territory might build a throne room, an extension of himself, decorated with Arabic calligraphy and the art of Mudejars, Muslims who remained in Christian lands after Christian conquest. Pedro I of Seville and his Alcazar Palace was one of many examples of this.[6] Sworn enemies praise the prowess and tragic circumstances of the other. We can only begin to explain the complex contradictions of the medieval Mediterranean if we first reveal the individuals in whose souls and experiences these contradictions are housed and in whose writings they are made manifest. While the modern tendency is often to contextualize and categorize the medieval past according to language, ethnicity, religion or culture, these categories can only go so far when it comes to the culture and the chronicles of the medieval past. Once the screen in front of a first reading of sources is lifted, the ambiguities of the Mediterranean and of Mediterraneans, sometimes absent from legal or religious writings, are laid bare.

Despite the importance of interactions between North Africans and the Latin West, European historians have often ignored or underestimated the contributions of North Africa to the common history of the Mediterranean, favoring stories of East versus West that leave out North Africa and that go back to the philosophy of Hegel in the nineteenth century.

Orientalizing North Africa in Western Historiography

In *The Philosophy of History*, G. W. F. Hegel (d. 1831) set the tone for subsequent European works on the broad strokes of world history. Although identifying the origins of "the West" in "the East", he made Protestant Europe, especially his own nineteenth-century Germany, the ultimate destination and apotheosis of the historical spirit.

> The history of the world travels from East to West, for Europe is absolutely the end of history. Asia is the beginning . . . Here rises the outward physical Sun, and in the West it sinks down: here consentaneously rises the Sun of self-consciousness, which diffuses a nobler brilliance.[7]

Although many modern scholars and many modern events would disprove Hegel and even his description of Europe and its culture forming "the end of history," the assumption remained that most of the "brilliance" in human culture moved from East to West. It was the East, after all, where the great monotheistic faiths were born. Later, both Baghdad and Constantinople (which went from being part of the West to part of the East with the splitting of the Roman Empire) saved Europe from the Dark Ages and preserved the classical traditions. Scholars have recently disputed this common assumption, indicating the central importance of an East "before European hegemony." The Indian Ocean and Asia has held the vast majority of the world's population and though scholars of world history are increasingly understanding the rise of Europe not as the "end of history," but as one periphery of a larger *oikoumene*, or "known world," interconnected by trade, current scholarship still often assumes that much of the movement of ideas, cultures, religious influences and trade occurred East to West or later, West to East. In the process of locating all that was influential to the origin of Europe in the East, the Near South and Near West – North Africa, and the continent of Africa as a whole – are left out of the migration of "world spirit". Hegel relegated North Africa to a traditional position as a peripheral tributary on the greater river of world history flowing from East to West. Even more so, however, North Africa, dominated by Islam, was thereby isolated from the great civilizational developments in "world spirit" that he saw fundamentally centered in the West. Although once a part of the West, after Islam, it could not participate in the great dialectic that Hegel saw as the center of his philosophy of spirit. Only Christianity, according to Hegel's philosophy, could link the realms of substance and spirit through the embodied God-head of Christ. Thus, long before Pirenne, Hegel created the intellectual foundations in his philosophy of history for the splitting of the Mediterranean, an ideological chasm created as much by philosophy as by actual history.[8]

Yet the flow from North Africa to Europe was far from a tributary or a mild cross-current, hampered somehow by the "barbarity" of the "Barbary, Berbers" in the mountains and desert who are among the most neglected peoples in all of English language historiography. North to south, northeast to southwest or southwest to northeast interactions were a primary means through which cultures in the Latin West, centered in the Western Mediterranean, and the medieval Maghrib, developed conceptions of themselves in contrast to the "Barbary" or "Saracen" or "Rumi."[9] Recent research has shown the vibrant level of trade and material cultural interactions between North Africa, Europe and Al-Andalus throughout the medieval period. Indeed, new academic working groups including the Spain North Africa Project are dedicated to this interaction.

Far from it being "no historical part of the World" with "no movement or development to exhibit,"[10] North Africa in the form of the Berber empires, the Almoravids and the Almohads, rose as a dominant player in the history of the Western Mediterranean. Far from Hegel's contention that "Historical movements in it – that is in its northern part [North Africa] – belong to the Asiatic or European World," North Africa was, and the culture it shared with Western Europe were, part of an important vertical and diagonal stream of political, social and cultural interactions, conflicts, encounters and influences.

The "East", indeed the very name Orientalism, suggested the temptations and luxuries of far off lands and Hegel's origin of spirit of human history. North Africa was itself often too easily "orientalized." The interactions between Europe and North Africa were ignored in favor of earlier, more exotic, Eastern origins. Yet North Africans, in adopting ideas from the East, also adapted and developed ideas of their own, before transferring them to Europe. These influences came through a Near West (Morocco goes further west than Iberia), a very Near West: the Maghrib was a land visible from Gibraltar or Sicily; the North African shore has always been a tempting target for trade, conquest, slavery and exchange. Many North Africans, especially Berbers, have, to this day, maintained a separate and distinct identity from the Arab East. The Mzabi Berber Ibadis, for instance, in the Mzab Valley of Algeria, created an exclusive zone of trade and community practices that lasted well into the twentieth century. For the most part, however, acculturation went both ways, with Berbers influencing Arabs and vice versa.

Throughout many of the mountains of Morocco, Berber is still spoken as the dominant language and is now being taught in schools. There are potentially countless examples of Maghribi cultural distinctiveness. North Africa, despite more than a millennium of Islamic influences from the East, continues to display its own culture, to not be simply an extension of the Orient. Yet, North Africa was also the first and closest place Europeans orientalized.

Just as North Africa was to Europe's south and west, Europe was also North Africa's near north. Even as movements East to West and West to East have been chronicled between Charlemagne and Harun Al-Rashid, Florence and Baghdad, Venice and the East, the Crusades in the Levant, movements, far more frequent and easy between North and South, and South and North in the Western Mediterranean remain generally neglected, especially in English-language scholarship. This book does not mean to suggest that East to West influences did not happen or were less important than they have been described. Rather, it proposes that movement of ideas and peoples and commerce should be seen through the prism of a mutual acculturation between both Berber and Arab culture that is still occurring to this day in North Africa. The Near West and Near South (North Africa), not just the Near East, should be considered a major contribution to the Western Mediterranean's historical development.[11]

Even works on Al-Andalus, Muslim Spain, have seemed to suggest that cultural brilliance jumped straight from the Islamic East (Damascus of 'Abd Al-Rahman and the Arab Umayyad rulers) to the Andalusi West (Al-Andalus), magically bypassing North Africa almost entirely.[12] For many, the accepted wisdom remains that North Africa divided the Mediterranean and pushed power to the north of Europe. Robert Kaplan's *The Revenge of Geography* summarized this limited view,

> While Portugal and Spain were the early beneficiaries of this Atlantic trade – owing to their protruding peninsular position – their pre-Enlightenment societies, traumatized by the proximity of (and occupation by) North African Muslims, lost ground eventually to the Dutch, French, and English in the oceanic competition. So just as Charlemagne's Holy Roman Empire succeeded Rome, in modern times northern Europe has now succeeded southern Europe with the mineral-rich Carolingian core winning

out in the form of the European Union: in no small measure because of geography.[13]

Recently, however, the Islamic world has been seen as more than merely a source of "trauma" and the Mediterranean and studies of the Sea as a whole, not as a place divided between Islamic East and Christian West, have gained in popularity.

Most histories, however, still focus on Europe and the East, the "Orient," Europe and the Crusades of the Levant are a primary focus of European and even World histories, leaving North Africa as the sideshow.[14] The Western Mediterranean from a North African perspective remains largely neglected. New studies since 2010, however, are revealing surprises. Scholars have shown, for instance, that after the Muslim conquests, the Byzantine cities of North Africa, far from collapsing, remained vibrant trading centers. Also, evidence of material exchange was significant in textiles, silks and ivory. Much work, however, remains to be done on North Africa in a Mediterranean context.[15]

Although scholars have traditionally located the birth of the Commercial Revolution and the Renaissance in the city-states of Italy, southern France or Iberia, historians of the broader Mediterranean have especially neglected the North African city as a locus of commercial and intellectual activity. Bringing medieval North Africa into the center of Mediterranean history, where it very much belongs, should shift basic assumptions about the nature of the Sea. The extent of northeast-southwest and southeast-northwest diagonal interaction across the Western Mediterranean showed that the Mediterranean was not split in two by Islam.

Neither Muhammad nor Charlemagne

The idea of a Mediterranean split between Christian Europe and Muslim North Africa was most famously articulated in the great Belgian historian Henri Pirenne's book, *Mohammed and Charlemagne*. In this book he argued that the "Arab" conquests split the Mediterranean in two and pushed Western civilization northwards; this had a major impact in revisionist scholarship. Entire volumes have been devoted to questioning the Pirenne thesis or defending it.[16] The coming of Muhammad created the conditions for Charlemagne. The main problem with this thesis when it comes to the Mediterranean, however, was that neither Muhammad nor Charlemagne was particularly close to the particular historical, cultural and economic concerns exisiting in either North Africa or Europe in the early medieval period.

To say the least, the debate about the divisiveness of Islam has a deep relevance to current maelstrom in countries such as France and Belgium about the compatibility of Western European and North African, Muslim culture. As the historian Patrick Geary has noted, the medieval period was especially important to European nation-states in their construction of their myths of nation, or myths of ethnic or linguistic national identity.[17]

This identity was often seen in contrast to one of the closest "others" possible: North Africans or Maghribis. In *Medieval Cities, Their Origins and the Revival of Trade*, Pirenne argued that after Muhammad, European cities were forced to build their own independent trading systems further north, divorced from the "closed" Mediterranean. North African cities and commerce were barely mentioned. Beyond early commerce, however, the twelfth century was also a period of renaissance intellectually and culturally. This Renaissance came out of both conflict and encounter between north and south shores of the Western Mediterranean.

Shared Commercial and Spiritual Histories

Far from being split into separate halves of the Mediterranean, medieval North Africans and Europeans shared parallel developments in understanding God, developments that, through debate, influenced one another but grew from the same, Mediterranean-wide causes. For example, during the twelfth century, height of the Commercial Revolution, both Latins and North Africans almost simultaneously embraced a new ideal of voluntary poverty. From the Franciscan movement in Europe to a burst in Sufism in North Africa, the pursuit of asceticism defined the age as much as the wealth of the period. On both sides of the Sea, new and profound explorations of meaning of the individual soul began, and they began around the same time.

Concomitant with this spiritual revolution in both North Africa and Europe was an intellectual one: instead of the religions of Islam, Christianity and Judaism developing theologies solely in spite of one another, all three religions were transformed by a renewed concentration on both reason and ascetic mysticism and the contemplative path of the individual soul was brought about, at least in part, by their interaction and competition. From Petrarch to Ibn Tufayl, from Abu Madyan to St. Francis and the *Zohar* of Jewish mysticism, the medieval Western Mediterranean became the nursery of an increasingly individualized understanding of the soul. The collective and formal, social adherence to a religion remained, but a new and, ultimately, more powerful stream became the lifeblood of all three faiths. In the midst of so much mixing and opportunism, in the midst of the exchange of mercenaries, merchants and missionaries, in the midst of a commercial explosion and the growth and fall of potential, but failed, empires and dynasties, from the Almohads to the Aragonese, there emerged a new religiosity based on poverty before fortune, sacrifice before success. Out of the medieval Western Mediterranean, in both Sufis and Friars Minor, traditionalists and rationalists, we see evidence for a Second Axial Age: a simultaneous revolution in the realm of spirit in all major religious traditions of the Mediterranean.

The Mongol invasions of the thirteenth century and other great ruptures, such as the plague, Crusades in the East, and even growth of neo-Confucianism in medieval China (even in Confucianism there emerged a more individualistic approach to a religion defined by social obligations to family), were important contributions to this worldwide revolution of spirituality. However, interactions between and developments within and between North Africa and Europe were, in many ways, a primary locus of spiritual transformation. The growth of the individual soul as its subjection to both spiritual and rational discipline in the North African and European West not only impacted the medieval period. Later, when the West – both the Christian West in Spanish Americas and the Muslim West in Morocco's expansion into Africa – came to conquer much of the world, this mystical legacy was spread far abroad.

This book tells the first part of this world historical transformation, locating a high tide of the Second Axial Age squarely, if not exclusively, in the twelfth century, mid-point between the first Muslim conquests in the seventh century to, roughly, the first half of the fifteenth century in the Western Mediterranean. Although stories for both earlier and later centuries will be told, the bulk of material will be from the twelfth century, a period when both

Latin Christian Europe and Arabo-Berber Almohad North Africa were fairly evenly matched and when the Commercial Revolution and Renaissance of the Twelfth Century was at its height both in Europe and North Africa. This book ends with the fourteenth century seen through the eyes of Ibn Khaldun (d. 1406), before the fall of Granada and the discovery of a new West. Rather than being a marginal footnote or simply the place of transmission from a superior East (*mashriq*), North Africa and North Africans are both scenes and dramatis personae of this great historical drama. At its roots, this story, the story of the emergence of the Western Mediterranean and the "West," was as much a North African story as it was a European one.

Limits of the Medieval Western Mediterranean

For the purposes of this book, the medieval Western Mediterranean was a cultural and geographical zone that included lands and ports bordering the sea from the western coast of modern-day Italy, Sicily, Tunisia, Algeria, Morocco, Spain and France. Yet some cities and places distant from the Western Mediterranean geographically could become close to it culturally – or at least be heavily influenced by the Sea. Following David Abualfia's notion of a larger Mediterranean, a Mediterranean that existed beyond strict, geographical categories, Marrakech is shown in the book as a city that became as much a Western Mediterranean city as an Atlantic or African center, despite being hundreds of miles from the sea.[18]

The Western Mediterranean is surrounded by diverse lands with many roots of what seemed, on simple analysis, to be completely different civilizations. Yet these roots often intermingled at different times. The medieval period was certainly one of those times. Western Europe and western North Africa (the Maghrib) combined, converged and tangled around the Western Mediterranean in the medieval period. Although opening with scenes in specific cities, Rome, Bèjaïa, Tunis, Marrakech, the book does not limit itself to these places, but shows connections between them, like trees tangled in a densely rooted forest. Exploring the history of these tangled roots, this book opens in twelfth-century Bèjaïa, a city on the north eastern coast of present-day Algeria.

1

BÈJAÏA:
INTRODUCING NORTH AFRICA, LATIN
EUROPE AND THE MEDITERRANEAN

The entire Mediterranean was his classroom. Bright-eyed and curious, the youth from the Italian port of Pisa roamed for his first time through the bustling streets and markets of the North African port of Bèjaïa, also known as Bougie. This commercial city in the northeast of Algeria, only a few hundred miles southwest of Sardinia and almost directly south of Marseille, gave the French their word "Bougie," candle, after the fine, tapered wax made and traded from there. Even as Europe's candlelight, essential for monastic scholarship in the dark northern winters, was made possible by Bèjaïa, Leonardo Fibonacci's time with the mathematicians of Bèjaïa would soon illuminate far more.

The name Bèjaïa referred to a Berber tribe from the region of the same name. The city is now the bustling capital of the region of Kabylia, a province that has maintained a largely self-professed Berber (*Taqbaylit*), as opposed to Arab, or French identity to this day. Indeed, the surrounding countryside was heartland of the "Berber Spring," an uprising against Arabization in the 1980s. The city in the mid twelfth century had a distinctly cosmopolitan character. In the time of Fibonacci, Berber, Arabic and medieval Italian as well French or Catalan and Castilian were spoken in its markets. Andalusi Berbers were especially numerous, carrying on a trade with Muslim Spain that had linked Bèjaïa to Europe for centuries. They maintained contacts with their extended tribe and families back in North Africa. For instance, before the Almohads, the Berber Zirids, had ruled both around Tunis and in Al-Andalus, and engaged in bustling trade. In terms of political power, Fibonacci's Bèjaïa was then tenuously under the control of the vast and powerful Almohad Empire. Although Arabs comprised part of their army and administration and many claimed Arab blood, the Almohads were primarily Berbers. They were not primarily from the Kabylia, but originated mostly among the Masmuda Berbers of the High Atlas Mountains in Morocco. This coming of the Almohads corresponded with the Commercial Revolution.

The Commercial Revolution of the Twelfth Century, a great increase in trade and commerce, was often associated only with the northern half of the Mediterranean and, perhaps, Egypt.[1] Yet the Commercial Revolution also occurred in North Africa. The alum for the dying of cloth in Europe came from Bèjaïa and it came often at a hefty price. But North Africa contributed far more than raw goods. It also shared with Europe some of most advanced spiritual ideas.

Shadhilis and Franciscans

A growth in commerce was accompanied by religious reform and an embrace of voluntary poverty and mysticism on all sides of the Mediterranean. Historians of medieval Europe have studied the foundation of the Franciscan and Dominican orders in the midst of this commercial revival. Less well known was the link between the commercial wealth, mysticism and asceticism in North Africa. Bèjaïa, as with other cities on the Mediterranean rim, was a great hub of commerce, was similarly a great center of religious and spiritual fervor within Islam. Abu Madyan (1115–98), one of the greatest Sufis of North Africa, would have walked the streets of this port, followed by numerous disciples. He was called the "Shakyh of Shaykhs" and the "Great Nurturer." Even as the Almohads established an empire of unity in this world, he asked questions such as "What is true unity (*tawhid*)?" and, "What is the Secret of the Secret?"[2] These questions would be asked over and over again, both by political forces, such as the Almohads, and Abu Madyan's many spiritual successors. His many disciples influenced the great Sufi scholar Ibn 'Arabi who traveled east, spreading ideas and ideals of spiritual unity from the Maghrib (North Africa) throughout the world. Ibn 'Arabi, traveling in his early life through the Western Mediterranean from Al-Andalus to Fez and Tunis, reacted against the prosperity of his surroundings and spoke of poverty or self-sufficiency found not in material goods or in wealth but in God.[3] He was inspired by the ancient practice of the *zahid*. A *zahid* was an ascetic, a voluntary renouncer of the goods of this world. They often lived as hermits in caves. The *zahid* had not only spiritual authority but also de facto political power over worldly rulers. Ibn 'Arabi's uncle, a *zahid*, reminded the powerful Sultan of Tlemcen, a city to the west of Bèjaïa, "You are a bowl filled with dirt. You ask me about your clothes while you are responsible for all the injustice that your subjects are suffering!"[4]

There were a great number of these Sufi ascetics in North Africa at this time. Some, such as the Sufi saint Al-Shadhili, came to have a great influence on the future course of Islamic history and created great orders by moderating their asceticism to appeal to merchants. The Shadhili order is still popular throughout the world from Sri Lanka to India and even in the contemporary, English-speaking community of Muslim Sufi converts. Although he started life as a wealthy son of a businessman from Ceuta, near Tangier, Abu Al-Hasan Al-Shadhili (d. 1256) became Sufi master and founder of a great order that still operates in various forms throughout the Islamic world. He taught that instead of searching for treasures of gold, one should seek "God's treasure." Accordingly, "the mystical sciences are garnered treasures." Although Islamic mysticism had been around for several centuries, Al-Shadhili attempted to form a consensus between elite and popular movements and to seek poverty and nearness to God beyond superficial displays of asceticism. Interestingly, Al-Shadihili was unlike some wandering saints who sought learning in the East and remained there. Al-Shadhili went seeking a true *qutb* or "pole" of mystical Islam in Baghdad. When he made it to Baghdad, however, the teacher there told him to turn around, to return to the Muslim West, the Maghrib, and seek guidance from Ibn Mashish, a great Sufi who retreated to the mountains near Tangier.[5] The Maghrib, the Muslim West, the story seemed to say, could be as much of a destination as the Muslim East for those seeking inspiration.

Around the same time, St. Francis, reacting to the riches of his own father, a merchant in Assisi, Italy went to war and became disillusioned with this world around 1204. He defenestrated his family's wealth, throwing his father's coins out of the window. He was inspired by the Gospel (Matthew 10: 9–10) passage saying none of God's disciples should, "keep gold or silver or money in their belts, nor have a wallet for their journey, not two tunics, nor shoes, nor staff." Many of the barefooted Friars Minor were at the forefront of evangelism. They went readily to North Africa. Some friars even went to North Africa to actively seek martyrdom, provoking the Almohad authorities, often themselves dependent on the protection of Christian mercenaries, through public blasphemy of the Prophet Muhammad. Thus, by the end of the Almohad period, there were poor mystics from both Christianity and Islam, contrasting their poverty with the wealth in the streets of the bustling Bèjaïa market. There was a new competition – not in the hoarding of wealth, but in displaying holy poverty.

Commercially and politically, by the time of Fibonacci, Bèjaïa had grown from its humble beginnings to a great prize. Almohad power, enforced from some distance, did not go entirely unchallenged. The rival Muslim Almoravid Banu Ghaniya regularly harassed the port, coveted by Muslims and Christians alike. In 1185, these recalcitrant Almoravid remnants even took the city briefly from the Almohads. The Almoravids, although they had transformed into great seafarers, actually started as Saharan Muslim Berber nomads, originally from the desert. They once were the great power in North Africa and Al-Andalus. It was only after their defeat by the Almohads in the 1140s that they had moved from the sands to the seas and to a Western Mediterranean island enclave on Majorca. Christians and their navies also captured the city on different occasions, hoping to turn it into an outpost for trade. Despite their sometimes-tenuous hold on this major trading outpost, the Berber Empire of the Almohads was still, without much doubt, the major power of the Western Mediterranean in the second half of the twelfth century. Surprisingly, much of Almohad history, as with much of Berber history, remains unwritten in English. Their contributions to the historical development of both shores of the Mediterranean remain underestimated or simply unmentioned. There has been a special neglect of the Berbers and North Africa, especially in history written in English. This oversight perhaps originated as early as the medieval period itself, in the Latin sources available to scholars of the medieval West.

Misunderstanding the Maghrib

Medieval chroniclers, themselves men of the Church writing in Latin, and, on the North African side, men educated in Islamic jurisprudence in Arabic accounts, often saw religious affiliation first, then language and culture. Faith was often a primary means of describing the other in chronicles if not in everyday life. North Africans were called Moors or Saracens by medieval Latin sources. Almost all Europeans, regardless of the diversity of medieval Christendom, were called Rumi (Roman or Byzantine) or *ifranj* or even, confusingly, *majus* (Persian magi) by Arab, Berber or Arabo-Berber chroniclers writing in Arabic. Also, instead of seeing the importance of distinctions and interactions between Berbers and Arabs, many Latin medieval sources called them all simply "Saracens" or "Moors."[6] Still today some modern scholars speak of medieval and early medieval North Africa under "Arab" control after "Arab" conquests, even though only a small proportion of the region was Arab or Arabized. Some medievalists, perhaps wanting to avoid the word "Saracen," have inaccurately identified all North Africans as "Arabs."[7] Even worse, perhaps, are some Arabists themselves who have developed the misleading phrase, the "Arab Conquest," suggesting that, soon after the rise of Islam, the pre-existing cultures of North Africa simply vanished into a massive, monochromatic blob of Arabization that could be neatly categorized on maps and in histories. North African contributions to Islamic culture are often minimized in favor of identifying the East as the true heart of everything Islam contributed to human civilization. Thus, V. V. Bartold, although rightly respected for his work on Persia and Central Asia, could still write dismissively of North Africa.

> North Africa and Spain did not contribute anything original but gradually accepted the systems elaborated in Hither Asia which were considered during a long time as absolutely unchangeable. In North Africa the unprogressive Malakite School became prominent and many scholars have attributed to this fact the cultural decadence of that part of the Mussulman world.[8]

Although Bartold's scholarship has been updated, some of his attitude towards North Africa as a much lesser player, on the periphery of the Islamic world, remains. Instead, the cultural and linguistic diversity of North Africa was far more complex than a single, linguistic label or school of Islam (Malikism) could express. At no point in its history was the Maghrib (North Africa) a homogenous extension of eastern Islam on the southern underbelly of Europe. North Africa's complexity reflected the diversity of the North. Diverse groups of Berbers from Marrakech to Awdagust (in the Sahara) to Tripoli changed most of the history of North Africa and had a major influence on countries throughout the Western Mediterranean in the medieval period; the sources of their history were not written extensively in Berber, but in Arabic or in the languages of European city states who were their trading partners.

The North African Almohad Empire had a major impact on even hostile European views of Islam. In addition to the Prophet Muhammad, polemicists and religious artists demonized a twin, a ruler they called "Miramolin" from the Arabic for "Prince of Believers", *Amir al Mu'min*, often used as the title of the ruler of the Almohads. Although derogatory, with this reference to "Miramolin," the Almohads were effectively promoted on par with the Prophet Muhammad in the worldview of Christians in the Mediterranean. Conveniently, the first Caliph of the Almohads was also called 'Abd "Al-Mu'min" or, for European writers, also the feared and fiercesome "Miramolin."

Indeed, this attempt to find one single representative of North Africa, whether as the "Moor" or his leader "Miramolin" may have reflected European frustration or misunderstanding of the diversity of North Africa itself. Even under the Almohad Empire, the first polity to unite all of North Africa in history, North Africa did not become a homogenous entity. The deep diversity of North Africa, both before and after the coming of Islam, continues to be misunderstood to this day. The importance of Berber culture and language in North Africa is still evident, especially in rural, desert or mountainous regions. Berbers from the Atlas Mountains of Morocco speak *Tashelhit* Berber as their main tongue and Berber has recently been recognized as a national language to be taught in Moroccan schools. Further north, in the Central Atlas, *Tamazight* Berber is spoken and several other language variations are found in Algeria. Ancient communities of Berbers are traditionally found as far to the east as the Siwa Oasis in western Egypt. Unlike the great port cities where acculturation into Arabic was the strongest, the great mountain ranges such as the Atlas or the deserts were where most Berbers and Berber language thrived. Berbers in the mountains or other remote areas were only slightly acculturated by Arabization. The Atlas Mountains of the Masmuda Berbers, for instance, loomed on the horizon over their recently captured capital city of Marrakech, which the Almohads finally captured in 1147 after streaming down from those very mountains. Mountains often served as nearly impenetrable natural barriers and hideouts, allowing Masmuda Berbers to maintain separate language and culture.

The Importance of the Almohads

After taking Marrakech and consolidating their power over the whole swath of North Africa, the Almohad Berbers under Ibn Tumart and 'Abd Al-Mu'min in the mid twelfth century had accomplished what no other power had achieved: even the Romans failed to really control most of North Africa. Roman client kings could never penetrate and unify the great mountainous spine of the Maghrib. These Almohads, in contrast, were the first to subdue the fractious tribes of North Africa and petty kings of Southern Spain. In this way, Almohad Berbers, speaking both Berber and Arabic, dominated the twelfth-century Western Mediterranean all the way from Marrakech to Seville to Libya during a time of great spiritual, commercial and political upheaval throughout the Western Mediterranean and the wider world.[9]

The great twelfth-century Almohad Empire, of which Bèjaïa became a part, was an expression of a great religious and political dream of what Almohads called *tawhid*, the absolute unity of God and God's community on earth. Although often relegated to a footnote in the history of the Mediterranean, the Almohads were founded on a successful combination of Arab Islam and Berber traditions and councils of rule. The Berbers, especially through the great Berber empires and dynasties, had a major and underestimated impact on Western Mediterranean economic, intellectual and cultural history.

Fibonacci, for example, would have almost certainly known about Almohad power and naval prowess on the Mediterranean. Saladin in Egypt pleaded for Almohad naval help against the crusaders. The Almohad admiral, Ahmad of Sicily, was renowned throughout the Great Sea and the Almohads, although dealing with typical problems of civil strife and a somewhat heavy reliance on the massive army of the Caliph, their ruler, seemed settled into the practical methods of governing their Empire. What made the Almohads amazingly powerful was the combination of control over the seas and the nearly unconquerable mountains that formed the spine of North Africa and acted as a great natural fortress.

Most importantly, by becoming a dominant force in the Western Mediterranean in the twelfth century, the Almohads caused a cultural and political rupture. It was not incidental that this rupture happened just as the medieval West, the European side of the Western Mediterranean and north to the Flemish and Champagne fairs, was experiencing the Commercial Revolution and the Twelfth-Century Renaissance. The Maghrib, finally united under the Almohad Empire, which also spanned the Mediterranean Sea, was very much a part of the Commercial Revolution and the Renaissance of the Twelfth Century experienced throughout the West.[10]

The Almohads started small with strict and revolutionary ideology that seemed most unlikely to prevail against the powerful reigning Empire of the Almoravids, those originally desert Berbers who were wealthy and prosperous with gold from Saharan trade. The charismatic founder and future "impeccable" Almohad Mahdi Ibn Tumart, called the "tent pole between earth and heaven," had visited Bèjaïa in 1117, before Fibonacci.[11] Yet, like many of this period, he was much less interested in trade than in spiritual reform. He was none too different from other, increasingly notorious, clerics with small groups of followers. Ibn Tumart entered the vibrant and diverse trading and port city seeing a hodgepodge of corrupting cultural influences. Originally a Berber himself but traveling back from the East with a new vision of true Islam, he now saw Bèjaïa as a transformed man. It was then under the rule of a Berber dynasty called the Hammadids, according to Ibn Tumart, a dynasty in a state of decadence and luxury. Bèjaïa suddenly seemed almost "pagan" to him, even as he witnessed Berber practices and traditions that he must have encountered on his initial journey to the East. He was especially concerned with the enforcement of what he saw as proper gender roles, a concern that will be a theme throughout this book, a concern that came to justify Almohad conquest of their effeminized rivals, the Almoravids. Men in Bèjaïa, according to Ibn Tumart, were dressing as women with luxurious sandals and turbans, tied with gilded ribbons, women and men mixed together. Music and celebration occurred in the streets, and the markets led to the intermingling of different faiths and tradition. If the *zahid* ascetic denied corrupting luxuries of commerce for himself, Ibn Tumart demanded such decadence be denied to society as a whole.

Berber Hammadid Civilization

Ibn Tumart's accusations of decadence went to the very top, to the Hammadid Emir who did not follow the "proper" legal strictures of Islam. The Almohad sources claimed proudly he publically embarrassed the powerful Hammadid

Berber prince of Bèjaïa, Al-'Aziz. In 1067, the Hammadids under 'Aziz's predecessor Al-Nasir had made Bèjaïa their capital, partially abandoning an inland site, the Castle of Banu Hammad. Al-Nasir called the new city Al-Nasiriyya, or "the victorious city". The Hammadids, perhaps faced with an influx of Arab tribes inland, were also wanting to establish themselves in a protected port away from their original capital inland. However, it was also possible they simply wanted to take advantage of maritime trade. The Hammadids built a splendid palace fortification called the Palace of the Pearl. Later Hammadid princes, including Al-Mansur, built a great mosque, planted elegant gardens on both banks of the Summam River, and built two new palaces including one called Castle of the Star. These Berber rulers, abandoning the inland Castle Banu Hammad and settling on the coast, built great civic works in their new capital, including an aqueduct bringing water from the Tuja Mountain. With up to seventy-two mosques (although this was possibly an exaggeration) Bèjaïa was at the peak of its Golden Age when Ibn Tumart came to visit. Its glorious architecture seemed to influence the rebuilding of Palermo by the Christian Normans in Sicily. Pope Gregory VII "The Great" (d. 1085) wrote to the Hammadid prince Al-Nasir, addressing him in terms from the Roman imperial past as King of Mauretania and the province of Setif.[12] In his letter, the Pope reached out with an air of religious understanding, saying God "wishes that all men should be saved and none lost . . . we believe in and confess one God, admittedly in a different way, and daily praise and venerate Him, the creator of the world and the ruler of this world." The Pope may have deliberately echoed the *fatihah* (opening of the Qur'an) in his last sentence. Gregory specifically hoped for the security and safety of the remaining Christians in Hammadid lands.[13] There had been an ancient community of Latin Christians in the region. He was probably looking for as many potential allies as he could find. The Pope, a humble son of a blacksmith, was familiar with the needs of Amalfi and other Italian traders who wished to increase lucrative North African trade. He regularly struggled against the powerful Holy Roman Emperor Henry IV.

In addition to receiving this papal diplomatic correspondence, the Hammadids were expert at trade. A massive gate, the Saracen Gate, and walls had to be erected to control the booming trade mentioned earlier. The

Hammadid ruler, obviously a sophisticated, Mediterraneanized ruler did not especially appreciate Ibn Tumart's challenge to their authority or to the peace of the market. He must have been especially horrified when Ibn Tumart accused him of spending too much money on a rare luxury, a decorated ostrich egg.

Ibn Tumart somehow escaped from elegant Bèjaïa unharmed, going west to the next city in the Central Maghrib (Algeria) where he found new mosques and forbade moral wrongs on his way to the Atlas Mountains of Morocco. Ibn Tumart seemed to have an uneasy relationship with the corrupting influences of the Sea. Once he entered the Mediterranean only for the sea to spit him back out. He miraculously survived an attempt by his fellow passengers on a ship to throw him into the sea when he complained about their un-Islamic ways. Staying afloat, seemingly by the grace of God, the passengers hauled him back on board. On land, he was constantly commanding right and forbidding wrong, often using his cane and his loud demeanor to overturn social norms that did not sufficiently fit Ibn Tumart's vision for a society prepared for the end of time and the day of reckoning.[14] Many of these practices were tied to Berber cultural norms, norms that may not have strictly followed Ibn Tumart's vision, a vision contrary to the Mediterranean economic, cultural and commercial exchanges that were accelerating at the time. Although he later professed a pure descent from the Prophet Muhammad, Ibn Tumart was himself a Berber, not from Kabylia, the Bèjaïa region with its own distinct Berber language, but a very different part of Berber North Africa, the Atlas and Anti-Atlas Mountains of Morocco.

Decades later, in 1152, the Almohad army, its core made up of Berbers from the Atlas Mountains along with several new followers collected along their way east, captured Bèjaïa. The city may have been bracing for a conservative, Islamic regime based on Ibn Tumart's vision. The Hammadid elite sailed for Sicily and the city awaited its fate.

The Almohads first conceived of North Africa as sacred as the land of Mecca and Madina in Arabia, a land of a new dawn that was destined to transform the Muslim world. They commanded all Jews and Christians to convert or be expelled, just as all Christians and Jews were forced to leave the sacred lands in Arabia centuries before.[15] Bèjaïa's Golden Age seemed doomed. Yet, in fact, the Almohad conquest of Bèjaïa did not lead to the permanent destruction of its cosmopolitan character.

The Mediterranean and the Almohads

After conquering the Hammadid Berber dynasty who had ruled Bèjaïa, the Almohads, despite having been founded by Ibn Tumart who criticized the luxuries of the city, themselves adapted and tolerated, even embraced the wealth that trade and openness of the Mediterranean port brought. Bèjaïa, even under Almohad rule, was "Mediterraneanized."[16] According to one scholar, "Bougie [Bèjaïa] remained an opulent mercantile town, into which Venetians, Pisans, Marseillais and Catalans imported merchandise made in Europe and from which they exported local products, especially candied [citrus] peel, wax [for candles], alum [a product used for leather preparation, dentistry and sugar production], lead and raisins."[17] The price of textiles in Europe, so dependent on alum for dyeing, was directly linked to the price of alum coming from ports such as Bèjaïa.[18] Unlike other North African cities such as Marrakech and Tunis, Bèjaïa had plentiful rain and was known for its cereal products and dried fruits. It was also known for the many Barbary apes in the Ape Peak and Valley near Cape Carbon.[19] There was even a debate among Jewish merchants and rabbis, including a son of Simon Duran, a great rabbi in the city of Constantine near Bèjaïa, about the legality of engaging in the trade of these animals.[20]

Bèjaïa was not only swept up in the North African Almohad revolution and the mystical Sufi revolution epitomized by Abu Madyan, but also in the Commercial Revolution: the revival of trade sweeping not only the European cities of Pisa, Barcelona, Genoa and Venice but also the cities of North Africa and Muslim Spain. In this way, Bèjaïa and other Almohad cities, even cities as deep inland as Marrakech, the once-inviolate capital of Almohad doctrine, were subject to the cultural and commercial flowering occurring in the Mediterranean, the great "corrupting sea."[21] Great wealth was produced not only on the northern shores of the Mediterranean but on the North African shores and deeper inland as well. Fibonacci's father, a very astute businessman and member of the rising Pisan elite, knew of the riches of North Africa when he brought his son there to learn the art of the merchant. But Fibonacci was no simple merchant.

A Dialogue of Numbers and of Faiths

A statue of Fibonacci, one of Pisa's greatest sons, stands prominently in a corner of the Camposanto, a majestic portico structure steps from the famous Leaning Tower of Pisa. The Pisans built the Camposanto around a pile of dirt brought from Golgotha – the place immediately outside Jerusalem where Jesus was crucified – by Pisans on Crusade. However, Pisa's relationship with the Muslim world was not simply about symbols of Crusade in the East, it was primarily about opportunities in North Africa. Traveling to Bèjaïa for many different purposes, Fibonacci encountered opportunities that would not only change his life but also the life of his city. Fibonacci, of course, was not a rare or exceptional traveler from the North. In fact, many Pisans had been to North Africa, both as traders and as conquerors. Latin Pisan poets recalled Scipio's defeat of Carthage and the ancient Roman province of Ifriqiya (Tunisia). Fibonacci's father, an influential customs official, would have been in charge of a whole community of Pisans in Bèjaïa. It was Fibonacci's father who encouraged him to study the mathematics and simple "calculation" skills that would be useful for the young man destined to become a merchant. Perhaps he envisioned the young Fibonacci following in his footsteps and taking charge of one of Pisa's many *duanas* – the customhouses that had been founded by Pisan traders throughout the Western Mediterranean. Pisa and its great competitors, Genoa and Venice, were all on the rise. Their military prowess was such that mercenaries from these Italian ports were hired by the Almohad ruler and sent all the way to Marrakech.

But the father's modest plans for his son would be far surpassed by the young man's natural abilities and intellectual ambitions, especially by his desire to learn from North African science. Leonardo was a precocious genius for numbers. Fibonacci experienced an intellectual awakening in Bèjaïa, most likely working with teachers who wrote in Arabic.[22] Bèjaïa's thinkers and polymaths exposed him to the use of "Hindu" numerals, or what we call "Arabic" numerals since they were transmitted from Hindu mathematicians in texts written in Arabic by both Arabs and non-Arabs. He used what became 1 . . . 2 . . . 3 . . . 4 as opposed to the clumsy I . . . II . . . III . . . IV. The journey of these numerals from India to the Middle East and eventually to the accounting books of the merchants and banks of Pisa, Genoa and Florence, and the rest of Europe, was long. Arabs had been using the numbers for centuries, advancing mathematics in ways unknown to the precocious Pisan. In fact, it was by using these numbers that he could begin to understand the works of the famed Al-Khwarizimi, the ninth-century mathematician from whose name was corrupted the Latin term *Algorismum* or algorithm. These formulae had more than an intellectual impact. They would indelibly change accounting and commercial practices throughout the West. The reigning Almohad Empire encouraged this commerce by providing a rarity in North African if not Western Mediterranean history – a large, politically united market that spanned the coast as well as Al-Andalus.[23] Far from being peripheral, the Almohads, having achieved unification of much of the coastline of North Africa and Iberia, were a major stabilizing anchor for the Commercial Revolution. Fibonacci's seemingly innocent "give and take" with the mathematicians of Bèjaïa was one of the sparks that enflamed the commercial relations of the Twelfth-Century Renaissance and the Commercial Revolution.[24] Historians noted an "explosion of Italian trade" would lead to one of the greatest advances in wealth, population and culture, halted only temporarily by the ravages of the plague.[25]

Between the twelfth and the fourteenth centuries the Bèjaïa of Fibonacci was one of the foremost intellectual centers of the Mediterranean, reflecting its commercial importance. The mathematician Al-Qurayshi used the works of the celebrated Egyptian Abu Kamil who taught higher algebra.[26] The elite of Bèjaïa were aware of their intellectual vitality. The historian Ibn Hammad wrote of the "princes of science" in Bèjaïa during the period of Fibonacci's visit. He discussed the work of a certain Al-Hassar whose symbols paralleled or influenced those of Fibonacci.[27] Fibonacci himself spoke to us breathlessly about his study of this Arab-Hindu math at Bèjaïa in a brief autobiographical note found in the front of his famed *Liber Abbaci* (Book of Calculation) first published in 1202:

> There, following my introduction, as a consequence of marvelous instruction in the art, to the nine digits of the Hindus, the knowledge of the art appealed to me before all others, and for it I realized that all its aspects were studied in Egypt, Syria, Greece, Sicily and Provence, with their varying methods; and at these places, thereafter, while on business, I pursued my study in depth and learned the give-and-take of disputation.[28]

This "give-and-take" disputation or "argumentative" method was not only an essential part of twelfth-century mathematics, it was also a preferred method of learning, education and truth finding throughout the region. Disputations, face-to-face occasions set up almost as trials for ideas and beliefs, occurred not only between mathematicians and philosophers of different cultures but between leading representatives of different faiths. It was believed that if formulae and scientific proofs could be discovered, so perhaps could that even greater truth – the nature of God – be known or defended. Truth revealed through argument was not relative, even if it appeared contested.

Dreams of Conversion

Although Fibonacci kept mostly to mathematics and accounting, intellectual dialogue and the exchanging of arguments as a means of transfer between cultures was not limited to numbers. Along with the spiritual revolution, sparked as a reaction to the increase of commercial wealth, came a renewed interest in conversion of the infidel. In fact, around the same time as Fibonacci, other great intellects were focused on the nature of God in a world seemingly divided between three related, but distinct faith traditions: Islam, Judaism and Christianity. Dialogue and contestation went beyond mathematics to even bigger questions about the nature of God, reason and human will. Far from being evidence of unbridgeable conflict and cultural misunderstandings, by the thirteenth century these dialogues and interactions between faiths instead revealed a common understanding of methods of argument and reason; the tools (based on both the writings of Aristotle and pseudo-Aristotles) were the same but the conclusions were different. Also, in preparing for any debate, one must get to know one's opponent, to predict their moves. Thus, even a sincere and dogged attempt to convert another, to confront the infidel on every possible point, led to transformations, not just of the intended target, but also of the person trying to do the converting.

It may be difficult for modern readers to understand the full importance of these medieval encounters, these highly competitive dialogues, disputations and debates between Western Mediterraneans. Modern understandings of tolerance do not easily apply to the interactions between different faiths in the medieval Mediterranean. Modern terminology and mindset, especially assumed dichotomies between faith and reason, between "practical tolerance" or religiously inspired fanaticism and violence, fail to describe the unique context in which these encounters took place. In fact, for all of their potential violence and great offensiveness to the modern ear, few alternatives existed outside of a faith community. Today, despite talk of a "clash between civilizations" faith leaders are often allied against secularism and the dangers of unbridled scientific progress and wealth. Before the seventeenth century, however, atheist secularism, at least amongst those intellectual religious elites writing history, was mostly hidden. There were some very rare exceptions to this, mainly in the Muslim world. Writers such as the blind humanist Al-Ma'arri (d. 1057) professed something close to atheism in his frustration with all religions.

For most medieval Muslims, Christians and Jews there was far more confidence than those from different faiths, even those who may have every reason to be stubbornly opposed to persuasion, could actually be converted or could, at least, concede some points in matters of faith. Science in the form of the writings of Pseudo-Aristotle and Aristotle himself was not purely for practical purposes, it was part of a religious-intellectual arms race with classical reason the main instrument for conversion by Muslims and Christians alike. Rationally based theological argument was fundamental to Islam, especially Almohad Islam, and this had an impact on Judaism and Christianity. This process of interacting with other faiths and borrowing their methods of argumentation and intellectual tools, often drawn from the same font of classical knowledge, deeply impacted all three faiths.[29] This growing "dream of conversion" was not relegated to non-state actors, evangelicals and missionaries. Unless minorities were under special legal protections, such as the Christian mercenaries of Marrakech, medieval Mediterranean kingdoms, both Muslim and non-Muslim, officially favored acculturation and conversion. Of course, this did not stop many Muslims from living in great numbers in medieval Latin Christendom, even at the height of tensions and religiously charged warfare. Neither did it stop Latin traders or mercenaries from living in Muslim North Africa. Yet, the dream of conversion or/and the encouragement to convert was often written into the law.[30]

Legal Boundaries

The Siete Partidas was the law code of the Christian king Alfonso X of Castile (d. 1284), a king so praised for his tolerance and his knowledge of Almohad sciences that he has been called "the last Almohad Caliph."[31] Yet under even his rulebook, considered perhaps one of the most tolerant rulers in Latin Christendom, Christians were encouraged to "endeavor to convert the Moors [Muslims] by causing them to believe in our religion, and bring them into it by kind words and suitable discourses, and not by violence or compulsion." Christian converts to Islam, in contrast, are put to death for apostasy, except at the discretion of the King.[32] In Norman Sicily, although Ibn Jubayr was also amazed at some examples of the tolerance of the Christian kings, the King was first and foremost a ruler who maintained Christian superiority. Thus, "should a man show anger to his son or his wife . . . the one who is the object of displeasure may perversely throw himself into a church, and there be baptized and turn Christian."[33] Christian missionaries could enter mosques and synagogues to preach and, in Aragon, Muslim subjects were also expected to fight for their Christian king.[34]

Many Muslims of Al-Andalus felt an obligation to leave Christian territory and flee to North Africa, bringing their culture with them but also encountering resistance and problems with acculturation and the sharing of power in their new, North African homes. Similarly, in North Africa and Muslim Spain, Christians and Jews were given special protections as "People of the Book" even though attempts to convince them to convert would have been constant.

Similarly, during the first decades of Almohad rule, many Jews were forced to feign conversion. Maimonides, the Jewish philosopher and doctor, for instance, blended into his surroundings in Fes, Morocco and possibly outwardly professed Islam. The Almohads, according to Jewish sources, had a devastating impact on their community.[35] Yet these restrictions and persecutions may not have been as systematic and did not hold long.[36] After 1164 and at the height of the Almohad Empire, Jews were once again allowed to move more openly through Almohad domains. Tolerance may have become a pragmatic necessity, not only to benefit the Empire but also to maintain the demands of commerce, trade and revenue.

A Convert to Islam

Conversions brought about by rational arguments, however, did sometimes occur. They occurred even among those debaters at the top of their respective religions who were supposed to be converting others. Although rare, some could in fact be convinced for reasons other than necessity. In most cases, conversion was often out of convenience or necessity a long process of minority acculturation under Christian or Muslim political rule. It was not theology or reason, but rather cultural and social change that explained most conversions. Nevertheless, there were rare exceptions to this rule.

Anselm of Turmeda, also called Abdallah Al-Tarjuman (Abdallah the Translator) in Arabic, was originally a Christian Franciscan monk who spoke Catalan and Arabic. After going to Paris, Bologna and other cities for his education, he traveled to Almohad Tunis as a friar. Interestingly, his process of inner conversion, although embellished in his autobiography, happened not while he was in North Africa but in Italy. While in Bologna, the great scholarly city in Christian Lombardy, he allegedly met a crypto-Muslim, a priest he called Nicolas Fratello, who had studied far and wide to identify the "Paraclete." This Paraclete, the prophet that Jesus predicted would come after him in the Gospels, was according to Fratello none other than Muhammad the Prophet.[37] Anselm and his crypto-Muslim had reason to be careful. After all, it was in this same city where Giovanni da Modena's late-Gothic fresco of Muhammad being tortured in hell was painted in the Cathedral of San Petronio in the fifteenth century. Anselm, apparently breaking with all cultural norms, was convinced by the argument that Muhammad was actually the true Paraclete, not a tortured soul. He was also awed by the simplicity of Islamic monotheism. After going to Tunis, Anselm sought out "somebody who could speak his language," in this case, the Jewish doctor of the ruler, and dramatically and publically converted to Islam in front of the Hafsid Caliph and his court in 1390.[38] In Tunis, he not only rose to head the customs house but became a powerful minister to the Hafsid ruler, the head of various trade monopolies in goods desired by Christian merchants and controlled by the Caliph. These Hafsid caliphs were descendants of the Almohad Berbers who had taken Tunis centuries before. Anselm used the same rational methods of his Christian predecessors, even, perhaps, his great namesake Anselm of

Canterbury (d. 1109), not to defend the Trinity but *tawhid*, the Almohad concept of God's unity.

Even as Christian rulers regularly invited him to return to his natal faith, Anselm's conversion was, at least from a broad perspective, somewhat minor, at least in terms of worldview. A man who transformed himself first from a Franciscan to a successful merchant and finally to a Muslim merchant, he seemed to reflect the crosscurrents of his age. He never lost his belief, common to Muslims and Christians alike, that the rightness of religion could be proven through argument and dialogue based on reason. Perhaps more imaginative than most, however, he cast characters of his imaginary disputations as animals, including a donkey. In a later tract, written in 1420 before he died around 1423, he sets out various arguments for the prophethood of Muhammad.[39] His tomb, still venerated and restored, can be found today in Tunis, built in the style of a North African Muslim saint or *sidi*.

A Common Search: Oneness of Being

Yet theological arguments such as Anselm's were not the only story. Religious difference and disputation was not the only defining factor of medieval thought in the Western Mediterranean. There were also compelling, even "modern" sounding appeals to a common humanity, a notion of belief beyond what seemed impossibly stubborn religious differences. Indeed, it was in the context of the religious debates and encounters between Jews, Christians and Muslims that some of the earliest and most eloquent proponents of a type of proto-humanism emerged, often breaking with the assumed categories of the past. In 1068, Sa'id Al-Andalusi, a philosopher from Almería, a great and prosperous port in the south of Spain, wrote a book called *The Book of the Categories of Nations*. In it he divided the world not between the realm of the infidel (*dar al harb*) and realm of Islam (*dar al Islam*) but between peoples "given to the art of knowledge" and those that do not pursue science and "resemble animals more than human beings."[40] In contrast to this bifurcation, the overarching mysticism of the Andalusi Muslim Sufi Ibn 'Arabi (d. 1240) evoked a "Oneness of Being" transcending all religions,

> All the revealed religions are lights. Among these religions, the revealed religion of Muhammad is like the light of the sun among the light of the stars.

When the sun appears, the lights of the stars are hidden, and their lights are included in the light of the sun. Their being hidden is like the abrogation of other revealed religions that takes place through Muhammad's revealed religion. Nevertheless, they do in fact exist, just like the existence of the light of the stars is actualized. This explains why we have been required in our all-inclusive religion to have faith in the truth of all the messengers and all the revealed religions.[41]

As modern, even new age, this approach to religious differences may sound, it was ultimately colored and expressed by Ibn 'Arabi's own particular cultural and religious approach. Even as he spoke remarkably of a Oneness of Being, Islam was the brightest Sun, other religions were the stars. Ibn 'Arabi harnessed the idea of humanity's common primordial nature (al-fitra) in which all are aware of the existence of God from birth, even as this awareness does not survive maturity. "Every child is born according to primordial nature; then his parents make him into a Jew, a Christian or a Zoroastrian."[42] Ibn 'Arabi did not come to his conclusions about Christianity and Judaism from the position of somebody ignorant of their traditions, in fact, as with many scholars of his caliber, he wrote a book describing the stories and lessons of the isra'iliyyat, traditions of Jews and Christians studied by many Muslim scholars.[43]

The idea of a common humanity was not merely an elite phenomenon. It was not just intellectuals or famous mystics such as Ibn 'Arabi who appealed, or seemed to appeal, to a greater and common God. Christians visited the Muslim scholar 'Abd Allah b. Sahl Al-Gharnati (d. 1158) in the town of Baeza "to profit from his knowledge in 'ulum al-awa'il, the ancient sciences." This occurred even as some scholars claimed the "era or convivencia" of peaceful "living together" had come to an end with the coming of the Almohads.[44] Oftentimes cosmopolitan communities, threatened by some natural disaster or some threat to all, appealed collectively to at least any god who might care to listen. While the elite might have some interest in highlighting the threat of the other, there are several fascinating instances where "common" people of different faith traditions are described as worshipping together. Most of these instances were during great natural disasters or emergencies such as shipwrecks, plagues or volcanic eruptions. At times of true desperation, both the common people and the elite could be united. One anecdote comes from the medieval world's greatest known traveler, Ibn Battuta (d. 1369). In 1348, on his first voyage, he witnessed "a remarkable instance of the veneration of the people of Damascus for the great Mosque." The Black Death had been spreading and the specter of plague hung around the city. The viceroy had ordered a great public fast of three days. People from all walks of life and from different faith groups and sects were crowded into the Great Mosque. Then, they went out barefoot, carrying their different books. "[M]ale and female, small and large; the Jews went out with their book of the Law and the Christians with their Gospel . . ."[45] There were also numerous instances of Christians, Muslims and Jews sharing in festivals and civic activities in Al-Andalus, Sicily and the North African Maghrib.[46]

Al-Qabisi (d. 1012), a mildly frustrated Maliki Sunni cleric in tenth-century Ifriqiya (Tunisia), then mostly under the control of the Sanhaja Berber Zirid dynasty, was scandalized by such cosmopolitan mixing of the common citizens of Kairouan. He wrote *fatwas* not only against the common people but also against the many educated Muslims clerics who joined Christians in their festivals or who accepted Christian gifts on Christmas, Easter, Calends and the Christian Festival of Saint Jean.

> It is wrong to accept [gifts] from the festivals of the polytheists [name used to describe Christians due to their belief in the Trinity]. These festivals include Christmas, Easter, the Calendes [of January?], Saint Jean of Andalus and the festival of Baptism among the Egyptian [*Ghitas* festival of the Coptic Christians commemorating the baptism of Christ]. These are all festivals of polytheists [Trinitarians]. For this reason a master who teachers the Muslims (*mu'alim*) should not accept or claim these gifts, even if they are given a gift in a gracious spirit that would benefit [the teacher].[47]

Such pronouncements calling for separation between religious groups were not necessarily an indication of generalized intolerance. Rather, they were reflections of a conservative reaction. These festivals, it seemed, were especially popular among young men and, especially, young Christian women who had emerged from the protective confines of the family to celebrate publically. The mixing of peoples during religious festivals reached the top of the social pyramid. Even Prince Tamim, son and successor of the great Zirid ruler Al-Mu'izz bin Badis (d. 1062), gushed in his poetry about the festivities and the beauty of those Christian women saying,

> Oh Allah! Does he not know that I am [helplessly] in love,
> With your beautiful countenance?
> That I [hopelessly] love your [strange] accent, even at the price of my
>   life-soul,
> When you read the words of [your] Messiah?
> I deliberately show affection to others [because of my faith],
> Yet [in secret] you are the only one I truly love.
> And, out of love of you, I [attend] the Christian feasts,
> and savor the sweet melodies of chanted psalms.[48]

Not all poetry by Muslims describing Christians was heterosexual.[49] Al-Mithqal, an eleventh-century Tunisi *bon vivant*, was notorious for his love for a handsome, young Christian wine seller. His romance was tolerated even as the young man seemed to seduce him toward Christ.

> He frequented a young Christian, a seller of wine, and his love for him was well known. He remained three years in the nightclub or singing house [?] (of his lover), close to the entrance and during this entire period, he went with him to the church on Sundays and festival days such that he became acquainted with a great part of the Christian tradition.[50]

Later, the young Christian left Ifriqiya for Egypt where he died. Al-Mithqal wrote a mournful poem. Descriptions of Berber homosexuality by Arab sources should be seen in context: often there was a motive to tarnish reputations. A few sources described the alleged homosexual practices of entire Berber tribes, including the Kutama (Kattama tribe that ushered in the Fatimid revolution), Mila and Stif, who, according to Ibn Hawqal (who may have been maligning them), "offer their body to their guests as an honoring act, and they feel no shame about it. Whether they be old or young or ugly, they offer their body for their guest and insist on that." This occurred, according to Al-Idrisi, even after the adoption of Islam, which condemns homosexuality in various hadiths (traditions of the Prophet Muhammad). Although some scholars have attempted to explain references to homosexuality in North Africa as a reaction to the lack of availability of women or matriarchal tribal structures, the scholar Mabrouk Mansouri explained this practice among prominent Berber tribes as part of a deep-seated code of hospitality.[51]

Evocative combinations of desire for the other, even as it conflicted with the deep-seated mandates of faith, were as alive in Zirid North Africa as in Cordoba in Muslim Spain.[52] The cosmopolitan mixing in medieval Tunis has left cultural artifacts in celebrations that have lasted to this day. The festival of the First of January remains vibrant among the Berbers of the regions of Yennar, Innair and Bubannani and others, who use green branches to signify the forces of nature. Well into the modern period, it was reported that children built tents of branches inside the homes of Tunis to mark the Mayday festival. "Native," or non-merchant, non-mercenary or non-Latin, North African Christians survived in isolated oases such as Djerid and Nafzawa up to the thirteenth century.[53]

Let Each Invoke the God He Worships

Ironically, perhaps, it was the story of one journey by a pious and self-righteous man that demonstrated the existence of a cosmopolitan ethos in the Mediterranean of the Almohad period. In the twelfth and early thirteenth centuries, Ibn Jubayr, strict follower of Almohad Islam, suddenly resigned his position in Granada and set out on a pilgrimage to Mecca. He went to this holy land of Islam, the Hijaz, in order to cleanse his sins after drinking wine, wine offered to him by an apparently, less-than-upright Almohad ruler. The Almohad rulers, no longer strict followers of Islam, seemed to have lapsed in Ibn Jubayr's eyes. The Almohads, at least of the more conservative variety, also had a reputation for religious intolerance. Yet, even Ibn Jubayr was saved by the tolerance of others and he even seemed, at times, convinced by the benefits of cosmopolitanism. It was through the somewhat dry eye of this "true" Almohad traveler that we see more instances of common people, Christians and Muslims, all appealing to God when under duress. Traveling back home from Acre in the Levant, he took a ship captained by a Christian from the Italian city of Genoa and even grudgingly described the beauty of some of the ceremonies on board, such as the lighting of candles in the night on All Saints' Day. Ibn Jubayr, like those of any age plagued with a weak stomach, really despised and feared sea travel. He dramatized the travails of his trip through the Strait of Messina, that narrow channel of water between Sicily and Italy that pours through with such force that it was here Odysseus fought against the mythical sea monsters of Scylla and Charybides on either side of the strait. Indeed, Ibn Jubayr seemed obsessed, like many a modern airplane traveler who fears flying, with all the reasons why ships were dangerous. He especially seemed to love reading warnings against sea crossings in Muslim tradition and especially in the Mediterranean, precisely because of the fierce reputation of the sea. One piece of Arabic verse seemed to express his attitude towards the sea. "The sea is bitter of taste, intractable; No need of it have I. Is it not water and we earth? Why then do we endure it?" It was perhaps not surprising the landlubber poet Ibn Rashiq Al-Qayarawani, or a man of Kairouan, wrote the verses. Kairouan was a city built inland in Tunisia by 'Uqba bin Nafi', the St. Patrick of Muslims and fabled seventh-century Muslim conquerer. According to legend, he tamed the snakes around the site of the city. Beyond a refuge from serpents and beasts, the city allowed great access to Saharan trade.[54]

For medieval ship captains, even for the highly experienced and wily Genoese who dominated the passenger route from the Levant to the Western Mediterranean stopping at many ports along the way, this narrow channel between Sicily and the mainland of Italy was as violent as it was dangerous. For Ibn Jubayr, there was so much water and it was moving so fast, it was as if the ancient Ma'rib dam in Yemen had burst.[55] The pilgrim's boat, captained by a tough Genoese and filled with a motley crew and cargo of Christian and Muslim passengers, a fleeting microcosmos of Mediterranean society itself, was crashed ashore.[56] At once, the captain urged the main sail be taken down to prevent further damage, but it would not budge. Suddenly it seemed certain that "the Last Judgment" had come. Ibn Jubayr's panicked travels demonstrated the cultural unity and connectivity of the medieval Western Mediterranean in the midst of violence, ambiguity and difference between faiths. There could be debates and disputations between the doctors and intellectuals of all three faiths, even dreams of conversion conjured and holy warfare pursued. Despite all this, when disaster struck the secure veil of exclusivity often seemed to fall. Everybody, especially the "common people", regardless of faith, together in these tight quarters, praised his or her God, asking for intercession in the middle of a natural disaster. Ibn Jubayr described the Christians on board as "giving themselves over to grief" and the Muslims as submitting to their Lord and uniting in prayer. Of course, Ibn Jubayr did his best to portray the Muslims as better in their faith than the Christians and it was likely that there were as many pious appeals to the Christian God as the Muslim one. Nevertheless, they were all, quite literally, in the same boat. Although driven aground in a mist and waiting for his death, and the dreadful possibility that the Christian captain would inherit all of his belongings as was the law of the sea among the Genoese, Ibn Jubayr's luck had not run out. It would seem the interfaith supplications worked. Ibn Jubayr had reason to hope. The cries of the ship did not land on an empty wilderness, instead,

> The sun then rose and small boats came out to us. Our cries had fallen on the city [Messina], and the King of Sicily, William himself, came out with some of his retinue to survey the affair . . . The strangest thing that we were told was this Rumi King, when he perceived some needy Muslims staring from the ship, having not the means to pay for their landing because the owners of the boats were asking so high a price for their rescue . . . ordered that they be given one hundred *ruba'i* of his coinage in order that they might alight. All the Muslims were thus saved and cried, "Praise be to God, Lord of the Universe."[57]

King William knew very well the value of learned Muslim men such as Ibn Jubayr. He even, it was said, ordered the detainment of Muslim astrologers and physicians passing through his land and forced them to "forget [their] native land."[58] Indeed, this kingly appropriation of great men of science, regardless of faith, was common practice throughout the medieval period. Ibn Jubayr, perhaps fearing capture, and thus wishing to return to the Almohad realm quickly, still explored the island as he awaited passage home. He learned that King William also spoke and wrote Arabic and the "handmaidens and concubines" of his palace were Muslims; even Christian women who came to the palace converted to Islam due to the influence of these women. When an earthquake occurred, many of the women and pages of William's household cried out to Muhammad the Prophet. William, however, did not punish them, saying, "Let each invoke the God he worships, and those that have faith shall be comforted."[59]

Ibn Jubayr witnessed that the "Christian women" of Palermo, the capital of Sicily, followed "the fashion of Muslim women, are fluent of speech, wrap their cloaks about them, and are veiled . . . Thus they parade to their churches . . . bearing all the adornments of Muslim women, including jewelry, henna on the fingers, and perfumes." Ibn Jubayr seemed titillated by the scene. Yet, instead of writing his own poem, as had the Zirid prince Tamim bin Badis, Ibn Jubayr quoted another poet saying, "Going into the church one day, he came upon antelope and gazelle."[60] He also met Ibn Zur'ah, one of the "learned doctors" of Islam who had been pressed into service with the Christian king and had eventually relented and converted to Christianity. He memorized the New Testament as he had the Qur'an. When a case arose between Christians he would judge it. He was qualified to judge the cases of Muslims as well. Even so, the straight-laced Ibn Jubayr could not believe the sincerity of the conversion, quoting from the Qur'an (Sura 16: 106), "Save he who, being under compulsion, yet in his heart believes."[61]

Pragmatic Universality

At times, appeals to a common faith seemed instrumental, and were even used to convince an enemy of a different faith to release captives. Upholders of *wahdat al-wujud* (oneness of being), such as the Sufi scholar Al-Harrali (d. 1270), used the concept instrumentally and tried to obtain the release of family. Al-Harrali wrote a florid letter to the authorities in the Spanish town of Tarragona, where several of his family were captive. He stressed the unity of the human race and asked the Spanish Christians to look beyond differences of religion.[62] One medieval pope used a similar appeal, recalling the greatness of Cyrus the Great, to ask a North African ruler to release some captive Franciscan friars who were arrested for overly open proselytizing on the streets.[63]

Yet oneness of desperation in the face of disaster was not the same as oneness of being. The dream for the unity of humanity under one faith was common in all three great monotheistic faiths, but that dream was, at least in its initial and most revolutionary stages, constantly challenged by the existence of the other. The "oneness of being" or *wahdat al wujud*, used to describe the universal concepts of Ibn 'Arabi, was a spiritual idea usually reserved for the path of the individual soul or his "way," his mystical school. But it was fostered in the context of much more real, political ambition, even an overriding dream of the medieval Western Mediterranean, a dream pursued by Muslim, Jewish and Christian thinkers alike. Although conversion of infidels could be part of this dream, it meant far more than that.[64] It was the dream of universality – the final leveling of differences between the sects and ways of humanity by apocalypse or day of reckoning. Universalism and "oneness of being" was not always, necessarily, a source of tolerance.[65] It could also be used to justify both retreat from the world and religious and missionary fervor. Similarities between faiths were both an opportunity and an intrinsic threat to the missionary believer: similarities could be a wedge for conversion, but also a temptation. Even so, some shifted focus from the quest for earthly unity, preferring an understanding of The One "worshipped by every tongue, in all states and in all times."[66]

Apocalyptic Visions of Unity

As Fibonacci's contemporaries realized, numbers were important for far more than commercial documents or algorithms. Some numerical truths, well reasoned by the logic of scripture, were thought by Muslim and Christian scholars to predict the future. Attempts to achieve oneness of being, that ultimate project of God, fundamentally shaped the religious and political terrain of the Western Mediterranean for Christians and Muslims alike. Living in a mixed, "corrupting sea" of many different faiths, cultures and tongues, many still appealed to a dream of a sea united by one faith. Predictions of apocalyptic purification often happened at times of greatest sharing and conflict between Muslims and Christians. When calling for the Fifth Crusade (1213–21), for instance, Pope Innocent III connected the time since the Muslim conquest and the numerical sign of the devil.

> The Christian peoples, in fact, held almost all the Saracen provinces up to the time of Blessed Gregory; but since then a son of perdition has arisen, the false prophet Muhammad, who has seduced many men from the truth by worldly enticements and the pleasures of the flesh. Although his treachery has prevailed up to the present day, we nonetheless put our trust in the Lord who has already given us a sign that good is to come, that the end of this beast is approaching, whose number, according to the Revelation of Saint John will end in 666 years, of which already nearly 600 have passed.[67]

In North Africa, a hundred years earlier, the time since the *hijra* of the Prophet Muhammad in the lunar Muslim calendar, 500 years, seemed to presage the coming of the Almohad Mahdi Ibn Tumart "from the West." Rather than being centered in the sacred sites of the Middle East and the Levant, apocalyptic expectation came bursting spectacularly from the mountains of North Africa. Beginning in the middle of the twelfth century, a concept of absolute divine unity (called *tawhid* in Arabic) was expressed in one of the most ambitious political experiments of the Western Mediterranean: the Almohad Empire.

The Almohad Empire was most clearly expressed in the *'aqida* (profession of faith) of Ibn Tumart, the founder and awaited one who was to herald the end of the world, the Mahdi. At least in the early days of their rise, the Almohads disrupted important aspects of the Berber society in the High Atlas Mountains. During the bloody *tamyiz*, or "sorting", it was mainly the old Berber chiefs who represented different identities and tribal affiliations that were driven off mountain cliffs to their deaths. The primary purpose of their leader, the Mahdi Ibn Tumart, was not to wipe out religious minorities but internal threats. Religious purity was part of an apocalyptic ideology – start a revolution to make the Maghrib, the West, the new Holy Land. Like the land of Mecca and Madina, Christians and Jews would, at first, not be allowed.[68] The conversion or expelling of Christians and Jews, seen briefly in the initial stages of the Almohad movement, was only secondary to the dream of creating a new caliphate and fulfilling an apocalyptic promise. It was, in fact, after the failure of Almohad *tawhid* and doctrine and military setbacks against the Almohad project that Sufi movements and ideas of spiritual oneness of being such as those of Ibn 'Arabi emerged. Also, as this book will show, Christianity and Judaism quickly returned to the heart and capital of the Almohad Empire – the city of Marrakech – even as that city was initially supposed to be closed to non-believers. There were many reasons why Almohad doctrine became the nest of Sufism and a spiritual revival.[69] The Almohads were not merely following established schools or traditions but proclaiming a new vision that called for the revival of Islam at its source. They upended the traditions of the past and provided a new opening for Sufis to thrive. Yet, unlike some modern movements such as Wahhabism,[70] the failure of Almohad political ambitions actually led to an intellectual and mystical opening, a rise of spiritual and mystical approaches to faith. Although scholars are uncertain over whether the two actually met, the inspiration for Ibn Tumart was Al-Ghazali (d. 1111), a great thinker who attempted to combine mystical spirituality with the particularities of faith. Also, for Ibn Tumart, reason, not simply blind adherence to the law, was essential for interpreting and understanding the Qur'an. Yet the Almohads were ultimately limited by political ambitions and power, by their attempt to create oneness of being in this world. Others would preach a far more successful vision of spiritual unity not based on political power.

Although he grew up during the height of the Almohad Empire, Ibn 'Arabi, unlike Ibn Tumart and 'Abd Al-Mu'min, spoke of "oneness of being" as a mystical not a political concept. He started his life as an Almohad, his father was a military man who served the Caliph in 1172, but he quickly grew beyond that original identity and became a man convinced by universal oneness of being in a spiritual realm not defined by political borders.[71] The Almohads embodied a faulty attempt to pursue unity in the earthly realm; Ibn 'Arabi would pursue it in the spiritual world. While the Almohad Empire lived on in the thirteenth century under the Hafsids of Tunis, the flotsam of empire and the dream of unity would continue to dominate the efforts and ambitions of North African emirs and successor states well into the fifteenth century. The Berber successor dynasties of the late thirteenth and fourteenth centuries, Marinids in the west (modern Morocco), Zayyanids in the center (around Algeria) and Hafsid emirs in the east (Tunisia), would continue to attempt, and fail, to reunite Maghrib, dreaming of reviving the Almohad Empire. Without a compelling and original doctrine, however, these states failed to recreate the revolutionary, historical rupture brought about by the Almohads.

Although now much subdued by Moroccan, Tunisian and Algerian nationalism and border conflicts, dreams to recreate the Islamic Maghrib of the Almohads remain alive today in North Africa. But the philosophical legacy of the Almohads would be even greater than their political prowess. When the apocalypse failed to fully manifest, the ambition to unite the world was focused in another direction: toward reason. Through the formulations of the Almohad Ibn Rushd (Averroes), the Almohads still sought to unite the world under one true faith in one true God devoid of attributes or limitations, even though their Empire's expansion was itself limited and inherently unable to produce the apocalyptical changes promised by its founder. This intellectual project, far from being inimical to "radical" understandings of Islam under the Almohads, was supported by a new confidence in the Islamic West produced by the success of the Almohad project. Rather than looking only to the East, the great cities of Cairo and Baghdad, Almohads were encouraged to gain the light of knowledge at home, in the Maghrib and in Al-Andalus, Muslim Spain. In fact, it has been argued that the rise of a unified, medieval Islamic Maghrib under the Almohads, based on reason not simply the inherited rulings of tradition, was the rise of the first West.[72]

Instead of asking if medieval Western Mediterraneans were part of a largely tolerant culture, or if this tolerance were "pragmatic" or "real", it is important to first ask what was being tolerated and why. Binaries of reason and faith, tolerance and violence, unity and disunity should be reformulated in a way that acknowledges not only fundamentally different visions of what truth was but also how that truth may be obtained. It was not a question of the role of faith or of practicality and "reason" behind tolerance or violence.

Arguments over truth and the nature of God had, by the twelfth and thirteenth century, moved far beyond what was useful for spreading the faith. It was part of a dynamic republic of letters, words and ideas – a battling, sometimes even to the point of martyrdom, between different views of truth. Fibonacci's "give and take" with the mathematicians of Bèjaïa, the doctor Constantine the African's highly influential book on medicine and the arguments it caused in Europe, Ramon Lull's foolhardy arguments with the people of North Africa, Ibn Rushd's, Maimonides' and Aquinas' remarkable rational systems borrowed from the same well and harnessing both reason and faith: all of these ventures in dialogue led to the growth of intellectual activity throughout the Western Mediterranean. The growth of a "culture of reason," eloquently described by Johannes Fried in his book *The Middle Ages*, was not limited to a European vacuum but occurred under the aegis of interactions with North African counterparts.[73] Although it has limits in the realm of spirit, reason was a tactic used in the great dialogues and disputations between Muslims, Jews and Christians alike.

As with Fibonacci in the market debating with the finest Berber and Arabo-Berber mathematicians of his day, competitive exchange and disputational dialogue at all levels, from math to commerce to religion and culture, compelled and propelled new investigations, not only between, but within faiths and cultures. While the medieval period has at times been held up as an unexpectedly Golden Age of tolerance, it was also a period of real conflict and challenges based on sincere religious beliefs. The peril of ignoring such arguments, such violent clashes and frank exchanges is great. It blinds us not only from understanding the medieval nature and meaning of "truth," but it may also prevent us from viewing these disputational origins of our modern world – a world that originated in an active, often polemical, but also often pragmatic, medieval Western Mediterranean.

The Spectacle of Disputation

One of the overriding intellectual efforts of the Almohad twelfth century, among Christians, Jews and Muslims alike, was the integration of faith, spiritual experience and reason. The great rationalist scholars such as Ibn Rushd, known as Averroes in the Latin West, defended reason as a means, not an end: God's higher truth. The idea that there was "tolerance" for modern "rational" or pragmatic purposes made little difference to the worldview of the time. There was no shying away from frank argument and disputation out of fear of violence – far from it.

Disputes as a means of determining truth or defending the faith were popular occasions in the medieval Western Mediterranean, both as spectacle and as an intellectual pursuit. Even though interacting and discussing with those of different faiths, especially when one was in the minority, was often actively discouraged, certain individuals reveled in such discussions, on the page or even on the streets or in royal courts. They sought out or accepted intellectual combat or dialogue even in places where their faith was not protected by political power. In the same way some judicial decisions in Spain were determined in a trial "by ordeal," so, perhaps, could the rightness of belief be tested by confrontation.[74] It was often too hard for these missionary visionaries to resist opportunities to show off their learning and to corner an opposing side.

Through the battling of beliefs and the emphasizing of differences and distinctions, whether in matters of mind or of the spirit, God's mystery might be uncovered. In this way, the Western Mediterranean world of Fibonacci was not simply a place of passive tolerance and "getting along" of those with different ideas and beliefs. Cultural borrowing, business and trade, no matter how vibrant, did not always equate with tolerance. Rather it was a dynamic, often-violent, often-opportunistic milieu where groups, often fully convinced of their own truths and beliefs, came into contact with others but where there were breakthroughs, conversions, exchanges and transformations. This competitive dynamic did not mean unbridgeable differences all the time. Even as the stew of religious and ethnic groups spoke of one another in often harsh and competitive ways, they were still able to debate using methods of "reason," to understand the basic tactics of the debate, if not the overall strategy of another's faith.

The Barcelona Disputation exemplified this sort of spectacle. Occurring in 1263, the leader of the Franciscans, Peter de Juana, and the Dominicans, Ramon de Peñafort, Ramon Martini and Arnold de Segarra, debated against a single Jewish representative named Nahmanides over four sessions, some of them presided over by the King. He was granted freedom to speak frankly. Accounts of the event from the Jewish perspective declared victory as the King, out of respect for Nahmanides' argument, visited the synagogue for the first time. Often these dialogues were as much about apocalyptic fervor as they were about conversion.[75] Yet it was not always the single Jew against the Christians. Some Christian thinkers singlehandedly and actively sought disputes with Muslims. Peñafort wrote to Thomas Aquinas (d. 1274), called the "Stubborn Mule" and the "Father of Scholasticism," to encourage Aquinas to write his famous *Summa contra gentiles*, "Tract against the Gentiles" and the Saracens.[76] This would become a guide to help Dominicans in their preaching and evangelism, especially in North Africa. Thomas Aquinas admitted he did not know very much about Islam directly, so he focused on defending Catholicism. A later tract, *De rationibus*, "Reasons for the Faith against Muslim Objections," written in 1264, showed that Thomas Aquinas did gain a better grasp of Islam in later years. He principally defends the Trinity, arguing that Muslims simply misunderstand Christian teachings and that by the Trinity, "we do not mean three gods." Interestingly, he also confronts accusations against the Eucharist and the notion that Christians "eat God on the altar, and that if the body of Christ were even as big as a mountain, by now it should have been eaten up." He also confronted the notion of pre-determination and suggests that Muslims believe that a man dies with his fate "written on his forehead." Interestingly, in this later tract, he already acknowledged the limitations of reason alone, saying,

> First of all, I wish to warn you that in disputations with unbelievers about articles of the Faith, you should not try to prove the Faith by necessary reasons. This would belittle the sublimity of the faith . . . Yet whatever comes from the Supreme Truth cannot be false, and what is not false cannot be reputed by necessary reasons.[77]

Reason was used not as the basis of faith but also as a defense of faith. In North Africa, after the Muslim Almohad conquest, jurists trained in the arts of reason and debate attempted to convince Jews in the Dra'a Valley, south of Morocco, and in Sijilmasa, a great caravan city known for the gold trade, to convert. They held public disputations over a period of seven months before forcing conversion or inducing false conversion by Jews who preferred outward apostasy to condemnation.[78]

One of the masters of disputation on the Christian side was the extraordinary polymath genius of his age, Ramon Lull of Majorca. In the year 1307, about a century after Fibonacci, he also traveled to Bèjaïa on a very different mission: to use reason and argument to convert Muslims to Christianity. An account of one of these disputations survives, published in 1308.[79] Where Fibonacci may have found in Bèjaïa a clearer way of expressing truth, Ramon Lull ended his life with a very different type of clarity. He learned Arabic, studied aspects of Islamic law and culture and grew increasingly convinced that he held the key that would convert the Islamic world to Christ. He traveled to North Africa several times and debated openly in markets and public spaces. He came to resent the obduracy of the Muslims in North Africa and eventually concluded that Muslims could only be converted once Christians had made them subject. Pagan Tartars and Mongols, in contrast, were compelling and realistic targets for Christian conversion.[80] Although considered an eccentric even in his lifetime, Lull was not alone in this firm belief. In fact, Christian rulers were so certain of their ability to conquer North Africa and convert its Muslims that their certainty was used against them. Although a school he set up to translate Arabic claimed up to 10,000 converts, almost none were from North African lands under Muslim rule. In many cases

Lull's disputations and methods were the product of wishful thinking. As the scholar Norman Daniel quipped, "Lull puts into his opponents' mouths words that sound more like that which Lull would have wished them to be, than like anything Muslims might expected to have said."[81] The same was true of other missionaries in Muslim territory, such as Riccoldo da Monte di Croce, once a professor in Pisa, who went all the way to Baghdad attempting to convert Muslims and Nestorian Christians. Around 1300, back in Florence, he wrote the popular *Contra legem Saracenorum* ("Against Saracen Law") using similar straw arguments.

Disputing Glories of Ancestry: Berber and Arab Boasts

This sort of disputational spectacle, imagined or real, most often failed to convince the infidel. Yet as fruitless as it seemed to be, when it came to encouraging actual conversions, disputations or dialogues between convenient outsiders were not restricted to debates between faiths. They could also tackle other forms of otherness, including language and culture. Although many studies on Al-Andalus and the Mediterranean focused on religious conversion and acculturation over time, one of the greatest cultural changes in the Mediterranean was not, at least not predominantly, religious. Perhaps the greatest story of acculturation in the Western Mediterranean was not on the margins of Muslim and Christian Al-Andalus or Sicily. Rather, it was an acculturation that occurred in the heart of North Africa and which was as much ethnic and linguistic in nature as it was religious: the Arabization of the predominantly Berber-speaking North Africa. But this acculturation went both ways. Berber culture also influenced Arabs in North Africa. Disputation existed in frank expressions of difference between rival members of the same faith. Thus it was with great gusto that the Arab writer Abu Al-Walid Al-Saqundi from Muslim Spain wrote his "Treatise on the Glories of Muslim Spain" by disparaging fellow Muslim Berbers of North Africa and trying to prove not only the rightness but the superiority of Andalusis (especially those who claimed Arab descent from the Umayyad Arab Caliph and his armies in Damascus, Syria).[82] Even as the elite Arabs of Al-Andalus spoke of the glories of Muslim Spain, the Berbers would write of their own "Boasts of the Berbers."[83] Not only in religion but in perceptions of race and ethnicity, cutting through and between religious communities, the medieval Western Mediterranean was a disputational culture: a culture that emerged not simply from "living together" but arguing and debating the "other" across a space made dynamic and accessible by trade in goods, ideas, peoples.

The Dream of the Conversion, Ramon Lull and the Council of Vienne

The Mediterranean, that corrupting sea, not only mixed religions and cultures in spite of efforts to prevent integration and impose uniformity, but also, paradoxically, because of these very efforts. A disputational atmosphere, as much as it seemed to be about contestants talking over each other, not with each other, could still bring about rich cultural borrowing and exchange. There was willingness to adopt the techniques, even the style and methods, but not necessarily the core beliefs of others. In fact, it was Ramon Lull who, although famously stabbed by his Muslim slave and Arabic teacher he failed to convert, preached the conversion of Muslims and Jews through prayer not force. Conversion could happen through gaining an intimate knowledge of, especially, Arabic language and the culture of North Africa. Ramon Lull's autobiography reveals his troubling relationship with his slave, a Muslim captive, who taught him Arabic. Included in one manuscript are a series of illuminated pictures of his life. Lull seemed to embellish many events, especially concocting an alleged martyrdom for him on the North African coast, in Bèjaïa.[84]

Convinced by scholars such as Lull, and perhaps also their own diplomatic needs, the Roman Curia and the Council of Vienne (1311–12) were open to the idea of establishing chairs of Arabic, Hebrew, Greek and Aramaic languages. This was to occur

> in the universities of Paris, Oxford, Bologna and Salamanca . . . translating books faithfully from those languages into Latin, teach others those languages carefully and transfer their ability to these by painstaking instruction, so that, sufficiently instructed and trained in these languages, they may produce the hoped-for fruit with God's aid and spread the faith salubriously to infidel nations.[85]

Also, crucially, these languages should be taught, "Wherever the Roman curia should reside." Although these chairs were not, in fact, set up immediately after the Council of Vienne, by the end of the medieval period there was an active community of Latin scholars with specialized interest in Arabic. The Council of Vienne showed a growing awareness of the specifics of Muslim religious practice, to the extent that local Muslims made pilgrimages to saint shrines (*ziyara* – often a way to fulfill the *hajj* without actually going to Mecca and a very typical practice in the Maghrib) and limited the call to prayer. Muslim rulers also came to limit public expressions of Christianity, from bells to other religious ceremonies.[86] Yet much more than gaining knowledge of religious practices, Muslims and Christians also competed in the realm of reason – trying to find ways to convert the infidel "salubriously," through intellectual effort.

It was thus in this very active clash and reforming of ideas, strategies and theologies on both North African and European shores that the Western Mediterranean world emerged.

Between Reason and Faith

Not wishing to foment tensions, mainstream religious leaders today tend to avoid debate with members of other faiths on the truth of specific myths or miracles. The realm of truth is now primarily contested by scientific method. Reduced to finding common cause against this godlessness, foundational beliefs remain untested and unremarkably accepted. Few mainstream religious leaders wish to bring up old, fruitless battles over a scripture that has become merely symbolic. The power and responsibilities associated with modern science seems at times a common enemy to modern believers. Even secular humanists have joined the fray, gaining common cause with religious leaders against the power of modern science to destroy its human creator. While the rise of religious extremism troubles the modern world, the primary struggle for many religious leaders and thinkers remains the consequence of unbridled scientific and technological change.

For educated Jewish, Christian and Muslim thinkers in the medieval Mediterranean, however, the exploration of the truths of this world and the truths of religion were not as easily divided into separate endeavors. Even spiritual matters could be seen in what we would consider today to be highly scientific terms. Higher levels of spiritual unity with God, according to the Sufi saint Ibn 'Arabi, were alchemical as well as spiritual. The "Red Sulfur" level of spiritual purity, for instance, used a precise chemical formula and the charts and diagrams of mystical writers in Jewish, Christian and Muslim traditions often have a mathematical or rational aspect that was not necessarily at variance with established, scientific knowledge. Indeed, science and the "rational" world could be harnessed in support of faith. Aristotle's logic, central to the theological arguments of Muslims, Christians and Jews alike, was not an impersonal or unstoppable force with its own Moore's law of institutional expansion shading the future in its shadow. Faith molded reason. When the "second Moses" Maimonides, the doctor of the Church Thomas Aquinas and the extraordinarily influential Ibn Rushd made arguments, they made them within the context of faith. Reason was a tool used either to defend the faith or even, sometimes, to push for the ultimate prize: conversion of the other or at least absolute confirmation of rightness in the face of difference. The use and integration of reason to support faith and to argue against the outsider was a common Mediterranean story, especially as the Twelfth-Century Renaissance, bolstered by the Almohad rupture, flung new ideas and approaches from West to North and East. These new approaches did not emerge only out of passive exchange of influences but also out of encounters and dialogues.

Growing Importance of the Individual Soul: Islam and Christianity

Contentious, transformative dialogue defined the intellectual and spiritual lives of the Western Mediterranean in the medieval period. Debate also defined the study of the Mediterranean. Mediterranean history has become central to discussions not only of what happened near the sea, but also debates about the nature and meaning of history itself.

The discussion between historians of the Mediterranean has been centered around a question at the heart of the historian's craft – to what extent is history a social science, a discipline that can predict and determine long-term reasons for change, and to what extent is history a humanistic discipline, one that allows for the free will of the individual despite impersonal forces? The French historian Fernand Braudel's argument was for a geographic "total history" of the Mediterranean, a history that seeks out "those local, permanent, unchanging and much repeated features which are the 'constants' of Mediterranean history." In one of his more extreme manifestations, Braudel saw "total history" and the *longue durée* as the great leveler not only of cultural difference but also of individual consciousness.

> When I think of the individual I am always included to see him imprisoned within a destiny in which he himself has little hand, fixed in a landscape in which the infinite perspective of the long term stretch into the distance both behind him and before. In historical analysis as I see it, rightly or wrongly, the long run always wins in the end. Annihilating innumerable evens – all those which cannot be accommodated in the main ongoing current and which are therefore ruthlessly swept to one side – it indubitably limits both the freedom of the individual and even the role of chance.[87]

Yet geography, like all social sciences, can only go so far. The humanistic element, the individual, the story, even the accidental, derail almost every attempt by economics or sociology either to predict the future or understand the past. Cultural commonalities existed in the Western Mediterranean not simply because of the crushing inevitability of a common geography, experienced over the very long term. Culture, like language, or ego grew out of contact, conflict and dialogue (in the original sense of a contentious search for truths) between individuals and groups. Freud famously argued humans are born almost undifferentiated from the unity of the universe: to define their place separate from the universe must set the boundaries between self and the world. Long before Freud, in fact, a similar concept existed in medieval Islam.

All humans, in this belief, are originally born into a natural state as Muslim. Only the corruptions and limitations of life lead people to abandon the original, primordial truth of God's unity. According to the saying of the Prophet Muhammad, no child was born as a Christian or polytheist, but as a Muslim. He or she did not inherent original sin but was a *tabula raza*, a primordial Muslim aware of the ideal unity of God himself. Only his parents or his culture teaches him to be otherwise. Thus, in Islam was recognized one of the foundational beliefs of modern cultural theory: the notion that racial or ethnic differences are ultimately constructed. At the same time, the specificities of Islam, learned only through experience, were not subjected to the same argument. Perhaps experience itself was the enemy of salvation, if not grounded in faith.

> No babe is born but upon *Fitra* [pure human nature]. It is his parents who make him a Jew or a Christian or a Polytheist. A person said: Allah's Messenger, what is your opinion if they were to die before that (before reaching the age of adolescence when they can distinguish between right and wrong)? He said: It is Allah alone who knows what they would be doing.[88]

This notion differed from Christianity that made infant baptism, not birth, the washing away of sins, the beginning of new life and the promise of salvation. Yet the basic notion of childhood innocence remained.[89]

As a child grew up, boundaries and differences appeared. These could be in the form of temptations or trials brought about by the discovery of difference between the child and others. Cultures and faiths, which are both social constructs of specific times and periods, similarly benefitted from individuals, often times powerful intellectual and cultural leaders, interacting in discrete periods and contexts. It was in the experiences, revelations, words, arguments of individuals and in discrete moments of time, whether during a religious disputation in Ceuta or on a missionary trip from Zaragoza to Marrakech or a return from pilgrimage to Mecca, that cultures and civilizations came into being. Thus, it was through experience itself, through human stories of individuals and the distinct places, the cities on both shores of the Western Mediterranean that they visit, that this book tells its story.

After all, the stories of great, transcendent individuals had a transformative impact on the Mediterranean. Alive or dead, these new saints on both shores, known for their voluntary poverty much more than their martyrdom or prowess, inspired the fervent devotion of populations in both North Africa and Europe, connecting vast numbers of followers to spiritual experience. Peter Brown, scholar of late antiquity, argued the cult of the saints was a Christian, Mediterranean phenomenon. Yet his argument should be extended far beyond Latin documents to include medieval North Africa as well. Spiritual transformation, although it could be modeled by others, was ultimately an experience of depth in the individual soul; "saints" on all shores of the Western Mediterranean were a primary force in challenging and shaping the social status quo both during their lives and after their deaths.[90]

Colonial Historiography and the Europeanized Maghrib

Even as the histories of the North African Maghrib and Europe were linked by disputation, by a competitive dream of conversion, by trade and by the compelling spectacle of voluntary poverty, there was no decisive winner, no religious system or empire that dominated the entire shore. The medieval Mediterranean, unlike the Roman Mediterranean, remained largely free of domination from one center. Even at the height of Almohad power, Christian kingdoms and city-states expanded their influence. Also, even at the height of Portuguese and Spanish power at the end of our story in the fifteenth century, Maghribis often resisted Christian incursions ferociously. Modern notions of a dominant nation-state, or common ethnic or religious domain, did not apply.

While Hegel, the German Dean of historical philosophy mentioned in the Introduction, simply seemed to sideline North Africa, some of his near contemporaries in France were just discovering the richness of Maghribi historical sources. In fact, interest in the history of the region grew along with colonial ambitions, especially in France. Yet this scholarship, valuable as it was, often came laden with racial cateogories and assumptions of the time. In the nineteenth and early twentieth centuries several colonial scholars, in addition to admirable work revealing the sources of North African history, attempted to make the argument that Europe and North Africa, especially "white" Berber North Africa and "white" Europeans, were racially, and hence, culturally the same. In this way, they wished to culturally homogenize North Africa into Europe. Scholarship ultimately supported the colonial project. The French state in the nineteenth and twentieth century would attempt to fuse Algeria into its borders, making it a full-fledged department of France. By demonstrating the deep roots of medieval French interests in North Africa, scholars such as Le Comte de Mas Latrie explicitly sought historical foundations for French colonialism. In fact, although it focused exclusively on the medieval period, the opening quote to Mas Latrie's influential work *Relations et Commerce de l'Afrique Septentrionale avec les Nations Chrétiennes* cited the "Battle of Algiers" as a greater victory than "Marignan, Rocroy" and even "Austerlitz" (Napoleon's greatest victory).[91] In the introduction he claims that the period "before the

Turks", that is, the Ottomans, was a time when "justice" reigned. Mas Latrie argued it was in this pre-Ottoman period when French relations with the Maghrib were at their height. Indeed, for Mas Latrie this medieval history of French presence in North Africa showed that Algeria was "irrevocably a part of France."[92] Mas Latrie's history was a history of connections and relations, a history that provided ample proof of interactions between the northern and southern shore of the Western Mediterranean. However, as Professor of Diplomacy, member of the Institute, head of the judicial and legislative department at the National Records, who was decorated with the Legion of Honor in 1851, Mas Latrie's main purpose was to show how these connections affirmed French colonialism. The sources of Mas Latrie's history, mainly commercial and diplomatic treaties, were not in themselves problematic. Indeed, some of his masterful research was used in this book. Instead, the problem was the way these sources were framed as part of the glorious rise of the West. It was a history of the Mediterranean that is one of domination, one that views the rise of the West, and of France in particular, as essential for the "freedom" of the Maghrib. He praised the Cardinal of Africa who had recently "realized the dream of Louis IX" by building the cathedral at Carthage. Indeed, he proclaimed it impossible to resist the inevitable "progress" of "Christian civilization" and the "*Gesta dei per Francos.*"[93] Although many were great scholars who brought documents and historical material to light that had not been seen before, it was often within the mentality of colonialism that much of French colonial history of the Maghrib and of the Western Mediterranean was written. This did not mean that all the writing of early French scholars should be dismissed out of hand. Despite holding views that have gone out of favor today, much of the scholarship of French colonial administrators and scholars was very meticulous, source-based work. However, much of their work was based on an essentialist notion of race – the idea that race as a biological category alone could explain the cultural and historical reality of the past. It was no wonder that North African scholars resisted fusing North Africa into Mediterranean history as a junior, subservient player in that history. Similarly, Italy reached into the past, to the time of Petrarch's writing of the epic *Africa*, the time of Pisa and Genoa's capture of North African cities, to justify colonial claims to Libya and Italian East Africa: *L'Africa d'Italia.*[94]

Reacting to the French and Italian schools, postcolonial scholars such as the Moroccan Abdullah Laroui shaped the writing of North African history. They wrote against the colonial historical narrative and also often reacted against annaliste assumptions. Rather than seeing North African history as inevitably dominated by Western culture, a culture that was transmitted largely through Mediterranean and Atlantic expansion after a supposed "great divergence," Laroui contended that the history of North Africa and the Maghrib needed to be understood in region-specific terms. Laroui critiqued seeing North Africa as changeless and ahistorical, as an extension of a dominant European culture or as subsumed under a euro-dominant, common Mediterranean system.[95] Such historical thinking, if interpreted in orientalist ways, could implicitly justify French colonial expansion in North Africa. Laroui called for a distinct history of the Maghrib from the Maghribi point of view, a history that was not dominated by the weight of the inevitable argued by Braudel. Not only were the contributions of North Africa to Mediterranean history largely ignored by those whose sources were filtered by colonial assumptions, it was made even more irrelevant by the imposition of their so-called "total history."

The post World War II world meant the eventual end of French, Spanish and Italian colonialism in North Africa. Literature and history focused on agency for the Maghrib, not only the agency of the individual but also the agency of nations and proto-nations. For North Africa, that means emphasizing regionalism, the distinctiveness of Maghribi, North African histories. Agency has been embraced by postcolonial narrative, especially since Said's *Orientalism* accused the essentialist of treating people in the Orient as a kind of cultural and international "proletariat" useful for the Orientalist's "grander interpretive activity." Said's contention that the Orient was an outsider and an incorporated "weak" partner to the West can certainly be applied to much of the French colonial literature on North Africa and to the resultant marginal status of North Africa in annaliste Mediterranean historiography.[96] In many respects, this postcolonial reaction came to be the heart of the so-called structuralist critique. Structuralists "tend to assume a far too rigid casual determinism in social life." Also,

What tends to get lost in the language of structure is the efficacy of human action – or "agency," to use the currently favored term. Structures tend to appear in social scientific discourse as impervious to human agency, to exist apart from, but nevertheless to determine the essential shape of, the strivings and motivated transactions that constitute the experienced surface of social life.[97]

Medieval North Africa and Europe: A New Approach

Although a full and comprehensive account is impossible, this book attempts to be a new approach that considers both the North African and the European histories together, not as a colonialist or an anti-colonialist reaction. While Abdallah Laroui and North African scholars such as J. Abun-Nasr, Mohammed Talbi and Malek Bennabi convincingly stated the need to study North African history in its own terms there are ample opportunities to integrate this "new" history of the Maghrib into the Mediterranean in a non-colonialist context.

Unlike modern national identities, with their claimed uniform myths and history, the medieval Mediterranean was a realm of conflict, encounter and dialogue. This space existed not in spite of instances of religious or cultural differences or commercial competition but because of them. Ultimately, underneath the labels of religious or linguistic identity, there was no single Muslim or Christian or Arab or Castilian or Berber Mediterranean. There was, however, a common zone of exchange.

Economic competition created a market for exchange between North Africans and Europeans. It also created internal disruptions and reactions to commercial development and the rise of the merchant class throughout the Western Mediterranean – a new spiritualism and a new mobility. Although still neglected by scholars writing in English, the medieval North African Maghrib was similar to medieval Egypt described by the historian Janet Abu-Lughod,

> Too often, European writings view the medieval Italian maritime states as "active" agents operating on a "passive" Islamic society. The Italians are credited with introducing enormous and innovative mechanisms for transport and trade into a presumably less competent region. That argument, however, illustrates . . . reasoning backward from outcomes . . . Although it is true that the "West" eventually "won," it should not be assumed that it

did so because it was more advanced in either capitalistic theory or practice. Islamic society needed no teachers in these matters.[98]

Up to the Black Death in the middle of the fourteenth century, North African rulers, whether Berber or Arab or a mix of linguistic identities, had power and influence equal to European rulers. This was recognized even in the Latin literature. After the fall of the crusader state of Acre to the Mamluks in 1291, the Pope attempted to ban all trade with Muslims and the Barbary Coast of North Africa. Yet many popes used this ban to their own monetary advantage, giving out special exemptions and exceptions to Christian merchants. Under Pope Clement VI (1342–52), for instance, the papacy gave out licenses to merchants dealing with specific approved Muslim trading partners.[99] Ignoring the papal embargo, the Venetians continued trading with the Hafsids, successors of the Almohads in Tunis. In 1273, the Genoese complained that their archrival Venice was revitalizing the infidel, forgetting of course their own long history of trade with North Africa. Charles II of Sicily proposed that the truest and greatest Crusade must be an "economic crusade" against the "Barbary coast." Northern cities did not always have the upper hand. Hilal le Catalan, a high-ranking Muslim minister born into slavery in Granada, overthrew the Zayyanid Amir of Tlemcen, Abu Hammu, in 1318 and put a ruler named Tashfin in his place. Representing Tlemcen, Hilal, that defiant son of Christian captives, said to King John II of Aragon, "If you accept our conditions there will be peace between us. If you have need for our supplies of gold we will make them available, but only if you give us guarantees. But if you reject our conditions all negotiations will be broken between us!"[100] Clearly, it was not always Aragon dictating all the terms of economic exchange in the Western Mediterranean. Just as the history of East-West interaction has been pursued with vigor, there is similarly a need to describe the interactions between North Africa, Aragon, Castile and Marseille. Learned friars submitted several proposals to the Pope in Rome. Fidenzio of Padua and Ramon Lull suggested a fleet of police ships to enforce the blockade and encircle the Barbary Coast: "source of the revitalization [of Muslims] in the Levant [Holy Land]."[101] Although none of these proposals were effectively implemented, they reveal a great deal of discomfort in the Christian West with the amount of profit the Muslims were gaining from commerce. The sins of greed and commerce, in this theory, killed the crusader dream.

Merchants and Saints

Yet the Commercial Revolution of the Twelfth Century, a great economic revival that scholars are increasingly understanding as a global phenomenon, was perhaps much less of a threat to religious fervor than Lull had feared. Certainly, many merchants were condemned for their avarice. Abbot Guibert of Nogent told of a wealthy man in Laon who nearing death,

> demanded interest from a poor woman who had already paid the debt itself . . . She sought for a penny, which she was scarcely able to find, and brought it to him when in the last conflict between flesh and spirit the death rattle was in his throat. Taking it in the moment of death, he placed it in his mouth; while he was swallowing it as though it were the *viaticum* (communion) he breathed his last and under that protection went to the Devil.[102]

Scholars have shown that many Muslims in Egypt also came to view poverty and charity as an important part of gaining favor in the afterlife.[103] Nonetheless, the rise of wealth and world trade, in historical terms at least, seemed to actually propel the practice of voluntary poverty, charity and mysticism.

Although the greatest mystics of the era such as St. Francis and Ibn ʿArabi spoke in very different languages, they both spoke of the sins associated with excess wealth in this world. As St. Francis broke from his wealthy textile merchant father, Ibn ʿArabi critiqued the gold and wealth of the markets becoming even a martyr against greed. He also critiqued the crusaders for relying on material success in this world for the spread of Christianity. In the Rule of St. Francis, friars "can behave among other people in two ways. One way is not to make disputes and controversies, but to be subject to every human creature for God's sake, and to witness that they are Christians. The other way, when they see that God pleases, is to preach the word of God."[104] Mere swords and armies could not bring about spiritual transformation. Rather, one had to go beyond the defeat of the Muslim stranger; the objective was to sympathize with his soul.

At the same time, this spiritual revolution, a Second Axial Age, was propelled around the world by the very wealth and excess St. Francis and Ibn 'Arabi deplored. Linked to the rise of the merchants and cities in both North Africa and Eurasia was not only a spiritual, ascetic reaction, but ways of marketing spiritual goods. The Commercial Revolution – and where there were merchants there were just as often, along with the cargo, itinerant and poor friars and Sufi masters who taught and redistributed a parallel economy of spirit.

In some instances, it seemed, there was even a crossing of the line between spiritual and worldly merchandise. The twelfth-century English St. Godric of Finchale, for instance, became the patron saint of merchants. He was fabulously wealthy, especially in the Rome trade – which would have most likely involved North African merchants. Over time, however, he meditated in solitude "on the saint's life with abundant tears" and "began to yearn for solitude." Eventually, he gave all his money to the poor and became a hermit.[105] It seemed possible to become a wealthy merchant and, at the end of life, give it all away and find favor with God. As mentioned previously, the Sufi saint Al-Shadhili appealed to merchant communities in North Africa with his refusal to display outward asceticism.

Finally, there was the example of Ibn Battuta (d. 1377). This indefatigable traveler from Tangier who went as far as China did not necessarily show great depth of commitment or mystical understanding towards the Sufi masters he saw. Always moving on to the next great master, however, he collected their honorary mantles and other trinkets, almost as a trader would collect the finest of gems. Commerce allowed the messages of particularly spiritual individuals to spread both between and within traditional political, social and religious boundaries. The exchange between North African and European cultures in the midst of conflict was true even in the symbolic heart of Latin Christianity in its nascent century: ninth-century Rome.

2

ROME:

NORTH AFRICA AND THE PAPACY

For years the frightful basilisk, a dragon-like creature that could kill with his foul breath or stun with a mere look from his devilish eyes, haunted the city of Rome. The serpent roamed around the city, cruelly taking victim after victim. One day, Pope Leo IV, like a courageous lion, "halted fearlessly over the cleft from which the breath of that plague-bearing serpent emerged. Raising eyes and hands to heaven, with abundant tears he besought Christ who is God above all to put to flight by his power the dire kind of serpent from that place."[1] The serpent died. Although historians say the monster was probably just some particularly bad methane gas expelling from the piles of rubbish around Rome, the death of this frightful beast, the embodiment of so many calamities, added to the reputation of the Bishop of Rome: the Pope. The papacy in the first half of the ninth century desperately needed these miracles. Popes were expected to prove their holiness through prayerful and successful appeals to God. Many popes before him were lackluster at this skill and the fate of Rome seemed dire. Leo IV marked Rome's turning point in the economy of miracles. Indeed, every trial under Leo IV came with its concomitant miracle, with proof of God's renewed favor for the desperate city of Rome. One of the greatest "divine interventions" would defeat another fabled monster from the outside, "Saracens." The so-called "Saracens" were actually Berber North African and Sicilian raiders who, according to papal accounts, sacked not only Rome but the very tombs of St. Peter and St. Paul in 846. They threatened Rome in 849 as well.

The city the North Africans and Sicilians were attacking had long been blessed and cursed by its fame. As with Jerusalem, Rome was, and is, more important as a symbol than as a place. Inevitably, there was always tension between what Rome was as a city for itself and what it was supposed to be for the outside world. There were two great Romes: one Rome of daily experience and political power and one Rome of symbol and ideals. There was the Rome of economic decline, malaria, earthquake and flood, the Rome of constant internecine struggle between families, the papacy and outside kings. There was the Rome invested with faith and history, the *capud mundi*, the head of the world and seat of St. Peter. One of the idealized roles of Rome of the popes was as a city that would uphold Christianity against the threat of infidels. In this way, Rome, seen as a bastion against the Muslim other, focused the attention and Christian passion of newly converted believers from Northern Europe. With the fervor of recent converts, they came to the city and settled as colonies around the Vatican, the site in the former imperial gardens where, by tradition, Nero killed St. Peter. Rome not only survived attack in the ninth century, it also became a headquarters for popes who encouraged the Crusades that ultimately transformed Europe. Despite all of this, Rome maintained a Mediterranean character. Popes traded and dealt with predominantly Berber (or Coptic) North Africans, as did the famous trading cities of Naples and Amalfi.[2] Pilgrims even benefited from a Berber presence. Kalfun, a Muslim Berber slave of the Aghlabid emir of Sicily, captured the Italian port of Bari in 847, only a year after the disastrous raids on Rome. Yet the capture of Bari by this Berber dynasty did not end Christian use of the port for journeys south or east. In fact, the Christian pilgrim Bernard petitioned the Muslim King of Bari, named Sawdan, for safe conduct all the way to Jerusalem. This safe passage was granted due to Sawdan's relationship with other Muslim rulers on the route to the Holy Land. Thus, a North African, Muslim Berber ruler on Bari may have helped facilitate early Christian passage to one of the holiest sites in Islam and the navel of the world for medieval Christians: Jerusalem.[3]

Centuries later, during the Gothic period, at the height of the Crusades, great cathedrals were built throughout Northern Europe to glorify not only God but the glories of those who had followed the Pope's crusading message at Clermont in 1095. One might expect Rome, above all other cities and as capital of crusade, to have been filled with such Gothic splendor. The city should be a city of many spires, an ocean filled with the waves of flying buttresses, a kaleidoscope of stained glass. Instead, Rome gave, and still gives, an impression quite different from northern cities. Although the Renaissance, at least the Renaissance as an Italian and Mediterranean phenomenon, would soon dominate the scene, the reason for this lack of Gothic splendor of lands further north was notable. Instead, as a great mixer of cultures, Rome throughout the medieval period had a Mediterranean culture even as it was a magnet to pilgrims from the north.

The popes have always been part of a secular geography as much as a sacred one. That secular reality was very much tied to a diverse Mediterranean. This was especially true when it came to relations between Rome and its southern neighbors, especially relations with North African and Muslim Sicily. These were relations that had existed long before the advent of Christianity. Romans only successfully sacked Punic Carthage with the help of Berber "Numidian" allies. The term Saracen or Moor, used well into the modern era by Christian chroniclers or playwrights such as Shakespeare for Muslims and Samaritans regardless of ethnic, geographic or linguistic background, was hardly descriptive. It referred to those who did not claim descent from Sarah but from Hagar and Ishmael. Due to its problematic character, many modern scholars have abandoned the term, preferring to call the Saracens "Arabs" or simply "Muslims". In fact, the tools of genetic analysis confirm what North Africans have long known: these "Saracens" and "Moors" were most likely predominantly Berbers, occasionally led by Arab commanders and adventurers, and Christian, Coptic shipbuilders and sailors. The caliph in Damascus, 'Abd Al-Malik Ibn Marwan (d. 705), moved around two thousand Copts to Tunis to construct a naval force.[4] Berbers left their genetic markers throughout Italy, Spain and Portugal. In fact, although the study provokes many questions about the notions of race in the modern academy, a recent article in a scientific, peer-reviewed journal showed that the region of southern Italy, Cantabria, showed the highest percentage of North African genetic legacy, higher even than Sicily, Portugal and southern Spain, areas controlled by Berbers for a much longer period.[5] Beyond questions of genetic analysis, however, Berber culture in the Mediterranean did not disappear with Arab invasions. Although most of our sources for North Africa are written it Arabic, only a veneer of actual Arab cultural influence existed, often at an elite level. Arabic became a language of rulers and Arab descent became, increasingly, a mark of nobility. Yet, in this earlier period, the acculturation of Berbers into Arab identity, an acculturation that has still not happened in many parts of North Africa, would not occur for centuries. Instead of Arab or Saracen, one could more accurately speak of the period of Berber domination of the Central and Western Mediterranean. Berbers were themselves hardly united into a coherent political or even linguistic entity and were often a greater threat to the power of the Arab caliphs than the Frankish Christians. It was not until the twelfth century that great migrations, some say invasions, of large numbers of Arab tribes into North Africa began. For centuries Berbers, both Muslim and non-Muslim, dominated the population and the peoples who came to "threaten" Europe. The Mediterranean, especially the Mediterranean west of Alexandria (Egypt remained primarily Coptic for centuries), was not really spilt into Arab and non-Arab spheres. Instead, North Africa maintained its Berber character with a light veneer of Arab and Arabic culture, often adopted by Berbers themselves. This was a veneer through which historians must read their sources. Language was the primary reason why more scholars spoke of the "Arabs" instead of the "Berbers" as masters of the Mediterranean. Unlike the Arab sources, there are pitifully few documents of any kind surviving in the Berber language, let alone archaeological and numismatic evidence. Thus, the Berbers have been seen by scholars of European medieval history through the lens of Arab language. This has transformed a people who had for centuries interacted with powers and peoples throughout the Mediterranean into exotic, orientalized Arabs.

Although held up as an infidel, these "Saracen" Berbers were as often a trading partner. Also, this trade in precious luxuries for the churches of Rome was procured through Jewish merchants in both Rome and North Africa. Even more importantly, the mostly Berber Muslims provided a convenient excuse for popes to form alliances with Christian princes to the south and, especially, to defy the Frankish Holy Roman Emperors. Also, it was North African Berbers, enslaved after the Battle of Ostia, who rebuilt the walls and churches of the holy city of Rome and erected a "Leonine City" named after the Pope. They not only restored the physical walls of Rome and the Vatican; they also fortified the reputation of the papacy and of the city of

Rome, making both far stronger than before. Far from disempowering the Pope and leading mayhem and disintegration on the northern shore of the Mediterranean, the Berber raids established the reputation and power of the papacy, renewing the greatness of Rome as a pilgrimage destination in a way that far exceeded their short-term threat.

Although it was possible that the Berber, Arab and Coptic forces were fully aware of the importance of the shrines of St. Paul and St. Peter, an argument could also be made that their raids were primarily about booty. Had they felt a fanatical need to capture Rome, the capital of Christianity in the Western Mediterranean, there would have been far more persistent raids and occupations and less hasty retreats. There would have been sieges and attempts to hold land immediately around Rome, tactics similar to those experienced by the far better defended city of Constantinople. That great eastern city, far richer than Rome at the time, was the real object of the great caliphs in Baghdad where most power in the Islamic world was then centered. Harun Al-Rashid even celebrated yearly, almost ceremonialized campaigns against the Byzantines. From the North African perspective, raids on Rome were probably based as much on economic opportunism and plunder as religious war. Rather than splitting the Mediterranean and leading to the decline of the northern shore, as argued by Pirenne, the North African raids into Europe spurred the growth of one of the world's most powerful institutions and one of the world's greatest cities: the papacy and Rome.

There had been contact between Christians and Muslims long before the famous sack of Rome in 846. Some of the earliest Christian writers, including John of Damascus, one of the first anti-Islamic polemicists, probably saw Islam as a misguided branch of Christianity, not a separate religion. For educated Christians, Muhammad was not a pagan but a heretic. Also, from the early Muslim point of view, Christians were "people of the book," people of Abraham who shared the same tradition of revealed prophecy as Islam. Questioning the earliest sources of Islamic history, many of them written in the ninth century, a scholar recently claimed that Arab Christians in the earliest years of Islam were all considered part of a common community of believers. In this theory, it was only after the rise of the powerful Muslim Caliph 'Abd Al-Malik (d. 705) that a marked distinction between Muslims and Christians developed.[6] Even during this period, when Islam seemed to emerge as a distinct religious culture in contrast with Christianity, there were plenty of instances of economic and political alliances of convenience. In 813, less than four decades before the sack of Rome, envoys from the Aghlabids rulers of present-day Tunisia helped a Christian Venetian crew to attack a rich merchant convoy of Andalusi, or Spanish Muslim, ships.[7] In the first decades of the ninth century, the Bishop and Duke of Naples joined the great Italian trading cities of Amalfi and Gaeta in an alliance with Berbers against Pope John VIII (d. 882).[8] Known for his efforts to stem Muslim gains in southern Italy, Pope John offered to pay off the threat from the Bishop and his Muslim supporters with a customs exemption and 10,000 mancusi coins. As the scholar Robert Lopez noted, "the *mancusi* in all probability were Islamic coins, and the papyrus used by the Pope for his diplomatic campaign was made in Egypt and bore at its top an Arab inscription praising Allah."[9] Raiding in the western Mediterranean was carried out not only by Berbers but also by Italian Christians, especially by the leading, adventuresome men of the burgeoning cities of Pisa and Genoa. Boniface, the Count of Lucca just north of Pisa, looking for an armada of Muslim ships to raid near Corsica, sailed south and entered the Gulf of Tunis and raided the city in 828. The Tunisians would fear these "Rumis" (a word they used to wrongly describe the Latin Christians in the same category as Byzantines) as much as the Christians feared the "Saracen."[10] The North African coast was left to defend itself as Arab leadership centered in Kairouan, south of Tunis, and on land routes through the Saharan desert.

In the midst of so many centrifugal currents, it may have seemed inevitable that the popes would need to bribe both Berbers and insubordinate Neapolitan bishops with coins minted in Arabic indefinitely. Indeed, Rome before the raid of 846, while increasingly a pilgrimage destination for many new converts to Christianity in northern Europe, was not a particularly promising place until Leo IV came along. Rome's difficulties were not primarily caused by the threat of invasion from the south. Popes were under the thumb of king and ruler with Frankish troops outside the walls. Centuries of "barbarian" conquest, plague and pestilence had dampened the fiery spirit of the population. It was only after the raid that Leo IV, one of the three most powerful "Lion" popes in history and possibly the most important, could build not only a newly fortified city bearing his name, but a new vision for the papacy. Yet the importance of Leo IV and the North Africans has been lost to many who focus on later Crusades in the East as the defining moment for Christendom and the papacy. Pope Leo IV solidified papal power due to a much more immediate threat, not from the Levant, but from North Africa. A partial explanation for this negligence of Leo IV's ninth century might be that after Leo IV the papacy went into a period of some decline.

Yet the legacy of Leo IV as a pope who used conflict with the infidel to increase his influence should not be underestimated. Romans proudly recognized the North African raids well into the Renaissance as one of the most important events in papal history. The battle against a common outsider unified the authority of a leader such as Leo IV. The "Saracens," most of them Berbers, far from destroying the unity of the northern Mediterranean, gave the papacy the ability to fortify itself, both in stone and in spirit. The Berber-built walls guarded the Vatican for centuries. They guarded popes not usually from Muslim threat but mainly from threats by other Christians, especially the Holy Roman Emperors. This set the stage for the Crusades.

Pope Urban II, calling for the First Crusade against distant Muslim lands in 1095, increased papal authority, allowing the unification of much of Europe around the authority of medieval history's most powerful pope, Innocent III. Yet it was the ninth-century naval struggle between these convenient, neighboring outsiders that began an escalation of papal power, a power that would culminate later in crusade. While later popes preached warfare against a distant enemy, Leo IV was faced by the prospect of the fall of Rome to the "infidel." There was nothing like disaster, whether fire, earthquake or "Saracen" threat, to found the reputation of the Bishop of Rome and seal the city as capital of Roman Christendom. Thus, far from destroying Christian claims to the Mediterranean, the conflict with Berber, Coptic and Arab raiders cemented the deep foundations of papal power, allowing him finally to organize the Christian merchant towns. Indeed, the seminal importance of Leo IV would be recognized well into the Renaissance.

Leo IV and the Transformation of Rome

As mentioned in the Introduction, the Belgian historian Pirenne theorized that the true end of the classical Mediterranean world happened when conflict with Islam, especially Islam in North Africa, drove the center of Europe to the north, splitting the Mediterranean. The rise of Rome under Leo IV contradicts this assertion. Rome, and much of Italy, was a magnet and an international destination for the rest of Europe, especially for recently converted Christians. German, Frisian (from the Netherlands), Anglo-Saxon and Lombard colonies surrounded the Vatican forming a neighborhood called the Borgo. The future King Alfred the Great of Wessex, first great king of the Anglo-Saxons, was the most famous among the English to visit the Borgo. According to the Anglo-Saxon Chronicle, Pope Leo IV vested him a Christian ruler and consul when Alfred was only four years old. Just as Pope Leo would fight against infidels from the land of Carthage, so too would Alfred fight against the infidel, barbaric Vikings. The Borgo "colonies" represented many of the barbarian tribes that had been successfully brought into the fold of the Church.

It would be these same colonists who attempted to fight off the North Africans as they sacked the church of St. Peter in 847, taking with them the hoards of jewels and precious metals. The North African and Sicilian raiders must have evoked memories of the Viking raids, especially among many of the Anglo-Saxon Borgo residents from England who protected the Pope and shrine of Peter.

Yet the pilgrims and residents of Rome were not necessarily the most holy or upstanding members of its society. Despite the expansion of Christianity into the north and its benefits for the papacy, Rome in the middle of the ninth century period saw many existential threats in Christendom both internal and external. Even the pilgrims from all around Europe who had come to Rome were not always a boon. Many of them criminals, murderers and miscreants, bishops sent them on their way to Rome granting them special protection and dispensation for forgiveness of their sin. Some described the city as a *refugium paccatorum*, a refuge of sinners.[11]

In addition to these local miscreants, the greatest threats to Rome came not only from North Africa but also from other Christian power centers. Before Leo IV, Rome was largely a tired shadow of her former self. Many of the great monuments and marbles in Rome had been carried off, plundered as much by Romans and Christians as by barbarians. On a visit to the city of Augustus, Byzantine Emperor Constans II, the same emperor who had been defeated at the great naval Battle of the Masts against Coptic ships commanded by Arab invaders, did much to damage the artistic heritage of Rome. After holding a great feast, perhaps to distract the leading men of the city, he took much that could be carted away and loaded it on imperial ships. It was conceivable that some of the same ships that defeated the navy of the caliphs thus contributed also to the deterioration of Rome. He seemed to have intended to return the capital of his empire to Rome, only cancelling this plan when stopped by the Lombards. Famously, most of the great public bronzes were taken, even taking tiles off the Pantheon church leaving only the statue of Marcus Aurelius, believed to be that of Constantine I, untouched. With his consolation prize of bronzes, Constans headed south to Syracuse, Sicily where he established himself for several years in a city especially vulnerable to the earliest raids from North Africa. In fact, Constans would later be defeated again at Syracuse by a Muslim fleet, causing treasures of ancient Rome, including the bronze tiles of the Pantheon, to fall into the hands of North African raiders.

Crumbling from these outrages and unable to fill the glorious extent of its ancient walls, Rome in the first half of the ninth century was divided into two sections, the *disabitato* (uninhabited) and the comparably small, inhabited or *abitato* part around the Vatican. Much of the city of Augustus had long ago been given up for pasture. In fact, the Roman Forum itself would remain a real *Campo Vaccino* or "Field of Cows" into the nineteenth century. The Vatican itself (although the Pope was resident in the Lateran) and the neighborhood around it, the Borgo, were especially vulnerable and unprotected without proper walls or defenses. This was despite the fact that it was on this very land that the greatest martyrs of Christian tradition had died at the hands of their pagan, Roman tormentors. The malarial marshes surrounding Rome had saved the city and the Vatican from many a sacking. Invading armies died more from the mosquito bite than the sword, but it seemed incredible that so important a site, the very place where the prince of Apostles was martyred, remained so exposed.

Although raids had a large impact, the greatest challenge to any burgeoning papal authority in Rome came mostly from the Holy Roman Emperors to the north, not from North African raiders. When the previous "Lion" pope, Leo III, crowned the Frankish ruler Charlemagne Holy Roman Emperor on Christmas Day AD 800 and prostrated himself before him, it seemed a new era of alliance between Holy Pontiff and Holy Emperor would begin. Instead, a struggle of epic complexity ensued. The greatest threat to the papacy came from the Franks and a succession of Holy Roman Emperors and monarchs. Before Leo IV, most popes were not as effective at maintaining papal authority. The relatively inactive Pope Gregory IV had died in 844 after constant struggles with the Carolingian monarchs, the descendants of the mighty Charlemagne, over the authority of the papacy. Sergius II, successor of Gregory, predecessor of Leo IV and member of a Roman family, came to power only after a divided election and without approval from the Emperor Lothar who commanded Louis, the King of Italy, to march on the city. Only after kneeling together at the grave of the Apostle Peter did king and pope come to some sort of momentary understanding. Yet the tension between secular and sacred authority would not disappear with prayer; it continued to linger between popes, kings and emperors for more than a millennium. The so-called "Donation of Pepin" (AD 754 and 756) had established the temporal power of the popes as rulers over their own lands when the Frankish ruler forced the Lombards. The Franks "donated" territory from the Tyrrhenian Sea to the Adriatic to the pontiff. Yet they also expected some sort of say in the selection of the Pope. In some ways, this embroiled the Pope in centuries of conflict between spiritual and worldly roles that lasts to this day.

Leo IV witnessed a growing threat from the North Africans arrayed on various islands around the Tyrrhenian Sea, including Sardinia. Yet, this did not mean that the North African and Sicilian raids were unimportant. Unlike threats from the Emperor, which occurred within a Christian orbit, he seemed to realize this was an external threat that would actually serve to bolster his power as a defender of the holy sites of Rome. First, however, Rome needed to avoid outright conquest by the North Africans – something that was not assured.

The Raid on Rome

Even as buffer states, small Christian kingdoms that protected the successors of St. Peter from fearful conquest by the so-called "Saracens," were beginning to crumble, Rome became more and more of an actual target. The Kingdom of Arichis divided; this division provided an underbelly allowing invasions from the heterogeneous Coptic, Berber and, only-rarely Arab pirates of North Africa who were raiding the coastlines, pushing people away from the fields and into fortifications and cities. Radelchis, Lord of Beneveto, had himself invited "these robber hordes" into the heart of Italy, just as in Iberia almost a century and a half earlier the Berber commander Tariq was invited to invade by a Christian ruler. In Italy, Berbers controlled substantial territory. "They made themselves masters of Taranto and devastated the whole of Apulia."[12] Even the miraculous arrival of Saint Bartholomew, famously swimming in his tomb from India to Lipari, did not protect the island from unpredictable Berber raids. Despite the short distance to the Italian shore, another miracle was not left to chance. The saint's body had to be carried to the mainland, to Beneveto, whose Christian ruler had actually invited the raids on Rome.[13]

In 845, raiders from Tunis, Sicily and Sousse, from Sardinia and Corsica, islands under the control of "Saracens," had already taken territory near Naples. Striking horror throughout Christendom, their ultimate destination after 845 seemed to be Rome, famed for its incredible wealth of relics and treasures. The great German historian of medieval Rome, Gregorovius, claimed, "They hoped to plant the flag of the Prophet on Saint Peter's."[14] Edward Gibbon, more famous for describing the possibility of Islam being taught in the colleges of Oxford had they defeated Charles Martel at Poitiers, spoke also of the raiders on Rome:

> In the sufferings of prostrate Italy, the name of Rome awakens a solemn and mournful recollection. A fleet of Saracens from the African coast presumed to enter the mouth of the Tiber, and to approach a city, which even yet, in her fallen state, was revered as the metropolis of the Christian world. The gates and ramparts were guarded by a trembling people; but the tombs and temples of St. Peter and St. Paul were left exposed in the suburbs of the Vatican and of the Ostian way. Their invisible sanctity had protected them against the Goths, the Vandals, and the Lombards; but the Arabs disdained both the gospel and the legend; and their rapacious spirit was approved and animated by the precepts of the Koran.[15]

In 846, a combined fleet entered into the Tiber River itself. One group of raiders went to Civitavecchia, another to the city upriver and another went towards the city of Rome. The Vatican and St. Peter's along with St. Paul's Outside the Walls were not, at this time, well protected. Even within walls, crumbling, neglected and in desperate need of repair, the Romans were not very safe. Not only that, Pope Sergius died in January 847, just after the raids were occurring. Even the German Barbarian invasions had not brought

Rome to a lower point. The city, even Roman-Christian civilization itself, seemed desperate for a savior.

We hear most about this Christian hero, Pope Leo IV, in the *Liber Pontificalis*, the Book of the Popes, a book that revealed interesting information not only about the papacy but also about the Berber Saracens. "A man very high up in the papal administration" who was the "mouthpiece" of Leo wrote this source for the life of Leo IV.[16] Nevertheless, even the *Liber Pontificalis* suggested that the "Saracen" raid was not primarily one of civilizational conquest, but one of economic opportunism. The fleets did not stay. They raided and then withdrew with their valuable booty. They did not set up permanent encampments.

The *Liber Pontificalis* showed how the raids, in fact, bolstered the Church. It also gave an intimate and exceptionally long portrait of the Pope's life. It was the longest life in the *Liber Pontificalis*, excepting only that of Leo III who crowned Charlemagne. The historian Pirenne focused on Leo III, the Pope under whom the center of power in Europe went north, to Charlemagne at Aachen. Yet it was Leo IV, through the excuse of the "Saracen" threat, who brought power back to Rome.

Leo IV's very ordination started because of the threat of invasion from the sea. It was, according to the *Liber Pontificalis*, the fear of the "Saracen" that led Leo IV to come to power without the approval of the Emperor as required by the *Constitutio*, the AD 824 agreement between emperor and pope. There were emergency circumstances brought about by the raiders.

> In his time [the time of Leo's predecessor Sergius's death] the churches of the blessed princes Peter and Paul were thoroughly plundered by the Saracens. At this distress and wretchedness all the vigor of the Romans melted away and was broken. When this happened, because of the two occurrences and perils, that is, the pontiff's [Sergius'] sudden death and the plundering that had taken place in the holy churches and their territories of all the Romans, the whole gathering of the Romans said that there was no way for them to escape the danger of death.[17]

The account goes on, indicating the needs of the Romans and the holy places above the legal requirements of an agreement between emperor and pope.

Instead of consulting the Emperor, it was in "common consultation" that the "dignitaries of Rome" itself thought about who would be the next pontiff.

> The late-departed pontiff [Sergius] had not yet been taken to his proper burial, and lo! Everyone from last to first with one voice and one heart, demanded the venerable priest Leo as their pontiff to be, and with many protestations and much clamor they said they would have none other over them as prelate but him.

Even if he wanted to obey Lothar and the *constitutio*, the Roman people would not allow it. They fetched him from the church of the Quattro Coronati where he was living, about a hundred meters away from the Lateran Palace, "by force and against his will, and with hymns and distinguished acclamations of praise conducted him to the Lateran patriarchate." In this convenient manner and with the threat "unanimously" uniting the people around his election, it seemed the Pope simply had to accept. The jewels and sacred treasures of St. Peter and St. Paul to wash upon the shore of Italy clutched, it was said, in the hands of many a dead raider. Even so, further attacks seemed on the horizon.

Pope Leo IV was a master at ninth-century public relations, uniting not only fractious princes in a naval campaign against the Saracens but, crucially, the highly volatile Roman population itself. In fact, we even have a visual example of his skill. Fortunately, in addition to the rich descriptions of the *Book of Popes* used above, there remains a painted portrait of Leo IV. This has miraculously survived almost twelve centuries in the basilica he restored in the triumphal heart of Rome. Now found under ground, there are few sites more evocative in Rome. Under the nave of the Basilica of San Clemente, just a short walk from the Colosseum, there still exists a surprising window onto the ninth-century world, several meters below the current street level.

In fact, it was Leo IV's restoration of the church of San Clemente that symbolized the revitalization of the legacy of ancient Rome. The frescoes (still seen today in the excavations of the lower church) depicting Leo represented "the most important groups of surviving material for the study of the art of the early Middle Ages."[18] Leo IV stands as a pillar of fortitude to the left side of a robed man dynamically cowering and ducking. It "reflects an accurate likeness." His head is framed by a halo. But unlike later medieval art, it is a rare square halo typical of the period, not round. He holds a codex, probably the bible and looks straight ahead with poise. Underneath is an inscription reading "Sanctissimus Dom(inus) Leo Q(ua)rt(us) P(a)p(a) Romanus": Holy Lord Leo IV Pope of Rome. Although the only surviving image, the Pope was represented not only in painting but also on vestments and metalwork.[19] Leo was especially eager to restore the tomb and altar of St. Peter, "violated and reduced to such dishonor and vileness by the infidel Saracens." It had become much less of a destination for the pilgrims, who did not come to the altar as eager to pray as they used to be. He restored the tomb and built new splendid panels. He erected one showing his likeness. This painting at the tomb of the triumphant St. Peter showed the new power relationship the Pope wished to clearly establish between himself and the Emperor. Emperor Lothar was demoted in the image and called "the spiritual son" of the Pope.[20]

As many acts of papal redecorating would evidence, little of permanent value was actually lost by the Berber incursion. The Pope gained much more in prestige. As Gibbon indicated, there was little centralized or organized about the "Saracen" threat:

> Had the Mahometans [Muslims] been united, Italy must have fallen an easy and glorious accession to the empire of the prophet. But the caliphs of Baghdad had lost their authority in the West; the Aglabites and Fatimites [Fatimids] usurped the provinces of Africa, their emirs of Sicily aspired to independence; and the design of conquest and dominion was degraded to a repetition of predatory inroads.[21]

Far better than a raid by a Christian rival or king, these raids by the "infidel" gave the papacy perhaps the greatest gift possible – an opportunity for leadership and, for posterity, the miraculous actions of God.

After a couple years consolidating his power, fighting demons and fortifying the walls of Rome, the Saracens gave Leo IV the opportunity to lead the papacy in a new direction. In fact, the best possible situation emerged for the Pope when the southern seaports of Gaeta, Amalfi and Naples, increasingly independent of Byzantium, formed an alliance with the Pope, what the German historian Gregorovius called the first medieval naval league.[22] The raiders had gathered on an island near Sardinia waiting to pounce on Rome. At first, however, the Pope seemed skeptical of help from the Christian south of Italy. He feared these rival cities at a time of weakness as much as he welcomed the possibility of assistance from their strong navies. One man, representing the men of Naples, Amalfi and Gaeta, promised that he wanted nothing but to "win a victory with the Lord's help over the pagans."[23] When the Pope came to Ostia to meet the Neapolitans and assembled allies, "they prostrated themselves on the ground at his feet, kissed them reverently, and gave things to the Almighty throned on high, who had decided to send such a bishop to strengthen them. That they might better be the victors over the Sons of Belial,[24] they begged him earnestly that they might deserve to receive the Lord's body from his sacred hands."[25] The Pope in prayer asked for the assistance of God, "whose right hand raised up St. Peter the apostle lest he sink when walking on water, and delivered from the depth of the sea his fellow-apostle Paul when three times shipwrecked."[26] The inclusion of Amalfi in this alliance was an especially important coup for the Pope as the city had frequently traded with North Africa.

The Neapolitan ships attacked first and many were destroyed or injured by the enemy fleet. The Berber raiders "would have been triumphant" were it not for a great storm that suddenly stirred up "such as no one in these times can remember . . . Almighty God, as we truly believe, had 'brought forth this wind from his storehouse' "[27] With their fleet destroyed, they were washed on shore in such a great number that many were killed by hunger and "by the sword." The Pope had not only triumphed over the "Saracens." He had shown the power of the two greatest patron apostles of Rome: St. Peter and Paul. Also, he had secured a large number of captives, Saracen slaves who were engaged in building the wall around St. Peter's church and various "manufacturers' tasks, whatever seemed necessary."[28] Gregorovius spoke breathlessly,

> Rome had again slaves of war, and after four hundred years celebrated another triumph . . . If the column of Duilius adorned with the rostra of vessels, restored by Tiberius, still remained erect in the ancient Forum, it is scarcely probable that any Roman now understood either its meaning or its inscription; and the victory at Ostia, in which papal galleys had doubtless taken part was celebrated amid solemn thanksgiving in the churches as a miracle due to the Prince of the Apostles.[29]

The Italian scholar and nationalist Michele Amari's contention that the destruction of the "Saracen" fleet "proved that the Italian fleet was better constructed and manned by sailors with more spirit" was perhaps a stretch too far.[30]

It was possible that the North African ships, less aware of the local geography, were in the wrong place at the wrong time. Yet the battle of Ostia should not be seen as simply a momentary victory that had a marginal impact on Roman society. The battle increased the prestige and power of Rome. Socially, these mostly Berber or Coptic slaves would eventually become integrated into the Roman population, putting their stamp on the character not only of its people but, possibly, of the buildings they helped build or the items they helped manufacture. Although there has been speculation that a market for slaves existed in Rome in the eighth century, these were primarily pagan, Slavic peoples, often sent to North Africa in exchange for goods.[31]

Captives in Rome and Papal Trade

What ultimately became of these "Saracen" Berber slaves remains an intriguing mystery. They obviously would have had an impact on the architecture and style of the Vatican but the exact extent of that influence remains obscure. There did not remain for art historians of Rome the same rich material left by the Mudejars, those Muslims who remained under Christian rule in Spain. Many of the captives may have converted, died during construction, perhaps even had families and acculturated into the polyglot, pilgrim society of ninth- and tenth-century Rome. Italian slaves, especially women, captured during raids also went the other direction, to North Africa. Both Italians and North Africans traded Slavic peoples. The full story of these captives on both shores of the Mediterranean and their integration into that society also remains an open question.

In only a few years, the North African captives had finished the Vatican walls. In 852, Leo was at the height of his powers. He ordered a triumphal celebration, the likes of which had not been seen in the city for decades. Having united the southern Italian cities, the people of Rome, and even having gained the support of Lothar, the emperor who helped financed the re-building of Rome, the Pope created a new city named after himself, the "Leonine City." This was the area now known as the Vatican district and portions of the walls, built with Berber, Arab and Coptic hands, still remain.[32] Yet, his efforts were not restricted to the walls. No expense was spared in returning the altars and shrines of the apostles to their former splendor.

In an ironic twist, much of what Leo IV used to restore these shrines came from lands conquered and controlled by the North Africans themselves. Restoring the churches using silk and purple velvet, pearls and precious stones, shows how great was the intercourse maintained with the erstwhile enemy. Trade was carried out with the help of the league that just defeated the raiders, the Neapolitans, and inhabitants of Gaeta and Amalfi who continued to have contact with Muslims (see book cover).[33] Metals, pearls and fine silks filled the churches of Rome. As the *Liber Pontificalis* noted,

> This noteworthy and distinguished bishop, boiling with love from on high, presented to St. Peter the apostle's basilica 1 fine silver crown weighing 24 lb; 2 chased bowls weighing 2 lb; 7 veils, 2 of them of interwoven gold, 2 of cross-adorned silk and 3 of Spanish. There he presented for the brightness and glory of that venerable basilica 1 Alexandrian curtain of wondrous beauty representing peacocks carrying men on top, and another representation of eagles and wheels and birds with trees.[34]

Some of these jewels, bought from North Africans, had been stolen not just by infidels, but also by Christian robbers who took the precious stones from one of the Pope's main crosses used in processions.[35] Much of the life of Leo IV in the *Liber Pontificalis* focused on his acquisition of great treasures for the churches of Rome. Long lists of the most opulent and luxurious items, most of them traded with North Africa or coming from lands under Muslim rule (Spain and Alexandria), filled his Leonine City. Leo IV was not alone in his seemingly curious willingness to buy from those who raided him. For centuries the interchanging roles of trade and warfare often meant merchant ships could be seized at port for the disposal of the ruler and the role of a vessel as either a warship or a trading ship was often indeterminate. Rulers on both Christian and Muslim shores could reserve for themselves the sole right to buy from a boat laden with goods essential for the army including such pedestrian goods as oil, wax and silk. Later sources showed that Muslim ships could be seized and emptied of their goods, including vessels coming from Muslim areas but owned by Jews.[36] Other parts of Christian Europe engaged in this trade. The Museum of the Bishops of Vic in Catalonia, north of Barcelona, contains stunning examples of North African *tiraz*, or fine fabrics, as well as Syrian and Egyptian fabrics imported during these early centuries.[37] In France, a document from AD 876 and written with the name of John VIII in Arabic and on papyrus contains the epigraph "Sa'id ibn . . ."[38] Unfortunately, we do not possess the complete name of this rare document. However, it was almost certainly from Northern Africa.

Beyond the complexity of his commercial relationship with North Africa, Spain and Alexandria, Leo IV's story entered the singing tradition of troubadours. The medieval French legend of the knight Fierabras tells of the "Saracen" sacking of Rome and Leo's rise after the death of Pope Sergius.[39] Later, in the Renaissance, it was immortalized in the new Vatican of Michelangelo and Raphael being built upon the old Leonine City.

The Sistine Legacy

After the Sistine Chapel, the most famous art within the Vatican is concentrated in the Room of the Signatura in the Papal Apartments. The room contains the famous painting of the School of Athens, one of the most iconic images in all of Western art, famous for including image of Averroes in a turban. Yet in the next room, even closer to the Sistine Chapel are two lesser-known paintings. The two rooms are mirrors of each other in form. These paintings in the same prominent positions reserved for the School of Athens and the Disputation of the Holy Sacrament, but in the "Room of the Borgo Fire" were designed and, at least partially, painted by Rafael. Their prominence in the Vatican exemplifies the legacy of the raids on Rome. The first painting, of the fire, shows Rome on its knees; the second shows the triumph at the Battle of Ostia. Fires were also opportunities for renewal. It was fitting, perhaps, that in a city such as Rome many incendiary moments turned into glorious opportunities to rise from the ashes. A magnificent domed painting designed by Rafael (d. 1520) in the Papal Rooms of the Vatican depicts the city of Rome in flames as a place of utter ruin and desperation during a crucial turning point in papal history.[40] Painted in 1514, the Borgo Fire fresco depicts the depopulated and badly defended city, resigning to the devastations of a great fire in the Borgo, a Roman quarter across the Tiber and right next to the Vatican, in 847, nearly seven centuries before. St. Peter's Basilica is a haven of refuge as a pope calms the crowd, protecting Rome from fire and chaos much as he later protected the city from the Frankish army of the Emperor and the ships of the "Saracens". Yet the Pope depicted in Rafael was not Leo IV, but another Leo, his Renaissance patron Leo X, a pope who was obviously appropriating the prestige of his namesake. Another painting in the same room depicts the great Battle of Ostia. The Pope, again depicted as a plump Leo X taking the spot of Leo IV, looks up to God as denuded bodies of "Saracens" are taken off ships to be killed or enslaved. In the distance, crusading ships gain the advantage. Only a few decades after this painting was finished, a combined force of Christian navies would defeat the Ottomans at the battle of Lepanto in 1571.

After being immortalized and appropriated by Rafael and Leo X, Pope Leo IV, even became a symbol of some lost republican virtue for French Enlightenment scholars. Leo IV gained some notice among skeptical classicists who generally despised the profligacy typical of many early, medieval popes. Voltaire said, "Leo was born a Roman; the courage of the first ages of the republic glowed in his breast; and amid the decline and corruption of a ruined age, he stood erect, like one of the firm and lofty columns that rear their heads above the fragments of the Roman forum. . ."[41] Leo IV, although he has not quite maintained his fame into modern times, was very much a symbol of the pre-Crusades, Christian or even Western Civilization battle against some perceived, long-term "Saracen" menace.

For the sociologist Georg Simmel, "war with the outside is sometimes the last chance for a state ridden with inner antagonisms to overcome these antagonisms."[42] Far from destroying Rome as the center of western Christendom, the Saracen raids secured its future. Even as centuries of infighting would continue between the Pope and his secular enemies, the Battle of Ostia became a symbol of the possibility of group cohesion; an outside enemy had been found. Later popes, such as John X (d. 928), also used the North African, Berber Muslim threat to consolidate support from allies and shore up the position of the papacy. John's victory at the Garigliano River in 915 against a combined alliance of Christian and Muslim forces to the south cemented the southern border of the Papal States. He personally led the papal army into battle. The results of conflict with the "Saracen" were, at least for that moment, highly beneficial to the papacy. The sacking of Rome and sinking of the North African fleet by the seeming grace of God would be remembered again and again as crusading popes sought to battle for the higher ground against their own, Christian rivals. Such rivalry was probably first and foremost from the very beginning, even in the mind of Leo IV. Victory for the Pope did not mean a break in relations with the south. If anything, trade and contact with North Africa only increased the bejeweled luxury of Rome's many holy sites, tantalizing magnets for the Christian world expanding to the north.

Captive Between Faiths: Philip of Mahdiyya

Not all slaves from North Africa were in chains building walls. Some held high positions in court. The story of one of these high-ranking slaves, Philip of Mahdiyya, was especially illuminating of the often-strained relationship of a slave who dutifully followed the interests of his Norman Christian king, Roger II (d. 1154) of Sicily, even as he subtly helped his fellows in Africa.

Philip was from Mahdiyya, an important port on the eastern coast of Tunisia founded by the Fatimid religious revolutionaries. He was a castrated slave, high functionary in the Sicilian court of the Norman King Roger II (1095–1154), and would have known the great Muslim geographer Al-Idrisi. Past scholarship speculated that Philip was Greek but recent research has proven North African, probably Berber, origins to be most probable. Philip spent much of his youth in North Africa. He was captured, turned into a eunuch early in his life. Philip's mentor was another peripatetic traveler who moved between Berber, Latin and Greek courts of the Mediterranean: the polyglot polymath George of Antioch (d. 1152).[43] George's parents had worked under Tamim bin Badis, the same Zirid Berber ruler who wrote poetry desiring the Christian festivals. After the successor of Tamim exiled George, the Greek fled to the court of Roger II in Sicily where he became a great "admiral of admirals." There he helped educate his protégé, Philip of Mahdiyya, in the art and science of naval warfare.

Born Muslim, Philip nominally converted from Islam to Christianity after entering the court of the Normans. According to some sources, sources that may have been biased against him, this conversion was never sincere. Philip allegedly made secret payments to Islamic charities in North Africa and sent money to the Tomb of Muhammad in Madina. He also visited the synagogue. Synagogues were often considered to be appropriate places for Muslims to pray at the time. *The Chronicle of Romauld of Salerno* said Roger II had a deep attachment to Philip of Mahdiyya. Roger entrusted him with control over the royal household and the navy. Philip led several expeditions, including one against the important port city of 'Annaba (also called Bona or the ancient "Hippo" Regius of St. Augustine) in what is now Algeria, to the east of Bèjaïa. The city, as many a port on the coast of North Africa, had gone in and out of Christian and Muslim hands, and had been captured a century earlier by Pisa in 1034. Philip captured 'Annaba in 1153, momentarily returning the ancient bishopric of Augustine to Christian control. This was only one year after the Almohad conquest and the surrender of the city to the Almohads by the Hammadid Berber sultan Yahya.[44]

Most of what is known about Philip of Mahdiyya, however, comes from accounts of his famous trial for un-Christian acts. Research by historians Joshua Birk and Jeremy Johns on the trial of Philip of Mahdiyya revealed the relations between Christian kings and their Muslim-born administrators.[45] Both Christian and Muslim accounts of Philip described him as a cunning deceiver of Roger II, acting officially as a Christian representative only to benefit his coreligionists. According to the chronicler Ibn Abi Al-Athir, for example, Philip warned a pious group of Muslims to leave town before he invaded 'Annaba with the Sicilian navy. While Ibn Abi Al-Athir used the story of Philip to discourage Muslims from working for Christian rulers, Christian chronicles used him as a foil for criticizing the "decadence" of the reign of Roger II. Accounts from both sides agree on the basic facts: Philip of Mahdiyya and all his fellow "Saracen" eunuchs in the Norman court were found guilty and executed despite having just triumphed in the capture of 'Annaba. Although he and his fellow group of eunuch administrators had been "forgiven" by the King several times, Roger II refused to grant clemency this time. Ultimately, 'Annaba fell into Almohad hands after the death of Roger II in 1154. One reason for this may have been the fact that Normans did not renew their agreements with the people of 'Annaba. The *'ahd*, an agreement between the Muslim city notables and the Christian Norman conquerors, protected the rights of Muslims in the community and protected trade with Sicily. Yet it was annulled and the population rebelled.[46] Incidentally, the existence of the *'ahd*, not just in 'Annaba, but in other beachheads of

Christian rule in North Africa, indicated not only the existence of an active city leadership but also an active civil community as was the case in medieval Italy. There were many good reasons for good relations with the city leadership of 'Annaba. Although perhaps not as large as Tunis, it was a rich port. Al-Idrisi described 'Annaba as having "beautiful bazaars and flourishing commerce." It was famous for wood "of excellent quality, important for building ships." Wheat, barley, millet, flax and fruits were abundant. There were also, "very good iron mines." Interestingly, in his description of 'Annaba, Al-Idrisi mentioned Philip of Mahdiyya indirectly saying, "having been conquered by one of the lieutenants of the great King Roger in 1153; it is now poor, not well populated, and administered by an agent of the King Roger, from the family of the Hammadites." Perhaps there was a subtle critique of the "great King Roger" buried here deep in Al-Idrisi's geography.[47] Roger also captured Tripoli in Libya. Although Al-Idrisi described it as having been ruined by "the Arabs," it still produced dates and other important goods.

Most of the royal functionaries under Roger II, such as Al-Idrisi, Philip and George of Antioch, were Berbers and Greeks, not Normans. In fact, official Norman documents were more often written in Arabic and Greek, not in the Latin used by Norman rulers further north. These powerful Berbers and Greeks allowed the King leverage against a Latinized nobility. The arts of the court of Roger II also reflected this hybrid, royal culture with the cathedral and throne room in Palermo, a prime example of hybrid Greek, Latin, Berber and Arab architecture. The original wooden roof beams of the cathedral contain a series of maxims and aphorisms in Arabic about the necessity of good governance and enlightened monarchy.

Al-Idrisi, the great geographer, helped the King build a sphere made of "pure silver" on which the "outline of the seven climates zones" would be "engraved along with their nations and regions, their coastlines and seashore, their bays, seas, rivers, and the mouths of rivers." It seemed Roger II was most interested in how this information could increase wealth and trade since one of his primary requirements was that not only "well-traveled" internal roads of each area of the known world should be recorded but also "the best known anchorages."[48] Al-Idrisi was aware of nautical details, revealing a superior knowledge of the seas. Indeed, it was only in 1133 that the scholar John of Seville, Spain had translated the great work on tidal theory by Abu Ma'shar

(Albumasar), a famed astrologer who linked the patterns of tides with the moon. Accurately calculating the tides could make a major difference in the success of a merchant's mission. The works of Albumasar, like many of these astrologers from North Africa, went north to England. Albumasar influenced Robert Grosseteste, considered a foremost English scientist of the period, and his influential innovations on tidal theory, essential for Britain's first, medieval forays into the sea.[49]

In the end, however, the power of Roger II waned, despite his efforts to expand trade, as Latin influences increased and the original Greek and Arab population of Sicily was forced to convert or leave the island. Although it is possible to underestimate the unpredictable whims of the King, the execution of Philip and the eunuchs occurred just at this turning point in the island's social and religious history. It also marked a change in history of African and Sicilian interactions. Sicily was as much an African island as a European one, both in terms of geography and in terms of political history.[50] For the popes, the convenient threat of the outsider "Saracen" was replaced in the south by an increasingly Christian opposition to their secular power when Frederick II took power until 1250 and defied the popes openly as "Wonder of the World." His adolescence under the tutelage of Innocent III, perhaps the most powerful of medieval popes who served as his regent after the death of Frederick's mother in 1198, did not go so well. Perhaps it was only inevitable that there should be conflict between pontiff and Holy Roman Emperor. Among the accusations against Frederick II was that he allowed the Muslim call to prayer when he was ruler of Jerusalem. He was also accused of employing Muslim mercenaries from Africa; many of these men were Berbers.[51]

Yet even in Rome there would continue to be contacts with North Africa, through the height of the Crusades. So close to the North African shore, Rome and the Papal States could not pretend to be a city divorced from geographical context. The popes, Norman kings and their agents would continue to play an important part in linking North Africa to Italy and Europe throughout the medieval period.

As late as the thirteenth century and in the throes of the Crusades, popes made entreaties to Almohad caliphs in Marrakech to protect Christian missionaries living in their land, appealing to the example of Cyrus the Great who tolerated the Jews.[52] This ease of understanding between the Pope and the Caliph of Marrakech had yet to fully mature. By the twelfth and thirteenth century, the Pope recognized a common Muslim-Christian heritage of the Jewish Captivity in Babylon and their freedom under the Persian Emperor Cyrus the Great, the sixth-century BC "messiah" of the Old Testament prophet Isaiah. A great deal more exchange would need to occur before such knowledge could be used by the papacy. Most or many of these exchanges were not of doctrine and religious texts but of medicine and astrology. Indeed, beyond building the walls of the Vatican and inspiring a revival of Rome, the Berber "Saracens" were the source of some of the most influential collections of medical texts, texts used in Europe for centuries.

Constantine of Africa: a North African Source of European Medicine

North Africa was far more than a source of slaves, precious jewels and cloth for Rome. Medical knowledge, especially knowledge carried by the famous Constantine the African, became a standard part of medical texts throughout Christian Europe. He interacted with the medical School of Salerno and also the Monastery of Monte Cassino, north of Naples.

Legendary and dramatic shipwrecks, so common in the treacherous seas around southern Italy and Sicily, seemed to be one of the archetypal stories of Mediterranean history. The right sort of shipwreck, especially with unexpected cargo, such as that held by Constantine, could transform a continent, changing the course of knowledge and experience for an entire culture. A scholar, merchant, man of many trades, ideas and expertise in the superior medical knowledge written in Arabic, Constantine had completed a fabled voyage deep into Egypt, Middle East, Persia, Ethiopia and India gathering all the great medical texts by Muslim and Jewish and Christian doctors or translators alike.[53] Far more precious than the grain, soap or even the gold coming from the African continent was the mind and experiences of this single man on board. It has been a challenge for scholars to separate the myth from fact in the story of his landing on the coast of Italy, his extraordinary travels, and his alleged conversion to Christianity. Constantine was called "the African" by Latin writers and translators to emphasize the fact that Ifriqiya, or Tunisia, was the source of his superior knowledge. His texts, used well past the fifteenth century, transformed the way Europeans thought about their bodies.

Medicine in North Africa was much more freely discussed than in the Christian West. This was true for even some of the most "conservative" of jurists and to questions of sex. Unlike Jesus, Muhammad the Prophet was not celibate and frequently spoke about issues such as sexuality and procreation. Even the Qur'an's first chapter revealed to the Prophet Muhammad showed knowledge of gynecology in seventh-century Arabia. The Qur'an spoke of humanity coming from a "blood clot." Indeed, it was Constantine from Muslim-ruled Ifriqiya who brought with him ideas and medical theories that were among the first since classical Rome to speak frankly about sex, including Constantine's tract *De Coitu* (*On Sex*) that had various herbal remedies for reproductive ailments, especially for male impotence. Some of these texts were condemned. Yet they were consumed by some later Christian writers, and his work became the basis for medical knowledge and every learned doctor's ideas, the advent of modern medicine.

Constantine the African may have first visited Salerno in his youth. Prince Gisulf II, the Lombard "pirate" Prince of Salerno (d. 1077), had a reputation for ruthlessness and for torturing his captives in gruesome ways. Yet Gisulf, it seemed, received Constantine; he probably recognized his potential. Constantine, however, was soon on his way from Salerno, perhaps engaging in trade of books and knowledge, searching the farthest places of the Islamic world for new information. Eventually, it was said, after many adventures and travails through Cairo, India and Ethiopia, Constantine the African returned to Tunisia. When he came back, however, he was welcomed by jealousy and intrigue and scholars of greater self-confidence, but perhaps of less knowledge and experience, drove him north. It was possibly on this journey that he was shipwrecked, his books, his most precious cargo, sinking into the waves.

Much of what we know about Constantine comes from a mysterious character: Petrus Diaconus, or "Peter the Deacon," a scholar from the famed Monastery of Monte Cassino, the great and early center of medieval learning inland from Salerno, a port city near Naples, Italy.[54] Before his fateful shipwreck near Salerno, Constantine had traveled to Sicily where he became a friend of the doctor and brother of the prince. It was over the course of this friendship that Constantine realized the lack of medical literature in Latin. Peter the Deacon asserted that Constantine only came to Sicily, then ruled by the Muslim princely dynasty, the Kalbids, after arousing suspicion and jealousy among scholars in Kairouan, the great caravan city where the famed ruler of the Berber Zirids, Al-Mu'izz bin Badis resided for some time before the city was destroyed by Arab armies. Al-Mu'izz bin Badis ruled a court filled with the some of the brightest luminaries of eleventh-century science and learning from 1016–62. Medical knowledge and the sciences were shared between Muslim, Jewish and Christian luminaries. In addition to Hebrew and Arabic and, perhaps, Berber in the private home, some scholars have suggested that Latin was still spoken as one of the surviving native languages in Zirid North Africa.[55] Constantine traveled as a merchant and salesman of books and ideas, perhaps making up some of his story or perhaps having his story augmented by his Christian monks and admirers. As many early medieval travelers, Constantine the African probably had many talents as merchant and scholar that he could use at various stages in his journeys.

After Sicily, he returned to Africa, gathered a large number of treatises on medicine and set sail, back to Sicily again. It was on this voyage, a voyage that would have otherwise seemed routine for a North African traveler, that his ship was blown far off course from Sicily and wrecked on the coast of Lucania on the Italian Peninsula. Although the manuscripts were badly damaged, Constantine is said to have bravely saved many of them. Eventually he made his way back to the port of Salerno in Italy.[56] Constantine's writings were part of a whole range of North African influences on Salerno and the Amalfi coast. Amalfitans traded silks from North Africa (Ifriqiya) in Cordoba.[57] North African and Sicilian art and architecture influence Salerno for centuries. The Cathedral of San Matteo, especially the courtyard and the geometrical designs on the twelfth-century Romanesque bell tower, evoke Arab, Berber and Byzantine styles of Sicily as well as the design of cathedrals and courtyards all along the coast, including those at Amalfi and Ravello.

While in Salerno, Constantine worked on his translations of Arabic manuscripts. Constantine omitted the names of many of the authors, perhaps because the names on many of the works were lost. The claim by historians that Constantine was a deliberate "plagiarist" seemed something of an anachronism. Neither Constantine nor many of the writers of the works he preserved wrote with the same expectations of scholarly citation used in the twenty-first century. Instead, Constantine may have seen himself as a vessel of medical knowledge, adding his own gloss or interpretation to centuries of Persian, Arab and Indian tradition.

Constantine the African brought this medical knowledge to Europe, knowledge that spread from Salerno and Monte Cassino to the great medical schools of Montpellier and north into France and England. Constantine probably died in Monte Cassino in AD 1098/99 according to a notation in the Monte Cassino obituary. The first known biographies of Constantine the African were written and modified by Christian monks from the monastery of Monte Cassino. This occurred within a decade of his death. As such, much of the information on the life of Constantine must be seen through the lens of these Christian monastic sources. In fact, some doubt that Constantine was even ever a Muslim: he may have been one of many Christians still living in Kairouan at the time. Christian festivals in tenth-century Ifriqiya, even in Kairouan, the Muslim religious center, were notorious to Maliki jurists, and Christians still lived in several parts of the Zirid realm.

Constantine did not seem to discuss religion very much at all. Preferring the *a capite ad calcem* form of translation that included the whole work from "top to bottom," Constantine drew on a huge range of works by Christian, Muslim and Jewish writers without much discrimination in terms of the faiths of these writers. He was most interested in what seemed useful, but also included plenty of the arcane. For instance, he translated an edition of the diet and medical encyclopedia of 'Ali bin Al-'Abbas Al-Majusi. Some of Constantine's texts were copied or revised from the work of this mysterious doctor who was influenced by the great medical writers of the East: Ibn Sina and Al-Razi.[58] Constantine also put his name on a famous work on depression entitled *De Melanchoila* by Ishaq bin 'Imran as well as many works by the great Al-Razi. Constantine's most popular works included the *Liber Pantegni* (Book of All Medical Arts) and the *Articella*, which was used to teach medicine up to the seventeenth century. Many of his manuals were already known among Jewish and Muslim doctors. For instance the *Viaticum*, another famous work, a compendium of medical knowledge often attributed to Constantine, was based on a medical manual composed by Abu Jafar Al-Jazzar who was himself a pupil of the famed Jewish doctor Ishaq bin Suleiman Al-Isra'ili, known in Europe as Isaac Judaeus.[59] Isaac Judaeus was the Jewish physician of the Fatimid Caliph 'Ubayd Al-Mahdi (d. 934) in Kairouan, North Africa.

Both the history of Constantine and the legend of Constantine written about him revealed much about interactions from south to north across the central Mediterranean. Just as the "Saracens" supported the spiritual and political claims of the Pope, the arrival of this North African, probably Berber, translator and traveler secured the intellectual reputation of the institutions throughout Europe where his works were adopted. The medical advances of Constantine's works spread almost immediately northwards, snatched up by physicians in northern European lands and leading to hundreds of copies of his many tracts. The story of Tunis, one of the cities Constantine the African would have known well, revealed the vibrancy of this world of early interactions between North Africa and Europe.

3

TUNIS:
AXIS OF THE MIDDLE SEA

Like Rome, Pisa and Genoa on the western coast of Italy, Tunis prospered in the ninth century from trade, slavery, naval-merchant exchange and raiding. Being on the coast was both an opportunity and a risk for residents of Tunis. Raiding always went both ways, the North Africans feared Italian pirates and vice versa. At any moment, an Italian duke or even another unfriendly Berber or Muslim ship, could arrive to take recently captured spoils. Overall, however, the opportunity of the sea still made a protected and strategic port city such as Tunis capable of thriving. Only a short trip from Sicily and the coast of Italy, Tunis was within the same commercial sphere as European cities to the north. The city of Tunis, nestled in a Lake of Tunis, itself protected within a Gulf of Tunis, faced out towards the Western Mediterranean. Following the legacy of Carthage, fewer cities could be better situated than Tunis to take advantage of Western Mediterranean trade. Tunis was to dominate the southern Mediterranean shore and north to the many islands of the Tyrrhenian Sea where boats were sent by steady currents. Although it never became a city at the level of Rome or Cairo, Tunis was often close to this status. It had been on the verge of empire at its height, a stopover point for ideas and movements far vaster than its immediate sur-roundings. Tunis at one point would be recognized in Mecca and Madina as the capital of the Caliph – leader of the Islamic world.

Tunis would eventually become the capital of Ifriqiya; the Arabized Latin name of the land that covers much of what is now Tunisia. Like a fat blade between the western mountains of Algeria and the deserts of Libya, Ifriqiya also seems to push northwards into the Tyrrhenian Sea, towards Sicily, with Rome and the strategic islands of Malta, Sardinia and the Balearics (Majorca, Minorca and Ibiza) easily accessible to trade, pillage, invasion or some combination of all three. The Bay of Tunis, in this respect, functioned like a net catapulting boats north and west and capturing them when heading east. Tunis eventually became not only a major port but also a significant center of learning, trade and commerce that not only raided but also rivaled European cities well into the medieval period. Tunis, like Bèjaïa, was originally a Berber settlement and its name, according to some scholars, came from the Berber word *Tunes* for "encampment" or "settlement." Tunis would come to be the center of a medieval North African revival of the fortunes of ancient Carthage, even as the ancient defeat of Carthage by Romans was very much in the minds of Italian Renaissance thinkers to the north and the Berber inheritors of Carthage's legacy in North Africa.

The Memory of Carthage

Africa, or at least the view that humanists had of Africa, helped inspire the birth of humanism. Near Tunis, on the hill there was Carthage, the great Punic and Roman city looking down upon the Berber Tunes. The fall of Carthage to Rome was in fact vividly remembered not only by Tunisians, but also by medieval Italians. They, at various times throughout the medieval period, attempted to revive the glories of Republican Rome's defeat of this rival and the Second Punic War. Petrarch, the great poet laureate in Rome, often called Father of the Humanism, wrote his famed epic *Africa*, leaving out references to current Muslim rule, references that would have been easily added by the listeners. After all, the Italian city-states and the cities of North Africa had been locked in rivalry, trade, military conquest and exchange for centuries. It was this poem that won him the poet's laurel in 1341, a crown that he then dramatically placed, in submission, to the Holy See. Not only the standard of Christ, but also the memory of Ancient Republican Rome, drove Italians into lands that they wanted restored, not only for Christ but also for the dream of a restored Republic.[1] One could argue that the Italian Renaissance started with this revival of Italian fortunes in Africa, or even with a poem entitled *Africa* – the epic that brought Petrarch his greatest fame. The poem had nothing to do with Africa as it was in the fourteenth century but everything to do with Africa as it was dreamed to be: its great resources conquered again and subject to Roman rule. Later editions of the work defined *Africa* as "a poem of the Mediterranean victory of Rome."[2]

Berbers and Arabs celebrated and attempted to revive the classical past as well, even before Petrarch wrote his epic poem on classical Africa. Far from dismissing the achievements of pre-Islam as an "age of ignorance", or the *jahiliyya*, many Muslim North African writers admired and studied the monuments from classical antiquity and the pre-Islamic past they saw around them every day. The Hammudid Al-Idrisi devoted long passages of his description of Africa to the ancient splendors of the city of Carthage, and seemed to want a return to that splendor. He dwelled on its theater with many "arcades", with "figures of humans, animals and ships, sculpted from stone with an incredible artistry." Even the Zaghouan aqueduct, "created geometrically with great knowledge of art" had been restored to some working order by the time Al-Idrisi described it in his geography. A later, Hafsid caliph added a branch to the aqueduct to his palace. Al-Bakri, an earlier geographer, similarly spoke of its many arcades. Al-Bakri was even a bit of a classicist and wrote in detail about "Anbil," Hannibal.[3] A full study of the interest in the classical past among medieval Mediterranean Muslim scholars has yet to be made, but would probably reveal a great deal. Even as the great humanist Petrarch was proclaiming a new Renaissance era and reviving classical Rome within a Christian humanistic frame, poets, historians and writers from North Africa also remembered, and perhaps even wanted to revive, elements of their own glorious antique history within an Islamic frame.

Today, a deceptively calm suburb surrounds the extant ruins of Carthage; it is an elite retreat overlooking the sea, which is exposed to the Mediterranean breeze. Although it was the scene of clashes during the 2011 Arab Spring uprisings, Carthage often seemed somewhat distant from the center of action. It was often a calm suburban haven for residents of Tunis living down in the bowl of the lake, wanting to escape the stagnant heat of summer. An eerie quiet remained around the ruins of Carthage, shadowed by the wealthy elite retreat as lonely, fluted columns attest to ancient grandeur. The "New" or Roman Carthage emerged from a great disaster, the devastation of the Punic

Wars and the famous, if legendary, "salting of its fields," to become a bustling Roman metropolis.[4] Vast amounts of grain from the surrounding fertile plains were exported to Rome and the hungry cities of the Empire. Even after centuries of Roman rule, however, Carthage would prove its imperial might again, under Vandal rule.

From Vandals to the Muslim Conquest

The Vandal king, named Genseric, seized Carthage in 439 after a march across North Africa and Spain.[5] He used this strategic base to strike a mighty blow against Rome – a blow that forever tarnished the name of the Vandals as "vandalizers" – launching the very same devastation threatened by Hamilcar and Hannibal in the First and Second Punic Wars. He conquered the strategic islands of the Western Mediterranean, Sardinia, Malta, and imposed taxes on clergy and the elite, forcing Pope Leo I to humble himself.

Over time, the Vandals lost their grasp on power. As the Eastern Roman Empire in Constantinople – often called the Byzantine Empire – strengthened, they established bases and revived classical Roman cities in North Africa, Sicily and the Mediterranean that had been conquered by the Vandals centuries before. Under the Byzantines, the dream of the Roman Empire had re-emerged. Byzantine successors to Rome attempted to establish their authority and exploit the lucrative grain supply of Ifriqiya, suppressing the local Berber population and "heretical" beliefs as they attempted to maintain central control.

By the time of the Muslim conquest, however, Byzantine control, never too strong to begin with, was beginning to falter. It was rife with internal revolts and dissention. One of the rebels against centralized Byzantine rule, Gregory the Patrician, although supported by Berber allies, had lost the city of Sbeitla in AD 647 to Muslim armies. After the conquest, it was as if time stood still; the city, overlooking vast grain and olive fields, remains one of the best-preserved Late Antique cities in the world. Carthage, on the coast, remained a Byzantine stronghold until the end of the seventh century. Looking only at Carthage, it may be tempting to describe the Arab and Berber conquest in the seventh century as finishing off Carthage, a great city, the one city that the Romans had refused to abandon for so long. Yet the Muslim conquest did not bring about a major decline in urbanism in North Africa, even if the make up of elites shifted from Byzantines to elite Arab and newly-converted

Berber families. Soon after taking Carthage, Berber and Arab Muslims and Christian Copts brought there from Egypt, built the city of Tunis only a few miles away.

Although the introduction of Islam shaped many social and economic structures over the long term, most of the initial social change was restricted to the elite crust of society. For instance, some sources described a mass fleeing of the elite rulers of Carthage, called the "Rumi" or Byzantines in Arab sources, as ships arrived to take many citizens away before the Arabs decisively captured the city in 698. Other sources said the Umayyad Arab commander Hassan Ibn Al-Nu'man "cut the aqueducts to the city."[6] Apparently, he wished to annihilate the possibility that the Rumi (the Byzantines) could return and retake the indomitable position at Carthage. The Arab commander seemed to have brought with him an army of thousands of Coptic Christians from Egypt to build a naval arsenal. In fact, the geographer Al-Bakri told that Copts were some of the first peoples settled in the city of Tunis.[7] Berber Tunes was re-founded as Islamic Tunis, according to Arab historians, in 699, although there had always been a large Berber population that eventually converted to Islam or mixed with the few, new Arab conquerors. The Arab commander Hassan bin Nu'man was far from a barbaric destroyer of infrastructure. He ordered the construction of a channel from the lagoon to the open sea, giving the newly built ships access to the Western Mediterranean.

As the Byzantine fleet retreated from Carthage to Crete, the Byzantine Apsimaros rebelled against the defeated admiral, John the Patrician. Apsimaros would later conquer Constantinople with his fleet, cut off the nose of the overthrown emperor and rule as Tiberios III. Despite his original efforts to recapture Carthage, he abandoned all future plans for Africa. The glorious memory of conflicts with the Byzantines did not fade. Interestingly, Arab writers, including the Tunisian historian Ibn Khaldun who wrote many centuries later (d. 1406), still called the Mediterranean the "Byzantine Sea."[8] The door to the Western Mediterranean had been wrested open by a handful of Arab commanders with the support of their Berber armies. Yet even at this point, politically shut to the main, Christian political power of the East, trade did not entirely cease with the Bay of Tunis.

For both Arabs and Berbers in North Africa, the Greek Christian, Byzantine exit from Carthage was an opportunity, an opening (or *fath*, the word for conquest in Arabic), as important as later conquests further west and into Al-Andalus. Along with their establishment of inland caravan cities such as Kairouan, the Western Mediterranean now allowed free reign for Arab and Muslim raiders and traders much as it was for Genseric in the fifth century. The rise of Islam did not "cut off" the sea any more than Genseric the Vandal king or the rebel Byzantine Gregory the Patrician. Byzantine cities continued. Commerce survived. Although the elite may have left, trade or economy was not destroyed in North Africa by the conquests as has sometimes been presumed.[9] The imperial potential of the Gulf of Tunis did not disappear, but would slowly develop under Arab rulers. The Berbers, led by their own leaders or occasionally by Arab captains, continued the raiding and opportunism reminiscent of the Vandals. The Muslim conquests, even the fall of Carthage in 698, were not a final, conclusive break from the classical past. Instead, the classical past continued to inform and influence Muslim Arab and Berber elites well into the medieval period.

Henri Pirenne, the celebrated Belgian historian, described the final conquest of Carthage and the spread of Islam throughout the Western Mediterranean in dramatic terms.

> With Islam a new world was established on those Mediterranean shores which had formerly known the "syncretism" of Roman civilization. A complete break was made which was to continue even to our own day. Henceforth two different and hostile civilizations existed on the shores of *Mare Nostrum*.[10]

There was change in terms of religious, cultural and political landscape especially with the settling of some Muslim soldiers and commanders from the East. Even so, many changes that did occur in North Africa after the conquest were the product of non-religious social changes, migrations, economic ambitions and political maneuvering that was not based solely on religion. Many Christians remained. Al-Baladhuri, the geographer, suggested that in the ninth century there were important cities or settlements of non-Greek, possibly Berber, Christians. A Berber freedman working for the Abbasid Aghlabid governor, named Kalfun Al-Barbari, would eventually conquer the Christian settlements, incorporating them into the Aghlabid governorate.[11]

In effect, Berbers resisted or deflected Arab attempts at outright control and assimilation, maintaining cultural norms and diverse practices; even as they converted to Islam they did not necessarily convert fully to Arab cultural norms or to an Arab identity. Far from being a unified coast arrayed against the northern shore of the Mediterranean, North Africa quickly became a patchwork of competing factions with Berber Ibadis in Tahert, Algeria rebelling against the Sunnis, Zaydi Idrissids in Morocco establishing their own dynasty despite attempts by the Caliph of Baghdad to send assassins to poison them.[12] Even in Sunni, Arab Aghlabid Ifriqiya, a dynasty roughly ruling over the area now known as Tunisia, power often did not extend consistently far beyond their inland capital city of Kairouan. Situated on the coast and well protected, Tunis experienced almost as much autonomy in the first centuries after the Muslim conquest as did the maritime cities of Italy. In Tunis itself there were constant rebellions against Aghlabid control from Kairouan as the militia in Tunis often disobeyed orders. The most famous of these officers was Mansur Al-Tunbudi who, for a time in the ninth century, had control of the city. Tunis was a "fractious city," according to the geographer Al-Bakri, and it bristled against control from the center.

The initial Muslim conquest of Carthage did not end the prospects for urban culture and economy in Ifriqiya. The ruins of Carthage and the new city of Tunis remained very close, both geographically and culturally. Arab and Berber commanders knew the strategic advantages of the region and the bay. By moving down to Tunis, they improved the defensive position of this capital and planted the seed of what would become a great port city. Other port cities were bolstered under Muslim and Berber control along the entire North African shore from Bèjaïa to Tangier, reviving old classical cities and stimulating the expansion of new ones. The city of Carthage did not simply die after the Muslim invasions. The esteemed scholar E. F. Gautier called Carthage and Tunis "one and the same city over three thousand years of existence."[13] The conquests moved the activities of Carthage to a much safer and strategic position at Tunis off the hill and on the lake.

Syncretism in the Tunis region continued to thrive after the departure of John the Patriarch, his rebellious men and the Byzantine elite from Carthage to Crete. In fact, the geographer Al-Bakri said that around one thousand

Coptic Christians were sent by the Caliph 'Abd Al-Malik to "Tarshish" (an early name for Tunis) to build an arsenal that would provision the Muslim armies.[14] He also ordered Berbers in the hills and mountains to provide, "in perpetuity," the wood needed to build the ships to combat Rum (the Byzantines) and to engage in organized raids of lands to the north.[15] Near the Tunis suburb of Rades, Christian Copts were brought by the Arab commander from Egypt to become sailors, using the wooden ships built by the Berbers.[16] Perhaps as an indication of the maritime tradition, now subsumed in Islamic terms, it was also near Rades where, according to the Qur'anic story, the Prophet Al-Khidr destroyed a boat of Moses to teach him a lesson about fate (Sura 18: 71). Tunis became a significant shipyard, an ideal place from which to launch naval power, even as the new caravan city of Kairouan, the new Umayyad capital of the province of Ifriqiya, moved the political center of gravity landward. Kairouan, according to the geographer Al-Baladhuri, was founded when 'Uqba bin Nafi' Al-Fihri, the Arab-Muslim conqueror, "saw in a dream as if a man called to prayer at a certain spot where he later erected a minaret."[17] Inland, the city of Kairouan, much the same as Marrakech centuries later, but very different from Tunis-Carthage with its ancient past, would be founded as part of an Islamic vision and on land where little had existed before. Yet, far from abandoning the Mediterranean, this Muslim city connected the port of Tunis with the caravan routes of the Sahara.

It was in 670, decades before the conquest of Carthage, when the Arab commander 'Uqba bin Nafi' moved the capital of Ifriqiya (Tunisia) inland from Carthage to the new garrison city of Kairouan. Kairouan, or *Al-Qairawan*, which literally meant "Caravanserai" or resting place for a desert caravan in Persian and Arabic, quickly became a spiritual center as well as a commercial one. It was less vulnerable to Christian naval raids. It also allowed Muslim raiding parties coming from Egypt a place to congregate and regroup as they spread west without having to return over the Libyan Desert. The mosque with its columns from ancient Carthage soon became a center of religious learning under the Aghlabids, the largely independent governors under the symbolic authority of the 'Abbasid Caliph in Baghdad. Extensive remains from the Aghlabid period (AD 800–909) survive today, showing significant technical skill in water management, impressive cisterns and irrigation, and architecture. Kairouan became a highly sophisticated city even as Tunis became the city where encounters with northern traders and raiders were most common.

The Myth of a Muslim Horror of the Sea

Some writers believed aversion towards the sea was a "universal trait" of Arab commanders, despite many successes in the Mediterranean. In one famous story the great Caliph 'Umar Ibn Al-Khattab wrote a letter to his commander 'Amr Ibn Al-'As. 'Amr had just conquered Egypt up to Alexandria and 'Umar asked him to describe what he saw in the sea. 'Amr said words of disdain, "[The sea,] it is an immense thing that carries upon its back [boats]: very frail objects built of worm-gnawed wood." The Caliph henceforth "banned Muslims from navigating on the Sea. No Arab could set sail and any who acted contrary to the wishes of the Caliph were punished."[18] This aversion seemed changed under the Umayyad Caliph Mu'awiya, ruling from Damascus. He authorized Muslims to navigate and use boats but only "during combat in protection of the faith." Ibn Khaldun described this hesitation to go to sea as a result of the Bedouin origin of the Arabs who had "no abilities upon the sea." The Byzantines and Francs, though, had a great deal of experience on the sea and "since their childhood" went out upon boats.[19] These rivals of Islam had perfected the art of navigation so, presumably, it seemed best to leave the sea largely to them. It would seem the Mediterranean shore was abandoned in favor of Bedouin land routes. Far from abandoning the sea, the coming of Islam linked the Mediterranean with the opportunities of desert trade.

The alleged Muslim horror of the sea was far from historical reality, especially in the Western Mediterranean. North African Muslims never abandoned the Mediterranean due to cultural proclivities. Ibn Khaldun, contradicting himself, described the "Command of the Navy" as an important function of government throughout the Muslim world, "especially in the Maghreb and Ifriqiya." The commander of the navy was called *Almiland*, a word he attributed to the Catalans or the Castilians.[20] Ibn Khaldun was pessimistic about the strength of North African naval commands and mentioned this as a reason why the people of the northern shore constantly put the Berbers under their submission. Yet this pessimism was much more a product of his own fourteenth-century context. In fact, naval raids from the coast of

Tunis to the Christian shores started almost as soon as the Muslim conquest of Carthage.

Raids on Christian Europe

It would take some decades after the conquest for Tunis-Carthage to reclaim its classical preeminence. Raids on Europe along with extensive trade through the port, however, set Tunis on a course towards growth and even a level of autonomy reminiscent of that achieved by some Italian cities. Despite the move of the capital to Kariouan inland, the people of seventh- and eighth-century Ifriqiya were not landlubbers.

As sources written from the North African perspective revealed, the potential and the possibilities of naval conquest and raiding in the Western Mediterranean were far too numerous.[21] There were Muslim raids on Sicily launched from Syria and Egypt in AD 666 under the reign of Mu'awiya (d. 680). The taking of Ifriqiya and the founding of Tunis, however, opened the gates to numerous raids and strikes against Christian territory.[22] Between the years 702 and 753 there are records of twenty raids, indicating a persistent, seasonal raiding cycle. One of the first great expeditions was led by a certain 'Ata Ibn Rafi' Al-Hudhali who arrived in Sousse, a city on the eastern Tunisian coast, with an Egyptian Coptic fleet. Al-Bakri, the Andalusi geographer, wrote of these Copts being sent by the Umayyad caliph in Damascus, 'Abd Al-Malik (d. 705). Ignoring the advice of the official superior commander of the Umayyad Empire, Musa Ibn Nusayr, and setting off on his own in harsh winds, his band of boats acquired booty from the mysterious "Island of Salsalah."[23] Later, his boats crashed upon the rocky shore of North Africa in bad weather. Some eight years later the Berber Tariq Ibn Ziyad would launch his famous raid in AD 711 against Iberia, also without approval from his superior commander. Although that famous and enormously successful invasion by Tariq into Spain has entered most history books, his was only one of hundreds. There were few details of many other uncoordinated *razzias*, or "raids," by rogue commanders only indirectly under the authority or power of the Arab, Umayyad, and caliphal command. Although the capture of booty seemed to be a primary object of these campaigns, they were engaged in forms of trade and commerce as well. Many of the commanders have Arab names but several seem to be Berber strongmen from the local population, taking advantage of the Islamic conquests for their own benefit.

That did not mean that these "Saracens," as they were perceived in European sources, were all rabble-rousers and that central authorities did not deign to set out to sea in search of booty or wealth. In fact, the appeal and success of these raids did not go unnoticed by the Caliph's commanders. 'Umar's policy for Muslims to stay off the seas now turned astern. There were dozens of official raids and campaigns directly supported by the Umayyad Caliph and his governors, often using the naval arsenal at Tunis. Throughout the eighth and ninth century, Tunis sent navies "towards the coasts of Rum (the Christians), ravaging and destroying them."[24] The island of Sardinia was a favorite target and, on the coasts, eventually came under the raiders' control. There were raids against the island in 705, 710, 732, 735, 737, and one, in 752, that ambitiously extended to the southern coast of France. Even more numerous, and presaging the eventual full conquest of the island, were campaigns against Sicily. These sea raids became highly organized, seasonal affairs. Inspired by economic gain as much as religious fervor, the eventual conquest of the islands of the Western Mediterranean can be directly linked to the naval prowess of Tunis.

By the year 800, when powerful Amir Ibrahim bin Al-Aghlab was made governor of Ifriqiya, he could demand almost complete independence from the Caliph in Baghdad. He benefitted not only from the spoils of these raids as much as the profit coming from trade in the caravan city of Kairouan. He founded a dynasty with his descendants succeeding him to the governorship for over a century, giving only token recognition to the Caliph. Tunis, especially as a center for the militia, grew in importance. One of the greatest successes for the Aghlabids came in 827 when Euphemius, Byzantine commander of the Sicilian fleet, rose against the Emperor. The Aghlabids agreed to ally with the rebel but soon took over, capturing Palermo in 831 and successfully repelling Byzantine counterattacks. In 849, as described earlier, raiders were defeated at the Battle of Ostia by a combined league of Naples, Rome, Amalfi and Gaeta. Despite some weak attempts to regain the island, soon it became apparent that the Byzantines would abandon Sicily much as they had Carthage. In 870, the highly strategic island of Malta, practically in the very middle of the Mediterranean, fell to the North African Aghlabids. Soon, however, decentralization and the weakening of the Aghlabids in North

Africa would lead to the rise of independent Muslim dynasties who maintained the tradition of raiding and who attacked mainland Italy regularly.[25]

Despite its own political disunity, Tunis benefited greatly from expanding conquests; even as enslaved North Africans under Leo IV rebuilt Rome, Tunis-Carthage was also revived. The geographer Al-Ya'qubi (d. 897–8), writer of *The Book of Countries*, described Tunis as one of the most vibrant cities of the region.[26] The Great Mosque of Tunis, later known as the Zitouna or "Olive" mosque, was restored in 864 under the last of the Aghlabid rulers and there seemed to be a general growth in urban activity and interest in controlling the urban space with the building of the city's first Qasba, or castle. Many chafed under the rule of the Aghlabid governors.

In Tunis there were several severe revolts against the governors. These revolts were brutally suppressed, leading to the enslaving of the rebels and the destruction of homes.[27] The instability and revolts against the Aghlabids seemed to follow the classic cycle of dynasties laid out by the historian Ibn Khaldun in his *Muqaddimah*, or "Introduction," to history. It was only a matter of time before a new movement took advantage of the internal decay. The initial, organizing impulse of Sunni Islamic conquest under Arab command seemed to have run its course. As the Aghlabids dallied in their palace, a revolution was stirring among the Berbers, specifically among the Kutama from the mountains with their powerful calvary.

The Fatimid Rise Among the Berbers

Living in the mountainous borderlands of present-day Algeria, the Kutama met the missionary Abu 'Abd Allah on their pilgrimage to Mecca. Perhaps knowing of their military prowess and potential, Abu 'Abd Allah claimed the Kutama name, with a similar root in the Arabic word *kitman* (secrecy), meant they were the people of a "pious age" as predicted by the sayings of Muhammad. One of their valleys was named Valley of the Pious and the Fatimid leader 'Abd Allah suggested to the Berbers that Muhammad meant their land also to be a sacred place, the very place from whence the salvation of the world would commence. Making lands outside the Arabian Peninsula sacred to Islam was to become a common practice, especially in the Maghrib and especially in an age when the centralized power of the Caliph in the East was increasingly challenged. The original, apocalyptic dreams of salvation and equality promised by the Prophet seemed late in coming. The revolutionary potential of Islam transferred from Arabs to Berbers who spread from west to east just as the Arab commanders had spread from east to west two centuries before. The Ismaili missionary Abu ʿAbd Allah introduced the Kutama to ʿUbayd Allah, the Mahdi, or the hidden Imam. Under the leadership of this awaited prince and taking advantage of discontent with Aghlabid rule, the Kutama stormed into Ifriqiya, taking the city of Kairouan, still a stalwart center of Sunni Islamic thought, in 909. By 920, the Mahdi had built the new "City of the Awaited One (Mahdi)" or Mahdiyya, centered on a citadel built on the shore near the Island of Jumma on the eastern coast of Tunisia.

The Fatimids, a new and powerful dynasty, had begun in Ifriqiya among the Berber calvary of the Kutama. ʿUbayd Allah was now a new caliph.[28] The Fatimid building of Mahdiyya, a major, highly fortified port city on the coast to take advantage of trade, set a pattern that would be mimicked by later dynasties throughout North Africa. From the Hammadids who built up Bèjaïa, to the Almohads who built a "New Mahdiyya" with Rabat on the Atlantic, Berbers set up fortified ports often immediately, during or after conquering the interior and gaining the loyalty of lineage groups and tribes. Although an empire or a dynasty might start in the mountains or the desert, the pull of the sea was almost always an immediate concern. The great ambitions of the Almohads at Rabat with its massive constructions and enormous, if incomplete, mosque and the still-preserved walls of Mahdiyya continue to attest to this strategic building of new ports.

Yet old ports remained important as well. Even as the Fatimid Mahdi and his successors attempted to establish themselves in Mahdiyya, Tunis (north of Mahdiyya) remained an important port and a center of revolutionary activity. Popular revolt in Tunis arose again, this time successfully, if briefly, under the "Man on the Ass." This was a prophetic man named Abu Yazid, known for riding in humble garb on a small donkey. Once he became ruler, however, the Man on the Ass began, at least according to the rather elite chronicles written after the events, to terrorize the population with "massacre, captivity and the taking of their things."[29] As Tunis dealt with a moment of political decay, Mahdiyya began to draw the attention of Jewish traders who were essential to the balance of power in North Africa and the Mediterranean as a whole. Al-Idrisi, the geographer for Roger II of Sicily, described the city as "beautiful" and wrote that

> this city flourishes, peopled by neighboring inhabitants and strangers from afar. It is surrounded by strong walls with three [main] gates. All the gardens and orchards are situated inside the city . . . [There is] honey and butter in abundance from which sweets of excellent quality are made.[30]

Trade was powerful not simply because of economic benefits; it could also influence the outcome of battles and the power of rulers. Traders could speak freely of great quantities of copper, of textiles, of bullion and jewels. Yet one commodity was far too precious to mention – at least in Arabic. This commodity could tip the balance of power: iron.

The Arabic word for iron was "next to absent" from the entire corpus of letters called the Geniza (Treasury), the most significant corpus of trading documents from the medieval Mediterranean ever discovered. This did not mean weapons made of iron metal, the strategic arms trade of the era, were absent from commerce. Instead, the word was written with Hebrew letters. The secret police would recognize the letters but not know the words. Although the letters of these great merchants can only tell us so much about the overall balance of trade, it was clear that Tunisia, and especially North Africa as a whole, contributed in a major way to the economy of the Mediterranean. Tunisian Jewish traders, especially, were famous as traders in metal and as metal smiths. One Tunisian even opened a bronze factory in India.[31] These traders, centered in Mahdiyya, Tunis, Sijilmasa, a desert city in Morocco, and Kairouan, with connections in Amalfi, Rome, Constantinople and much of the Near East to India, created a trading economy that went beyond the Mediterranean. There were also names of Christian traders in the Geniza documents. A source by a Jewish merchant mentioned a Christian trader from Amalfi and possibly Tunisia named Yuhanna (John). The document was written in Arabic, with Hebrew letters and stored in a synagogue.[32] North Africa under the Berber Zirid dynasty had a vibrant Christian-Arab community and they had a direct link to other parts of the Western Mediterranean.[33] The influence of the Zirids, through their partner, a related dynasty ruling in Al-Andalus, Muslim Spain, spanned the Western Mediterranean. Although Fatimids regularly employed local Christian artisans and employed Jewish doctors, it was the Zirids, a dynasty left to rule Tunisia after the Fatimids captured Egypt, who fostered an intellectual renaissance in Ifriqiya.[34] The Zirids created these centers of intellectual activity despite challenges such as plagues, in-fighting and Christian invasions.

The Berber Zirids

Even as they maintained trade and accommodative policies towards Christian and Jewish communities, a main concern of North Africa's political leadership was religious legitimacy and suppressing revolts. This role was especially important during revolts led by figures such as the "Man on the Ass," based on religious feeling. Despite many ill-fated rebellions by the populous, Tunis, especially under the Fatimids and their successors, the Berber Zirid emirs, remained prominent not only as a port but as an intellectual and cultural center. Far from being marginalized for being near the sea and vulnerable to attack, Tunis had a period of efflorescence under these sophisticated Berber rulers. The Zirids were left to rule in Tunis after the Fatimids had conquered Egypt. The Zitouna "Olive" mosque, the main Friday mosque, had to be expanded to accommodate a larger population of merchants and the traders in the "Sunday Market." Zirid intellectuals and luminaries went back and forth between Zirid domains, connecting Ifriqiya directly to Spain. A quantity of "Ifriqiyan" coins in Al-Andalus attested to the vibrancy of this trade.

Following the pattern set by the Aghlabids who declared independence from the 'Abbasids, it was only a matter of time before the Zirids claimed autonomy from the Fatimid rulers who had left for the wealth of Egypt. One of the greatest Zirid rulers, Al-Mu'izz bin Badis, responded to popular upheaval and massacres against Shi'ites, the agents of the Fatimids, and declared independence from the Fatimid leadership in Egypt. It was the court and long reign of Al-Mu'izz bin Badis (1015–62) that fostered the intellectual climate of Constantine the African, of great Jewish and Arab astrologers such as Abenragel, and of cultured, cosmopolitan poets such as Ibn Hamdis and Tamim, the son of Al-Mu'izz bin Badis.

In a pragmatic break from the revolutionary ideology of the Fatimids who had conquered Egypt and built their new capital called Cairo in 969 CE, the powerful and long-reigning Berber Zirid governor for the Fatimids in Kairouan, Al-Mu'izz bin Badis, renounced Shi'ism in 1048. He minted new coins, acknowledged the 'Abbasid Caliph in Baghdad and returned to the Sunni orthodoxy common among the larger population. This change of heart only came about after encouraging the very intellectual debates and disputations that were to be a central part of courtly life throughout the Mediterranean. Asking both Fatimid and Sunni scholars to present their points of view, Al-Mu'izz bin Badis considered himself something of an intellectual king. His teacher, Ibn Abi Al-Rijal, known as Abenragel in Latin, was one of the foremost astrologers of the day. He equipped Al-Mu'izz bin Badis with the tools of dialogue and debate.[35] After fatefully deciding for the Sunnis, he renewed formal recognition of the 'Abbasid Caliph in Baghdad and minted coins that no longer mentioned the Shi'ite imam and clerics were asked to replace their white, Fatimid robes with the black mantle of the 'Abbasids who ruled from Baghdad. At Sabra Al-Mansuriyya, a city established by the Fatimids to rival Kairouan, he built a new oratory and formed alliances with other Sunnis and Berbers throughout the region, even threatening distant Egypt, having formed an alliance with Al-Muntasir Ibn Khazrun, the independent ruler of Tripoli. Incidentally, some art historians have claimed that the unique stucco design at Sabra Al-Mansuriyya may be the "missing link" for the origins of Romanesque style in southern Italy.[36]

The Fatimids responded to this threat to their power, it was said, by "unleashing" the Banu Hilal and Banu Sulaim Bedouin Arabs across the Nile into Ifriqiya. For dramatic effect, the great historian Ibn Khaldun called these tribes a "cloud of locusts" that devastated North Africa. The Banu Hilal were blamed for every possible decline and caused, according to some historians, a great "historical breach" that devastated the Berber culture of the region. This story then became the basis for later, colonial arguments by French administrators, in particular, for a separation in the recognition of legal and cultural systems between Berber and Arab in North Africa. In fact, there were already Arab tribes on the other side of the Nile and the movement must have been as much a voluntary migration as a weapon of reprisal. As the Arabs migrated in thousands, the Bedouin were often blamed for the breakdown of central authority in North Africa and the decline in agriculture. More Arabs and Arabic cultural influence came from the Arab tribes of the Banu Hilal and later migrations than from the original invasions of the seventh century. Although much scholarship has critiqued his work, the French scholar

George Marçais even counted the Banu Hilal and the Banu Sulaim as the major turning point in North African history, the point when large swaths of North Africa, particularly the plains and the urban ports, tipped from Berber to Arab cultural and linguistic predominance. The mountainous areas and the deep desert have remained predominantly Berber through modern history.[37] Nonetheless, even the great epic of the Banu Hilal recognized the centrality of Berber cultural influences and indicated the existence of several intermarriages between Berber and Arab. General turmoil and revolt was already a problem for the region, long before the Banu Hilal.

The so-called "invasion" was as much a massive, disorganized migration as a purposeful punishment. Historical sources, often written by Arabs in Arabic, have both glorified the Banu Hilal and admitted to their brutality. Also, their cultural and linguistic legacy was far from simply destructive; the poetic "Epic of the Banu Hilal" described the relationship between Arab and Berber tribes as one of competition and accommodation, not simply annihilation and dominance.[38] The story of the Banu Hilal has been preserved in the great epic that continues to be recited to this day among those of both Berber and Arab ancestry. In fact, the coming of the Arabs, at least in literary form, has many parallels with the Latin entry into Etruscan Italy. A new people, in this myth, did not set out to "destroy" the existing Berbers, but to find a place beside the Berbers in their new home. Even as they struggled with one another, they also traded and intermarried.

The Berbers in Arab Song (*Geste Hilalienne*)

Similar to the "Song of Roland" and the *chansons de geste* in Europe that chronicled the rise of the Franks, the *Geste Hilalienne*, or songs of the Banu Hilal, still sung in the streets of Cairo to this day, told of the epic struggles of the Arabs. The "Roland" of the North African Arabs was Diyab, a semi-legendary Arab chief and a primary character in the most important medieval Arab epic, the *Sirat al-Hilaliyya*, "The Epic of the Banu Hilal." The epic glorified the story of the great "western march" or *taghriba* in Arabic.[39] Rather than describing the Berbers as dissolute and in need of conquest, the work did not concentrate on Fatimid retribution. Rather, the Arabs were as much independent agents as clients of the Fatimids, unleashed to punish the Berber Zirids. The epic described the noble resistance they encountered from Berber peoples as they spread across the continent in the tenth and eleventh centuries. The first part of the *Sira* takes place in Arabia and details long struggles between warring factions and the eventual displacement of one tribe, the Banu Hilal, to the land of "Jaziya" in North Africa. Driven from Arabia by famine, drought and a series of trials, the Banu Hilal make their way to the pasturelands of the Berbers thousands of miles to the west. The epitome of the epic is the "sublime pearl" on the war of Diyab and the slaying of [the Berber] Al-Zanati Khalifa.

As in the epic poems of the early Greeks where the enemy is portrayed sympathetically, the Berber enemy is depicted as a noble adversary. The Arabs themselves are praised as much for their wiles as their bravery. Set in the Maghrib, the Banu Hilal infiltrate the lands of the Arabs through disguises and ingenious measures such as dressing up as "troubadours" to seek out the best pasturelands. Some of the Arabs such as Abu Zayd, the man of "ten masks," are clever enough to learn the language of the Berbers. As the Arab tribes reach Tunisia they encounter the ruler whom they call Khalifa Al-Zanati. The actual Sanhaja Berber ruler of Tunis at the time was Al-Mu'izz bin Badis. Khalifa Al-Zanati may refer to a particularly effective general who served the prince of Tlemcen in modern-day Algeria. The daughter of Khalifa Al-Zanati was Su'da. She falls for one of the Arabs and vows to assist the Arab enemies of her father who refuses to allow his daughter to marry the Arab. In fact, Khalifa Al-Zanati imprisons the Arab lover of Su'da. Diyab and the leaders of the Arabs are incited to ransom Su'da's lover. Their attempts, however, are met with Herculean labors against impossible odds. Khalifa Al-Zanati is vested with peculiar powers: his headdress renders him invisible except for his eyes. He particularly offended the Arabs when, without releasing the imprisoned Arab, he demands the hand of one of the most beautiful of the Hilali women, Jaziya, in return for the right of the Banu Hilal to use pastureland. Jaziya eventually escapes after tricking Al-Zanati into a dare and a game of chess that she wins decisively.

The heroes of the Arab Banu Hilal and the forces of the Berber Khalifa Al-Zanati meet in battle. Diyab's two brothers are slain in the battle and Diyab is called upon as the last chance for the loosing Arab side. In one version, he eventually manages to pierce through the eye of Khalifa Al-Zanati in an epic single combat scene. The Arabs capture Tunis and the "fourteen castles" of the Berbers. In this description of the final victory by Diyab over Khalifa Al-Zanati, the immigration of the Arabs into Berber lands is memorialized and justified in epic terms. Diyab, however, becomes haughty with his new powers and is described in the poem as a tyrant who mistreats Su'da, the former princess of the Berbers. "He ordered his servants to increase the burden of her labors and they obeyed his word. For two weeks she continued to weep and lament. . ." She writes a letter to another hero of the Berbers, Al-Hasan, who fights with Diyab to liberate Su'da. The epic continues in this vein with wrongs being inflicted on both sides, usually centered on the treatment of women. Diyab is portrayed as a complex character, as both protagonist and antagonist, as hero and anti-hero. At the end of the story, Diyab is eventually finished off by the orphans of the many warriors he has killed. New migrants of Banu Hilal from the East refuse to bow to Diyab's unjust authority. A successor of Khalifa Al-Zanati comes to rule the land of Tunis and Khalifa Al-Zanati's image as a paragon of true "Arab" virtues is restored.

Although there are several oral version of the Hilal epic still being sung among the Rwala and Shuwa Bedouin of the Empty Quarter in Arabia, they refer to the defeat of the real Zirid Sultan Al-Mu'izz. Arab tribes routed Al-Mu'izz and the full wealth of his convoy was looted at the Battle of Haydaran. He retreated with his personal contingent of black guards, the 'abid, from the Sahara.[40] Even after his defeat, Al-Mu'izz strategically married the daughters of some of the Arab chiefs, perhaps hoping for an alliance with the new migrants in his territories.

Al-Mu'izz bin Badis retired to Al-Mahdiyya on the coast and, conceding defeat, allied again with the Fatimids and ordered the minting of Fatimid coins. Even as Zirid power diminished and the Zirids had to create new agreements for the collection of *iqta*, or land taxes, from the Arabs, the new population of Bedouin Arabs may have inspired the growth of the independent city. Tunis would increasingly break from Kairouan and Kairouan from Tunis.

The Republic of Pisa and the City of the Mahdi

After the death of Al-Mu'izz bin Badis, Ifriqiya was faced with the disintegration of political power in the hinterlands. Urban centers such as Tunis were now ruled by independent dynasts that built up their fortifications and expanded. In this respect, Tunis functioned as an independent city-state, focused on protection and trade, even as Italian city-states of Pisa, Genoa and Venice were flourishing. It was a capable officer, 'Abd Al-Haqq bin Khurasan, following a tradition of army-officer revolts in Tunis going back to the ninth century, who started a petty dynasty ruling over Tunis and the surrounding territory from the middle of the eleventh to the middle of the twelfth centuries. Now a small, independent principality, Tunis under the clan of Khurasan enjoyed a small building boom with a palace for the princely family and a new "mosque of the fortress," *Jami' al-Qasr*. The prince Ahmad bin 'Abd Al-'Aziz (r. 1106–28) renewed the city defenses. The famed Sicilian poet Ibn Hamdis, ensconced in Kairouan, described the port of Tunis as a place of poets and doctors.[41]

Although prosperous, the city was regularly challenged by Christian raids from the north. Where Tunis was once the base for building the boats that rained on the Western Mediterranean, it now had to defend itself against Christian attack. The port city of 'Annaba on the Algerian shore had already been taken by a coalition of Genoese, Pisans and Provençal navies in 1034. Pisans, although not invited by the Normans, joined in the sack of Palermo, bringing back building material for the cathedral of the Virgin Mary, according to an inscription.[42]

Revival of the Republic and Prequel to the Crusades: Mahdiyya 1087

Pisans had boldly threatened the great city of Mahdiyya, south of Tunis and on the east coast with access to eastern Mediterranean markets, in 1057. Zirids took back the city only to lose it again some thirty years later. In multiple, devastating attacks, Pisa, with the support of the Pope, Amalfi and other Italian city-states, had sacked what remained of Carthage. Pisan and Catalan forces also attacked the governors of the Balearic Islands who had declared autonomy from their Muslim Slavic ruler (many Slavic slaves had risen through the ranks to become rulers in their own right) Al-Mujahid (d. 1044). Al-Mujahid wanted to create a commercial empire centered in Denia, the southern Iberian port just north of the Balearic Islands. Calling for assistance from the Almoravid of Marrakech against the Pisans and Catalans, the Balearics would be ruled by Almoravids from 1116 until well into the Almohad period. Although much scholarship has focused on the impact of the more-famous Crusades in the Levant on European history and the role of the Church in medieval society, these other campaigns, many of them well before the First Crusade, revealed a different story. The Pisans and Genoans, for instance, attacked Mahdiyya in 1087 not simply out of a feeling of religious fervor as was the case in the First Crusade ten years later, but also as an expression of the revival of the ancient Roman Republic. The Mahdiyya campaign was an early expedition to prove far more than Christian values, but also republican virtues, proof of the success of Pisa.

Pisa and Christian allies, including Genoa, took the strategic port of Mahidyya in 1087, only a decade before the famous capture of Jerusalem in 1099 during the First Crusade. Mahdiyya was a great prize. There were thousands of captive slaves.[43] Al-Idrisi, geographer of Roger II of Sicily, described in rich detail the wealth of the city and the merchant suburb Zawila. The region was full of iron ore and timber, useful for shipbuilding. It had a reputation for silk and cloth manufacture and goldsmiths who had access to the metal coming through Saharan trade routes. Mahdiyya was actually only the name of the residence of the Sultan and his troops, dominated by a large castle of the prince, "constructed in the most solid manner possible." Zawila was full of rich markets and solid buildings with large, wide streets. Its inhabitants were "rich merchants gifted with cleverness and admirable intelligence." Their flowing white clothes gave them a dignified aspect, "they take care that they remain clean, along with their bodies." The city was surrounded, both on the side of the sea and on land, by a great stone wall as well as a large moat. There were enclosed gardens. Facing defeat of their great capital, "the pivot of Empire" in the words of Al-Idrisi, the Zirids paid a huge amount of gold to the Pisans and to Roger when he campaigned against them later in the mid twelfth century.[44] The Pisans hauled off their booty to Lombardy and displayed North African plates and other fine captured items in their churches and squares.[45] The battle, likened by the Pisans to ancient Rome and Scipio's destruction of Carthage – which was, however, some 170 kilometers north of Mahdiyya – became a central part of Pisan civic legend.

The Pisans commemorated the battle of 1087 in a poem written on a twelfth-century manuscript called "Song on the Victory of Pisa" (*Carmen in Victoriam Pisanorum*). In 1092, the Pope recognized the Pisan victory against the "Hagarines" who during the siege, the poem says, vainly "appealed to

Muhammad, enemy of the Trinity and Holy Men of Faith." Pisa was raised to an archbishopric and made the churches of Corsica subject to it. In North Africa, a fragment of a *qasida* (or epic poem) in Arabic survived, written by the poet Abu Al-Haddad about the defeat. Yet the Pisan win against the Zirid Berbers did not mean Pisa was inherently hostile towards North Africans or Muslims. Pisa was increasingly becoming a cosmopolitan center, similar to the ports of North Africa where Pisans traded and, sometimes, conquered. Mahdiyya later passed between Christian and Muslim hands, being ruled by the Normans from 1148 until the Almohads conquered the city in 1160.

Fibonacci, the twelfth-century Pisan mathematician, would have spent his youth in Pisa knowing about earlier Pisan conquests in North Africa. He was surrounded, as were many Pisans, with what one scholar called "Other People's Dishes:" ceramics from North Africa, Al-Andalus and Sicily literally stuck into the walls of churches such as San Sisto. North African ceramics were displayed on the tops of churches, looking out on the public squares of the city. One can see the plates just below the roofline of these churches (Figure 1).

These magnificently decorated North Africa, Sicilian, Egyptian and Andalusi plates, once probably much more colorful and bright than they are today, were known as the "bacini."[46] One of the world's greatest collections of Western Mediterranean Islamic ceramics can be seen in the back rooms at the medieval Museum of San Matteo on the banks of the Arno River. Many were decorated with fantastical birds and beasts. Some of them even contained verses of the Qur'an. Within San Sisto, as well, are ancient Corinthian column capitals captured from a mosque. Thus classical, pagan decorative works, adopted by Islam, were then reclaimed for the churches of a confident Pisan Republic. Perhaps Fibonacci's voyage to Bèjaïa would not have induced as much homesickness as might be assumed. While Tamim, the Zirid ruler, was described in Pisa's triumphal poem as a "dragon of the antichrist" who "sacked cities from France to Spain to Italy," who performed "wicked arts," in his advanced construction of the sea walls of Mahdiyya, many North Africans were integrated into Pisan society.[47] There were records of Muslim neighborhoods in Pisa during this period and several names of leading citizens in an 1188 peace treaty between Genoa and Pisa revealed as many as twenty people of high status with Berber or Arab origin. There

Figure 1 Bacini plates from North Africa, Sicily and Al-Andalus decorate the top of the façade of San Sisto, Pisa. Photo by Author.

were, for instance, the Benzerri (Ibn Ziri), Solemani and Ismaeli.[48] Some of these men may have been among the notable Pisans, including the two Consuls (following classical Roman tradition) and other city officials, who had a prominent place in urban governance and mercantile associations, even though they were also subject to clerical and aristocratic powers. The conquest of Mahdiyya and the many raids on North Africa was a revival of Roman, particularly Republican Roman glories.

The many North African plates and columns from Mahdiyya, proudly displayed in the church squares of Pisa and preserved to this day, exemplified not only the success of Pisa's navy but also the wealth of Pisan traders who not only attacked the Saracen but traded and learned from them. Later, in the twelfth century, Norman invaders, who came to the northern Mediterranean at about the same time as the Banu Hilal Arabs came to

Africa, reached south and took control of the coastal cities of Gabes, Sfax and Sousse, a city known "to voyagers from all over" for "its fabrics and turbans that give us the name 'Turban of Sousse.'"[49] These were prosperous and well-fortified cities on the way to Tunis. Conquest seemed inevitable; Tunis seemed next in line for conquest by these new and fiercely competent Christian invaders.

At the last minute, Tunis was saved from the Italians and the Normans. The Almohads, the Berber dynasty from the Atlas Mountains of Morocco that invaded from the west, came upon the scene. Even as the Fatimids had begun among a group of Kutama Berbers declaring a new era, so too did the Masmuda Almohads from the High Atlas Mountains hundreds of miles to the west. In 1157, 'Abd Al-Mu'min, the first successor to the Mahdi (the awaited one) Ibn Tumart, thought the city important enough to besiege personally. Tunis and the Banu Khurasan resisted for two years against overwhelming odds and finally fell to the Almohads in 1159. Christian forces were pushed out of Ifriqiya. Tunis emerged as the capital of the rich Almohad province of Ifriqiya and central axis of Mediterranean trade.

Tunis: Hafsid Capital, Mediterranean Axis

After the Almohad conquest, Tunis became one of the most important cities of the new Almohad Empire, an empire that united much of the Western Mediterranean under its rule, from Al-Andalus, to the Atlantic, to Libya in the east. The Almohad governors, descendants of the important Abu Hafs Al-Hintati, an elite Berber family loyal to Ibn Tumart from the beginning, maintained Almohad orthodoxy in their court. Over time, however, the charismatic message of the Mahdi and his successors began to diminish. The apocalypse promised by the Mahdi was slow in coming and, in the words of the father of sociology Max Weber, Almohad doctrine and Ibn Tumart's charismatic message became "routinized."[50] While charisma flourishes with the overthrow of exisiting structures and bureaucratic institutions, over time routine activities, the actual governing of society, takes precedence and old cultural and legal norms (Maliki Islam reformed by Almohad doctrine) rise again to the surface. This routinization was already occuring during the reign of the first great Almohad caliphs or their successors who maintained a united empire. Over time, however, the doctrine of the Mahdi faded, new caliphs in distant

Marrakech decided to break from Ibn Tumart and his doctrine. Despite being farthest from the birth of the Almohad movement in Marrakech, it would be the Hafsids, the Almohad governors, who would steadfastly maintain their Almohadism as an elite identity, even as a majority of their own population remained Maliki Muslims. Transforming from a revolutionary doctrine that was embraced across North Africa, over decades Almohadism became an elite identity associated with the Berber Hafsids who traced their ancestry to the distant Atlas Mountains hundreds of miles away, the place where Ibn Tumart had first preached. In 1229, the Hafsids under Abu Zakariyya formally broke from the Almohad Caliph of Marrakech, declaring their loyalty to the doctrine of the Mahdi. Yet the Hafsids had changed into something quite different from the original Almohad society of the mountains. As the Almoravids of the Banu Ghaniya had transformed from Saharan desert warriors to traders and raiders on the sea, the Hafsids, rooted in the mountains, became rulers of a great Mediterranean port. Following an Almohad identity, however, did not necessarily mean enforcing or following all aspects of Almohad doctrine as preached by Ibn Tumart. In fact, the Hafsids, while proudly proclaiming themselves as successors of the Almohad caliphs, opened their courts to the Mediterranean cultural diversity around them. In this Mediterraneanized way of rule, the Berber Hafsids, originally from relatively isolated Atlas Mountain villages, were able to rule a vibrant port city for many centuries, much longer than the Almohad Empire itself, surviving until the rise of the Ottomans. As Almohad elite rule became routine among the Hafsids, it also became Mediterraneanized, a part of the long-term, cultural norms that Ibn Tumart had once preached against with charismatic fervor. The independent Hafsids made Tunis on the Mediterranean Sea, not old and inland Islamic Kairouan, their capital and center of power. In choosing Tunis they thrived on maritime trade and commerce.

From around the middle of the thirteenth century to the fifteenth century, Tunis became the "incontestable capital" of the eastern Maghrib under the Hafsid caliphs. Other North African cities were important, but Tunis was supreme. It was even the capital of the Islamic world for a brief moment when Hafsid caliphs were proclaimed in Mecca. Bèjaïa and Constantine and Tlemcen to the west (in Modern Algeria) became the headquarters of various dissident dynasties, but they never had the "geographic advantages" of

Tunis.[51] Moreover, Tunis further developed its character as a nexus of East and West, North and South, Berber and Arab interactions and exchanges. The Hafsids went from strict followers of Almohadism to patrons of art and heads of diverse and vibrant courts that came to a peak by the thirteenth and fourteenth century. Although they claimed to be adherents of Almohad Islam, they did not necessarily follow the example of the Almohad founder and Mahdi, Ibn Tumart. As time passed, perhaps, the memory of the Mahdi and their origins in the distant High Atlas Mountains began to fade. Soon, the Maliki school of Islam, practiced by the vast majority of the people living in Hafsid domains, became predominant and the Hafsid dynasty itself became effectively Maliki and moderated. Yet this moderation was not simply about adopting a new school. It had to do with exposure to the Mediterranean culture of Tunis itself as well. This could be seen especially in Hafsid attitudes towards music.

Musical Culture under the Hafsids

While Ibn Tumart, the Almohad Mahdi, smashed musical instruments in Ifriqiya on his way back to Marrakech, his Hafsid successors ruling the same lands centuries later would embrace music and poetry. Although the religious use of music was in principle not allowed, Sufis and Sufism had so suffused the culture and had so embraced the power of recitation and music that it soon overwhelmed attempts to stop it. Cymbals and other instruments would accompany religious holidays such as the birth of the Prophet. Trumpets might sound in the mosque during Ramadan and great bands of musicians accompanied the army during wars against Christian armies. Froissart, the Christian chronicler, noted the Muslim use of "tymbres et tabours" during St. Louis' siege of Mahdiyya in 1390. Leo the African mentioned that "everybody" in Bèjaïa owned his or her instrument. In addition to singing slaves and musical experts, an organ was offered by the King of Naples to the ruler in Tunis in 1472.[52] In addition to embracing music, the Hafsids also realized the need to maintain a tolerant attitude towards non-Almohads. Quickly abandoning the original Almohad policy of converting or exiling non-Muslims, the Hafsids would also benefit from the counsel of Jewish doctors and translators and would welcome Christian merchants back into their ports.

The Relaxing of Ibn Tumart's Doctrine

There were several additional reasons for the relaxation of Ibn Tumart's Almohad doctrine in Hafsid Tunis. First, the particular origins of the Hafsids, originally strict followers of Almohadism, revealed they were always a bit separated from Marrakech, able to maintain their own power base. From the beginning, it seemed the Hafsids, the successors of the Almohads, knew the power of their exclusive relationship with Almohad doctrine and, as with the Fatimids who were above the doctrines of the common people, Almohadism in Hafsid North Africa was transformed from a doctrine of unity to a doctrine of elite exclusivity. The Almohads, despite their compelling claims to unity, were a diverse mixture in linguistic and ethnic terms, if not, at least at first, in religious affiliation. The Mahdi and spiritual founder of the Almohad Empire, Ibn Tumart, claimed both *Sharifian* (descendent from the Prophet Muhammad) and *Ugallid* (high Berber chieftain) ancestry. 'Abd Al-Mu'min claimed the Berbers of his ancestry were originally Arabs. As was the case with the Fatimids, once the power of the Almohads had been established, the practicalities of rule tended to take over the initial, apocalyptic ideology. During conquest, 'Abd Al Mu'min had to put down several rebellions and attempts by various Berber factions to contest his authority. The same challenges came to his successors as well. It was therefore even more remarkable that the Hafsids managed to maintain a link to the doctrine of the Mahdi Ibn Tumart, whose memory was becoming more and more distant, for centuries after the fall of Almohads in their heartland around Marrakech. The Hafsid governors in Tunis maintained many aspects of Almohad ideology and formal ritualized recognition of Almohadism in court; they also eventually returned the masses to the legal Maliki school of Islam the Almohads had overthrown. The Maliki school of law was maintained, although it was now reformed. At the same time, Almohads quickly encouraged trade with Christians, used Christian mercenaries and Jewish doctors and encouraged a boom in arts, sciences and architecture. For travelers from the West such as Al-'Abdary of Morocco, Tunis would become the new shining capital of North Africa. It even briefly laid claim to be the first city of the entire Abode of Islam.

After the Almohad Empire eventually decentralized in the first half of the thirteenth century, the imperial administration lost grasp of far-flung territories. Yet the Hafsid Almohad elite maintained prestige and even med-dled effectively in distant Moroccan politics. Tunis enjoyed the height of its power and influence under the Hafsids, the Almohads in Tunis. The Hafsid Almohads had gone from provincial governors to caliphs. Tunis, as Hafsid capital, went from a provincial capital subject to Seville and Marrakech, to the first city on the Mediterranean coast of North Africa. The Hafsids, in addition to their claim of being part founders of the Almohad dynasty, also claimed Arab descent from the second Caliph 'Umar.

When Abu Zakariyya Yahya (r. 1228–49), Hafsid governor of Tunis, proclaimed independence from the Almohad Caliph Al-Ma'mun in Marrakech, he started a dynasty that would last into the fifteenth century. Abu Zakariyya, his family descending not only from a top lieutenant of the Mahdi Ibn Tumart, but from 'Umar, Muhammad the Prophet's own lieutenant, was upheld as restorer of the Mahdi's doctrine. He and his ancestors had halted the many attacks of the Almoravid Banu Ghaniya from Majorca and had consolidated power, or at least allegiance, among the fractious tribes of Ifriqiya. Linking himself to Almohad Marrakech, he even reproduced many of the same elements of the Caliph's *qasbah* in Marrakech in his own *qasbah*, or palace, in Tunis.[53] There was a great esplanade for the Hafsid prince's ceremonies, called the *Asarg*, a Berber name that meant "court," with a principal gate facing the west. He built a "Mosque of the Almohads" in his citadel, establishing the elite status of the Almohads, despite the fact they would increasingly rule over a population with far more diverse affiliations.[54]

Near the *qasbah* was the fortress of the Christians, *Rabad al-Nasara*, where the Christian mercenaries who guarded the Sultan were quartered. Despite the difficulties the Almohads would have in Marrakech with their Christian mercenaries, the Hafsids would continue to use Christians as reli-able guards, elevated above the factions and jealousies of the Sultan's own population. Christian, some Jewish, and Muslim merchants engaged in the booming trade in the markets of Tunis, including the *Suq al-'Attarin*, "Market of Spices," near the Grand Mosque, the Suq of Cloth Printing, and the *Qaisariyya*, a market grouping weaving and textiles together. There was also the important bookseller's suq, the notary suq and the leather suq. Many of these have retained some of their character to this day.

The Caliph Proclaimed in Tunis

Abu Zakariyya's son and successor, Al-Mustansir bi'llah (r. 1249–77), came into power just as the great 'Abbasid capital of Baghdad was threatened and then conquered by the Mongol Hulagu in 1258. The Almohad dream of a reigning influence over the East finally came to fruition, if for a fleeting moment. The Hijaz, the land of Mecca and Madina, and Egypt, the great cultural center and crossroads of North Africa and the Middle East, both gave their formal allegiance to the Hafsid caliphate. Thus, for perhaps the first time, a Berber ruler was recognized widely as the most powerful and most stable force from Mecca, the center of the Islamic world. Far from being a mere peripheral interest, Tunis, relatively far away from the Mongol threat, briefly became the heart of Islam.[55] Ambassadors even from Scandinavia visited. In 1260, the brother of the King of Castile, Don Henry, who had fallen out with his brother, appeared before the Sultan in Tunis who gave this Don Henry a high place in government.[56] The Caliph co-opted rebellious Arab tribes and formed strategic alliances that allowed him to pit one tribe against another and ensure loyalty to Tunis. Connections were forged further south as well, into the continent of Africa, including the kingdom of Bornu in the east of Nigeria. Great gardens and palaces were built in Tunis and the city became a major urban center and seat of caliphal power. Christian crusaders, influenced perhaps by Dominicans and Franciscans who were preaching and evangelizing in Tunis, threatened this period of Hafsid prominence, only to leave in 1270. If anything, the Crusaders, divided between Hohenstaufen and the Anjou, had more to fight about with one another than they did with the Hafsids.[57] The treaty of 1270 that Charles of Anjou signed with the Hafsids after the death of St. Louis IX was relatively generous to Tunis' Christians and allowed churches to be maintained and Dominicans and Franciscans to evangelize. One writer, Father Ellemosnyna, reported that a large number of Christians and merchants in Tunis were able to receive the sacrament but there were almost no converts from Islam.[58]

Tunis – Briefly Capital of the Muslim World

Al-'Abdary, the thirteenth-century jurist and pilgrim from Morocco, gave us a description of the flourishing culture and splendor of Hafsid Tunis in his travels. First he described the role of Tunis as "axis," an inflection point between the Eastern and Western Mediterranean. "We arrive in Tunis, the high goal of all hopes, a point of convergence for the sight of all, a rendezvous for voyagers from the East and the West." He then described the sight of caravans from the desert meeting the ships of the sea. "It is there where fleets and caravans converge." It was in Tunis where one could find "anything that a human could desire." He asked, "Do you wish to go by land? Here there are many guides who can take you. Do you prefer to go by Sea? There are vessels going every conceivable direction." He then described the quarters of the city. "Tunis is a crown. Each neighborhood is a jewel in that crown. Its suburbs are like a royal audience, constantly refreshed by the breeze." He described the many intellect pursuits of scholars in the city where "every branch of science is explored . . . many are mountains of erudition, others beat the gazelle with the speed of their pens." Living in an era after the decline of the Almohads in the West, he said, "had I not entered Tunis, I would have declared that [true] science has left no trace in the Occident and that its name had been forgotten . . . but I found in this city a representative of every sciences . . . this constellation shone with a brilliant light." Confirming the status of Tunis as a capital of Islam, he even compared Tunis to rival cities in the East and West, and declared Tunis as "sovereign."

Al-ʿAbdary gave the city a voice, saying that if it could speak, it would say these verses of defiance, comparing the city to an independent-minded virgin in remarkably erotic ways. He identified Tunis as a city attached to East and West, sea and desert, Arab and Berber, even pagan and Muslim, a true inflection point of the world. Tunis said,

> I am the beautiful, the superb one,
> Who never submitted myself to marriage.
> Let other women (cities) give up their virginity,
> For me, I despise this (deflowering).
> When I wish, I can see the gazelles leaping through the desert,
> Or contemplate the fish of the deep blue sea.
> It is within my inner walls that pilgrims incessantly come to rest.
> I am the support of an antique temple,
> Upon which is erected the vault of the skies.[59]

The city as a woman, or at least a feminine character, capable of being deflow-ered (conquered) seemed to be more than a literary trope, one we will see later with Marrakech.

One weakness of Hafsid Tunis, a weakness that would eventually lead to the defeat of some future Hafsid rulers, was the lack of water. Nonetheless, there was still an impressive infrastructure in place. Most drinking water was collected in cisterns or in the Aqueduct of Zaghouan Mountain, which brought water to the gardens of the Hafsid Sultan and the Olive Mosque through lead pipes. There were about fifteen public baths in Tunis during the rule of Caliph Al-Mustansir.[60] The very Aqueduct of Carthage that had been damaged by the first conquerors had been restored. The main Olive Mosque had been adapted or expanded since Aghlabid times. Al-'Abdary, however, was not always so florid in his description of Tunis, he hinted at problems with the weakness of governance.[61]

Christian Hopes and Jewish Settlement

After the death of Al-Mustansir, power was decentralized as his succes-sors fought for control. The sons were vulnerable and sought alliances with Christian kings such as Peter III of Aragon who used the Hafsids in his battle against the Anjou. The Catalans and Aragonese become a major force in the Western Mediterranean with the commercial rise of medieval Barcelona, rival to the Genoese. Hafsid rulers resorted to the use of Christian mercenar-ies, mostly from Aragon, commanded by the Aragonese King. One Hafsid successor, was, according to rumor, a "Christian convert" who arranged a coup that brought him to power in 1311. Understanding the Christian "urge for crusade" and the desire for a type of medieval, Manchurian candi-date who would overthrow the Hafsids from within and turn North Africa to Christianity, this Ibn Al-Lihanyi may have pretended to be Christian to appeal to various Christian allies, especially the Aragonese. Likely, the Aragonese may have simply made up the story of his Christianity out of misinformation or crusading fervor. In fact, Ibn Al-Lihyani proved to be very much a Muslim ruler. He met the conservative jurist Ibn Taymiyya during a pilgrimage to Mecca. When he returned and took power he reclaimed the title of Caliph.[62] Although there were some good rulers, most succes-sions became unpredictable and the rival dynasties surrounding Tunis and centered in Bèjaïa or Constantine caused instability. Hafsid power and stability would not be restored until the reign of Abu Al-'Abbas (1370–94). He was a patron of the great scholar and source of much of the history of North Africa, Ibn Khaldun (d. 1406). Abu Faris, the successor of Abu Al-'Abbas, ruled with Anselm of Turmeda, the Catalan turned Muslim mentioned in the Chapter 1, as his translator and minister, and a court full of luminaries. Also, there was a thriving community of Andalusi Jews, escaping the persecutions of Castile and other Christian kingdoms. In the fourteenth century, the Hafsids, despite some formal adherence to Almohad doctrine, welcomed large numbers of Jews from Muslim Spain, especially after the great persecutions of 1391 when thousands of Jewish families were butchered in Seville, Barcelona and other cities enflamed by the preaching of Ferrand Martinez, confessor to the Queen Mother of Aragon.

Thus, centuries after the Almohads expelled Jews or compelled false conversion, they were welcomed to Tunis and other North African cities. The migrations continued for centuries. Even in this refuge, however, Jews were subject to arbitrary impositions of the *jizya* or head tax for non-Muslims, and were required to wear distinctive clothing, going back to a pronouncement by the Almohad Caliph Al-Mansur at the end of his reign in 1198 that all Jews wear blue caps in place of turbans. Later, the fashion changed and Jews were required to dress in yellow. During certain parts of the Hafsid period, Jews wore a yellow cap on their back or their heads. There seemed, however, to be some distinctions within the Jewish community in their choice of how to wear these markers with "native" or indigenous Jews wearing slightly different designs than Jews from Muslim Spain. Jews were important and powerful members of court, serving as doctors and as ambassadors who could negotiate the release and ransom of Muslim captives in Christian hands. Jewish traders and merchants had a major impact on the commerce of Tunis. One group of Tunis Jewish merchants had almost a monopoly over trade with Marseille in France in 1248.[63]

One sign of the continued flourishing of Tunis in the fourteenth and fifteenth centuries, despite many instances of political instability and plague, was the multiplication of infrastructure projects, including vast cisterns and projects built by Abu Faris near the Bab Al-Jadid. Abu Faris also founded the famous Bardo (Bardu) Palace, first mentioned in a source from 1420, and built royal roads for chariots six horses wide that linked city palaces and pleasure gardens together. The Bardo is now a world-class museum, recently attacked in 2015 by those who seemed to despise the classical past and the foreign tourists it attracted.[64] Although Tunis was later made a part of the Ottoman Empire and then a French Protectorate, the city remains an inflection point for Mediterranean exchange and voyages to this day. Since the Arab Spring and the Jasmine Revolution, Tunisians, fully aware of their medieval heritage as capital of the Islamic world, have seen themselves, perhaps rightly, as the center of a new form of Middle Eastern politics.

Moving across North Africa to the Far Muslim West and to Marrakech, the focus of the next chapter, we encounter a place very different from Tunis but with also a surprising number of parallels. Unlike Tunis, Marrakech was inland, far away from the Mediterranean. Yet, as capital of the Almoravids and then the Almohads, it became to a great extent, a Mediterraneanized place: highly influenced by the mixing and cosmopolitanism of medieval Mediterranean culture. One might reasonably expect the story of Marrakech – not founded on classical ruins, closer to the forbidding Atlantic, much deeper inland and built initially as a sacred, exclusive city of a resurgent, Berber Islam – to be a much different story. In fact, Marrakech, the heart of the Almohad Empire, showed how exchanges originating in both the Sahara and the Mediterranean could transform a sacred city. It was claimed twice as exclusive for Islam, then changed into a diverse city, teeming with friars, Jewish traders, Sufis, Saharan and mountain Berbers and Arabs. Changing from a place of exclusive intolerance to a cosmopolis, Marrakech would become not only a market but also an intellectual center, a spur that accelerated the Twelfth-Century Renaissance and Commercial Revolution. Although not directly on the Mediterranean, this capital of the Almoravid and Almohad Islamic revolutions, deep in North Africa, became cosmopolitan and diversified, even "Mediterraneanized." To begin, however, we encounter a ruler of another great Western Mediterranean city, Seville, a city that would become intimately intertwined with Marrakech due to the influence of the Berber empires, the Almoravids and Almohads. These empires, for a time, united Al-Andalus and the Maghrib.

4

MARRAKECH:
THE FOUNDING OF A CITY

In 1091 a humbled prisoner in the town of Aghmat wrote a poem. Yet, this was not just any prisoner.

I say to my chains
don't you understand?
I have surrendered to you.
Why, then, have you no pity, no tenderness?
You drank my blood.
You ate my flesh.
Don't crush my bones.
My son Abu Hasim sees me fettered by you
And turns away his heart made sore.
Have pity on an innocent boy
Who never knew fear and must now come begging to you . . .[1]

After a long and healthy reign, Mu'tamid, King of Seville, and his family, a noble dynasty that had risen from rough warlords to cultured gardens of splendor and luxury, was captured, taken across the straits and hundreds of miles deep into Almoravid territory. The Almoravids reduced this poet king to prisoner at Aghmat, the old capital of the Almoravids located about half a day's journey from the new and growing city of Marrakech. It was here where this cultured king, enslaved by his own desperate act to save his kingdom, spoke "to his chains." There was one child Mu'tamid did not speak of in his lines: a daughter, named Saida, who had converted to Christianity and married Alfonso VI of Castile.[2] According to a mix of legend and history, she brought with her a dowry gift, the fortified city of Cuenca, and bore Alfonso a son named Sancho.

From Seville to Marrakech

Returning in his mind to the splendid pleasure gardens of his Alcazar, he must have recalled often the golden colored city of Seville on the Guadalquivir River. Muslim trade and commerce in the Mediterranean was increasingly threatened by Christian ships including the Pisans and Genoese. One poet from Sicily, explaining the difficulty of traveling to Seville, wrote to Al-Mu'tamid saying, "The Sea is of the Christians; vessels do not traverse it except at great risk; while the Arabs have the solid ground."[3] Yet despite some setbacks at sea, Seville was still a great port. Seville was a place of irresistible pleasures. Mu'tamid assembled poets, epicureans and writers from around the Mediterranean, including the mercurial Ibn Hamdis, the itinerant poet who connected Mu'tamid to Tunisia and the Zirid Berber court at Kairouan. This caused both cities to flourish as refined worlds of cultural and intellectual exchange. Although a defender of Al-Andalus, Al-Suqundi, that panegyrist for the virtues of Al-Andalus, could not help but mention the love of drinking, singing and dancing in the city.

> On both its banks are the merriest people on earth, always singing, playing various instruments, and drinking wine, which among them is not considered forbidden, as long as it is used with moderation . . . It is true that there have been at times in Seville governors and Sultans, who, being firmly attached to religion, and the strict observance of its ordinances, have done every thing in their power to check the evil; but all their attempts have been in vain.[4]

Mu'tamid certainly enjoyed his wine, his women and his young men. In one poem about his cupbearer he said, "Now we both are masters, both are slaves!" Yet, he was also ruthless with his lovers. Ibn 'Ammar, the great *wazir* and poet, who was Mu'tamid's mentor and several years older, proclaimed his love of Mu'tamid to Mu'tamid's strict father who exiled the *wazir*. After the death of his father, Mu'tamid was said to invite Ibn 'Ammar back, only to kill him in a fit of rage.[5]

Mu'tamid was most famous not for his love life, or even his poetry, but for inviting the Almoravids into Muslim Spain. These Almoravids were the mainly Sanhaja Berber Muslims of the Saharan desert who had recently and fervently converted to Islam. Mu'tamid, although from a powerful and confident family, invited them into Al-Andalus to stem the advance of Alfonso VI, the Castilian king who had just recently entered the city of Toledo in triumph.

Yet it would not be only the Castilians who would be stopped by the Almoravids. Seville and the great, fertile plain surrounding it, called Aljarafe, was too tempting a prize for the Almoravids. Mu'tamid's wealthy and prosperous city fell into their hands. Many medieval chroniclers described the Almoravid invasion of Al-Andalus as a great imposition of moral severity and political unity on the dissolute and effete "Petty Kings." Turning over of the wine containers, their capture of wealthy and luxurious cities, their renewed imposition of Maliki Islamic law with the fervor of a recently-converted people, seemed ample evidence, not only of the power and internal cohesion of the Almoravids, but also of the decline and decadence of the Andalusi kings and their courts. In essence, for writers such as the historian Ibn Khaldun (d. 1406) decadence was effeminacy and homosexuality or lack of fertility made a place ripe for decline, ruin and invasion. Even orange blossoms, justly famous to this day on the thousands of citrus that line the golden streets and squares of Seville, symbolized luxury. Their purpose was only aesthetic and not of use to man. Sevillian oranges were (and still are) not the mandarin oranges we are familiar with today – famous for being edible with their sweet juice. Rather, if one picked up a Seville orange and tried to eat it, one quickly realized its bitter, inedible truth. "This is the meaning of the statement by certain knowledgeable people, that if orange trees are much grown in a town, the town invites its own ruin."[6] Prosperity and pleasure, for Ibn Khaldun, held within itself the bitter juice of its own fall from the tree.

It seemed surprising then that these Almoravid men who overturned the rule of seemingly effete rulers such as Mu'tamid, proudly dressed with a male mouth veil called the *litham*. Seemingly so stern against the sexual depravity and intermixing of the Andalusis, the Almoravids were themselves a hybrid of diverse influences. While their ideology may have been inspired by the missionary preaching and discipline honed in the *ribat*, the military-monastic schools and warrior training camps built on the coast of Mauretania, their culture was more matriarchal than that of the Andalusis. Yet the supposed sternness of the Almoravids, especially towards the effete nature of Andalusi rule, was more complicated than a comparison of the use of sweet-smelling fruit trees. As with their future enemies, the Almohads, who would also need to reconcile their new and radical doctrine with the particular culture of the mountain Berber tribes, the Almoravids conveniently found a way to fit themselves into the Qur'anic Arab tradition while still maintaining their own. This occurred through a convenient legendry reading of the obscure legends of pre-Islamic Arab history. The old dichotomy between a paternalistic North Africa invading an effete Andalus that fell purely out of unmanly culture was an illusion written into our sources.

The Mirage of Luxury and Decadence

Even as they invaded the palaces of Mu'tamid, the Almoravids were building themselves a great city, a city that started as a statement of their embrace of a version of Islam, walled off and sacred. Yet this idealized, religiously pure vision of the city of Marrakech would not last long, if at all, in a sanctified state of purity. Perhaps even from the moment of its founding as a religious and political center, it evolved, as many great cities must, into an urban cosmopolis of wealth, luxury and diversity. Born on an empty, red-dusted plain, it started as a new citadel of religious reform. It became, in almost every sense, a cosmopolitan city similar to Tunis and Seville, with vibrant communities of minorities, Jews and Christians, Arab and Berber tribes of every sort. Seeing the wealth of what they created, the Almoravids could not help but tax the commerce coming through the mountains, adding further fuel to the fire of revolution that was brewing amongst the Berbers who controlled the passes through the Atlas and the Anti-Atlas. The city also welcomed peoples from the south who had never completely given up their pre-Islamic beliefs and practices, peoples who were a part of the Almoravid's vast Saharan Empire, linked to the Mediterranean in the north.

The Male Veil

While the men were veiled with the *litham*, the mouth veil, the women of these Saharan tribes went unveiled. This was far different from the conditions of Mu'atamid's court in Seville. If anything, women, at least culturally and socially, still seemed to dominate many aspects of internal Almoravid dynamics, even as they were recorded as portraying an image and ideology of Islamic purity. The anonymous fourteenth-century Arab writer finds no issue with the male veil, however, because of the following extraordinary myth he used to explain the alleged origins:

> One of the Tubba (Yemeni pre-Islamic) Kings had no like among the kings who had preceded him and not one of them had attained the virtue and the might of kingship which he had attained . . . A certain rabbi had informed him . . . that God would send a messenger who would be the Seal of the Prophets and would be sent to all the nations. He had faith in him and believed what he would bring and said about him, "I testify that Ahmad is the Messenger of God". . . Then he travelled to the Yemen and summoned the people of his kingdom but none would assent to his summons except for a group of the Himyar. When the people of unbelief overcame the people of faith and all those who had faith in him and followed had become either killed or exiled, or pursued and scattered, they took to wearing the veil as their women did at that time and fled . . . The *litham* [mouth veil] became the costume with which God had honored them . . .[7]

This association with the Himyar from "pre-Islamic times" may have been related to another Arab tradition recorded by Al-Baladhuri that "Ifriqiyah was subdued in pre-Islamic times by Ifriqis Ibn Qais Ibn Saifi *al-Himyari* and was named after him. He killed [the Byzantine General] Jurjir [Gregory] its ruler and said, regarding the Berbers, How barbarous they are! Hence the name, Berbers."[8]

The supposedly "Arab" origin of the *litham*, the male mouth veil of the Saharan Lamtuna (and present-day Twareg), was constructed in medieval Arabic sources as a response to the political and religious ambitions of both the Lamtuna, desert-dwelling Almoravids, and the Masmuda, mountain-dwelling Almohads. The extraordinary mythical account of the male mouth veil as a legitimate Arab and Islamic custom, as cited above, developed after the conversion of the Lamtuna to an evangelical, Maliki Islam preached by the Almoravid spiritual founder 'Abd Allah Ibn Yasin (d. 1059). It was these Lamtuna veil-wearers who formed the core of the Almoravid army and elite.

In sources written by the Almohads, the later, purifying Berber enemies of the Almoravids, the male mouth veil was described as either un-Islamic or femininizing. Yet those in favor of the Almoravids, of course, denied this. Some sources described Lamtuna not as effeminate Berbers, as most geographers had identified them in previous centuries, but as a lost tribe of true Arabs, proto-Muslims who had even greater faith, perhaps, than the original converts and followers of Muhammad. After all, they lived in exile for their beliefs in one true God without the comforting message of the Prophet reaching them until centuries later. According to these sources sympathetic to Almoravid customs, the Lamtuna, the major tribe of the Almoravids, were descendants of the Himyar, a pre-Islamic, exiled Yemeni tribe that professed that "Ahmad is the Messenger of Allah" centuries before the coming of Muhammad. The men wore the veil and dressed "as women," according to this story, to avoid capture, escape the ignorance of enemy tribes in the age of ignorance (the *jahiliyya*) and flee to the pure lands of the Saharan desert where they roamed as primordial Muslim Arabs lost in a sea of Berber lands and customs. In this legend, they lived a nomadic life, but often crossed through the city of Tadmakka, a name that means "Mecca-like" because it was the Saharan town whose setting looks most like Mecca.[9]

The Lamtuna Almoravid male mouth veil was thus not a symbol of gender confusion or of Berber custom as it was described in earlier Arab sources. Rather, the male veil was transformed into a gift from Allah to the lost "Arab" tribe, an Arab tribe that only reclaimed its rightful inheritance with the establishment of the Almoravid Empire and the founding of Marrakech (c. 1060). Ironically, a symbol of profound difference, a male veil became a sign of integration, integration into a wider Islamic mythology of legitimate Arab origins: the notion that in order to be legitimate, an empire must be Arab in origin. The *litham* was thus no longer a garment or a custom that distinguished the Lamtuna from the Arabs. The male veil became a symbol of Allah's special protection over Lamtuna and the Almoravids as "true Arabs" and primordial Muslims who had recognized the authority of the Caliph in Baghdad and established a strict form of "orthodox" Maliki Islam.

This reforming of the legend of Almoravid Arab origins was probably a reaction against the attacks of their later rivals, especially the polemic preaching of Ibn Tumart (d. 1130), spiritual founder of the Almohads. It was the ambition of Ibn Tumart and his Almohad followers to conquer Almoravid lands and to portray the Almoravids as feminized and, therefore, ready for conquest. As part of this ambition, Ibn Tumart described the Almoravids as feminine and weak, bathing in the corruption and luxury of power. In Ibn Tumart's logic, their wearing of mouth veils not only proved that they were like women; it proved inherent, effeminate degeneration. Instead of being "true Muslims" who happened to wear a mouth veil, Ibn Tumart claimed that the prophet Muhammad opposed such practice.

> The Messenger of God commanded opposition of people false in their dress, their actions, and their affairs . . . He said: Oppose the Jews, oppose the polytheists, oppose the Magians, and likewise the unbelieving anthropomorphists who resemble women by covering their faces with a *litham* [mouth veil] and *niqab* [face covering], while their women resemble men by revealing their faces without a *litham* or *niqab*.[10]

Preaching to the first Almohad followers in the Atlas and Anti-Atlas Mountains south of Marrakech, Ibn Tumart explicitly described the *litham* as licentious, as proof that the Almoravids were ripe for penetration and conquest by the masculine, unveiled Almohad mountain Berbers.[11]

Medieval scholars writing in Arabic were our main source for the history of the *litham*, the veil of these ancestors of the Twareg, the heavily romanticized "blue men of the desert." Known sources on the early history of the Almoravids of the Sahara and medieval West Africa more generally, were written outside of the Berber context. Almost all sources on the *litham* were written by Arabs in Arabic. Even the name *litham* was Arabic in origin. The Saharans almost certainly used variation of the words *alechcho* or *asenged*, Tamahaq for mouth veil and head veil respectively.[12] Medieval sources on the veil thus must be seen primarily through the cultural and historical lens of the Arab geographers and historians. These writers, whether pro-Almoravid or anti-Almoravid, attempted to explain the visibly different cultural practices of another that was also, perhaps most disturbingly for Arab writers, very similar. From the earliest Arab point of view the Saharans were a society that had many similarities with Arabs – an appreciation for oral poetic expression, for long-distance trade, tribal honor and nomadic ways of life – but they manifested their culture very differently.

Before the successful Almoravid conquests and their need to legitimize their practices in an Arabo-Islamic origin story, the earliest Arab geographers explained the mouth veil in a way remarkably similar to modern French anthropology: part of the vague theory of "shame." Without any notion of why such shame should exist, the mouth veil was worn simply because the Saharans thought it was shameful to show the mouth. The mouth veil, according to these early Arab authors, was more foreign and less familiar than it was to later medieval Arab writers. According to these earliest Arab writers, writers who felt no immediate historical or political affiliation with the Saharan peoples, the veil was worn out of a sense of shame.[13] The Andalusi geographer Al-Bakri, writing with a tone of cultural and religious superiority in the same years as when the Almoravids began their movement, listed the wearing of the veil among the "ignorant," "peculiar practices" of 'Abd Allah bin Yasin, spiritual leader of the Almoravids, who was supposed to teach them how to follow proper Muslim ways.

> All the tribes of the desert preserve the custom of wearing a veil which screens their foreheads, above the other veil which covers the lower part of their face, so that only their eyes are visible. They do not remove these veils under any circumstances. A man does not distinguish his relative or friend unless he is wearing the veil. Thus if one of them is killed in battle and the veil is removed, nobody can recognize him until the covering is put back, for it has become for them more necessary than their skins.[14]

Al-Bakri went on to say that the veil was used most improperly. The male veil was simply another example of the ignorance of the Saharan Berbers in Al-Bakri's view.[15]

According to Ibn Tumart's writings, especially his book of doctrine or the *A'azz ma Yutlab*, the Almoravids were essentially ruled by their women.[16] By actively feminizing the Almoravid enemy tribes in his polemics, Ibn Tumart helped rally the Almohad mountain tribes and justified the eventual conquest of their feminized, Almoravid desert rivals. According to Ibn Tumart's proclamations, a good masculine tribe must control its feminine or feminized neighbor. Among their greatest sins, according to Ibn Tumart, was the way their "women wore their hair [unveiled] high on their heads" like a bees' nest.[17] This was one of a long list of traditional Lamtuna practices that Ibn Tumart used to justify *jihad* (holy war) against the Almoravids.

For Ibn Tumart and the mountain tribes of the Atlas, the fundamentally feminized nature of their Almoravid rivals was embodied by Sura, the Almoravid princess and sister of the Amir 'Ali bin Yusuf, who rode proudly unveiled on her horse without any regard for what Ibn Tumart and the Almohads viewed as the strict norms and ideals of Islam. According to the historian Ibn Khaldun (d. 1406), who wrote for the Almohad Hafsids and was at times sympathetic to the Almohad cause, Ibn Tumart "encountered Sura, sister of this prince ['Ali bin Yusuf of the Almoravids] who was going around in public with her face and head exposed, as did all the Almoravid women and upset at this spectacle, he gave her a vigorous reprimand. She ran crying to her brother and recounted the insult. [In response] Ali subjected Ibn Tumart to questioning. . ."[18] Thus an eminent Almoravid Lamtuna woman, the sister of the Lamtuna leader who, according to Lamtuna tradition, was afforded special honors and whose son would normally inherit power, would become symbolic not of honor but of decadence. In the midst of tribal feuds and tribal polemics, the women of the Almohads and the women of the Almoravids would face this feud as respective embodiments of Almohad and Almoravid honor.

Thus, the story of the mouth veil was as much about the transformation of religious and ethnic identity as it was about gender and the flipping of gender symbols in the midst of conquest. Culture could be reframed under a new religious category, even if it remained unchanged and the Almoravid conquers of Andalusi excess, the jailers of Al-Mu'tamid who attacked the cosmopolitanism of Al-Andalus, were themselves the product of a spread of the Mediterranean south into the Sahara. Not all important conflicts between convenient "outsiders" in North Africa were strictly between different religions. In fact, the Almohads made good use of the Almoravid male veil in their propaganda and their message against these degenerate effetes who had just done, decades earlier, what the Almohads themselves hoped to do – conquer much of Al-Andalus and North Africa. The conflict between Almoravid and Almohad ideals, even as they paralled one another, could be best seen in the history of the city of Marrakech.

Founding Marrakech

Marrakech was an unlikely spot to start a city. It was not on any navigable waterway. From Seville, in contrast, ships could sail easily to the Mediterranean. Marrakech, instead, was an inland crossroads. Rooted in the red soils of the Haouz Plain north of the Atlas Mountains, connecting great Saharan desert trade routes, the founding of the city of Marrakech transformed the Western Mediterranean. It created a great churning gear, one that accelerated connections between the Sahara, Maghrib and the Mediterranean. Marrakech was construed as a purely original Islamic city, a citadel to the unifying reforms of the Almoravid and Almohad Berber empires. Over time, despite some efforts to stymie religious diversity under both Islamic empires, the city almost irresistibly emerged as a cosmopolis.

During the early thirteenth to fourteenth century, Christian mercenaries, Jewish traders and Sufi mystics rubbed shoulders with Saharan nomads and strict adherents of the theology of the apocalyptic Mahdi or Awaited One, Ibn Tumart. Iberian cities are often credited as sites of encounter between Muslims, Jews and Christians, especially the golden-yellow Seville that was sanctified as the second capital of the Almohads. However, these encounters also occurred deep in the Maghribi heartland. The red city of Marrakech, a major city and true holy site of the Almoravids and Almohads, was the beating heart of power in the Western Mediterranean from the end of the eleventh to the beginning of the thirteenth century when the Almohads began what medieval chroniclers described as a major decline, a decline into the same "decadence" supposedly experienced by the Andalusis to the North.

Gaston Deverdun, the French scholar, claimed a main reason for the foundation of this red city on the open plain was the "horror of the Saharans, like all nomads of the world, towards every edifice or confinement, for them only the tent is noble! Inhabitants of the immense horizons of the deserts, they were not used to living in a permanent place. . ." Deverdun seemed swept up in an image of the desert nomad: the idea that nomads had an inherent "nostalgia for space."[19] He also suggested several possible, practical reasons for the foundation of Marrakech. Situated on a plain, a surprise attack could be detected and easily avoided. Certainly, the Lamtuna Berbers of the desert were more adept at fighting in the open than in the mountains. They did not build directly on the banks of the Tansift because "rivers did not agree with the habits of the Saharans."[20] In Deverdun's view, Marrakech was an attempt to recreate the desert on the Haouz plain. But if Deverdun was correct, if the Almoravid's underlying purpose of building Marrakech was to remember the desert, they could have easily returned to those vast, desert expanses where they originated. Instead, there was something holding them to that place that became the holy city of Marrakech, something that kept the Almoravids from being more than a glorified troop of marauding desert nomads that arrived on the plains, demanded booty and disappeared back into the sands. This something was an idea – the idea of creating a common Islamic community, the idea of uniting the tribes of the Maghrib under the rule and promise of Almoravid Islam.

The Almoravid Founding of Marrakech

The Almoravid Berbers of the Sahara created Marrakech as a completely new spiritual and political center, a manifestation of the power, legitimacy and permanence of Almoravid doctrine. The origins of Almoravid Islam were found both in the urban centers of North Africa and in the deep desert. The Sanhaja Saharan tribes were split roughly into three groups: the Lamtuna, Guddala and Massufa tribal confederations. These three fierce confederations held sway over huge swaths of the Sahara and the gold trading routes through the Maghrib. These trading routes developed after a shift in the desert climate that made a direct route to the rich markets of Egypt and Damascus almost impossible. The Egyptian Sultan Ahmad bin Tulun (863–83) ordered the diversion of all trading routes through the Maghrib, creating a boon for the western Saharan tribes.[21] Moreover, a new, Islamic ideal was emerging in the Muslim religious center of Kairouan, the city in Ifriqiya south of Tunis. The two worlds of desert and city were brought together when the leader of the Guddala, Yahya bin Ibrahim, visited Kairouan on his pilgrimage to Mecca in 1035.[22] Yahya was determined to establish the Maliki code of life in his own marginally Islamic tribe. To help him in these endeavors, his colleagues referred him to the existence of Wajaj bin Zalwi, a cleric who had built a *ribat* or spiritual retreat in Sus.[23] The Almoravids were disciplined into a strict adherence to Maliki Islam by their spiritual founder 'Abdallah bin Yasin who was sent by Wajaj into the Guddala Desert to impose Islamic law. Within years, the tribes had united around Yasin, building a *ribat* of their own. They called themselves the *Murabitun*, Arabic for the Almoravids, "the people of the *ribat*." The Almoravid's very identity was thus centered on the foundation of spiritual centers, centers that represented strict adherence to Maliki Islam, one of the schools of Muslim jurisprudence.

The Almoravids conquered the great trading city of Sijilmasa linked to the Sahara east of the Atlas, and smote the Berghwata with their uniquely Berber interpretation of Islam. The Berghwata read a Qur'an written by their founding, eighth-century prophet Salih bin Tarif, in *Tamazight* (the Berber tongue) and with eighty suras, much like the Qur'an of the Arabs. By the sheer overwhelming force of confederated tribal cooperation under the banner of Islam, the Almoravids had burst from the desert and created a patina of unity over the tribes of plains, deserts and mountains throughout the Maghrib. They promised to make Almoravid Islam the new standard of belief. There were, in fact, no major urban centers in the region of Marrakech at the time, certainly none built boldly on the plain without the protection of mountains. Small rural communities and the occasional medium-sized mountain trading settlement like Aghmat or Naffis were the only concentrated population centers in the region.[24] Before the rise of the Almoravids, the Berbers of this region, especially the Berbers of the desert and the mountains, had little or no experience of urban government or urban life. Some of the Almoravid desert nomads may have never even seen bread, but only the products of camels and date palm. They emerged from the desert, their hearts enflamed with what they believed to be the pure truth of Islam.

As the center of Almoravid power, Marrakech was to be boldly new, Saharan Berber city; it symbolized the first birth of a new order, the first beginnings of specifically Berber Islam combined with great imperial power. It would not be going too far to claim that it represented the first beginnings of a collective civilization and identity united under Almoravid Islam. Certainly, the tribes would remain divided according to their ancestry and descent, despite a thin veneer of Almoravid power. Nevertheless, the Almoravids had created something new: the idea of unity. Even if their ideology was derived, and based completely on the preaching of Yasin, spiritual leader from the East, the Almoravids had started something: a combination of tribal vigor and religious certainty, solidarity and divinity. As a new civilization, the Almoravids would need a new city invested with a holiness usually reserved for cities in the East such as Kairouan, Jerusalem, Mecca and Madina. The power of the Almoravid idea had been shown in blood, battle, and booty; now it could be founded in brick, beam, and stone.

Abu Bakr, the great Almoravid leader, was not satisfied with his temporary capital at Aghmat-Urika. There may have been pragmatic reasons to move the capital. His dissatisfaction with Aghmat was rooted in a desire to create a new holy city. If he was concerned with purely practical reasons, he could have made Aghmat the permanent capital. Although not approaching the wealth of Sijilmasa, Aghmat was a rich trading center at the time.[25] Almoravids had nothing but the best relations with the mountainous Huwara people of Aghmat-Urika. Several Lamtuna tribesmen seemed to be settled there or have close connections with the city's merchants. Far from wanting to hide their riches from the Marrakech tax collector, Al-Idrisi mentioned, "during the time of the Almoravids, there were no richer people than the inhabitants of Aghmat. They had the custom of placing, at the doors of their houses, signs of their wealth . . . the proprietor planted beams or joists to indicate how much wealth he possessed."[26] Abu Bakr did not leave Aghmat as a type of punishment against its wealthy population. Aghmat-Urika was slightly cooler than the lower plains of Marrakech. "During the winter the stream flowing through the center of town freezes and is covered with ice that will not break, allowing the children of the city to play games and slide upon it."[27] But weather alone could not explain the motivation behind Abu Bakr's purposeful foundation of a new city on the plains.

The main reasons for the foundation of Marrakech were not notions of nostalgia, fear of raging torrents of water or even fear of mountain Berbers. Although it started as a mere camp, Marrakech became much more: the wet clay molded by the desert Almoravids soon turned into their citadel of Islamic unity. The sources contradict on matters of exact date and seem particularly steeped in legends about the foundation of Marrakech. Nevertheless, the sources suggest planned purpose behind the permanent establishment of Marrakech. The *Bayan Almoravide*, an Almoravid source, claimed that Abu Bakr (d. 1072), the great Almoravid conqueror of Awdagust, Sijilmasa (1054–5), and controller of the entire trade route between sub-Saharan, golden Africa and the North, ordered the departure from Aghmat on May 7, 1058.[28] The entire court at Aghmat picked up and moved to the empty plains to build a new city. Marrakech would be a city built seemingly in the middle of nowhere.

In the very beginning of their movement, the Almoravids had built a *ribat*, a fortified monastery, on the remote desert island of Tidra off the coast of Mauritania. From this *ribat* the movement's leader Yasin literally whipped the tribes into a disciplined observance of Maliki Islam, demanding that every lapse in observance or loyalty be punished with rough justice and the rod. But the rewards for joining were also great: the promise of a new religious spirit, the promise of new lands and wealth.[29] Marrakech would have also started as a type of *ribat*, but not a usual type of *ribat*. While the Almoravids built earlier *ribats* for strategic purposes, Marrakech would be a permanent citadel of ideals and doctrine that represented not the abolition of tribal solidarity but the unification of tribal differences around both religious ideal and practice.

An important part of this ideal was to create a community that would uphold the ultimate equality of believers, despite important tribal identities that remained the building blocks of Almoravid society and the mountain tribes of the region. The new city also represented an attempt to reconcile different tribal cultures. The *Hulal al-Maushiyya*, citing earlier sources, claimed that Marrakech was built deliberately on the boundary between two rival tribes, the Haylana and the Hazmira.[30] The small river Issil probably separated the two tribes. The purpose of this was not merely to avoid dispute but to found the city on some sort of neutral territory, a space defined by religious identity, not tribe or ancestry. The city would represent the making of an Islamic community, the deliberate creation of a religious and political center not based on any previous settlement or history. As the desert tribes set up their tents, the mountain tribes built mud brick houses: the tribes inhabited the new city encampment side by side. The first large structure made of stone was the *Qasr al-Hajar*, or the Stone Palace.[31] Abu Bakr probably conceived this palace as the new axis of power.[32]

Just as he began his ambitious city building project, members of the Guddala tribe revolted.[33] They threatened the vital trans-Saharan trade. In 1071, Abu Bakr returned to the desert with his army. He left his cousin Yusuf bin Tashfin in charge of Marrakech and of his beautiful and intelligent wife, Zaynab (the former wife of a defeated Berber king from the mountains). In an early indication of the notion of the city as feminine and decadent, the sources suggested that Zaynab would not have withstood the harsh conditions of the desert.[34] Yusuf bin Tashfin and Zaynab solidified the Stone Palace and oversaw the development of Marrakech as a permanent urban center. Some sources, like the Sicilian geographer Al-Idrisi, did not date the beginning of Marrakech as a city until 470 н (1077–8), well into the reign of Yusuf bin Tashfin.[35] Despite having a capital somewhat far from the sea and lacking a navigable river, the Almoravid ruler encouraged seafaring. Al-Idrisi told of an Almoravid admiral named Ahmad Ibn Umar, or Raqsh Al-Auzz, sent by Yusuf bin Tashfin to explore the far western reaches of the Atlantic. There he encountered many curiosities in this Western Sea, perhaps even reaching the Sargasso Sea.[36]

Benefiting from trade on land and connected to trade on the sea, Marrakech linked markets from the Sahara to the Atlantic and the Mediterranean, but it was in the reign of the Sultan 'Ali bin Yusuf that Marrakech began its true flowering. It was also during his brilliant reign, however, that subtle threats to Marrakech and cracks in the confident Almoravid edifice began to emerge. The two most important building projects of 'Ali bin Yusuf were the mosque and the city walls.[37] The only significant remains of the Almoravids in Marrakech, after the destruction of almost every Almoravid building by the Almohads, is a finely detailed *qubbat al barudiyyn*, a dome. It may have been 'Ali bin Yusuf's ablution fountain and an inscription, defaced by the Almohads, barely reads his name and calls for God to grant him victory. Much of the ornamentation came from Al-Andalus; the very place the Almoravids had conquered and critiqued for cultural excesses became the basis for their own art. At the same time, there were references to the 'Abbasids, to whom the Almoravids gave nominal allegiance by recognizing the Caliph in Baghdad.[38]

Archaeological evidence, suggested that the Mosque was a large and imposing structure: around 120 by 80 meters, significantly larger than the mosques of Fes Qarawiyin (90 by 70), Tlemcen (70 by 75) and Algiers (90 by 70). The surviving *qubba* gives but a glimpse of the intricate and refined line characteristic of Almoravid style. The French scholar Deverdun claimed, "Islamic art has never surpassed the splendor of this extraordinary *qubba*." At no one point can the eye rest, the elaborate shell and acanthus motif seems to encircle itself in a pattern of delicate, confident but fragile splendor. This was in marked contrast with the starker, linear style of the Almohads. The mosque was intended as a massive and permanent statement of Almoravid power and doctrine. As the florid details of the Almoravid style seemed to suggest an interior, delicate complexity, so too was the original, confident, Almoravid ideal becoming increasingly immersed in the complexities of urban life.

The Maliki cleric, the 'alim, and the faqih with his complex and encircling web of commentaries upon commentaries, was replacing the believer and the Imam as the real basis of power and legitimacy. The Almoravid Empire was at the peak of its power but underneath the massive façade, at least according to Almohad propaganda, the founding ideals were slowly eroding into disputes over minuscule matters of doctrine and practice.[39] The rulers were further and further divorced from the people of the city; the people of the city in turn were becoming further and further isolated in their style of living from the people of the surrounding countryside and the lifestyle of their nomadic ancestors. The Almoravids introduced taxation of the Masmuda mountain tribes who bought items in the markets. The geographer Al-Idrisi mentioned this illicit introduction of a qabala tax by the Almoravids on several items of merchandise including perfumes, soap and yellow leather. The Almohads promised to do away with this tax when they conquered Marrakech.[40] At this point, spiritual leaders such as Ibn Al-Qasi in the Almoravid Algarve (southern Portugal) and Ibn Tumart in the Atlas Mountains, looming above the city, began to gather their support. The façade of Almoravid power was strong, but the fundamentals of their movement were being challenged.

Almohad Propaganda Against Marrakech

Before discussing how that challenge was mounted, some more observations about the significance of the mosque as a defining element of Almoravid doctrine are in order. In his article on the architecture of the Middle Eastern city, Oleg Grabar described how the first Muslims built the city around a common place of prayer, a space owned by God, a masjid that could contain the entire male community.[41] Like the Almoravid sultans, the first leaders of Islam were careful to prevent the development and ownership of mosques by individual tribes or factions. The city mosque, at the center of the city would not be owned by any one tribe but would represent the development of an overarching religious identity composed of different tribes.[42] The founders of Marrakech built deliberately between and over tribal lines creating almost a haram, a forbidden, holy space similar to the Haramayn: the two holy cities of Mecca and Madina in Arabia. Tribal identity itself was not rejected, the community was still built as a hodgepodge of styles and dialects and ancestries. Nevertheless, the core of urban development was not simply the building but more importantly the idea of the *masjid*, the place of prayer. As the Qur'an reads, "Verily sanctuaries (*masajid*) are but for God."[43] Extending this idea, the founding purpose of new cities, which house these sanctuaries, was ideally but for God. Commerce, trade, practical considerations of war were all important, but only secondary to the founding principle of the Muslim city as the gathering place of God's community.

In a seminal article on the Muslim city, Georges Marçais described the Muslim city as "a place of contact and exchange."[44] This contact and exchange was not simply commercial or based on the market. The commercial aspect of Marrakech was important but perhaps even more important was the contact and exchange gained from common religious worship. The Great Mosque was literally "the gathering place;" it occupied the role of the agora or forum of classical cities. Writing in the fourteenth-century Maghrib, Ibn Khaldun considered the "leadership of prayer" as the highest of all functions and "higher than royal authority as such." In early Islam, Muhammad the Prophet chose Abu Bakr as prayer leader; this helped the case for making him the first Caliph or successor to the Prophet. The mosque thus represented leadership. In the Great Mosque, believers of all tribal backgrounds were equal before God. Ibn Khaldun described "minor mosques restricted to one section of the population and one quarter of the city." But these "are generally not attended for prayers."[45] Rather, the common prayer in the Grand Mosque was possibly the single most important unifying activity of the population. Surrounding the central mosque were the main markets and commercial activities. Although questioned by current historiography, which resists a single category for describing the Islamic city, the main mosque (and its transformation by the Almohads) was, in fact, an important part of the rise of Marrakech.

Yet the religious unity envisioned in the founding of Marrakech and the Almoravid mosque did not last long. The Almoravids were distant from the central events of the Islamic Middle East, yet still they claimed nominal allegiance to the 'Abbasid caliphate. This stunted some of their authority when compared with the new Almohad movement that did proclaim independent religious authority. Ibn Tumart was a Mahdi who did not answer in any respect to the 'Abbasids. Similarly, his successor 'Abd Al-Mu'min was to be a caliph. Also, by the reign of the last great Almoravid ruler 'Ali bin Yusuf, a certain dissolution between religious scholars, political power and the community was seen in Marrakech, a division of community from religious ideal caused by the development of a clerical class that sought to dominate both secular and sacred spheres. There was a growing, even inexorable domination of urban Maliki jurists in almost every aspect of public life. "By the twelfth, thirteenth, and fourteenth centuries, the domination of the city's intellectual atmosphere by the concerns of the clergy marks the end of any intellectual model which would bind together the ruler and the ruled . . ."[46] Intellectual activity was still strong during the brilliant reign of 'Ali bin Yusuf. The ideal of the Islamic city, however, as a place embodying the concept of the *umma*, an equal community of believers ruled by a rightly guided Imam, was affected by the rise of a strong, if not completely dominant, legist-bureaucracy and the reliance on legal manuals and interpretations as opposed to a new or original ideology.[47] This, at least, was certainly the perception of Ibn Tumart and the Almohads who were emerging in the mountains among those heavily taxed Masmuda Berber tribes.

At first, the Almoravid rulers, like the first 'Abbasid and Umayyad caliphs, may have attempted to co-opt the mosque and those learned in religious science. Soon, however, the Almoravid Maliki jurists began to claim more and more exclusive power. Their strict and meticulous law books replaced the original sources of religion as the basis for legitimacy and power. This had happened before in the East. In the 'Abbasid caliphate in Baghdad the learned jurists had gradually whittled away not only at the power of the Caliph, but also the original Muslim ideal of the equal community, the *umma* of equal individual believers who ideally had no need for cleric, spiritual bureaucrat or intermediary.[48] In the case of the Maghrib and Marrakech, however, the clerical domination may have been more pronounced. In the East, the four major legal schools were constantly competing with each other to dominate urban religious life. In the Almoravid Maghrib there was no such competition: the Malikis and their complicated legal manuals far divorced from the foundations of Islam dominated almost every aspect of religious and intellectual life.[49]

The development of this class of cleric and spiritual administrator represented, at least for the Almoravid enemies, the Almohads, a decline of the original idea of the city as a divine community, a space owned by God. Soon, the Almohads, organizing against the Almoravids in the purple-colored High Atlas Mountains that loomed over the city, could claim that the "idea of Marrakech" as a spiritual citadel of common believers had become dominated by clerics and determined to cut off and control trade through the Atlas. As Marrakech became more and more a center of legalized religion, walled off from the surrounding countryside, it became less and less a symbol of unity and legitimate royal authority and more often a symbol of injustice, taxation and inequality to the innumerable Masmuda tribes in the mountains near Marrakech.[50] Inspired religious doctrine, the promise of the super tribal confederation of God, even the promise of the end of time, not law books, procedures, and the superficial forms of urban civilization, was what animated the Berber tribes.

Even as they preserved the city from attack, the building of the magnificent defensive walls of Marrakech signified the new, interior-looking nature of the city and the growing disintegration of the idea of Marrakech as an Islamic spiritual center open to the entire community, both rural and urban. The anthropologist Clifford Geertz observed that Muslim cities were not "crystal islands set in a shapeless sea." But they could become that way when the city deliberately walled itself off from the surrounding community, defensively preserving and exploiting commercial wealth while becoming vulnerable to attacks and infiltration by more strident ideologies and doctrines such as those of the Almohads. The walls of Marrakech did not make the city hermetically sealed from the outside. The *abwab* (doors) through the Almoravid walls, seemed to take the shape of a *mihrab*, leading those outside to the central mosque. Marrakech could not survive completely cut off from its surroundings. That was one reason why the Almohad threat was so real.

It seemed clear that the fluid interaction of the High Atlas mountainous, Almohad homeland and late Almoravid Marrakech was becoming more and more problematic. "The fluidity of town life was hardly less that that of rural, just somewhat more confined, while the forms of tribal society were just as clearly outlined as those of metropolitan. In fact, adjusted to different environments, they were the same forms, animated by the same ideals."[51] In the region of Marrakech, however, the countryside and the city were increasingly animated by different ideals: the Almoravid city looking into itself, the Almohad countryside animated by a new revolutionary ideal. "The ancient camp open to all had become a closed city of Islam."[52] At least, this was the message that Ibn Tumart was attempting to promote.

The Almohads, having gone on their *hijra* (immigration) from Igilliz (the Almohad Mecca) in the Anti-Atlas Mountains to the village of Tinmall (the Almohad Madina), days away from Marrakech and protected by the fierce terrain of the Atlas Mountains, were creating an expansive Islam led by Ibn Tumart. The idea of Almoravid Islam, in contrast, was based increasingly on law books and a class of clerics rather than the flame of faith and revolution. According to Ibn Tumart, Marrakech had become defensive and inward looking. It was this break with ideals, this slow decay of Marrakech into commercialism, concentration of wealth, government taxation and the breakdown of the original Berber system and its link with the Sahara and the Lamtuna tribes that seemed to threaten the strength of the Almoravids. Taxation, cosmopolitanism, centralization and the support of legal schools did in some sense contribute to the wealth of Marrakech but all this wealth came at a price: the image of Marrakech as a center of Berber, Islamic ideals.

Nonetheless, Marrakech did not completely break from all tribal support from the countryside. Counter revolutions did occur even after the eventual Almohad conquest of Marrakech in 1147. The major rebellion by Al-Massi, who opposed the Almohads but ultimately failed against their superior forces, erupted – but mainly from lands and peoples not newly incorporated into the new, Almohad hierarchy.[53]

Jewish Aghmat and Mellah

An interlude in the relationship between the Muslims at Marrakech and the Jewish minority was important; it pointed to further evidence of a Marrakech conceived from the beginning as a type of exclusive, spiritual citadel to Berber Islam yet eventually transformed and Mediterraneanized over time. One should not mistake Aghmat-Urika for Aghmat-Ailan, a small, rich town six miles to the east and about four miles from Marrakech that was, according to Al-Idrisi, "inhabited exclusively by Jews." The Jewish minority seemed to remain in this town a few miles outside the city.[54] To preserve the sacred, exclusively Muslim space of Marrakech, but also allow for vital commerce, the later Almoravid Sultan 'Ali bin Yusuf allowed the Jews from Ailan to enter the city at certain hours and perform what Idrisi called the "services for which their nation is specialized." They then return to Aghmat-Ailan before the setting of the sun. Al-Idrisi mentioned, "their life and their well-being are at the mercy of everybody. Thus, the Jews were careful not to violate this regulation."[55]

One can safely assume there was a Jewish quarter, or mellah, in Marrakech at this early stage. Although divorced from the city, with Aghmat-Ailan we have an early indication of the many purposes of the Marrakech Jewish quarter as Dr. Emily Gottreich described.[56] The original exclusion of the Jews from Marrakech at night, when their vital trade was still allowed during the day, indicated that Marrakech was still seen as an exclusively Islamic city, a manifestation of Almoravid Islam: a city as doctrine, even if certain compromises had to be made to maintain its position as a center of trade. It is well known that the Qur'an specifically calls for the tolerance and protection of the "people of the book," including the Jews. Although Muhammad expelled the Jews from his early community in Madina, there was no indication that he felt it necessary to exclude them completely from the Islamic community as a whole. They were a vital part of many a normal Islamic city. In the minds of the Almoravids, however, Marrakech held a status in the region similar to Medina or Mecca. Allowing the Jews to settle permanently in Marrakech was possibly seen as compromising the idea of Marrakech as a sacred, exclusively Islamic center. Nevertheless, the decision was made to allow the Jews to enter for economic purposes only. Like the holy city of Mecca, the holy city of Marrakech would restrict the entry of non-Muslims. 'Ali bin Yusuf may have been the first sultan to even allow the Jews to approach the city. Was this a compromise on the part of 'Ali for the sake of commercial development or was he actually being more restrictive than his predecessors? The sources were unclear, but given the original idea of Marrakech as a citadel to Almoravid Islam, it was most likely a compromise for practical interests. Trade in the "crafts of the Jews" may have been conducted in Aghmat-Ailan itself before they were allowed into Marrakech. Even so, Jews were taxed heavily by the Almoravids. When the Almohads conquered Marrakech, they would once again expel the Jews, not only from the city, but from much of the Empire.

Even Jewish converts in Fes, the city where Maimonides resided for part of his life, were required to wear distinctive clothing and not to mix with the rest of the population.[57] The historian Al-Marrakushi could say, "the status of the dhimmi (minority) has not been granted to Jew or Christian since the Masmuda (Berbers of the Almohads) took power, nor in a Muslim land is there synagogue or church."[58] Even so, Al-Marrakushi's history, usually sympathetic towards a hard-line Almohad ideal, was written around the same time Marrakech was about to be opened not only to Christian mercenaries but also to the Jewish community throughout the Empire. By around 1164, the later more refined Caliph Abu Yusuf Ya'qub allowed Jews to live openly.[59] Al-Marrakushi and other sources did reveal, however, the extent to which Almohads saw themselves as purifiers of what they saw as the un-Islamic practices of their Almoravid predecessors.

Ibn Tumart visits Marrakech

When Ibn Tumart, the Mahdi of the Almohads, entered the splendid mosque of 'Ali bin Yusuf in 1120 (514 H) in Marrakech after his journeys through the East, the Sultan apparently had nothing to fear. His reign appeared the culmination of Almoravid power; he had every reason to be confident of the strength of the Empire. Ingenious irrigation canals allowed for lush palm groves, gardens and orchards, seeming to rise out of nothing as a sign of God's blessing, God's city on earth. All around him was a city that manifested the power and legitimacy of Almoravid doctrine. Marrakech had become a magnificent and prosperous commercial center, much larger than any urban center ever seen in the region. It was not only a symbol of the success of Islam but the success of the Berbers in founding a civilization. At first, 'Ali bin Yusuf seemed to have little idea of the internal weaknesses of his reign, nor of what Ibn Tumart, inflamed by millennial prophecy, could do.

Ibn Tumart himself manipulated and turned on its head the system of legitimacy and doctrine originally manifested in the building of Marrakech. When 'Ali bin Yusuf entered his mosque, that great monument to Almoravid Islam, and found Ibn Tumart sitting there silently in the place reserved for the Sultan he should have known that trouble was coming. The space at the very heart of Marrakech, the very center of legitimacy in the Almoravid Empire, the prayer space of the leader of the community had been usurped.

The story itself may have been a fabrication, used by the Almohad historians to bolster the image of the Mahdi. Even so it symbolized the main reasons for the Almohad conquest: they had gained the high ground, not only literally in the mountains of the Maghrib but morally in defining the meaning of Berber Islam. When he left the city and the palace of the Sultan and encamped in the cemetery, Ibn Tumart seemed to suggest that the city of Marrakech, despite its splendor and greatness, had lost its original Islamic ideals. Ibn Tumart has sometimes been described as a Kharijite, insisting on commanding right no matter what the circumstance. He could also be called a Mu'tazilite, a philosopher insisting on the absolute unity of God and the blasphemy of all forms of anthropomorphism. He could even be called a Shi'ite or a Fatimid who believed in the infallibility of the Mahdi over the fallible consensus of Islamic clerics. In reality he was all of these, and none of these. Ibn Tumart represented the growing desire among the Berbers not only to define their own version of Islam but also to reform and rejuvenate the entire Islamic world.[60]

Although there may have been some plans for a wall as early as 1120 (514 H),[61] the original reason for strengthening the walls of Marrakech was probably the battle of Buhayra in 1130 (524 H), a battle of epic importance to the Almohad movement. Unaccustomed to fighting on the plains, and possibly deluded by an absolute belief in their movement, they lost decisively. They fled back to the impenetrable mountains and, under the leadership of the new Caliph 'Abd Al-Mu'min, slowly took control of all the major mountain chains in the Maghrib before successfully conquering Marrakech in 1147. Like the lost battle of Uhud three years after Muhammad's *hijra* from Mecca, even the battle of Buhayra and the clear military supremacy of the Almoravids did not destroy the Almohad spirit.[62] It was not cracks in the walls of Marrakech that the Almoravids had to worry about: it was cracks in ideology, cracks in the doctrine and founding ideals of the city. It was through these cracks that the Almohads would mount their most effective attacks. There was thus a paradox. At the same time as the renewed openness and flexibility in doctrine strengthened the economic vitality of the city of Marrakech, they also made it open to accusations of excess from a new group of Berber reformers – the Almohads. Later, the Almohads themselves would expand and then collapse internally.

Ibn Khaldun, the fourteenth-century historian from whom much of this history derives, believed that societies lived roughly the same lifespan as the human body: starting off young and vibrant, they passed into an established, confident adulthood and eventually descended into the somber decadence of old age before disintegrating into catastrophe.[63] When Ibn Tumart sat down in the mosque of Marrakech in the place of 'Ali bin Yusuf and petulantly commanded right and forbade wrong to the Sultan himself, the Almoravids had reached their last years on the steady, high plateau of middle age and had begun a relentless, accelerated decline. Both historians of the time and enemies of the Almoravids expressed this decline in a variety of ways. In effect, however, the underlying dynamic behind all of these descriptions of decadence, effeminacy, and moral decay was the break between Almoravid civilization and its surrounding social environment. Jared Diamond wrote that the decline of great cities and societies could be explained by the break-down in the relationship between a civilization and its physical environ-ment.[64] In the case of the Almoravids however, the physical environment was not really the issue. The trade routes were still in use; the Almoravids had never been so rich. Rather, the real reason for decline was a break with the social web of relationships between the new city of Marrakech and the surrounding rural system.

Our main source for polemic against Marrakech under the Almoravids came from Ibn Tumart himself. One of his first arguments was economic. The Almoravids originated from nomadic desert peoples. Ibn Tumart claimed that nomadic shepherds suddenly settling and building cities was predicted by Muhammad the Prophet as a sign of the last coming, "nomadic herders rising up buildings – this is among the signs of the end of time."[65] This rising up of buildings was likely meant to refer to the foundation of Marrakech. The result of this was the growth of "unlawful trade," taxation and illegal property charges used by the Sultan to host vast and decadent banquets where forbidden food and drink were served. Ibn Tumart thus complains against tax revenue being farmed from the countryside and concentrated in the Almoravid power center of Marrakech. The second argument against the city was based on morality and sex. Ibn Tumart engendered the city. By identifying the city of Marrakech with the effeminate and the decadent, Ibn Tumart strengthened the masculine imperative of the tribes to conquer, to penetrate the walls of feminized urban space. The city was idle and settled; the tribes were mobile and active. In short, Ibn Tumart was saying that the only "real men" were the men of the tribes. Ibn Tumart claimed their women dominated the Almoravids. The women of Marrakech, in particular, went unveiled and flaunted their outrageous hairstyles. They had far too much influence over government and the court.[66] This view of the city as effeminate was not limited to Ibn Tumart. Ibn Khaldun expressed similar views in his *Muqaddimah*.

> Sedentary people have become used to laziness and ease. They are sunk in well-being and luxury. They have entrusted defense of their property and their lives to the governor and ruler who rules them . . . They find full assurance of safety in the walls that surround them, and the fortifications that protect them. No noise disturbs them, and no hunting occupies them. They are carefree and trusting, and have ceased to carry weapons. Successive generations have grown up in this way of life. They have become like women and children, who depend on the master of the house. Eventually, this has come to be a quality of character that replaces natural [human] disposition.[67]

Ibn Khaldun saw walls and fortifications as signs of weakness as much as strength. The walls of Marrakech may have been in mind. In Ibn Khaldun's view, heavily influenced by his extensive experience as an envoy between tribe and government, the people of the city were "for the most part . . . more cowardly than women upon their backs."[68] He even suggested that city life effeminized so much that it encouraged homosexuality.[69]

For Ibn Tumart and the mountain tribes, Marrakech and the Almoravids were symbolized by people like Sura, the Almoravid princess who rode proudly unveiled on her horse without any regard for what Ibn Tumart and the Almohads viewed as the strict norms and ideals of a revitalized Berber Islam.[70] This polemic engendering of the feminine city verses the masculine countryside was but one more indication of the rift developing between the two systems.[71] Ibn Khaldun would say that the Almoravids were loosing their 'asabiyya (tribal solidarity). The social and moral cohesion between tribe and ruler was fracturing. Out of this fracture the Almohads emerged.

Even the Qur'an recognized the destruction of a city was punishment for the excesses of decadence.

When we decide to destroy a town (*qarya*), we first send a definite order to those among them who are given the luxurious, good things in life and yet transgress; so that the word is proved true against them. Then we destroy them utterly. (Qur'an, Sura 17: 16)

But what did these accusations of decadence and luxury really mean? Decadence meant several things in practical terms: inflation, over taxation, the development of a weighty government or religious bureaucracy, the division of society, a growing split between the urban and tribal life: all of these factors contributed to the decline of a dynasty.[72] It was no surprise that Ibn Tumart acted so scandalized by the decadence of the Almoravid cities, destroying illegal instruments, breaking wine amphorae, and ruining wedding parties whenever he entered a cosmopolitan city.[73] His actions meant more than commanding right and forbidding wrong in the immediate sense. He was commanding right and forbidding wrong against an economic and social system that seemed to be gradually loosing its balance and legitimacy, a system symbolized by moral decline in cities like Marrakech. He commanded right and forbade wrong in a way that was appealing to the increasingly marginalized tribes surrounding Marrakech. Ibn Tumart's message was clear: the city would have to be transformed in a way that manifested the new doctrine of Almohad Islam. Ibn Tumart promised to restore the founding principles of Islam. He promised to restore the power of the Masmuda tribes by making Marrakech, the first citadel of native Berber Islam, their own. With this promise the city of Marrakech was to be born anew.[74]

The Almohads dominated not only the high ground but also the waters of the Western Mediterranean and they had a significant impact on Christian European history. Unlike previous Islamic empires, empires that based their power almost exclusively on land armies, the Almohad navy was one of the greatest Muslim fleets ever created. The famed fourteenth-century historian Ibn Khaldun claimed, "The Almohads organized their fleet in the most perfect manner ever known and on the largest scale ever observed . . . The Muslim fleet was of a size and quality never, to our knowledge, attained before or since."[75] This unchallenged control of the seas gave the Almohads access to Western Mediterranean markets, trade and taxation.

5

THE ALMOHADS:
EMPIRE OF THE WESTERN
MEDITERRANEAN

The fascinating life of the Almohad admiral Ahmad Al-Siqilli (of
Sicily) mirrored the close interactions between Christian and Muslim
Mediterraneans in this period. The Normans under Roger II of Sicily, also
known for his patronage of the geographer Al-Idrisi, had captured Al-Siqilli
as a young man. Ahmad Al-Siqilli was then trained in the arts of the admiralty. After the death of Roger, Ahmad fled to Tunis and Marrakech where
he joined the court of the Almohad Caliph Yusuf bin ʿAbd Al-Muʾmin. The
Caliph declared him commander of the fleet. Ahmad and his ships were able
to fight Christian forces so effectively that his fame spread throughout the
Muslim world. Even Salah Al-Din Yusuf bin Ayyub (the famed "Saladin"
who drove the crusaders out of Jerusalem in 1187) sent a close member of his
family to the court of the Caliph Yaʿqub Al-Mansur begging for the support
of the Almohad navy. Perhaps for the sake of prudence or perhaps because
Yaʿqub Al-Mansur felt he was the greater anti-crusader, the true leader of the
Muslims, Saladin's envoy was sent back.

The almost unprecedented power of the Almohads over the seas was
reflected in the confidence of their architecture and art. Just as the success
of the Italian city-states in the Eastern Mediterranean produced a flowering
in architecture and culture, the success and confidence of the Almohads in
the Western Mediterranean was expressed in their massive and austere architecture. The Almohad Giralda Mosque of Seville, whose minaret remains

as the bell tower of the cathedral of Seville, outshone most mosques of the East. The Almohads often used architects and artists from throughout the Mediterranean. Many of these came from as far away as Sicily (then under Christian control). Like the admiral Ahmad Al-Siqilli, the architect of the Giralda was Abu Layth Al-Siqilli (from Sicily), showing the lasting Mediterranean influences of the architectural styles of the Almohad Empire.[1] If finished, the enormous Hassan Mosque in Rabat, now the capital of Morocco, could have quite easily been one of the largest mosques in all of Islam, as great as Damascus, Baghdad or Mecca. Rabat itself was founded as a monumental city, a proclamation of *jihad*, a statement in stone and mortar to the duty to spread the universal ideal of Almohad doctrine, the ineffable unity of God. The remains of Almohad influence are scattered everywhere through-out the Maghrib, a distant but powerful reminder of a once magnificent unity under Berber rule. Not only the famous Abubacer and Averroes, whose works brought classical knowledge to Christendom, but a whole school of scholars, thinkers, poets and philosophers, swelled the biographical dictionaries of the time. An enormous burst of spiritual energy and unity among the Berber tribes of the High Atlas had been transformed into a civilization.

Berber Roots in Almohad Influence

In terms of governmental organization and military power, the Almohads were clearly one of the largest and most dominant political entities of the twelfth-century Mediterranean, just as Europe was on the cusp of a period of rebirth. Remarkably, the Almohad Empire was a civilization and govern-ment based firmly on tribal Berber structures and society, even as those tribal structures were consolidated into a coherent government. The Berber *agrao* or tribal councils, the *mizwars*, tribal mediators, who maintained rules between pastoralists and agriculturalists, *tamyiz*, a method of ordering a con-federation for battle, the system of developing pacts and alliances between tribes, even the traditional Berber mystical beliefs, became the basis for Almohad hierarchy and ideology. The *Ait al-Arba'in* (*Ait* is Berber for clan or tribe, *Arba'in* means forty in Arabic) was a classic Berber social formation that, along with the closest council of ten in the Almohad hierarchy, became the elite of the Empire.[2] Berber tribes and tribesmen became the bureaucracy of the Empire.

Yet, despite their undeniable influence on the course of Mediterranean history, the Almohads are most often depicted as stern spoilers of the Andalusi dream world.[3] Traditional, nationalist history marginalized the Almohads as a largely peripheral force. Even recent studies of Andalusia have focused largely on the early Umayyad caliphate centered on Cordoba, that ornament of the world. The Almohads, like their Almoravid predecessors, are still too commonly dismissed as "African" and "Berber" and "fundamentalist" and hence alien to European culture, unworthy of the same attention as the Umayyads of Cordoba. The Almohads are often considered intolerant and backward Berber invaders into Europe from the African shore. Even as the Almohads repelled the Christians, they are often blamed for the ultimate ruin of the Andalusi dream. In a typically unsympathetic and dour description of the Almoravids and Almohads, Maria R. Menocal lamented the coming of the Berber Almoravids and Almohads,

> Andalusian Muslims would be governed by foreigners, first these same Almoravids, and later the Almohads or "Unitarians," an even more fanatic group of North African Berber Muslims likewise strangers to al-Andalus and its ways. Thus did the Andalusians become often rambunctious colonial subjects in an always troublesome and incomprehensible province.[4]

The Almoravids and Almohads introduced a strict form of revivalist Islam and Mahdism to the peninsula, a doctrine and discipline that was not always welcomed by the urbane but notoriously fractious Andalusis. Yet this doctrine often quickly accommodated local conditions to survive. Also, far from being mere foreign overlords and colonizers, the Almohads and Berbers already possessed many cultural and ancestral ties to Al-Andalus. The geographer Al-Ya'qubi spoke of established Berber tribes and clan-like structures in the Valencia region as early as the ninth century. There were enough Berbers in Andalusia for a certain Ibn Al-Qitt, one of many Mahdi precursors, to raise an army of some 60,000 men, although this number is very much disputed. Although a professed Arab, who was from the family of the Umayyad caliphs, he had a great deal of Berber support. Also, there was Shaqya bin 'Abd Al-Wahid of the Miknasa Berber tribe who claimed descent from 'Ali and, using the mountains around Cuenca, rebelled against central Umayyad power in Cordoba.[5]

Several place names and towns bore the stamp of Berber tribes, often from the Atlas Mountains where the Almohads originated. Today's Mequinenza in Aragon, Azaneta in Valencia and Axuaga in Badajoz are Spanish versions of the Berber Miknasa, Zanata and Zuwagha tribes.[6] Berbers often ruled in rural or mountainous outposts such as Albarracín near Teruel, where there were perhaps as many Berber Taifa "petty kings" as there were Arabs. Other Berber Taifas included Elvira, Granada, ruled by the Ziri Berbers of Kabyle, around Bèjaïa, until 1090. The Dammaris, Zanata Berbers, ruled the city of Morón near Seville until 1065. Other Berber rulers were "absorbed" by Mu'tamid and the Abbadids of Seville: these were the petty kings of Algeciras, Ronda, Carmona and Arcos. Seville was taken and the Almoravids imprisoned Mu'tamid in 1091.[7]

Later, in the twelfth century, the Almohad Berbers were not distant overlords but were welcomed into Andalusia by Al-Qasi, a Sufi rebel from Portugal, to establish unity over the warring petty Muslim kingdoms.[8] Nor would it always be accurate to depict the Almohads and Berbers as always less educated than Andalusis. Books, manuscripts and learning were portable arts and not necessarily contingent on the existence of numerous walled cities. This was especially true in Berber North Africa.

Ibn Tumart's voyage to the great centers of learning in the East was not unique. Pilgrimage east was considered a rite of passage for prominent sons of Berber chiefs or Ugallids. Indeed, Ibn Tumart met several Berber scholars who were on similar journeys, bringing back new ideas and knowledge as they returned home to rule their tribes. 'Abd Al-Mu'min, the future Caliph and successor of Ibn Tumart, was but one of these many traveling scholars and pilgrims. Ibn Khaldun provided evidence for expansive and impressive libraries held by Berber chieftains in the most remote and seemingly inaccessible regions of the Atlas Mountains. A great Saksawa chief of the Haddu family, from the highest regions of the Atlas, was famed for his learning. It would not be far fetched to assume that camels to and from Ghana and the gold routes were laden not just with raw merchandize but also great quantities of books. The Almohad mosque in Marrakech was named the Kutubiyya, a name deriving from the Arabic for "books" because of the large book market that thrived in the shadow of the famous minaret, that impressive monument to Almohad ideals (Figure 2). A similar minaret survives as the bell tower

Figure 2 The Almohad Kutubiyya Mosque in Marrakech. Photo by Author.

of the Giralda Cathedral of Seville (Figure 3) where another great Almohad mosque was built, symbolically linking North Africa to Al-Andalus and its Mediterranean empire in architectural terms.

As the most honored of trades, the stalls of booksellers were always closest to the mosque. A culture of books and literacy, even in the largely rural

Figure 3 The Almohad "Giralda" Minaret is now the bell tower of the Cathedral of Seville. Photo by Author.

areas of the Maghrib, was not surprising. Indeed, the rural *zawiya* culture of tribal libraries, mobile madrasas, is still very strong in even the most remote Moroccan regions. The library at the twelfth-century madrasa at Tamegroute (the foundations are medieval but the madrasa is now a modern building), twenty miles from Zagora, still holds one of the richest collections of medieval manuscripts written in Berber with Arabic script.[9]

Also, despite the reputation of the Almohads as radical Islamic dogmatists, the vision of Ibn Tumart, the founder of the Almohads, was as much intellectual as it was merely dogmatic, stern and radical. Rejecting idolatry and anthropomorphism in all its forms, Ibn Tumart and the Almohads, like Muhammad and the first Muslims, promoted the written word as the medium through which humans could understand the divine. While largely illiterate Europeans were educated in the stories of the Bible by visual, ecclesiastical art, the Almohad Berbers of North Africa, regardless of birth or status in the egalitarian milieu of the tribes, were expected to actually read and understand the word of God. It was not surprising that a book burning may have initially launched Ibn Tumart's fervent mission to restore the true nature of Islam. A main justification for Almohad rule expressed in the chronicles was outrage at the burning in Al-Andalus of Al-Ghazali's *Revival of the Religious Sciences*, a massive treatise on the synthesis of reason and mystical experience. Ibn Tumart's impressive book of doctrine, the *A'azz ma Yutlab* was admired by medieval Christian monks and scholars like Marc of Toledo who considered the work of Ibn Tumart superior in its argument for God's unity than the Qur'an itself.[10]

Many of the common Europeans and Andalusians of the pre-Almohad period were probably more illiterate than some of the Berber tribesmen who made up the core of the Almohad forces. The development of literacy, the memorization of Almohad doctrine and Qur'anic passages was an obligatory duty for every Almohad, not just the ruling elite. The *Rawd al Qirtas* described a scene where Ibn Tumart lined up a group of mountain tribesmen, assigning each of them a name corresponding to a word in the Qur'an. Ibn Tumart would pass in file each day and expect a new passage to be learned.[11] In fact, in addition to the prominent role of the Berber tribes in the hierarchy of the Almohad Empire, the rise of the Almohads let to the creation of a local, Berber-speaking literary and religious tradition based in the Sus valley. The Berber-speaking Salim Ibn Salama as-Susi (d. 1193), for example, translated Islamic jurisprudence into medieval Tashelhit Berber dialect.[12] Almohad sources, even from a later period, were scattered with Berber phrases, transliterated into Arabic letters, creating a puzzle for twentieth-century French Berberists.[13]

Ibn Tumart's charisma among these Berber students, followers and writers was so powerful that it became necessary to conceal his death while his successor, 'Abd Al-Mu'min, consolidated power.

Ibn Tumart's Influence after Death

When Pope Leo IV restored and embellished the tombs and churches of St. Peter and St. Paul in Rome (see Chapter 2) and secured St. Peter's with a wall built by defeated "Saracens," one of his main concerns was the return of those pilgrims who had abandoned the altars of the great apostles after the attack. Leo IV knew that the cult of these saints was essential not only to Rome but to centuries of ecclesiastical practice. The reverence of dead saints and their remains, especially those saints closest to Jesus, had become an integral part of Christianity by the ninth century. Far from being merely a popular practice, such reverence for the dead was endorsed by bishops and popes from St. Ambrose and St. Augustine to Leo III. Yet it would be a mistake to believe that such veneration of the dead was distinct only to the north of the Western Mediterranean, that it was absent from Islamic North Africa. Although they may have simply invaded for plunder, there was also the intriguing possibility that the "Saracens" who desecrated the shrines of St. Paul and St. Peter in Rome may have been fully aware of the holiness of these shrines and the damage their raid would inflict on the morale, not only of Romans but of Christendom and the thousands of pilgrims who came to Rome.

In *The Cult of the Saints*, the late antique historian Peter Brown suggested the unique status of the great saintly pilgrimage sites of the Christian Western Mediterranean. For Brown, these sites came to "form the basis of lasting ecclesiastical power structures." This cult of saints and, especially of dead martyrs, was seemingly a uniquely post-classical, Christian phenomenon. The dead had come to find an intimate place in society. "Thus, in Christian belief, the grave, the memory of the dead [martyrs], and the religious ceremonial that might surround this memory were placed within a totally different structure of relations between God, the dead, and the living." The boundaries between God and humans were no longer firm, as they had been in classical myth. The promise not only of eventual resurrection, but also of intersession by the saints, instead of being rejected as common and pagan, was embraced by the early bishops of Western Catholicism. Drawing on the fieldwork of famed anthropologist Clifford Geertz, Brown contrasted this with the Islamic world where, although there were holy tombs, they "existed always a little to one side of Muslim orthodoxy." For Brown, although holy graves exist in Islam, "to exist was not enough. Public and private, traditional religious leadership and the power of the holy dead never coincided to the degree to which they did in Western Europe."[14]

Almost everything about the curious conditions surrounding the death of the Almohad Mahdi Ibn Tumart seemed to disagree with Peter Brown's assertion of an essential difference between North Africa and Europe regarding tombs. Ibn Tumart was allegedly "kept alive" for three years even though his body had died. The ceremonies that surrounded his house included voices and sayings coming from his room. In fact, the date of his death was a matter of debate in the sources; such was the mystery that there are several different accounts.[15] Later, Atlas Mountain Berbers would venerate Ibn Tumart as a type of Mahdi saint for centuries.

While Brown and Geertz noticed some broad differences in the place of the dead in North African and European society, the North African historical record has revealed that, in fact, the holy graves did indeed coincide with "religious leadership" especially under the Almohads. While in Marrakech, Ibn Tumart deliberately retreated to the graveyard after his encounter with the Almoravid 'Ali bin Yusuf, seeking the protection of the dead. 'Abd Al-Mu'min, the first Caliph of the Almohads, grew sick while on pilgrimage to see the tomb of Ibn Tumart in 1162.[16] He later died in Rabat after that winter pilgrimage.

Writing in the mid twelfth century, Al-Idrisi described the cult of Ibn Tumart who died on "the Mountain of Stars . . . In our time his tomb is considered by the Masmuda Berbers as a holy place, and it is a pilgrimage destination. The tomb is surmounted by a building with a dome but not highly ornamented, conforming to their legal precepts."[17] There was a beautiful mosque built, still seen today, at Tinmall. Ibn Khaldun, in his history of the Berbers, mentioned that Ibn Tumart's tomb was still a focus of veneration in his own time in the fourteenth century, hundreds of years after the Almohad Empire had dissolved and its last caliphs had either fled to Christian Spain or had been executed.

The tomb of the Mahdi [Ibn Tumart] still exists among them, as honored, as revered as ever. The Qur'an is recited day and night; men still come there. There is a corps of guardians, conserving the same organization and following the same ceremony as that followed during the time of the Almohad Empire, receiving pilgrims and devotees from afar who are introduced into the sanctuary with an order and solemnity that inspires profound respect.[18]

It would be difficult to verify Ibn Khaldun's report. He may have written this glorified account of a lost remnant of the defeated Almohads to please his patron, the Hafsid ruler of Tunis hundreds of miles away, who maintained a semblance of an Almohad tradition in his realm.

Nevertheless, what Ibn Khaldun indicated was the pull of a certain powerful myth, a myth about the rise of Almohad doctrine and Almohad ambitions to reform the Islamic world as a reflection of claimed, innate Atlas Mountain Berber virtues, and the power of the mountain Berbers when united under a common cause. In fact, it was possible Ibn Tumart's body was actually removed from its tomb in Tinmall and taken to a secret location where Berber tribesmen have venerated it ever since by remembering the period when Almohad and Masmuda Berber power was at its height.[19]

Even after the death of the Mahdi and the building of the intricately ornamented mosque at Tinmall, the Almohads were not adverse to destroying and purifying in the name of conquest. Like the growth of many civilizations, the Almohads did replace elements of their rival, the Almoravid's, legacy. They resanctified the art and architecture of the past to reflect a specifically Berber cultural milieu and their new vision of divine unity.[20] They introduced a new, geometric style to the art and culture of Andalusia. They claimed no need for the *jizya*, the tax imposed on religious minorities, and under 'Abd Al-Mu'min gave many Christians and Jews the choice between conversion or death.

Yet, as with perhaps all absolute doctrines established in the corrupting realm of power and politics, there were exceptions and realities to Almohad *tawhid* and revolutionary fervor from the beginning. The Almohads were inspired by a strong founding principle, the principle of absolute divine unity.

However, instead of halting the vibrancy of Western Mediterranean culture, as is often wrongly assumed, much of the most important architectural, philosophical, literary and cultural achievements of Al-Andalus occurred under the reign of the Almohad caliphs. Yet this initial intellectual confidence trained into young students and functionaries of the early Almohad Empire often had a price. Some ancient customs of tolerance, especially towards Jews and the few remaining native Christian communities in North Africa, were rejected, only to be restored at the height of empire under later caliphs. Yet this did not mean the end of Christianity in North Africa. Ironically, Almohad caliphs would use the services of Christian mercenaries from the north almost from the beginning of their conquest.[21]

Despite their simple message of unity, political rule for the Almohads was never very simple to achieve. The contradictions and complexities of role of the Almohads in the Western Mediterranean deserve some reassessment. In those few accounts of Almohad culture that are available, they hold an undeserving reputation as a crazed horde of intolerant clans who ruined the promise of a tolerant Andalusia, yet the Almohads were a central and powerful player during the development of the intellectual and cultural revival in the twelfth-century Mediterranean. Almohad Islamic culture and civilization had a far-reaching impact at least as powerful as heavily studied, Christian European cultural and political centers.

There was serious economic and political exchange between the Almohads and Europe: an embassy from an English king, a trading pact, and a letter from a caliph to a pope. Also, the surprising wealth of Almohad material culture and literature and its influence on the West, despite some of the puritanical aspects of Almohad doctrine – fine ceramics, austere architecture – will be described. Finally, this chapter provides a brief reassessment of the influence of Almohad doctrine on famous Islamic scholars of the period, scholars who became renowned throughout Europe. Ibn Rushd, known as Averroes in Europe, was one of the brightest stars of intellectual history in both the European and Islamic worlds. A defender of logic and an advocate for the accommodation of reason with revelation, the fact that Ibn Rushd was an Almohad was sometimes overlooked. He was directly influenced by the aims and doctrine of the Almohad Berber civilization in which he lived.

Political and Economic Exchange in the Midst of Decline

The influence of Almohad civilization was felt as far north as England. In many ways, England was a natural ally of the far Maghrib (Morocco), especially with the potential mutual rival developing in Castile, Spain. This was certainly the case in the sixteenth century. Yet signs of a rudimentary alliance developed much earlier. In 1213 Matthew Paris, a reliable chronicler, wrote that King John sent a special embassy to the Almohad Caliph Al-Nasir. The King of England offered to convert to Islam and become a vassal if the Caliph offered help against the rebellion of the Magna Charta nobles and the invasion of France. The Caliph rejected the offer. He commented that no free man should ever reject the faith into which he had been born.[22] It was somewhat doubtful King John actually made this offer to the Caliph. Caliph Al-Nasir had just suffered a major defeat at the battle of Las Navas de Tolosa (1212) and was in no position to support a weakened English monarch. Nevertheless, the reference to the power of the Almohad Caliph in the chronicles of England revealed the important role of the Almohads, as far away as Runnymede, the site where King John sealed the Magna Carta in 1215.

Despite their eventual defeat by the combined armies of Europe at Las Navas, the Almohads, both before and after Las Navas, still had a direct part to play in the economic and political history of the Italian city-states, their natural trading partners and rivals for Mediterranean supremacy. In her book *Venice and the East*, Deborah Howard revealed the strong impact of Eastern Islamic culture on the Italian Renaissance.[23] Although most of Venetian trade seemed to occur with Eastern markets in Syria, Egypt or Constantinople, there were extensive trading contacts with North Africa and Andalusia, the Almoravids and the Almohads. Economic exchange was so extensive that the distinctive and highly valued, square-shaped dirham coins of the Almohad Empire were still a standard form of currency in Western Mediterranean markets as late as the sixteenth century.[24] Trading routes criss-crossed the Mediterranean and North Africa allowing for the export of gold bullion along with other precious items from North Africa: asbestos, skins, alum, ebony, spices, intricately carved ivory boxes, books and rare stones. Finely crafted Almohad ceramics, bronze work and textiles can be found throughout Italy.[25]

An expert on Andalusian ceramics wrote that under the Almohads "there appeared a previously unknown decorative and plastic splendor."[26] Such was the fame of Marrakech that Dante mentioned the city in the twenty-sixth canton of his "Divine Comedy."[27] Recent studies have pointed out the influence of Muslim education on the development of Western European universities. Although most research has focused on influences from Eastern Islam on the ceremonies and structures of the European university, there were also significant influences from the madrasas and universities of the Almohad Empire.[28]

Considering its powerful geographic position in the heart of the Mediterranean, the involvement of the Almohad Empire in European political and economic developments as far away as London, Rome or Paris was not surprising. Stretching over half of the southern Mediterranean coast, and the entire southern coast of the Iberian Peninsula, the Almohad Empire held a strategic geographic position straddling Africa and Europe. The increasingly powerful mercantile centers of Italy clearly coveted the rich trading opportunities in the ports of North Africa. At the apparent instigation of the Pope, Genoa and Pisa had already attacked Mahdiyya in Tunisia in 1092–3. The Catalans and the Pisans both attacked the Balearic Islands in 1114–15. By the middle of the twelfth century, the Normans of Sicily occupied almost the entire coast of present-day Tunisia. The Almohads expelled the Normans from their Tunisian trading ports, driving them back to Sicily with the capture of Mahdiyya from the Normans in 1160. In the process, the Almohads created a powerful naval and military presence throughout the Western Mediterranean. Before the Almohad capture of the city, the Christian Archbishop Cosmas I fled to Sicily with the "treasuries of two Mahdiyya churches." These included precious silks, emblematic of the silk and cloth trade that had existed between Ifriqiya, Norman possessions and the rest of the Western Mediterranean. Even Roger II's royal mantle (made c. 1133) included a long inscription in Arabic.[29] It was unlikely the Almohads would have destroyed this trade even as they cut the Normans off from their coastal possessions.

If Byzantine Constantinople was the main rival and trading center of the Venetians on the east coast of Italy, the Muslim Maghrib Al-Andalus ruled by the Almohads was now both a primary rival and trading partner for the Pisans and Genoese on the west coast. Although perhaps not influenced by Islam to the same extent as Palermo, Pisa and Genoa were constantly attempting to strengthen their position in the Western Mediterranean despite Almohad rule. Situated at a most favorable position for trade with North Africa and the Almohads, Genoa actively cultivated contacts with the Almohads. An Arabic language school was founded in Genoa in 1207 for this purpose.[30] Like the Venetians on the eastern side, the Genoese adapted and adopted many of the cultural styles, ideas and customs of their Berber and Andalusian trading partners and rivals. Interest in North Africa was not limited to the port cities of Italy. As Modena and Ferrara, cities far from the sea, increased in prosperity during the Commercial Revolution, they formed treaties with North African Berber rulers.[31] Evidence in the form of the many treaties between North Africa and multiple Italian city-states pointed to extensive trade contacts.

An 1181 peace treaty between the Almoravid prince of Majorca, remnants of the Almohad rivals and predecessors, and the republic of Genoa revealed the extent of Genoese involvement in the Western Mediterranean trade and their desire to expand contacts.[32] The Almohads would have benefited from this increase in trade. Even as, in the realm of ideas, especially the spiritual relationship between individual soul and God, the Almohads brought a unique perspective, they also influenced everyday life.

Almohads and Mediterranean Culture

Far from being a marginal movement of Berber tribesmen, as has often been argued; the Almohads greatly influenced twelfth- and thirteenth-century Mediterranean culture and daily life. One of these important, but less studied, areas of cultural impact was in food. Food was one of the most intimate markers of home and private life. The Almohads even left a legacy in the arts of cooking.

A manuscript from the late Almohad period, before Ferdinand III conquered Cordoba and Seville, contained some "five hundred" recipes of diverse origins from both North Africa and Spain.[33] Several recipes including *al-banadiq* or "Albondigas" meatballs are still familiar to travelers and Sevillianos today. In addition to instructions for wedding dishes and ceremonies, food could be a mark of status. Even some personalities were associated with the recipes: the Sayyid Abu Al-'Ula, governor and admiral of Ceuta, was partial to several meat dishes. The extent of combined North African and Iberian influences could even be seen in the type of equipment used. The earth oven of Fes was considered the best for cooking Asado en Sartén: roast skillet.[34] There were also variations on cuisines from the East including the *zirbaya* – chicken in sweet sauce. Still other recipes indicated the far-flung origins of the ingredients: the cook book of Abu Salih Al-Rahbani, for instance, called for cinnamon from China, ginger, cumin and thyme, "two dirhams each."[35] Almohad square dirham coins, respected for their value, were a regular part of daily commerce, not only in North Africa but also in Europe. The Almohads had deliberately chosen the square shape, with half dirhams being actual square coins and full dirhams having a square border printed on them, to differentiate themselves from the Almoravids.

A Sea of Ideas, a City of Philosophers and the Dream of Unification

Just as Almohad doctrine was based on the unity and oneness of God, so too were philosophical and spiritual movements at the time focused on the importance of singular solitude, primordial unity of all humanity. One thinker who spanned both shores of the Mediterranean during the Almoravid period and had a major influence on both Almohad and Christian philosophers was Ibn Bajja (d. 1139), known in the medieval Latin world as Avempace. Ibn Bajja's ancestors were possibly Andalusi or Sephardic Jews. His connection to Africa began in 1110 when the city of Zaragoza fell to the Almoravids of the Saharan Desert. As a *wazir* (or minister) to various Almoravid governors, Ibn Bajja traveled frequently between North Africa and Al-Andalus, Muslim Spain. The Almoravid capture of Al-Andalus united the Sahara, North Africa and Al-Andalus as one political unit. He was known primarily for his deeply philosophical works on the nature of the divine and the individual soul, works that would became widely popular in translation throughout Christendom. In addition to his famed rationalist writings, Ibn Bajja also composed poetry, music and songs. Ibn Bajja often came into direct conflict with the Almoravid political and religious establishment of the time even as he often found employment in that establishment. Often his poetic repertoire contained Christian elements. According to the Tunisian Al-Tifashi, he "often combined the songs of Christians with those of the East, thereby inventing a style found only in Andalus, toward which the temperament of his people inclined such that they rejected all others." This was the famous *muwashshaha*, a poem written as a mélange of both Arabic and Romance languages. Maimonides even told us these poems were performed at Hebrew weddings and were allowed by Jewish doctors, despite their salacious content, because they were performed in Hebrew, not the original Arabic.[36]

Although a great poet and philosopher, there are very few details about Ibn Bajja's early life and education in the last years of Muslim Zaragoza. One of his first positions was as a minister and ambassador for the Berber Almoravid governor, Abi Bakr bin Ibrahim Al-Sahrawi or Ibn Tifalwit. One of his first, rather unfortunate, embassies was to 'Imad Al-Dawla bin Hud then at the town of Ruta. 'Imad was the prince who had ruled Zaragoza before the Almoravids took the city. When he arrived in Ruta, Ibn Bajja was thrown in prison as a traitor. When he was finally released he soon found himself the target of charges of heresy and was imprisoned by the Almoravids. He was only released after the intervention of the grandfather of another famous philosopher, Ibn Rushd (Averroes).[37] Having regained favor with the Almoravids, he then worked as minister for the Almoravid Yahya bin Yusuf bin Tashufin. In the 1130s he was stationed in Oran, Algeria. He died after moving to Fez, Morocco in May 1139. There was a rather extraordinary story associated with his death. Some sources claim that the father of Ibn Zuhr, known in Latin as the famed doctor Avenzoar, served Ibn Bajja a poisoned fruit, perhaps out of jealousy. Ibn Bajja died just as the Almohads were growing in prominence in the Atlas Mountains (in 1130). There were several surviving works by Ibn Bajja both in the original Arabic and in Hebrew translation. Also, many known fragments of his work were quoted in the Latin translations of Averroes and in the writing of Albertus Magnus. One outstanding example was the *Tadbir al mutawahhid* or "Rule of Solitude."[38]

The political realm would soon reflect the philosophical. The word for solitude, *al-Mutawahhid*, was from the same root *wahid*, of "one," as *al-Muwahhidun*, the Arabic word for the Almohads who sought unity under the authority of the Mahdi and his caliphs. It seemed more than a coincidence that as Ibn Bajja and his successors in the philosophical realm sought unity within themselves, the Almohads sought unity in the realm of politics, and powerful crusader popes in Europe, such as Innocent III, sought unity under the authority of the Church. The main dream was not simply the dream of conversion, but the dream of unification.

Ibn Bajja focused on a theme repeated throughout Sufi literature: the steps and levels achieved by the soul on its path to union with the divine. Ibn Bajja was much more of a rationalist in his approach to the relationship between the self and God. Rejecting the idea that the traditional Sufi steps or *tabaqat* toward union with the divine were the reward of ritual and doctrinal devotion, Ibn Bajja posited that the ascent toward the divine was primarily intellectual, even a rational process. Following a neoplatonic philosophy of forms, Ibn Bajja developed a complex set of abstractions that eventually led to the ultimate light of the divine presence.[39] Humans could ascend through mere material forms by this process of abstraction until the ultimate intellect was reached. Avoiding the potential, heretical charge of combining the soul with God, Ibn Bajja described this ultimate intellectual presence not as God himself but an emanation from God.

Ibn Bajja's work was influenced by earlier philosophers including the famous Al-Farabi (Al Farabius in Latin) who, like Ibn Bajja, decried the difficult situation of the philosopher whose mind and access to rarified, intellectual forms was stuck in a society that favored more mundane pursuits and understandings. Al-Farabi, the great philosopher originally from Turkestan, believed in the philosopher's elite access to knowledge, knowledge that should not be shared with the common masses. Following a similar trend, Maimonides, the famed Jewish philosopher, believed in an elite and exclusive realm of theological knowledge.

Leo Strauss, the German-American political philosopher, in his book *Persecution and the Art of Writing*, suggested that the greatest medieval thinkers wrote in esoteric terms, trying to avoid detection by political authorities but also trying to avoid the possibility of escape: when philosophy negatively impacts the popular masses.[40] Focusing on the medieval period, Strauss held up both Muslim and Jewish scholars, especially Maimonides, Al-Farabi and Ibn Bajja, as exemplars of this dissimulation. Yet, Strauss may overestimate the presumed risk from both Almoravid regime and the Almohads. Often, it was rival philosophers and ministers within the court, indeed other intellectuals, who were the greatest danger. After all, it was the father of the doctor Ibn Zuhr who served the poisonous dose to kill Ibn Bajja.

On a Primordial Island: Almohad notions of Solitude and Belief

Whether influenced by politics or by academic backstabbing, Ibn Bajja suggested withdrawal from the world of imperfect human contact and emigration to an ideal community or "city" of philosophers, full of thinkers devoid of political motivations.[41] If such a community did not exist – Ibn Bajja claimed it did not exist during his own life – he suggested withdrawing into isolated contemplation. Solitude allowed for perception of the divine.[42]

It was this philosophical angst over the imperfections and disappointments of the natural, ideal medieval Islamic polity that led the North African scholar Ibn Tufayl (Abubacer in Latin) to write *Hayy Ibn Yaqzan*, the life of a man born without parents, growing up without parents away from all human contact. Supported by the courts of the Almohad caliphs as a doctor and advisor, Ibn Tufayl wrote his work fully aware of the mission of Almohad doctrine. This man independently comes to the realization of God's unified and singular nature. Similar to Rousseau's later concept of the "noble savage," humanity in this pure form was a true Muslim and believer in a single God. Ibn Tufayl would, in turn, teach Ibn Rushd (Averroes), the Almohad philosopher who would have the most influence on the Christian and Islamic West.

Ibn 'Arabi, born into the Almohad world, focused on this notion saying,

> original faith is the primordial nature in accordance with which God created mankind. It is their witnessing of His Oneness (*wahdaniyya*) at the taking of the Covenant. Every child is born in keeping with that Covenant. However, when he falls through the body into the confines of Nature, the place of forgetfulness, he becomes ignorant and forgets the state he had had with his Lord.[43]

Only the corruptions of this world divert every human spirit from his original beliefs. Thus, "if an individual has faith that the Qur'an is God's speech and is absolutely assured of that, let them take their creed from the Qur'an itself, without any interpretation or bias."[44] This, in political form, was what Ibn Tumart and his successors tried to achieve. The full history of the success of Ibn 'Arabi's doctrine, despite instances of official persecution, cannot be told here. Ibn 'Arabi's approach, a concept of unity directed inward, mostly restricted as it was to the realm of the soul, and able to navigate as a movement between and among political boundaries, turned out to be even more successful than the political approach of the Almohads. Even so, the birth of the Almohads provided the climate in which such reflections on unity and the nature of God could be renewed and travel from West to East, just as Islam had originally traveled from East to West.

The concept of a "natural Islamic man," an original state or, at least, susceptibility to true religious inspiration, would centuries later be expressed by the great philosopher of history who remains the most important source for medieval North Africa: Ibn Khaldun (d. 1406). Rather than seeing the possibility of a "city" of pure thought and spirit, Ibn Khaldun saw the countryside as the idealized incubator. Tribes from the countryside embodied the natural state of human society. As man who pursued, but failed, to adhere to the rigors of Sufism himself, Ibn Khaldun instead seemed to see the primordial, pure state of human society in tribes, as opposed to the corruption and decadence inherent in urban life.

Arab and Berber tribes were not merely threats to an existing, corrupt and divided political order. Their natural cohesiveness, called 'asabiyya – a vague term basically meaning the God-given ties that bind people together through blood – when combined with true religious inspiration, was the real reason for the success of empires and dynasties. This belief in a natural, original state of purity, corrupted by time and experience, the life of man being seen in the lifespan of society, was in many ways not so different from the original belief in God bestowed to every infant, and would form the building blocks of a successful and divinely sanctioned society. As Ibn Khaldun viewed the disintegration of the Almohad Empire from its original, primordial ideals, he may have just as easily described, as did Ibn 'Arabi and Ibn Bajja before him, the very corruption of every soul as it broke from the oneness of God.

Bishops of Almohad Marrakech

Even as a doctrine of oneness was being spread over the whole expanse of North Africa and eventually transformed the whole Islamic world, there remained a powerful Almohad dream. Practically, this dream of empire was difficult to implement. Politically and militarily the Almohad caliphs became increasingly dependent on diverse sources of power, even the power of Christian mercenaries. Although the dream of an exclusive realm for free, philosophical reflection would continue through the intellectual history of the Western Mediterranean, constructing an elite city of philosophers was not the central concern of religious and political powers of the Mediterranean. In terms of trade and exchange, Genoa and Pisa were not the only Italian city-states influenced by the Almohads; there were contacts between the Almohads and the Pope himself. A letter from the Almohad Caliph Al-Murtada to Pope Innocent IV (1243–1254) confirmed the existence of contacts between the Almohads and papal Rome as late as 1250.[45] The Pope had earlier asked the Caliph to convert to Christianity and give over the palace he lived in to the very Christian mercenaries who guarded it. Clearly aware of the intricate power politics of the Italian city-states, and desperate for assistance as their position weakened, this Almohad Caliph, formerly an advocate of *jihad* against Christians, reacted to the Pope's many letters to him and called for some understanding with the leader of the Christian West. Clearly, the Almohads had been fundamentally transformed since the early decades of their empire when they set the terms.

Pope Innocent IV had his own problems in Europe. Emperor Frederick II, who was practically adopted by the Pope, had been excommunicated by a previous pope for lack of commitment to the Crusades and was none too pleased with his former mentor. Even so, the very fact that the letter was written from a Muslim caliph to a pope fighting vigorously to extend the Crusade seems astonishing, revealing an extensive amount of contact between the Almohads and the Christian West. The letter mentions the envoy of the Pope, the Franciscan Lope Fernando d'Ayn. Lope was made "Bishop" of Marrakech in 1246. In a letter given to Lope to present to the Caliph, the Pontiff asked for a way to establish a church for the large number of Christians, especially mercenaries, in Marrakech. Like the missions of Jean de Plan Carpin, William of Rubruck and André de Longjumeau who had been sent as envoys to the Mongols around the same time, the Pope gave great importance to Lope's mission. Nor was Lope a mere provincial priest: chronicles from the time indicate that Lope had become one of the papacy's primary advisors and contacts – he was, in many regards, a type of plenipotentiary envoy. The Pope saw Lope's mission as an essential diplomatic endeavor:

he recognized that the Almohads were still a dominant force in the Western Mediterranean despite their famed defeat by a combined force of Christian armies at Las Navas de Tolosa in 1212. Most of the Christian rulers in Spain were still in their infancy at the time and the Almohads were left to attempt to shore up their losses. This was made difficult by the short reign of many of their rulers and conflicts between the conservative Almohad shaykhs and the Christian mercenaries brought in to protect the Caliph.

To minister to mercenaries, and other Christians, the Pope sent not only letters but also prestigious legates. Like the philosopher Avempace (Ibn Bajja) before him, Lope d'Ayn came from the region of Zaragoza, only recently conquered by Christians in 1118. As was the case for later Christian conquests in the Iberian Peninsula, much of the architectural, cultural legacy of the Muslim rulers remained. Still today stands the fabulous Aljaferia Palace of Zaragoza, filled with chambers for poetic recitation and gardens for "drinking companions." Even amidst its wild arcades, reaching out and intermingling into a seemingly unapologetic decadence of style and refinement, the palace also displayed scripture that appealed to a conservative audience.[46] It was a testament to the height of Andalusi culture built by Ahmad Al-Muqtadir of the Banu Hud dynasty. Zaragoza churches took over mosques with North African designs, keeping minarets intact as iconic bell towers, such as the unique, octagonal bell tower where a *mudejar* bell tower echoes Almohad designs. The Kutubiyya Mosque (Figure 2) would have recalled the designs on churches and cathedrals throughout the lands in Al-Andalus the Almohads once held.

The new Christian rulers of Zaragoza did not want to destroy this luxurious palace or beautiful designs. In fact, after the Banu Hud had been ousted by the Almoravids, they joined Alfonso "the Battler" to take it from the North Africans. The Christian king and the Church seemed to revel in their new surroundings. Even so, there were some Zaragoza Christians, such as Bishop Lope d'Ayn, who wished to go to North Africa to convert Muslims to Christ and minister to the Christian merchants and mercenaries already there.

Born in the town of Gallur near the city of Zaragoza, Aragon in 1190, Lope d'Ayn, also known as Beato Agno or Agno de Zaragoza, was Bishop of Marrakech from 1246 to 1260. From the beginning of his life, Lope was associated with several miracles and good deeds in Aragon. His name is still known in Aragon where a parish bares his name. Many of his writings and journals from his time in North Africa were, unfortunately, destroyed in a fire. However, it is still possible to trace the basic trajectory of Lope's fascinating career.

Lope rose quickly in the church hierarchy and held the position of Canon of the massive cult shrine and church of Santa Maria del Pilar in Zaragoza. In 1220, however, he was one of the first in Spain to embrace the newly established order of the Friars Minor, the Franciscans. As St. Francis' famous visit to the ruler of Egypt indicated, one of the main missions of the Franciscans was to convert and preach to the "infidels" in Northern Africa. In was in this spirit that Lope accepted the position of Bishop of Marrakech in 1246 in a papal bull written by Pope Innocent IV.

The Bishopric of Marrakech was established in 1226, some two decades earlier, when Archbishop Jimenez de Rada of Toledo was given the authority to consecrate a bishop "to the lands of Miramamolín [the Latin name used for most rulers of the Maghrib] so that from this time forward the Christians there should have the Bishop they have lacked for time immemorial." There had been some bishops in North Africa before, especially a long line of ancient ones before the Muslim conquest, but Marrakech did not yet exist – these would be among the first bishops to Marrakech, a city established in the eleventh century and considered sacred to Maghribi Muslims. Lope was, by far, the most important and powerful of Marrakech's bishops. During his long term, the Pope granted him extraordinary authority. Unlike most bishops, he only had to visit Rome once every ten years, instead of every five. He communicated regularly with the Pope. Lacking other leaders in the community, he became not only the spiritual leader but also, in many real ways, the temporal authority and representative of the Christians of Marrakech. He learned Arabic and negotiated regularly with Muslim rulers on behalf of the Pope himself to allow a fortification to protect the Christian community. The importance of his mission to the Pope and to the Catholic kings of Castile is evidenced in their financial and political support. After the Christian conquest of Seville, Lope and his Bishopric were given the rents off tracts of the newly acquired land to support their mission in Marrakech.[47]

Within Marrakech there were at least four main groups of Christians in Lope's flock. First, there were the local Christians who had lived in North

Africa for more than a generation. The sources called them "Farfanes." Scholars are still debating their obscure origins. Although they may have claimed ancient origins, before even the Almohads, scholars have concluded that although "we can admit to the possibility that they were descendents of ancient (pre-conquest) Christian populations, this possibility is highly doubtful."[48] The Farfanes left Marrakech for Seville in 1390 and established a church there. The term "farfanes" was still used in Christian chronicles to describe North African Christians as late as 1432.[49] They are also mentioned by an Arabic chronicle dating to the fifteenth century, the *Rawd al Qirtas*, with a description of the destruction of the "Church of Marrakech" and the killing of many of the people of the "Banu Farfan" by Yahya, an Almohad chief who had rebelled against the Almohad Caliph who was himself under the control of Christian mercenaries.[50] The second group of Christians were missionary "lay men" who in the words of one chronicle, "gave up their livelihood, land and possessions" to come to North Africa and preach the word of Christ. Third were the Minor Friars and monks of other orders who came to Marrakech with similar, evangelical missions. Finally, there was a substantial population of Christian mercenaries and knights who fought in the armies of the Amir, the Muslim ruler. The mercenaries often brought their families with them. There may have also been some Christian merchants.

A papal bull put all these Christians under the protection of the Pope, Father of the Church in Rome. Lope's role as representative of the Pope was sealed when he was formally announced as "African Legate."[51] Lope's influence extended beyond Marrakech and he wrote letters to the rulers of the cities of Bèjaïa and Tunis (the Hafsids) asking for the safe passage of various Friars Minor.[52] Other bishops in North Africa, including Lorenzo of Portugal, were among some of the most distinguished and well-traveled Spanish friars. Lorenzo went on missions to Tartary before being stationed in the Maghrib. Pope Nicholas IV sent Rodrigo of Gudal, incorrectly called "archbishop" of Marrakech, with letters to the rulers of Tunis and Tlemcen in what is now Algeria. Bishops would be sent from Iberia to Marrakech until the height of the inquisition and the death of one of the last Spanish bishops of Marrakech, T. de Espinoza, in 1631.[53]

In 1254, Lope returned to Al-Andalus, was named ambassador and plenipotentiary, traveling to Toledo to help form a pact between the royal families of England and Castile. He ensured that they would promise to combine their efforts against the Muslims. In 1255, Lope was able to extract promises from King Alfonso X "the Wise" to declare a crusade against North Africa. Preparations began in earnest and Lope was named Predicador (lead preacher) of the Crusade by the Pope. The plans fell apart when Alfonso grew increasingly occupied with rivalries in Europe. Extraordinarily, despite all of his attempts to foment crusade against them, Lope maintained his relationship with the rulers of North Africa and would remain Bishop until around 1257 when he expressed his desire to give up the Bishop's miter and go on a pilgrimage to the Holy Land. The opportunity for a strident evangelist, such as Lope, to maintain these relationships came after a dramatic shift in Almohad doctrine.

Al-Ma'mun and the Decline of Almohad Doctrine

Despite the original exclusiveness of Almohad doctrine preached by Ibn Tumart and maintained by the first caliphs and strict enforcers, the situation had changed dramatically for Christians and other minorities by Bishop Lope's time. Marrakech, although originally touted first by the Almoravids and then by the Almohads as a purified city, was by no means violently opposed to all forms of Christian influence and evangelism. Even as Ibn Tumart's doctrine of *tawhid* was being translated in Spain by the cleric Marc of Toledo, Christianity and Christian doctrine possibly influenced the late Almohad caliphs and two Christian religious orders were established to assist the Christians of North Africa. Al-Ma'mun, a late Almohad caliph, ultimately rejected Ibn Tumart as Mahdi.[54] He was not adopting Christianity; his view of the Mahdi as the prophet Jesus was also an orthodox view of most non-Almohad, Sunni Muslims.

This break with Almohad doctrine had an immediate consequence for the once far-flung authority of the Almohad caliphs. Responding against this move away from Almohad orthodoxy, Abu Zakariyya Yahya, the Almohad Hafsid governor of Ifriqiya, already enjoying a great deal of autonomy from Marrakech, no longer mentioned the name of the Caliph in Marrakech in prayers in the Zitouna Mosque in Tunis.

Al-Ma'mun's fateful pronouncement was an extraordinary claim to make at the height of the Christian conquest of Al-Andalus. Perhaps as a sign of his submission to the Christian mercenaries who were his only real guarantee to power, the Almohad Caliph constructed a new church in Marrakech; the original had been destroyed in 1231 during the insurrection of Yahya Ibn 'Abd Al-Haqq.[55] The death of five Franciscan martyrs, protégés of St. Francis himself, who had been killed for preaching and evangelizing openly in the street was not the end of the Christian presence. If anything, the martyrs provided cohesion to the community and a site of reverence that connected Marrakech to the friars and Franciscan movement throughout Europe.[56] Before entering Almohad territory in Seville, the group of Franciscans had already declared their intention to be killed by the Muslim government. They tried to break into the Great Mosque (now the Giralda) and then went to the Alcazar across the square to publically renounce Muhammad. It was actually the local Christian community itself that asked for these trouble-makers to be deported. It was only after much prodding by the populous and attempts to offer them wealth, women and reward for conversion that they were killed.[57]

Nonetheless, the deeper influence of Christianity, especially the role of Christian mercenaries, inspired reactions from the population even if the government was slow to move against a few missionary zealots. In Marrakech, insurrectionists were concerned about the growing influence of the Christian slaves, merchants and mercenaries. The use of Christian mercenaries was unpopular. Al-Ma'mun's reign saw the stationing of 12,000 Christian troops in the Maghrib, the creation of a North African bishopric, and the ringing of church bells from a cathedral in Marrakech, the very heart of the Almohad Empire. Unlike Muslim Spain, which had known and tolerated the presence of Christian communities for centuries, Marrakech was so sacred that it was, at one time, forbidden for non-believers to remain inside its walls after sunset. Al-Rashid, the successor to Al-Ma'mun took Marrakech with an army made up almost entirely of Christian mercenaries and Arabs. He roundly defeated rival Almohad Berber shaykhs, led by the prestigious Atlas Mountain Haksura tribe, supported by Yahya Al-Mu'tasim. The Haksura left for the region of Sijilmasa. Even as negotiations with Berber shaykhs convinced Al-Rashid to restore Almohad doctrine, his Arab allies changed their loyalties and sided with the Haksura who returned from Sijilmasa to raid the town.[58] Al-Rashid captured Marrakech once again, but the glories of the Almohad Empire had long passed. Lacking significant means to enforce authority, a successor of Al-Rashid, Al-Sa'id (1242–8), lost large swaths of the Empire as regions such as Hafsid Ifriqiya defected from Marrakech (Chapter 3).

In the Central Maghrib, the Zayyanids under their leader Yaghmurasan bin Zayyan also proclaimed their autonomy in Tlemcen, an important city across the border of Morocco in Algeria close to the Mediterranean port of Honaine but still protected from coastal raids. Tlemcen was also something of a spiritual center for Sufis. The strict ascetic Abu Madyan (d. 1198) was buried in a magnificent tomb: the Sidi Boumediene (Abu Madyan) mausoleum and mosque, which survives to this day in the outskirts of the city. As with the Hafsids in Tunis, the Zayyanids took advantage of the spiritual and economic transformations of the twelfth century. They encouraged religious pilgrimage (Abu Madyan) and centered power and commerce close to the Mediterranean Sea.

Ferdinand III of Castile, realizing the weakness of Al-Rashid in Marrakech, reduced Muslim Spain and raided into new territories. One of the very last of the Almohad caliphs, the son of Abu Dabbus, having lost control of the capital Marrakech to a new Berber Zenata dynasty, the Marinids of Fes, fled to Aragon in Christian Spain.[59] Ironically, it had been from Aragon where Reverter, Viscount of Barcelona who converted in Islam and became an Almoravid general, had been captured centuries before. The last Almohad shaykhs were executed at Tinmall in the mountains. Even so, the mosque of Ibn Tumart was not completely destroyed and remains in ruins to this day. The historian Ibn Khaldun warned against the use of mercenaries as a primary cause for the decline of dynasties. His warnings had no better exemplar than the Almohad Empire.

The transformation of Marrakech from the capital of a revolutionary Berber Islam to a citadel for mercenaries, and the caliphate from an institution of the Mahdi to a puppet of Christian soldiers seemed an extraordinary development to North Africans. Just as Mecca and Madina were off limits to non-believers in Arabia, Marrakech was, hypothetically, off limits to non-Muslims in North Africa. Marrakech, as mentioned earlier, had been the symbolic core of the Almohad Empire, the main Kutubiyya Mosque, rebuilt on the site of the Almoravid mosque but with a new orientation towards

Mecca, was an expression of their rule and doctrine. Afterall, it had been rebuilt and its *qibla* (prayer direction) "corrected" from the corrupted calculations of the Almoravids. Even so, this did not prevent 'Abd Al-Mu'min himself, the first Caliph of the Almohads and the one who codified the doctrine of the Mahdi, from using Christian mercenaries who had served the Almoravids to defeat a rival "false" Mahdi named Al-Massi from the Atlantic coastal city of Salé who rose up against him. The tribes and tribal leaders that joined the rebel Al-Massi were purged in a fashion similar to the original *tamyiz* massacre under Ibn Tumart. Taking advantage of divisions between Spain's Christian kingdoms, the Almohad armies also regularly allied with Christian rulers such as Fernando II of León who conquered Badajoz and gave it to the Almohad Caliph Abu Ya'qub Yusuf in 1168.

This close affiliation with Christian armies showed the advantages of their training and eventually made caliphs desirous for their services. The Christian mercenary presence would only increase under later Almohad caliphs, especially as the loyalty of the original Atlas Berber tribal leaders, the so-called "Almohad Shaykhs," began to waver in their support and as they attempted to select their own candidates for Caliph. They saw caliphs moving away from the original message of the Mahdi Ibn Tumart and making the concessions necessary for imperial rule. Indeed such was the power of the mercenaries that they, in a fashion similar to ancient Rome's Praetorian Guard, proposed their own caliphs. The shaykhs eventually had to contend against these mercenary caliphs. The mercenaries became so numerous that under later Almohad caliphs church bells would compete with the Muslim call to prayer of the Muezzin. The Marrakech that the Almohads had taken and resanctified from the Almoravids as an exclusively "Islamic" city did not remain that way for long. The increasing Almohad use of Christian mercenaries required a compromise.

This shift, however, seemed anathema to some of the more conservative Almohads, especially some of the original Berber tribes who still held up the belief in the doctrine of the Mahdi Ibn Tumart. There were many revolts and factions that arose to try and restore the original doctrine, in vain. As mentioned earlier, the crucial break was when Al-Ma'mun had abandoned not only the sacred status of Marrakech but the original Almohad doctrine. He claimed that Ibn Tumart, the esteemed founder of the Almohads, the original charismatic force behind the creation of the Almohad movement, was not in fact the Mahdi, the awaited one. Instead, the Mahdi was Jesus, the Mahdi expected by most Sunni Muslims. According to one fourteenth-century chronicle, Al-Ma'mun proclaimed, "You know that we have suppressed error and published truth, that there is no other Mahdi than Jesus, son of Mary, who alone has a right to the title of Mahdi . . . This is the reason why we have abolished that Almohad innovation and have removed the word infallibility (ma'sum) . . ."[60] This abrogation of the central, distinguishing pillar of Almohad doctrine, the infallibility of the Mahdi Ibn Tumart and his writings contained in the A'azz ma Yutlab, the "second Qur'an" of the Almohads, would have the same impact as a proclamation by the Sunni Caliph in Baghdad that Muhammad was not, in fact, God's messenger, but a fraud. Replacing Ibn Tumart with Jesus seemed to be popular with those mercenaries who destroyed the tribal forces of Yahya, the favorite of the Almohad tribal shaykhs, and put Al-Ma'mun in power. These were the very Christian mercenaries purchased from the Castilian King Ferdinand III.

As a price for his support, King Ferdinand specified the stringent conditions under which he would allow his troops to be borrowed by Al-Ma'mun. Al-Ma'mun was also forced to pay Ferdinand an enormous amount of money, 300,000 maravedis, a gold and silver Iberian coin of the period.[61] Yet more damaging than the monetary costs were the conditions imposed by the Castilian King. "I will give you the army only under the condition that you give me ten fortresses on the frontier of my reign, selected by me. If God favors you and you enter Marrakech, you must build a church in the middle of the city for those Christians who go with you, where they will practice their religion and ring their bells at the time of prayer." In other words, the whole character of Marrakech as an exclusive Muslim city at the heart of a Muslim empire, an idea at the heart of Almohad ideology, seemed threatened. The King, perhaps fearful that some of his mercenaries would try to curry favor through conversion, even required Al-Ma'mun to refuse the conversion of any Christian to Islam. "If a Christian attempts to convert himself to Islam, he shall not be received as a Muslim and will be returned to his brothers so that he may be judged in accordance with his laws and if a Muslim converts to Christianity, none shall do a thing to him."[62] Not only was Marrakech no longer a sacred city exclusive to Islam, Muslims were forced to be treated as lesser citizens than these mercenaries; they became, as it were, *dhimmis* of the *dhimmi* (religious minorities under Islam).

The old guard of the Empire, the powerful Berber Hintata and Tinmall tribes of the Atlas Mountains, had rebelled against Al-Ma'mun and installed a rival Caliph in Marrakech. When he regained control of Marrakech he massacred large numbers of powerful tribal chiefs and advisors. Moreover, he even rejected the original doctrine of the founder of the Almohads, Ibn Tumart, the doctrine that provided the social glue for the fractured, tribal landscape of twelfth-century North Africa. Unlike his predecessors, Al-Ma'mun could not depend on a disciplined cohort of tribal fighters. Instead, after conquering Marrakech in 1227, he immediately made his pact with Ferdinand. Instead of gaining loyalty freely, he purchased it. He would rely on Ferdinand's European mercenaries, disciplined troops under his control, troops who seemed a better alternative than gaining the fickle loyalty of the Berber tribes.

The Almohad Empire faded as the once-powerful Berber governors and loyal followers of Ibn Tumart's doctrine retreated back to their homelands in the Atlas Mountains. In the fourteenth century, Ibn Khaldun (d. 1406) described some of the last Almohad adherents gathering at the grave of Ibn Tumart deep in the mountains south of Marrakech. Even as Al-Ma'mun's reign was a decisive blow to the Almohad movement it did not completely extinguish the fervent flame lit by the Mahdi Ibn Tumart a century before. The fall of the Almohad may have had less to do with ideology, however, than with some of the peculiarities of North African warfare. While in Iberia, where citizens were increasingly armed, and even in Turkey under the Ottomans or Egypt where trained and armed Sufi youth protected their cities, in North Africa there was an increasing dependence on mercenaries from Europe, even from long-standing enemies and rivals such as Castile. Nonetheless, the suggestion that there was no resistance or no urban organization in North Africa needs some reconsideration.

Mercenary North Africa: A Society Not Organized for War?

Using European mercenaries, often a mix of Spaniards, Catalans and even Italians, was a way of delaying inevitable decline, a way of avoiding the cycle of history and preventing the rise of a new, tougher, more unified, tribal dynasty. The most common tactic of Berber and Arab tribal armies, both from the mountains and from the desert regions, was to attack and withdraw to a defensive line that included their women, children and their entire livelihood. In traditional warfare one of the main reasons for fighting was survival, sustenance and defending their own blood. The most effective battle tactic, a tactic used during the first Islamic conquests, was to attack a fixed target, such as a town or village, and withdraw back to some inaccessible campsite in the mountains or desert. At this campsite there was a rally line of women, children and supplies. Traditional Berber and Arab warfare was, however, no longer used as an originally tribal dynasty grew and matured with urban luxury. As Ibn Khaldun noted,

> [W]hen luxury penetrated the various dynasties, the use of the rally line behind the fighters was forgotten. This was because when they were Bedouins and lived in tents, they had many camels, and the women and children lived in camp with them. Then they achieved royal luxury . . . When they traveled, they left their women behind. Royal authority and luxury caused them to use tents both large and small. They used these things to form their (protective) line in war . . . These things, unlike one's own family and property, do not inspire willingness to die . . .

Unlike tribal armies that simply returned to their homelands and abandoned an unpopular ruler, European mercenaries were trained to hold the line, to keep a tight formation.

> We have mentioned the strength that a line formation behind the army gives to the fighters who use the technique of attack and withdrawal. Therefore the North African rulers have come to employ groups of European Christians in their army, and they are the only ones to have done that . . .[63]

Scholars of Spanish history, in contrast, attempted to show that Christian citizens of cities were organized for war differently and, perhaps, more effectively. In Cuenca and other frontier towns on the "marches" or battle zone between the Castilians and the Almohads in twelfth-century Iberia were societies "organized for war." Unlike North Africa where armies were composed of rural tribes or mercenaries, the entire social network of Christian towns was directed at conquest and preparing for battle. This meant not only that Christian towns were better organized against a common enemy, but also that they could maintain a level of independence and autonomy from the King, demanding *fueros* or power concessions from the ruler. The famous *fueros*, or municipal constitutions, of Spain were even an inspiration for the United States of America's second President John Adams.[64] Drawing on Ibn Khaldun, scholars have focused on the necessary reliance on Christian mercenaries and Arab or Berber tribal armies as the Achilles heel of medieval North African dynasties and ultimately, perhaps, a reason for the decline of the region in relation to Europe. The transplantation of Arab tribes from the East to the plains of the Morocco by Almohad caliphs, in particular, has been seen as a source of instability and constant raiding within the Empire. Although his form of combat was highly effective in battle, the Caliph had to move his massive army from crisis to crisis. Without trained, urban militias fighting for the cause of Islam he may have avoided rebellion, but he also made his borderlands vulnerable to Christian raiders. Faced with the growth in power of Arab tribes, the Almohad Berber tribes retreated to the Atlas Mountains just as the Berbers of the Central Maghrib, Algeria, seemed to retreat from the Banu Hilal Arab migrations decades before.

This did not mean that urban citizens under Almohad rule lacked any desire for resistance to invading, pillaging armies. The people of Marrakech regularly took sides in conflicts between rival Almohad caliphs and the population of Seville rose up and tried themselves to fend off the army of Ferdinand III of Castile when the Almohad army of the ruler Al-'Adil stood down and allowed the city to be taken. They were defeated almost without a fight.[65]

The Independence of Urban Populations

Despite the possible benefits for defense, the arming and training of an urban population had inherent risks for any ruler who wished to extend influence beyond the walls of the city. Simply because European cities may have been full of armed citizens ready to fight did not imply a superior or more stable form of urban organization. In fact, new research comparing cities in medieval and late medieval Europe and the Islamic world has begun to call into question assumptions of a superior, European model of urban organization.[66] In many instances, the multifarious centers of power within European cities, from neighborhoods to guilds to aristocracy, were, as with Near Eastern urban spaces, highly fractious hindrances to development or defense. They cannot always be seen as seeds of the modern city of today.

Although many cities in Christian Italy and Spain may have been full of well-armed adventurers, mercenaries and merchants, such as the *almogovars* of Barcelona, populations could just as well rebel against attempts at centralized rule. Cities around the Western Mediterranean were notorious for struggles between old and new families, between the under classes and the growing, commercial elite. Even Rome, the heart of western Christendom, was a site of popular rebellion. Popes in Rome, despite their spiritual claim to power, were often subject to popular urban rebellions. One of the most famous and successful was that of Arnold of Brescia (d. 1155). Disgusted by the extreme wealth of the Commercial Revolution, Arnold of Brescia established a Commune of Rome (1144) based on the old Roman Republic and an overthrow of the nobility. Arnold called for the Church to abandon property and wealth it had been gathering with the rise of pilgrimage and donations to the Church. He was only defeated by the combined forces of Frederick Barbarossa and Adrian IV – one of the few times an emperor and a pope could see eye to eye was when the urban population gained control. Arnold's ashes were thrown into the Tiber to prevent his becoming a martyr.[67] Just as Ibn Tumart had called for a restoration of the original principles of Islam, calling especially for the repeal of oppressive taxes and the marginalizing of the Atlas Mountain tribes, Arnold of Brescia appealed to the original principles of Christian poverty, even as the Commune seized the wealth of the ruling class. In one instance, an empire was created. In the other, the citizens of Rome and the Pope eventually came to an understanding with the creation of one of medieval Europe's first municipal statutes. Yet North African cities also had their rebellions and rabble-rousers. In his autobiography, Ibn Khaldun described the Moroccan port city of Ceuta as having its own council of city leaders in the fourteenth century who made most of the decisions. The people of Bèjaïa and Tunis often revolted and changed their allegiance.

Tunis, as we have seen, was the site of religious revivals such as those inspired by the "Man on the Ass" and municipal leaders in 'Annaba and, as mentioned earlier, other port cities in North Africa formed pacts, the 'ahd, with Normans, indicating the same potential for civic independence that was the norm among Italian cities at the time.

Even as he was aware of these urban rebellions and municipal councils, according to Ibn Khaldun cities were not as significant in his broader picture of power and history. The main source of power in much of North Africa came from the surrounding rural tribes. Ibn Khaldun's concentration on rural, tribal power may have had as much to do with his own political position as "minister to the tribes" as it had to do with a complete reflection of North African historical reality. Ibn Khaldun, as we will see in a later chapter, possibly had an interest in portraying North African history in a way that downplayed the very urban dynamics that historians saw as key to the eventual success of Europe.

Almohad Legacies in Mediterranean Art, Architecture and Literature

Like the road that papal and caliphal letters took between Rome and Marrakech, the road between the northern Andalusian culture of Seville and the Southern Berber culture of Marrakech and the Maghrib went both ways. This may seem obvious from the available historical, archaeological and artistic evidence so far presented. Nevertheless, several historians, starting with Ernest Renan in the nineteenth century, called fanaticism "the soul of the Almohad revolution" and depicted the Almohads as the destroyers of Andalusian civilization. Yet the invasion of the Almohad Berbers and the patronage of the great Berber caliphs may have preserved the remnants of learning and cultural vitality in Andalusia.

Nor were books being produced only in Al-Andalus. Starting with Renan, most Western scholars have inevitably focused on the archives of Spain and Europe, especially the Escorial monastery near Madrid, for their sources. Maghribi archives, however, are yielding a rich array of books and manuscripts from the Almohad period written primarily in Maghribi script by Maghribi, probably Berber authors. Many of these authors could have easily been educated at schools for the training of young Berber tribesmen established by 'Abd Al-Mu'min in Marrakech at the famous Menara Gardens, an encampment for indoctrination and also learning, still found outside of the walls of the city today. The Menara Gardens were not just for book learning. An indication of the Mediterranean ambitions of the Almohad Empire remains today in the gardens: a large pool, used for exercises and naval training for the religious-military elite, would have seen group swimming lessons for these newly literate Berbers of the Sea.[68]

Although we do not possess all of the encyclopedic works inspired by the Almohad intellectual effort, there are some examples. The magnificent Shihab Al-Akhbar manuscript from the Royal Library in Rabat is dated 1172, decorated with gold, blue and red medallions, and reveals the intricate style of the Almohad Maghribi scribe.[69] Maghribi script has shown up even in some European libraries. One of the few illustrated manuscripts to survive, the *Hadith Bayad wa Riyad*, was without equal. Found in the Biblioteca Apostolica Vaticana in Rome, the work is written in Maghribi script and is illustrated throughout with images from a story of forbidden love. A merchant, Bayad, falls in love with the handmaiden Riyad, who is under the tyrannical control of Al-Hajib the chamberlain.[70] It is unknown how this manuscript ended up in the Vatican archives; perhaps it was brought back by one of the so-called Bishops of Marrakech. Almost certainly there remain several undiscovered riches from this synthesis of Maghribi and Spanish styles in the Almohad art of the book.

In addition to books and ceramics, Almohad craftsmen were also especially skilled in the art of textiles, bronze and ivory. The Tortosa ivory and wood casket in the treasury of the Cathedral of Tortosa represented the Almohad style at its height. A marquetry menagerie of deer, bulls, peacocks and lotus flowers and the tree of life decorate this splendid box with the writing "my house is the seat of the Caliphate."[71] The Almohad Monzón Lion, presently housed in the Paris Louvre, shows a type of bronze metal sculpture "that appears to have substantially influenced Mediterranean taste."[72]

There was perhaps no better representation of the power of Almohad civilization than its architecture. Three major Almohad religious structures, the Kutubiyya of Marrakech, the Giralda of Seville and the Hassan Mosque of Rabat, remain defining symbols of the cities in which they were built. The Kutubiyya in Marrakech and the Giralda in Seville (later turned into a cathedral bell tower), designed by a Sicilian Almohad architect, show the compelling and enduring unity between the cultures of North Africa, Spain and the wider, Western and Central Mediterranean created during Almohad rule (Figures 2 and 3). Almohad Rabat, where the magnificent Almohad doors at the Qasbah and the massive unfinished tower of the mosque can still be seen today, was called Al-Mahdiyya, perhaps to mimic Al-Mahdiyya, the Fatimid city of the "Mahdi" similarly situated in a strategic coastal position in Tunisia, which the Almohads conquered from the Normans in 1160. In this way, the Almohads linked the Atlantic into the Mediterranean with these two ports of the true Mahdi.[73] Almohads used religious architecture in Marrakech to re-establish the city as a symbol of Almohad ideas, making stone the substance of doctrine. That Almohad legacy survives vividly today throughout North Africa and Muslim Spain in both small towns and major cities.

Much of the main structure of the great Giralda bell tower of the Cathedral of Seville, still the third largest cathedral in the world, was originally Almohad (Figure 3). The Giralda was built to represent a link in a chain of Almohad power that included the imperial cities of Rabat, Seville and Marrakech. At the same time, their vigorous building campaign was not limited to the major cities. An astonishing number of architectural remains of the Almohad past are scattered throughout North Africa and Andalusia, in small towns such as Niebla, showing the deep impact of the Almohad movement beyond the urban scene. Ibn Tumart personally founded several mosques in the smallest villages of Tunisia, Algeria and Morocco on his journey back from the East. Unfortunately, there is still no complete catalogue of what are possibly hundreds of Almohad architectural and archaeological remains throughout the Maghrib. Again, like the art of the book, one is faced with a situation where most research has been completed in European languages and in Spain, leading to an unfortunate ignorance of the Maghribi and North African contributions to Almohad civilization. Compounding the problem, several important place names mentioned in historical sources remain to be reliably located on modern maps.

Almohad architectural taste was not guided solely by the more European sensibilities of Andalusis, as has often been assumed. Again, the line between Andalusi and Berber was not so distinct. As one architectural historian explained, "the pacifying power of the Almohad caliphate fused the outer Maghrib and Al-Andalus into a totally unified artistic sphere."[74] Yet, again, the prejudice seems to be directed against both Andalusis (passive) and North

Africans (intolerant and invasive). Instead, the striking similarities between the Giralda of Seville, later transformed into the Cathedral of Seville, and the massive but incomplete Hassan Mosque in Rabat attested to this fusion of styles, not the inevitable conflict between them.

The Almohad Caliph 'Abd Al-Mu'min called for Andalusi architects to help design the Kutubiyya in Marrakech, yet this did not exclude the highly probable use of North African resident craftsmen. Ibn Tumart had built spare and simple mosques in the Atlas Mountains decades before. It was in the fusion of the fine decorative style of Al-Andalus and the powerful simplicity of Berber style that the Almohad architectural tradition emerged. Whatever the relative influence of Andalusi or Maghribi craftsmen, it would be absurd to think Almohad mosques were simply expressions of Andalusian decorative arts. The architecture was meant to be a massive statement of unity, an embodying of the revolutionary doctrine of *tawhid* (divine unity). Yet, even after the Almohad Empire of worldly, political unity was established and experienced its Golden Age, the question Abu Madyan asked at the beginning of the book "What [really] is divine unity (*tawhid*)?" was still being asked. Instead of resolving the question, it seemed the Almohads only blew open the doors of both rational and spiritual investigation.

Ibn Rushd, the Almohads and the Philosophical Dream of Unity

If the fusion between Andalusi and Maghribi styles produced a revolution in architecture, the fusion of Andalusian philosophy and the doctrine of the Almohads produced a revolution in ideas, a revolution that has had an immeasurable influence on the Western intellectual tradition. Known in English as Averroes and Abubacer, Ibn Rushd and Ibn Tufayl were two of the most famous and prestigious scholars of the Almohad court. Treating him almost as a proto-European, many studies of Averroes, beginning with Renan, have wrongly considered the philosopher completely outside of the context of Almohad civilization. In fact, Ibn Rushd's philosophy, a philosophy that was translated throughout Europe and arguably became the basis of the European scholastic tradition, was as much the product of a vibrant intellectual climate supported by the Almohad Berber caliphs. Beginning with 'Abd Al-Mu'min (d. 1163), the Almohad caliphs patronized a whole host of scholars and intellectuals. A dynamic intellectual arena developed that could have rivaled the House of Wisdom in Baghdad or the court of Hakam II.[75] Like Averroes, many of these scholars, both Jewish and Muslim, became famous in the West. Moshe bin Maymun, known as Maimonides, the most important Jewish philosopher of the entire medieval period, was a part of this intellectual climate, even if he was possibly forced to hide his faith while living under Almohad rule in Fes. In his letter, *On Apostasy*, Maimonides argued that it was better to pretend conversion to Islam than face martyrdom.[76]

The most striking achievement of the Almohad intellectual tradition was in the attempt by Almohad scholars to reconcile faith and reason, religion and philosophy. A true sign of intelligence is the ability to hold two contradicting thoughts in one's mind simultaneously. The Almohad philosophers went even further. Rather than merely accept apparent contradictions they strove to bring unity, *tawhid*, the founding principle of Almohadism, to the rational and the spiritual. Ibn Rushd described this seemingly impossible endeavor in the introduction to his *Decisive Treatise*, the *Fasl al-Maqal*:

> Our goal in this treatise is to examine, using religious speculation, if the study of philosophy (*falsafa*) and the logical sciences is permitted or forbidden by religious law (*shari'ah*) . . . If the work of philosophy is nothing other than speculation over the universe in order that one might know the Creator . . . and since the religious law (*shari'ah*) both invites and incites one to develop knowledge from consideration of the universe, it is thus evident that the study designated by the name of philosophy is, by the religious law both obligatory and meritorious.[77]

Thus, with remarkable confidence, Ibn Rushd proposed to demonstrate the coherence of philosophy, religion and reason.

Instead of seeing Ibn Rushd as a product of his own time and context, the standard story of Ibn Rushd, first told by the famed orientalist Ernest Renan in his classic *Averroés et l'Averroisme* ("Averroes and Averroism"),[78] was that of a besieged philosopher, the end of the road for Islamic philosophy, the last gasp of reason, marginalized and despised by the supposed "fanaticism" of the Berber Almohads. Renan believed that

> Ending more and more its dependence on the essentially skeptical Arab race, and becoming through the accidents of history the propriety of races

susceptible to fanaticism, like the Spanish, the Berbers, the Persian and the Turks, Islamism, in these new hands, followed the allures of an exclusive and austere dogmatism.[79]

Versions of this problematic analysis of Ibn Rushd and his role in Islamic civilization can still be found in standard texts on medieval philosophy. The author of *The Medieval Foundations of the Western Intellectual Tradition* wrote,

> While Averroes was immediately hailed as providing the most accurate introduction to Aristotle in his day by Jewish, Christian, and Muslim philosophers alike . . . in Islam he represented everything that was most to be feared from philosophy. In his own community his doctrinal innovations were rejected as incompatible with Muslim faith.[80]

Yet, in many ways, the philosophy of Ibn Rushd was a reflection of core Almohad principles. Ibn Rushd made numerous references to the 'aqida or Ibn Tumart's profession of faith and philosophy of *tawhid* throughout his works. Ibn Rushd wrote a separate commentary on Ibn Tumart's doctrine.[81] In his commentary on Plato's *Republic*, Ibn Rushd applied Greek philosophy to the structure of the Almohad state. The Almohad and Almoravid states are compared with the ideal *Khilafa*, the rightly guided caliphate of Islam and the ideal *Politeia* of Ancient Greece. Like the reconciliation of philosophy and reason, a type of synthesis was attempted between two different cultural and political systems.[82] As Madeleine Fletcher aptly noted in her recent study of Ibn Tumart's doctrine, "It was through forcing the introduction of new content, which could not possibly fit the dry old conventions of Maliki *naql* and *taqlid* (traditional references), that the Almohads promoted mystical and rational traditions that have survived in some form, in Western Europe, up to the present day."[83]

Far from being shackled by fanaticism, Ibn Rushd seemed relatively free to criticize established social norms, even such sensitive topics as the role of women in society. In his commentary on the *Republic* he criticized Muslim states where women are not given a significant role in society. Thus, perhaps ironically, it would be an Almohad philosopher who would provide one of the most eloquent defenses of the role of women in society, even though it was the Almohads who had so viscerally criticized their desert Almoravid predecessors for the prominence of their women.

In these states . . . the ability of women is not known, because they are only taken for procreation there. They are therefore placed at the service of their husbands and to the business of procreation, for rearing and breast-feeding. But this undoes their other activities. Because women in these states are not being fitted for any of the human virtues it often happens that they resemble plants. That they are a burden on the men in these states is one of the reasons for the poverty of these states.[84]

One would expect such radical thinking to gain some notice among conservative forces in Ibn Rushd's time. On that theme, much has been made of the banishment of Ibn Rushd by the Caliph Al-Mansur.

In fact, Ibn Rushd was temporarily banished to Lucena as part of a plot by rivals on the eve of the Caliph's departure and *jihad* against the Christians. He may have been caught up in the continuous tensions between Arab and Berber factions and the attempt by Almohad caliphs to claim a Sharifian, Arab lineage back to the Prophet. In his *Book of the Animals*, Ibn Rushd "mentioned that he had seen a giraffe at the court of the king of the Berbers."[85] This mistake, whether it was legendary or not, indicated the sensitivity of the Almohad elite towards their non-Arab Berber origins, especially as they entered into the culture of the highly acculturated and Arabized elite of Al-Andalus.

Ibn Rushd's philosophy, while a reflection of the core Almohad principles, gained him many enemies in the jurists and theologians of Andalusia who wished to maintain their status and thwart the reforms that Ibn Rushd proposed. He was soon restored to his post at the side of the Caliph. He died in Marrakech in 1198 in favor with the Almohad court and Almohad civilization as a whole.[86]

Even if Rushd were executed for his philosophy, it would be problematic to follow Renan in condemning the entire Almohad project, indeed, the entire Berber race, as fanatical and dogmatic. If this were so, it would be necessary to condemn the entire civilization of Ancient Greece as fanatical and dogmatic for their decision to execute Socrates with the charge of corrupting the youth of Athens with his philosophy. Almohad civilization, as a whole, although starting from an apocalyptic premise and violent towards minorities, cannot be dismissed as completely peripheral to Ibn Rushd's intellectual achievements. Averroes was soon recognized throughout the West as a great pillar of philosophy, finding a spot in one of Raphael's most famous paintings in the Papal Palace, "The School of the Philosophers," a favorite poster for the walls of many a college student today. Of course, Ibn Rushd would be depicted very differently from the rampaging Saracens of the Battle of Ostia who sacked Rome in 849. In this way, Raphael showed at least two of many contradictory images of the "Saracen" in the European mind.[87]

Just as many scholars have tried to isolate great thinkers such as Ibn Rushd from the Almohad Berber context, Almohad civilization has also often been described as driven by select, almost exclusively northern, Andalusi elite. In the words of the scholar Le Tourneau, "Between the rural masses and the leading elite, there was nothing . . . since the middle class, existing only in some cities, was very small." In Le Tourneau's view, "The Almohad civilization, as we see it, had been built up by a very small elite."[88] Living in a rural region made one automatically susceptible to divisiveness, lack of imagination or intelligence. Almohad civilization was based on Berber tribal structures that were, in fact, quite sophisticated. The Almohad Empire at its height was not merely a civilization of a few, elite, Spanish and hence honorary "European" city dwellers. Ibn Tumart and 'Abd Al-Mu'min and the Almohad elite built the Almohad Empire at least as much on Berber traditions and educated Berber tribesmen as on the work of a few Andalusi scholars and architects. Nor was the line between Andalusi and Berber, town dweller and rural tribesman as distinct as Le Tourneau imagined. The history, art, literature and architecture of the Almohads developed from a cross-pollination of Berber and Arab, Maghribi and Andalusi cultures. The Almohads and their intellectual and artistic legacy constantly influenced the wider Mediterranean as an important stimulus to the Renaissance and Commercial Revolution that was sweeping through the world. Indeed, even as the Almohads lost their grip on empire and began to disintegrate into warring emirates led by various Berber families, their successor dynasty, the Hafsids, lived on in Tunis for many centuries and, far from excluding contact with non-Almohads, grew highly pragmatic and officially embraced trade and, over time, developed a cosmopolitan attitude that contrasted from the original impulse of Almohadism. As the experience of Fibonacci in Almohad and Almoravid (Banu Ghaniya) Bèjaïa indicated, commerce especially necessitated a high level of cosmopolitanism in legal commercial matters.

Late Almohad Trade and Commerce

For the later Almohads, especially the Hafsid successors based in Tunis, Christian Italian merchants were even accorded a special status under Almohad rule that was different even from the *dhimmi* (protected minority) Jews living within North Africa. The Genoese and other Italian cities such as Pisa were allowed significant latitude to pursue commercial interests.[89] The scholar Michele Amari recorded the extensive commercial treaties between Italian city-states and North African Almohads discovered in the Florentine archives.[90] Similar evidence from the Archives of the Crown of Aragon uncovered extensive documentation of the links between Almohads, their Hafsid successors in Tunis, and Barcelona. The following is a translation of a contract from 11–21 August, 1277 (Rabia 2, 676):

> Shams al Din Abu 'Abd Allah, son of the Jeque Abu al Tahir Isma'il, son of Mayhub the Sailor, bought from Petrus Lonkira [Longuera] the Christian [of Pisa?] in a single act and contract, three eights [octavas] of the ship (the ship possessed by the two signers of this contract) that is now in the Port of Tunis. (How Great is God!).[91]

The ship was bought for a total of 1,000 dinars using "current money" and the contract was clear to point out that Shams Al-Din would have no right over the inheritance or full ownership of the ship.

This practice of renting out ships or portions of ships, called the right of *nolis*, was clearly laid out in treaties between Catalonia and the Hafsids, successors of the Almohads, ruled by the Banu Hafs, an elite tribe originally from the Atlas Mountains who were second only to the family of Ibn Tumart and his successor 'Abd Al-Mu'min. In fact this renting out of ships was so common that a law was instituted to restrict the renting of ships to a third of the combined Catalan commercial fleet. In one treaty of 1323, according to Capmany, the great scholar of medieval Aragon, there were no limits to the right of *nolis*.[92] This was despite the fact that the Pope had outlawed commercial relations between Christians and Muslims, especially during periods of crusade. The practice of *nolis* seems to be an example of "ideology" taking a "back seat to expedience and personal interest" in the words of the scholar of medieval Iberia, Brian Catlos.[93] Yet this document does not seem to be an example of *nolis* between Catalan and Hafsid Almohads but between Pisan and Hafsid. A parallel could be found in the medieval *commenda*, common in Italy and similar to the Islamic *qirad* contract, a contract in which many different borrowings occurred from different sources. Yet these may have an even more ancient origin in the Jewish *'iqta* and the Roman *societas*.[94] In this sense, as in many others beyond commerce, Almohad North Africa was integrated into a Western Mediterranean system of religious, cultural and mercantile interaction that was multilayered. Thus, although the original, apocalyptic Almohad doctrine was an ultimate weakness, later Almohads were certainly capable of adapting to the new Commercial Revolution and Renaissance of ideas that the Almohad revolution – or the refocus of power to the Maghrib from the Middle East – originally produced. World historians are only now beginning to recognize that the Almohads represented the first "West" even as Western Europe was also rising commercially and culturally.[95]

The Almohad Influence on Theological Disputation

Debating the nature of God could often be seen as the ultimate hubris. Reason, and even its spiritual cousin, wisdom, have long had a difficult relationship with faith in the Judeo-Christian-Islamic tradition, long before the advent of modern science. A passage from Paul's letter to the Corinthians, an inspiration for mystics and saints such as St. Francis, and an explanation for the eventual abandonment of reason and embrace of mysticism by great scholastic philosophers such as St. Thomas Aquinas, explicitly showed the limits of human thought. Centuries before the great rationalist debates and disputations of the medieval Mediterranean, St. Paul knew that "the greatest debaters among you" or "the debater (philosopher) of this age" would ultimately not be successful in convincing others of Christ's divinity through reason.

> For the message of the cross is foolishness to those who are perishing, but to us who are being saved it is the power of God. For it is written: "I will destroy the wisdom of the wise; the intelligence of the intelligent I will frustrate." Where is the wise man? Where is the scholar? Where is the debater of this age? Has not God made foolish the wisdom of the world? For since in the wisdom of God the world through its wisdom did not know him,

God was pleased through the foolishness of what was preached to save those who believe.

Paul went further to establish the foundations of Christianity's ambiguous relationship with reason, especially from the Greeks,

> Jews demand miraculous signs and Greeks look for wisdom, but we preach Christ crucified: a stumbling block to Jews and foolishness to Gentiles, but to those whom God has called, both Jews and Greeks, Christ the power of God and the wisdom of God. For the foolishness of God is wiser than man's wisdom, and the weakness of God is stronger than man's strength. Brothers, think of what you were when you were called. Not many of you were wise by human standards; not many were influential; not many were of noble birth.

Foolishness and faith seemed better for Paul than a reliance solely on wisdom and reason.

> But God chose the foolish things of the world to shame the wise; God chose the weak things of the world to shame the strong. He chose the lowly things of this world and the despised things – and the things that are not – to nullify the things that are, so that no one may boast before him. It is because of him that you are in Christ Jesus, who has become for us wisdom from God – that is, our righteousness, holiness and redemption. Therefore, as it is written: "Let him who boasts boast in the Lord." (1 Corinthians 1: 18–31)

At the same time, however, Jesus himself seemed to provide a counter-example when he visited the Temple as a boy and argued with men of learning. Yet even as they were "amazed at his understanding," Jesus respectfully listened as well as questioned (Luke 2: 41–52).

Still, a basic theological problem with debates remained. In many respects, dialogues and disputations, both real and constructed, in the medieval Western Mediterranean seemed to contradict the basic message of the sacred literature of Islam, Christianity and Judaism – the message that God was ultimately the all-knowing. The Qur'an is full of reminders of the limits of human wisdom. On spiritual issues of dispute and debate, Sura 2: 269 states,

Say, "O Allah, Creator of heaven and earth, Knower of the unseen, and the witnessed, you will judge between your servants concerning that over which they used to differ."

At the same time, the Qur'an left open the possibility of hidden wisdom, reserved for those "men of understanding." This opened up the possibility of "*batin*" or the hidden nature of the Qur'an, and all existence known to an exclusive group. The Fatimids certainly believed in this exclusive knowledge and Ibn Tumart's access to the secret *Book of Jafr*, predicting the future of the earth, seemed to indicate his connection to esoteric knowledge:

He [Allah] grants wisdom to whom He pleases; and he to whom wisdom is granted indeed receives a benefit overflowing. But none will grasp the Message except men of understanding. (Qur'an, Sura 2: 269)

Also, the Qur'an, Sura 39: 21 stated,

Do you not see that Allah sends down rain from the sky and makes it flow as springs [and rivers] in the earth; he then produces thereby crops of varying colors; then they dry and you see them turned yellow; then He makes them [scattered] debris. Indeed in that is a reminder for those of understanding.

Attempting to use human wisdom to force uniformity was against God's will.

And among His Signs is the creation of the heavens and the earth, and the variations in your languages and your colors; verily in that are Signs for those who know. (Sura 30: 22)

Thus, scripture, although providing for the limitations of wisdom, also embraced forms of knowing that were not fully rational but merely given to the believers. The men of understanding are determined by God who will eventually reveal, at the end of time, which sect among the seventy three sects of Islam predicted by the sayings of Muhammad will be deemed correct. Bacon, the Oxford scholar, in his *Opus Majus*, divided the world into specific numbers of groups of different faiths and their divisions. Likewise, Muhammad Shahrastani (d. 1153) of the prestigious Nizamiyya madrasa in Baghdad sought a "mathematical system" to understand other faiths. He wrote that "the sects following a religion are definite in number, as tradition [the sayings of the Prophet] tells us, the Magians being divided into seventy sects, the Jews into seventy one, the Christians into seventy two and the Muslims into seventy three." Then in one striking sentence, he proclaimed the prevailing belief that "Salvation belongs to only one sect." This was because "It is impossible to hold of two disputants who are wholly in conflict in rational principles, that both are right and in possession of the truth."[96]

In the Western Mediterranean, Ibn Hazm (d. 1064), having abandoned politics after witnessing the disintegration of the great Umayyad caliphate in Muslim Spain, wrote a book "Of Religions and Sects," almost a century before Shahrastani.[97] Ibn Hazm argued a Zahiri, or "literalist," interpretation of the Qur'an was the one correct way of understanding God's revelation. Delving into polemic, and backing his argument with historical sources, he famously claimed that the Christian Gospels were corrupted and that God only gave Christians one, not four books. To come to the truth, Ibn Hazm encouraged his readers to examine the nature of their spiritual beliefs by reading his logical handbook, *An Approach to Logical Definitions*.[98] Even though God may be able to reveal through his logic the truth of Zahiri Islam, Ibn Hazm also saw its limits and he has been described as "an extreme example of the tendency hostile to human reasoning."[99] Nonetheless, reasoning based on God's established truths could be employed to, as the Qur'an (16: 126) states, "call men to the path of your Lord with wisdom and kindly exhortation. Reason with them in the most courteous manner." Even so, "Your Lord knows best those who stray from His path and those who are rightly guided."[100]

It was clear that God, not humanity, was often in the position of determining ultimate truth in the scriptural traditions of Islam, Judaism and Christianity. In the Kabbalah, a mystical interpretation of the Torah, reason was similarly reduced to a role secondary to revelation. There was certainly a role for the wise and "men of understanding" but this seemed to be reserved for judges and wise leaders of the community, not debates over the ultimate meaning and nature of God.

Nonetheless, warnings about the limitations on reason contained in the scripture of all three traditions did not limit the vibrant era of debate or disputation. The rise of the Almohads seemed to spark an era of debate both within Islam and by Christians and Jews. The Almohads, who were influenced by Zahiri belief in returning to the original sources of the Qur'an and the Sayings of the Prophet, also explicitly believed that reasoning was necessary to prevent seeing God as having a body. The Almohads were also probably following what the scholar Maribel Fierro indentified as a newly "reformed" Maliki school of orthodox, Sunni Islam.[101] The Almohad creed of Ibn Tumart commanded figurative interpretation of scripture to prevent literal notions of an embodied God "sitting" on his throne as described in the Qur'an 2: 255. God could not be limited by shape or form and these verses must be read symbolically. Instead of being an actual seat, the throne represented God's power over all creation. "His seat [Kursi] extends over the heavens and earth, and their preservation tires him not. . ." In addition to the accusation that they were effeminate, Ibn Tumart explicitly accused the Almoravids of taking the Qur'an too literally, of giving God bodily form. He called them anthropomorphists due to their mistake of not using proper reason and interpretation.

Under 'Abd Al-Mu'min, the first successor of Ibn Tumart, and the later great Almohad caliphs of the twelfth century, Abu Ya'qub and Ya'qub Al-Mansur, there was a conscious effort to determine a theologically correct interpretation of the Qur'an and Hadith. Rather than relegating matters of faith to narrow legal interpretation, as was the case of the Almoravids, these caliphs, seeking a renewal of knowledge that might crack the mystery of God's true nature, not only sponsored the works of great scholars such as Ibn Rushd, they also encouraged the writing of treatises on mathematics, the sciences, and knowledge on a large range of themes. They also encouraged the writing of manuals to educate children in proper doctrine and belief as well as the new knowledge they had encouraged.[102] The *talaba*, literally "the students," were a special class of Almohads drawn from Berber and Arab tribes who were versed in debate amongst themselves and even with the Caliph himself. This activity was not reserved for the fluent, Arab urban elite. Instead, new blood and new perspectives came into Western Mediterranean Islam as these *talaba*, or indoctrinated students from the mountains, but now trained bureaucrats, engaged in intellectual exchange across the Empire. Many creeds and didactic works were originally written in Berber as were "Berber formulas for the call to prayer."[103]

The Almohad doctrine, the *'aqida*, came to influence Christian writers directly. It was translated into Latin by Marc of Toledo (d. 1239). Marc was a physician and canon of the Toledo cathedral. He had also translated the Qur'an, which led to important theological debates between Christians and Muslims. As part of Archbishop Raimundo of Toledo's famed School of Translators, Marc of Toledo's translations of these essential religious works inspired dialogues between the Mozarab (Arabized Christians), Christian Latins and Mudejars (Muslims under Christian rule).[104] King Alfonso VI had recently taken Toledo in 1085. During this period, many converts from Islam to Christianity who knew Arabic were determined to show their adherence to their new religion. For instance, there was a tract called *Liber denudationis*, a translation of an Arabic original that justified the writer's conversion from Islam.[105] Similarly, Petrus Alfonsi, a Jewish physician and philosopher who converted to Christianity in 1106, wrote a dialogue between his Christian self and "Moses" his former, Jewish self.[106] Yet he also brought up the question of Islam and why he chose Christianity instead of "the faith of the Saracens, with whom you were always associated and raised."[107] He showed a fairly accurate knowledge of Islam. Like Ibn Rushd, Maimonides and others before him, Petrus Alfonsi used logic and reasoning, based on Aristotle or Pseudo-Aristotle, to defend the Christian Trinity of God.

An anti-Christian text written by a Muslim from Cordoba, Al-Imam Al-Qurtubi, was written against a converso, a Muslim who had converted to Christianity. This man sent Al-Qurtubi his own tract called *Tatlit al-Wahdaniya*, from the Arabic word for three (*tatlit* or *tathlith*) that defended the triple nature of God. Interestingly, scholars have suggested that both the text of the converso and Al-Qurtubi's response were "especially reminiscent of works written by Ibn Tumart . . ."[108] Responding to the Almohad doctrine of "absolute oneness" or *tawhid*, the Muslim convert to Christianity seemed to write the work to negate the appeal of Ibn Tumart's message. He sent the tract to Cordoba to convince Muslims there to give up Islam and embrace the rising tide of Christianity on the Peninsula. But the Almohad legacy went beyond theology and disputation. It's alive today.

Abdu among the Almohads: A Post-Almohad Man?

In *Abdu 3inda al Mouahidin*,[109] "Abdu among the Almohads," a 2006 film by Said Naciri, the Moroccan comic, the continued relevance of the Almohads to Moroccans was used to critique the current social and political order in

North Africa. In the film, Abdu, a man reduced to harassing wealthy Western tourists, who flees the corrupt police on a motorcycle, was sent by a time warp to the medieval past, to the time of the Almohads. Although from the modern world, he is continually astounded by the progressiveness and knowledge of these Almohads under Caliph Ya'qub Al-Mansur. Abdu's experience and the fact that the Almohads are still a central part of the popular culture of the region, shows the continued role of the Almohads as a Golden Age, even for dual national Maghribis such as Said Naciri. Even though the Almohad Empire fell after some 130 years, it left a memory and legacy of a unified government across a vast and geographically varied territory of peoples and tribes, and languages, built on a synthesis of Berber, Arab, Jewish, Christian and Andalusi culture. This legacy continues to this day. Malek Bennabi (d. 1973), the famed Algerian philosopher of history, spoke of the dream of Almohad unity and the rise of the "Post-Almohad man" that caused intellectual bankruptcy and the undermining of ideas in the Islamic West. Indeed the dual imagined nature of Almohads, as either a shining example of cosmopolitan intellectual revival or as a return to the purity of Islam, now inspires both modern secularists and Islamists alike.[110]

While Bennabi's search for a divergence between the Maghrib and the Latin West was meant as a tool for national revival, it was when the Almohad Empire began to interact with the Latin West that the Almohad Empire, and arguably Maghribi cultural greatness, was at its height. It was in that period after the death of Ibn Tumart, and to a lesser extent, during the Hafsid era, when the Almohads embraced the complex contradictions of unity and diversity, art and austerity, faith and reason that the Almohad impact on Mediterranean culture, intellectual history and even commerce was most evident. Although beginning and maintained by a vision of absolute monotheism that did not allow even vague representations of the divine, it was in the flowering of a diversity of cultural interactions between the Maghrib, Andalusia and the twelfth-century Mediterranean that the Almohad Empire left a lasting influence. Beyond being a major source of political and economic unity over a rich part of the Mediterranean, the mountainous spine of the Maghrib, the initial success and spectacular dismantling of the Almohad Empire did not mean the end of their impact. The possibility of Maghribi unity represented by the Almohad Empire would continue to inspire successor dynasties for centuries. North Africa had arrived as a place where Islam was not only folded into a Berber cultural context but actually renewed and reborn. Almohad doctrine, a doctrine based on the unity of God and a rationalist interpretation of scripture, spurred debate and opened spiritual avenues among intellectuals in Europe and North Africa alike. For long after their political disintegration, the Almohads sparked a new era focused on the interplay of reason in faith in the Western Mediterranean.

The Almohad Empire undoubtedly inspired a great deal of disputation and debate between converts and theologians of all three faiths. Its revolutionary focus on *tawhid* and new, rationalist notions of the nature of God led to a flourishing of intellectual dispute. Beyond their doctrine, the Almohads also had an impact on North African understandings of the meaning of history and the relationship between history and religious inspiration. This relationship was discussed in the histories of one of the greatest writers of the Islamic world: Ibn Khaldun.

6

BETWEEN CITY AND COUNTRYSIDE: IBN KHALDUN AND THE FOURTEENTH CENTURY

In 1291, a Genoese adventurer named Benedetto Zaccaria, then working for King Sancho IV of Castile, defied all odds and defeated the much larger, but unwieldy fleet of the Berber Marinids, the Almohad successor dynasty in Morocco.[1] Zaccaria would help create an Aragonese and Castilian fleet ready for centuries of naval war and set Christian Spain on a path to dominate waters that were once patrolled by North Africans. This was perhaps as important as the defeat on land of the Almohads by a combined Christian force at the land battle of Las Navas de Tolosa in 1212. The fall of the Almohad and post-Almohad North African fortunes reflected a crisis in late thirteenth- and fourteenth-century North Africa. Of course, much of Europe was also entering a calamitous century. Full of outbreaks of plague, the Hundred Years War, and major fiscal challenges associated with a bubble in trade, the Commercial Revolution and capitalist expansion of the previous centuries seemed to implode.

The situation was increasingly dire for North African shipping in general. After the fall of the Almohads, according to Ibn Khaldun, "Maritime habits were forgotten . . . The Muslims came to be strangers to the Mediterranean."[2] By this time Muslim shipping was, compared to the glories of the Almohad past: in tatters. Although the office of the admiralty still existed in Hafsid Tunis in the Zayyanid court and in the Marinid realm, Maghribi shipping activity was largely reduced. The army of the Marinids seemed demoralized by the disastrous battle of Rio Salado in 1340, one of the final major attempts by Marinids to control Iberia. Ibn Khaldun always encouraged continued advances against Christian Iberia; he did not lose all hope. Foreshadowing the rise of the Ottomans, he predicted the rise of a great, new Muslim naval power, a power that would conquer all the lands of the European Christians beyond the sea according to the "books of predictions."

Yet the polymath, minister and historian Ibn Khaldun (d. 1406) did not give up hope of a more immediate change in affairs. As an ambassador between urban rulers and the tribes of the countryside, Ibn Khaldun realized that new dynasties could arise, take power and set the stage for a new era. He wrote a great history of the Berbers to illustrate his point, perhaps to give hope that a new unifying dynasty would emerge in the midst of the disintegration of North Africa and the misfortunes of the Almohad successor dynasties. Only late in his life did he seem to realize it might be tribes from Central Asia, not the Berbers, who would fulfill this vision of a renewed era of unity for Islam.

It would be extreme to say that by Ibn Khaldun's fourteenth century the Muslim east–west axis of Mediterranean trade had disappeared completely. However, a north–south, European axis was becoming more prevalent as the Northern European market became an increasingly important trading partner for Iberian merchants. According to some scholars, this north–south axis eventually enticed European merchants into the Atlantic world and began the age of discovery. It would be a mistake, however, to assume that no Muslims or North Africans were engaged in the north–south scheme, that the rise of European hegemony in trade was a result only of European initiative and Jewish middlemen. Despite the disillusion of the Almohads and a consequent decline in the North African admiralties, Muslim trade, commerce, and travel, as Ibn Khaldun's work richly attested, was still bustling in the fourteenth-century Western Mediterranean.

Ibn Khaldun was well aware of some of the new, scientific and philosophical accomplishments of Europe saying,

> We further hear now that the philosophical sciences are greatly cultivated in the land of Rome and along the adjacent northern shore of the country of the European Christians. They are said to be studied there again and to be taught in numerous classes. Existing systematic expositions of them are

said to be comprehensive, the people who know them numerous and the students of them very many.[3]

Although Ibn Khaldun recognized this rising potential of Europe, it did not mean the complete end of North Africa. His contemporaries, Ibn Al-Khatib and Ibn Zamrak, continued to write great works and different courts and dynasties competed for the services of intellectuals and scholars. Cultural unity and memory of past Almohad or Almoravid unity remained, especially amongst the elite. Still, a lack of political unity and the impact of external factors such as plague caused problems for the region. Having split into three evenly divided, but never very effective, dynasties, North Africa was, as with Europe, impacted by plague and the decline in trade. In Tunis in the 1340s, Ibn Khaldun lost nearly his whole family to sickness. Al-Andalus, Muslim Spain, the beautiful land of his ancestors, was shrinking and the rulers of magnificent Granada, that last outpost of Islam in Iberia, were virtual vassals of Christian kings. North Africa was divided between factions and Berber tribal dynasties, mainly the Marinids in the west, Zayyanids in the center and the Hafsids in Ifriqiya. Many of the dynasties were attempting, but failing, to achieve sufficient long-term legitimacy to revive the unity of the Almohad past. Trying to explain the horrible events of his century, this man, Ibn Khaldun, no longer accepted the assumption that all of history was a reflection of God's will.

The plague was a breaking point in Ibn Khaldun's worldview. So many died, it was as if the whole world had changed. Instead, history must be studied in a rational and meaningful way, distinguishing, as did Aristotle, the merely accidental from the patterns and meanings of events. Much as calamity in Europe influenced the intellectual climate there, the calamities in North Africa would lead Ibn Khaldun to write one of the most stunning and famous histories of the world. Yet Ibn Khaldun was, perhaps, overly pessimistic on many points. Ibn Khaldun's contribution as a major, primary source for the history, not only of North Africa, but also of the world, his concentration on the importance of tribal solidarity, may have skewed perceptions of North Africa as a region with history but without the possibility of long-term civilization due to geographical limitations.[4]

Studies of the post-Almohad crisis of legitimacy in the medieval Maghrib have considered political, religious, social, and economic power, but rarely have they examined the political motivations of those such as Ibn Khaldun who wrote the sources of the era. Although archaeology has made some promising advances, the basis for our understanding of these factors comes primarily from historical sources written by a particular class of scholar. Historians who were also ministers and advisors with their own specific and highly political interests wrote most primary sources of the medieval Maghrib. These writers were far from passive referees on the sidelines of history – they were very much in the field. Their portrayal of what was legitimate or even of what was history often had to do with their own political interests as learned ministers. Ibn Khaldun's autobiography revealed reasons for his possibly over-emphasizing the power of tribes. By studying Ibn Khaldun and his intellectual network, a type of "community of letters" of ministers and writers in the medieval fourteenth-century Western Mediterranean, we can contextualize some of the key problems of North African history. Finally, Ibn Khaldun's personal struggles between political power, worldly fame and a desire for spiritual transformation and withdrawal occurred at the apex of a Mediterranean characterized by such struggles among intellectuals of very different religious persuasions. Unlike Ibn 'Arabi, who stressed maintaining distance from the power and temptations of the Sultan, Ibn Khaldun gave into them, seeking not only to understand human interactions, but to redirect them.

Finding Legitimacy

Philosophers, at least since Plato and Aristotle, have long struggled to answer why humans form tribes, groups, societies and civilizations. While the tribe or the family seems a natural unit, the status of the city is problematic – is it natural and stable or was urbanism a forced condition bound to break apart over time? Are we "political animals," capable of being organized into city states for ends outside of blood-relations, or are we ultimately familial animals, driven primarily by a deep genealogical loyalty or affiliation? Is humanity's most natural, and therefore also most potentially holy (holy is used here in the broadest terms possible), state in the city or in the countryside? Ibn Tufayl placed Ibn Yaqzan, the Robinson Crusoe and noble, believing man of the twelfth century, in an isolated wilderness. For Ibn Khaldun, the natural state was not nearly as lonely, but it certainly was not in the city. For the polymath, historian and political operative, a government with this indispensible ingredient he called 'asabiyya or "social solidarity" was a dynasty with most of the necessary ingredients of legitimacy. 'Asabiyya, especially the 'asabiyya of hardy tribes from the countryside, seemed to function not only as a political force but also as an expression of God's favor. Ibn Khaldun stated, "religious propaganda cannot materialize without group feeling."[5] For such an important concept, however, Ibn Khaldun was somewhat vague about precisely what 'asabiyya really was. Translations of 'asabiyya – Franz Rosenthal's more narrow "group feeling," Y. Lacoste's global *esprit de corps* – reveal the imprecise nature of answers to this basic question. Ibn Khaldun may have preferred to keep the exact meaning imprecise. Aristotle simply declared that humans were social animals. In much the same way, Ibn Khaldun's own somewhat abstract and vaguely dissatisfying answer to the foundations of human society and government was a vague term, 'asabiyya. That said, even as he avoided a direct definition, there were clues in his writings that point to what he meant by 'asabiyya and what the relationship was between 'asabiyya and legitimacy most of the time.

For Ibn Khaldun, 'asabiyya usually, but not always, consisted of those abstract "natural" bonds, real or perceived, that form societies united by ties of blood. 'Asabiyya was usually strongest in the countryside among tribes far from urban luxury. He linked 'asabiyya to legitimacy and stated that those dynasties lacking in 'asabiyya would lose power and legitimacy over time. An exception to this was dynasties inspired by true religious prophecy. But, as stated above, religious prophecy, or at least the "legitimate form," must have a politically and socially effective following: it must obtain the support of 'asabiyya.

Ibn Khaldun's concept of a natural, social instinct differs from the classical philosophers in many important respects. Unlike Aristotle, whose concept of "social animal" was expressed ultimately in terms of the ideal city, the legendary Atlantis, the gleaming *polis*, Ibn Khaldun largely saw the true source of society's mysterious bonds as originating in and existing most effectively in idealized societies living far from urban influence, in the real and imagined ties of blood that formed the *qabila* or tribe. Natural 'asabiyya, originating from tribal bonds of blood, for Ibn Khaldun, was a necessary condition for political legitimacy. 'Asabiyya was a condition, legitimacy was the result, the *khabar*.[6] In this sense, Ibn Khaldun applied rationalist theory to the "natural" origins of human society, making the tribe the prime mover of humanity.

'Asabiyya, tribal solidarity, as a concept and a theory of political and social organization in the medieval Mediterranean remains a compelling reference for scholars. It allowed giants of modern North African anthropology, from Ernest Gellner to Jacques Berque, to develop sweeping theoretical and methodological backdrops, not only for studies of North Africa but for studies of what Gellner called "Muslim society."

However, recent research has chipped away at the automatic deference to Ibn Khaldun's conclusions. His work may have distorted some of the dynamics of North African medieval society in a way that benefited his career as a negotiator between rural tribes and urban dynasts. Several scholars, from Michael Brett, Ron Messier and others, questioned the supremacy of Ibn Khaldun's theory of tribal *'asabiyya* as the only and essential cornerstone of dynastic legitimacy in the fourteenth century.[7] There is also new anthropological and archaeological evidence questioning Ibn Khaldun's assumption that urban communities in North Africa were always weak and somehow continually at risk of overthrow by the Arab and Berber tribes of the countryside. The works of Yvon Thébert and Jean Louis Biget as well as studies by Boone and Benco have shown evidence of extensive urban communities in North Africa up until the plague.[8] Even as his version is contested by some archaeological evidence, however, the notion of ideal Arab and Berber rural groups as kingmakers, expressed in Ibn Khaldun's theory of the role of *'asabiyya*, has retained much of its primacy. The concept continues to be the best known, the standard that even critical scholars must first address and argue against.

Ibn Khaldun's theory remained a salient subject of debate, his own motivations, often political in nature, for tying legitimacy to *'asabiyya*, specifically, forms of *'asabiyya* based on lineage, were largely unexplored. The personal and political in Ibn Khaldun's life were crowded out by the compelling elegance and seeming originality of his argument. Many modern scholars saw in Ibn Khaldun a thinker to relate to, an intellectual, not simply a chronicler. For some scholars in the Arabic-speaking world he is also held out as something of a proto-nationalist, intellectual hero, lionized by modern states and identity politics. As such, his theories and interpretations often pass through without a great deal of critical scrutiny of his own, often bald, political motivations. The factors that influenced his particular view of human nature have been given less attention even as they likely influenced his theory of and its role in the rise and fall of dynasties in the medieval Islamic West. Rather than seeing Ibn Khaldun as simply a source of fourteenth-century Maghribi history, he can also be seen as an active shaper of events he describes with distinct motivations for describing human society and history as based in tribal *'asabiyya*. He was an individual who, for much of his life, embodied the contradictions of his era and the complexities of the fourteenth-century, Western Mediterranean.

Ibn Khaldun repeatedly expressed his regret for engaging in the political realm and seemed disappointed at his inability to simply withdraw from the world. He was a man who could not help from plunging into political quagmire. Even at his ultimate retreat at the remote watchtower of Ibn Salama where he wrote the first draft of the *Muqaddimah*, Ibn Khaldun could not get away from the politics that filled his pages. Constantly sidelined and buffeted by the whims and political turbulence of the fourteenth-century Islamic West, Ibn Khaldun became profoundly skeptical and critical not only of the politics of the time but of his own choices in life. This skepticism had an impact on his observations about how social and political legitimacy worked. For Ibn Khaldun legitimacy was almost an unapproachable ideal. Examples of idealized simplicity, sincere honor and generosity such as those displayed by his father were encountered in Ibn Khaldun's autobiography as examples of legitimate, idealized leadership. His own decisions, in contrast, were often viewed with a sort of regret and *anomie*. Ibn Khaldun not only elevated certain individuals such as his father; entire peoples or ways of life were idealized above others. He portrayed the Arab and Berber chiefs and tribes as legitimated, romanticized examples of an ideal form of leadership lost by later dynasties of his own time. Ibn Khaldun's disappointment with the political realities he encountered in Al-Andalus and the Maghrib was not wasted. His difficult experiences in the Maghrib and Al-Andalus, even more than his later and much-studied life in Egypt, shaped his theory of history and society. In most studies of Ibn Khaldun's thought, his ideas are considered out of context, in the abstract or in theoretical terms, often as a baseline for explaining modern phenomena. Yet Ibn Khaldun's ideas were political tools, not simply intellectual abstractions.

Ibn Khaldun as Political Actor

Ibn Khaldun's influence as a political actor in the fourteenth century was important. Far from sitting on the scholarly sidelines, Ibn Khaldun repeatedly attempted to personally implement his plans to restore legitimate rule to the Maghrib and, less so, to Al-Andalus. Ibn Khaldun was inspired to do this not only out of a sense of idealism but also for very realist reasons, for his own political aspirations. By focusing on *'asabiyya*, particularly the *'asabiyya* of the Arab Bedouin tribes and rural Berbers and by attempting to maintain excellent relations with them, Ibn Khaldun communicated the necessity of his role as an intermediary between sultan and countryside, as a vector through which the legitimacy, honor and *'asabiyya* he so praised can be assured. One of many incidents from the beginning of Ibn Khaldun's career served as an example.

It was 1358 and the powerful, if much maligned, Marinid Sultan Abu 'Inan had died, strangled. The death of Abu 'Inan was a relief to Ibn Khaldun, who sat languishing in prison for conspiring against him. Ibn Khaldun's friend, the minister Al-Hasan Ibn 'Amar, was now the regent. Ibn Khaldun was given robes of honor and set free to continue his work as an intermediary between the city of Fes and the remote oases, the man who was tasked with maintaining communication between the government and the Banu Marin tribes.

It was years before he began writing the *Muqaddima*. Nevertheless, Ibn Khaldun, the political actor, not the scholar, was already implementing some of the key ideas he would later expound in his writings. Seeing an opportunity in the unstable conditions left by the death of Abu 'Inan, Ibn Khaldun rode out of Fes and headed straight to the Banu Marin. There he organized the tribes for a coup against his friend Al-Hasan and the child prince Abu Zian Al-Sa'id. Despite the legitimacy of Al-Sa'id and his regent's claims to power, without the support of the Banu Marin tribes, their claims could be easily disputed. Ibn Khaldun had effectively helped usurp power with the assistance of his co-conspirator Ibn Marzuq and the Banu Marin whom he visited in the countryside. While all of this conspiracy was taking place, a rival sultan, Abu Salim, was waiting. The Castilian King Pedro, the Christian monarch whom Ibn Khaldun would famously meet as an ambassador, supported Abu Salim. With the Banu Marin withdrawing their loyalty, Abu Salim crossed the Strait of Gibraltar to claim the Marinid capital as his own. It was Abu Salim who had called on Ibn Khaldun to aid him in his overthrow of the child-prince. Instead of refusing out of some sense of loyalty to Al-Hasan, Ibn Khaldun readily agreed. Ibn Khaldun was well placed for this betrayal as one of his duties was as secretary to the minister in charge of the Marinid chiefs and Marinid tribes.[9] Ultimately, he saw legitimacy not in the ruler and his court in Fes but in the Banu Marin. Their *'asabiyya* was shifted to another ruler by Ibn Khaldun's persuasions. It was little wonder that Ibn Khaldun described the *'asabiyya* of founding tribes as the essential ingredient for rule. Ibn Khaldun's theory of *'asabiyya* was not simply an academic or intellectual matter; it was an essential ingredient in his arsenal as an active, political agent.

Using his special access to the Marinid chiefs, Ibn Khaldun went out and rallied the chiefs of the Marinids against the child-prince and in favor of Abu Salim. In his own words, "I took the affair into my own hands, went out on my own accord, and met with the great chiefs of the Banu Marin confederation. I pushed them to favor the side of Abu Salim."[10] One could imagine Ibn Khaldun leaving the city walls in the dead of night, riding hundreds of miles to meet with the Marinid chiefs. With his knowledge of Berber society and vast interest in Berber and Arab history, Ibn Khaldun was able to maintain good relations with the Marinid chiefs, a position that provided him with a great deal of power: a position as negotiator between rural tribes and urban rulers, be they Arab or Berber, that he would exploit throughout his career in the Maghrib. This was not the only time Ibn Khaldun capitalized on his position as an intermediary between urban and rural, sultan and tribe. Ibn Khaldun, like other minister-historians of the medieval Maghrib, was certainly not an impartial observer. In fact, the role of minister-historians in shaping the "legitimacy" of their masters should be carefully considered when making conclusions about the true strength of tribal raids and their relationship to the rise and fall of dynasties. As his autobiography has slowly received more attention, scholars have started to recognize the importance of Ibn Khaldun's political contexts. As scholars of the Hafsids (another dynasty where Ibn Khaldun tested his own political theories) have noticed, "Ibn Khaldun's concerns were firmly grounded in the politics of his time. His ideas were steeped in the intellectual traditions that formed the basis of political strategy . . ."[11]

He used his connections as a negotiator between dynasties and tribes of their origin to advance his position in court, even when he was not necessarily plotting the Sultan's overthrow. During his tenure as minister to the powerful Hafsid Sultan Abu Al-'Abbas, Ibn Khaldun wrote several panegyric poems found in the autobiography and dedicated to the Hafsid ruler. There is a distinct sense, both in these poems and in the *Muqaddima* dedicated to the same sultan, that Ibn Khaldun was using his writing not only to illuminate and inform but also to subtly advertise his political weight. Even as he deftly praised the power of the Sultan, he suggested that power would best be vested in those ministers who know best how to negotiate that power.

In a long passage that subtly reinforced his own position and his own theory of the importance of tribal solidarity, he evoked those powerful tribes who gave Abu Al-ʿAbbas obedience and loyalty. These tribes were the specific sources of group feeling, of *ʿasabiyya* available to the Caliph: "The Salwa available with their great force . . . the Dhuwayb and the Maʿqil who organize attacks."[12] He described those important tribes and allies who followed the Caliph's commands. Ibn Khaldun demonstrated, in poetic form, the power and importance of tribal support, the type of tribal support he could confer not only as an expert but also as an emissary to the Dawawida,

> Amazing men, always in motion . . .
> Demigods, they have nothing but the desert mirage for drinking,
> And for their subsistence, a lance that they manipulate skillfully . . .
> They inspire fear in rulers because of their nomadism . . .
> But you have given them your favors,
> Thus they have given in to your power.[13]

In these last two lines, a reciprocal relationship, a give and take, not a relationship of absolute authority, was admitted. Thus, even in a panegyric poem allegedly written to enforce the power of the Caliph, Abu Al-ʿAbbas was portrayed as submitting to deals with the tribes, deals that were often conveniently brokered by Ibn Khaldun. Indeed, it could be argued that the *Muqaddima*, a text originally dedicated to Abu Al-ʿAbbas, is a subtle and well-crafted augur, a warning about the power of *ʿasabiyya* and the power of Ibn Khaldun's influence as a man who could secure the support and *ʿasabiyya* of rural tribes, be they the Banu Marin in Fes or the Dawawida Arabs in Tunis.

That is not to say that Ibn Khaldun was purely political and devoid of a sense of moral purpose. The failure of political legitimacy Ibn Khaldun saw around him during his life and travels created a basic ethical obsession: a theory of political legitimacy in the *Muqaddima* that was, at root, ultimately tied to his notion of honor, an honor that was a divine characteristic of "natural" human society. Although honor without power and legitimacy was commonplace, legitimacy without honor was ultimately doomed to failure. Honor, for Ibn Khaldun, was a necessary ingredient for dynastic success. In rare instances rulers or governors such as the Sharif of Ceuta possessed this honor. But it was also an honor possessed by the Arab and Berber tribes whose *'asabiyya*, or solidarity, was what brought dynasties and empires into existence. Ideally, this *'asabiyya* was a reflection of that same *'asabiyya* that God empowered the Arabs with during the rise of Islam itself.

The Turmoil of his Age

Thus, Ibn Khaldun's profound disappointment and personal turmoil, a turmoil expressed so often in the autobiography, reflects and mirrors the turmoil of his age. Ibn Khaldun's disillusionment was expressed repeatedly. Ibn Khaldun's younger brother Yahya, an aspiring historian of the Wattasid dynasty, lovingly following the example of his older brother, was imprisoned and killed on a political assignment that Ibn Khaldun had suggested for him. Hearing of the news, Ibn Khaldun "renounced the mirage of title and rank. . ."[14] There were many examples of profound psychological crises and guilt in his work. Shortly after hearing about the death of his wife and children in a storm, he says, "The thought of renouncing the world came back to my spirit anew."[15] He resolved to resign from his post. At first the Sultan refused. Yet Ibn Khaldun was saved by the grace of God. Having pity for his situation and seeing how depressed he had become, he released Ibn Khaldun from "his chains."[16]

Ibn Khaldun wrote how his sadness made him unable to function; unable to express the sorrow he had for the loss of his family. He spent three years dedicated to teaching, reading, and writing "with the hope that God would allow me to spend the rest of my life in his devotion and to vanquish the obstacles in the way of happiness."[17] He also spoke of his father's decision to pursue the simple life of a devoted Sufi, abandoning the ways of the world and politics. He may have also thought of the simple life chosen by his older brother Muhammad, who remained behind in Tunis. In these many instances of regret Ibn Khaldun's autobiography reads as much as a warning to those who were like him as a young man, tempted by the trappings of power and wealth.

In much the same way, Al-Ghazali wrote his life story as a model and manifestation of his ideas, and Sufi masters used their lives and actions as examples to follow. Ibn Khaldun's autobiography was a mirror of the ideals and patterns he details in the *Muqaddima*.[18] Scholars have seen the auto-biography of Ibn Khaldun as an appendage, a mere add-on to his magnificent *Muqaddimah*. But the inverse was also possible. History was, in some respects, in the service of autobiography. Far from being an impersonal and "scientific" study of human history, the *Muqaddima*, in this reading, was an account of the way Ibn Khaldun thought his world should work, an expression of what political legitimacy should mean; a work of idealism in the midst of a life of skepticism, self-criticism and disappointment. In the opening pages of the *Muqaddima*, Ibn Khaldun boldly claims to reveal the "secret meaning" of history. The search for this secret meaning was as much an obsession derived not simply out of curiosity but out of a need for self-justification. As well as an extraordinary work of history and social philosophy, the *Muqaddima* is Ibn Khaldun explaining himself to himself. One can presume that the other historian-ministers of the medieval Maghrib, from Ibn Marzuq to Ibn Al-Khatib to Ibn Khaldun's brother Yahya, also wrote history to reflect certain ideals and political ambitions – even if those ambitions were not quite as clearly stated.

It was argued, most strikingly by the famed translator and scholar Franz Rosenthal, that such a deep reading of the autobiography is not really possible. Ibn Khaldun seemed to be using the text to settle old scores, to put himself in a good light. A long list of ancestors is punctuated with sparing accounts of their accomplishments and duties. That was followed by yet another long list of his teachers and mentors. Ibn Khaldun then proceeds to describe his somewhat pained, dour, and directionless journeys from court to court in the Islamic West and, finally, Egypt. At least initially, when compared to the depth of intellectual reflection and deep analysis evident in his wildly famous *Muqaddima*, Ibn Khaldun's autobiography, *The Life of Ibn Khaldun and his Travels West and East*, may seem, at first reading, less than enlightening.[19] It might be easy to agree with the negative assessment of Franz Rosenthal, the Arabist who translated the *Muqaddimah* in loving detail but left out the autobiography from his efforts. The autobiography, for Rosenthal, lacked what he termed psychological depth.[20] Rosenthal decided that the *Ta'rif* was not worthy of the same attention as the rest of Ibn Khaldun's work.

Recent scholarship, however, has shown that medieval Muslim autobiography should not be so easily dismissed. It was not simply a rote exercise. It was part of a complex and sophisticated Marinid culture and society. In the words of one scholar, "It was a heterogeneous and individualistic society, with a deeply mystical religious streak to it . . . The great number of autobiographies written by contemporaries . . . attest to a greater sense of the self."[21] Ibn Khaldun's autobiography was certainly an example of this deeper, and in some sense, more fraught and individual sense of self amongst the intellectual elite.

Ibn Khaldun's autobiography, when read carefully and in combination with his other works, revealed not only profound psychological complexity but provokes many questions about the nature and portrayal of political legitimacy in the Maghrib in the sources. Although they provide no single, definitive answer, Ibn Khaldun's writings provoke several questions. The very act of determining the meaning of legitimacy was itself political and dependent on the sources we use to analyze the question.

However, Ibn Khaldun was not a pure Machiavellian (and neither was Machiavelli).[22] He was also concerned with legitimacy not simply to understand the world around him but to legitimate himself. After all, the self as an object of legitimation, especially within the Sufi tradition that Ibn Khaldun knew and experienced so well, was an obsession. As the scholar Marshall Hodgson famously suggested, the late medieval period in the Islamic world was a time of individualism and relative freedom. While the guilds and class hierarchies of the Occident militated against social mobility and freedom of movement, in Islamic lands

> there remained wide personal liberty for a man to make his own choice within a reasonably predictable framework and in a range that was relatively broad . . . Such freedom was essential for a further sort of freedom of action – freedom of historical action, freedom to initiate new ideas and teach them . . .[23]

The individualism of thirteenth- to fourteenth-century Maghrib was an individualism of a sort very different from the individualism of contemporary

Britain or America or Enlightenment France. Most importantly, it was an individualism that was defined largely by a spiritual struggle, a struggle embodied by the great masters of Sufism in the Maghrib and Al-Andalus – the symbols of a new religiosity. This awakening seems to be part of a wider trend of individuals standing up to corrupt political power. In the Maghrib, Vincent Cornell has shown how those who arbitrated over this spiritual journey of individual Muslims held not simply the typical political powers but authority and influence.

Sufism Confronts Political Power

The masters of the Sufi realm of spiritual legitimation had at least as much influence as the sultans of ephemeral earthly kingdoms and realms. The reclusive Sufi and patron saint of the Moroccan town of Salé, Ahmad b. 'Ashir Al-Ansari, who commanded a wide following throughout the Maghribi countryside, famously criticized Sultan Abu 'Inan and questioned the legitimacy of his rule. Decrying the Sultan's lack of social justice, Ibn 'Ashir said of Abu 'Inan, "The commander of the Faithful [Abu 'Inan] must remember that neither his servants nor his bodyguard will save him. Instead, they will flee from him on the Day of Judgment as he will flee from them."[24] In reply, Abu 'Inan recognized his faults but commented rather skeptically and unapologetically that, "all who hold power are unjust and despotic, are deceived by their confidants, and allow their intimates to carry them away with their passions."[25] Indeed, his lack of specific religious legitimacy was, in Ibn Khaldun's view, one of the reasons for the transience of Abu 'Inan's project to reunify the Maghrib. It could have also been the reason for Ibn Khaldun's disappointment with some of his own highly political decisions. Legitimacy in fourteenth-century Maghrib, in many ways, was what writers such as Ibn Khaldun told us it was.

Many of these writers, part of an educated class of counselors and ministers who often held more power and influence than initially revealed, expressed the importance of the great spiritual and mystical movement emerging and maturing in the Maghrib. Rulers and their ministers responded to this movement in various ways, wanting to shore up their right to rule in every way possible. The scholar Amira Bennison described how the façade of the ruler's authority was constantly, and perhaps somewhat defensively, proclaimed as he roamed through the countryside where many of these Sufi shaykhs were found.[26]

Writers such as Ibn Khaldun and Ibn Marzuq supported the possibility of this façade of power. Yet as much as Ibn Khaldun was a panegyrist and a proud student of the master-minister Ibn Al-Khatib, his autobiography also revealed another possible sentiment: perhaps legitimacy was not just political or founded in 'asabiyya, but also part of the medieval Maghribi and Andalusi mystical project. Sufism encompassed not only following holy men, but also the project to legitimate the individual self and the soul to God. The state and sultans were important, but also in many ways secondary, to this much greater legitimation related to those breaking points of religious awakening that so defined not only moments in Ibn Khaldun's life but also the experience of many living in that era.

Ibn Khaldun – Promise of Sufism and Frustrations of Power

To question what really was the legitimacy provided by 'asabiyya is also to ask who Ibn Khaldun really was. Both of these questions cannot be definitively answered. Instead, we can conclude that he was an individual as troubled and mercurial as the times in which he lived. Ibn Khaldun revealed obsessions of the fourteenth-century, North African cultured mind. In the end, his autobiography expressed a sense of frustration. The autobiography showed that he longed for justification for his life in the spirit as much as in the mind or in a sense of political accomplishment. He often saw with regret his own decisions in life, a man who searched for ideals in himself. It was a search that was mirrored by the search for legitimacy among states and governments he described. Ibn Khaldun would end his life unquenched by the ultimate futility of worldly power, a power he simultaneously hungered after and despised. Ibn Khaldun was certainly not alone in his struggles between the draw of a vigorous and developed spirituality, Sufism, and political or even monetary power. In fact, he lived in the last decades of an age that, around much of the Mediterranean, was defined by this very struggle.

7

CONCLUSIONS:
A SECOND AXIAL AGE

I bn Khaldun experienced profound angst and internal conflicts between spiritual enlightenment and the appeal of worldly power. In this way, he reflected
a much larger trend in the medieval Mediterranean. The conflict between
money, power and spirit, the simultaneous rise of both a commercial revolution and a spiritual revolution on all shores of the Western Mediterranean,
was one of the most defining struggles of the medieval world. Ibn 'Arabi, for
instance, was the great Unlimited Mercifier who, coming from the Almohad
West, transformed the Islamic world with his teachings and spiritual exercises,
far from the realm of political power and its allures. His followers and disciples
as well as the disciples of many more Sufi saints spread throughout the Islamic
world, following trade routes deep into Eurasia and Africa. St. Francis, and
many others, similarly rejected worldly goods, war and the life set before him
by his father and by society. Strategically embraced by the Church, his movement and his friars, from William of Rubruck to Lorenzo of Portugal, Lope
d'Ayn, spread out through the known world, from Marrakech to the Mongols,
following the mercenaries and merchants whose fortunes were being made
with the rise of global trade. Yet along with this trade and new wealth, for both
merchants and rulers, came profound spiritual crisis.

In the period covered by this book, roughly between 900 and 1450,
and especially in the twelfth century midpoint, major religious traditions
throughout Eurasia and North Africa, well into the Sahara, experienced

a great spiritual transformation. The rise of commercial wealth and trade and the interactions between different faiths it caused sparked this spiritual revival. This could be called a Second Axial Age: a world historical transformation marked by profound changes and encounters both within and between matured religious traditions and cultures. While conflict has often been downplayed in favor of studying tolerance and commercial exchange, informed recognition of, and then reaction to, other, rival religious traditions characterized this age.

Rather than being marked only by passive dismissal, tolerance or cross-cultural conversion, encounters between different universal faiths provoked profound changes and reactions *within* those very traditions. Although the "dream of conversion" was not always the central concern, it could lead to angst. After initial bursts of expansion and triumph, often supported by empire, the "stubbornness" and resistance of rival universal traditions to conversion or conquest caused crises calling for an explanation. It caused a turning inward, an attempt to recast and revive faith from within. These reactions were, at first, highly complex and limited to what might be called an intellectual and spiritual elite. Spiritual mystics and esoteric fraternities, often appealing to notions of a higher, spiritual revelation, dealt directly with the "problem" of cosmopolitanism, arguing in one way or another for the unity of faiths under the "true" faith even if that unity was not encountered in the outer world. Finding fault neither in the diversity of faiths, nor in the stars, mystics were soon joined by spiritual rationalists (those who proposed an accommodation between reason and spiritual or mystical truth), a process that started in the Islamic world and caught fire in Christian Europe.

In this way, reason, sometimes considered a dangerous inheritance from the pagan classical world, was captured by spirit. The enveloping of reason by faith traditions, however, did not occur in isolation. Indeed, disputes, whether imagined or real, between different religious traditions required the use of reasoned debate and logic, not only to uphold the faith to some universal truth but, even more crucially, to uphold the faith in often spectacular debates between faiths. Through high-stakes debates, disputations and wrangling between representatives of different religious tradition, reason, as well as luck, was an essential part of one's arsenal. These debates, often rigged and often accompanied by military forms of conflict, were popular not only in real, historically documented encounters but also in fantasy, with animals or stock characters taking the role of different faiths or religious points of view. These disputations, real or not, often seemed staged by a particular faith, often with an expected outcome.

Yet there were instances, for example, disputations held by powerful pagan rulers such as the Mongols, when great conversions seemed most possible. These conversions involved especially high stakes, as they shaped not only the history of central Asia but also, potentially the entire world, when the playing field did seem relatively even. Even though the object of the debate was the triumph of one's particular faith, the result was often profound changes within traditions that went beyond recognition of inherent truths within other belief systems and within reason itself – that lodestone of conversion that ended up changing its bearer as much as its intended target. Thus, out of the intense realization of the implications of cosmopolitanism and the necessity of reason emerged a new religiosity that often surfaced as a threat to the status quo. The realm of universal spirit and mystics and the particular demands of worldly rulers were often in conflict as mystics and saints often went directly to the people, outflanking rulers and institutions and forcing them to accommodate new religiosity or risk loosing not only to rival faiths but to new movements from within. A rise of mystical thinkers and esoteric knowers of universal spiritual truths, although these movements started among a select few, came to expand and profoundly change the nature of religious traditions throughout Eurasia, sub-Saharan Africa and the Mediterranean. Perhaps the most profound changes occurred in Islam, Christianity and Judaism and the twelfth-century mystical awakening of Sufism, Kabbalah, and the Minor Friars. Although these highly influential religious movements, friars and Sufis were to be found in some of the highest governmental and political posts as ambassadors, bishops and qadis, and seemed interested in the "dream of conversion" of non-believers, their foremost concern was with spiritual unity and perceptions of mystical revelations achieved through individual effort and known only to the individual soul. Although many scholars have identified the eighteenth-century Enlightenment in Europe as the birth of the "individual" mind,[1] the individual, mystical journey of the soul and attachment to the unification of that soul with the divine as a spiritual pursuit, laid the foundations for later, Enlightenment-based individualism.

At the same time there were similar transformations happening in other parts of East Asia. In China, the rise of Neo-Confucianism in the Song Empire sought an accommodation between concrete obligations in this world and more spiritual dimensions of Taoism and Buddhism. In the Indian Ocean basin the spread of Islamic trading communities had a major impact on Hinduism and vice versa. Ostensibly shaped by encounters with the other and based on an interior spirituality that challenged outward orthodoxy, this Second Axial Age changed religions to focus less on establishing this world and focus more on the spiritual path and transcendence experienced by individuals within the outer confines of faith.

The Second Axial Age thus transformed and fortified many major religious traditions, arming them with the twin prongs of reason and spiritual transcendence in the midst of constant encounters with recalcitrant others unwilling to convert to the "true" doctrine. This spiritualism may have allowed believers to deal not only with the challenge of each other but, also, centuries later, to survive and then re-awaken from the greatest existential threat to spirituality the world has ever seen: the rise of modernity, relativism and, even, self-interested individualism.

In economic history, scholars described a world that, in economic terms flourished, "before European hegemony." This flourishing commercial world, leading to encounters between different cultures and religious traditions, disputations, dialogues and debates and the need to adopt reason to fortify those debates, as well as the final realization that reason was not enough to prove a particular spiritual worldview, led to a near-simultaneous transformation of Jewish, Muslim and Christian thought – a shift towards spiritualism and mysticism all along the great trade routes of the world's twelfth-century commercial revival.

Karl Jasper's Axial Age

The concept of an axial period, an age when there seemed to be a simultaneous religious transformation throughout the world, emerged in 1949, the year Karl Jasper's book *The Origin and Goal of History* was published. Nazism and the horrors of the "final solution" had freshly wounded the philosopher and psychiatrist's worldview. Science, in the form of eugenics and technology, in the form of atom bombs, machines of war, seemed to have negated the human spirit. Focusing on the role of religion in history, especially the nearly simultaneous appearance of new religions throughout Eurasia from 800–200 BC, Jaspers identified the so-called first "Axial Age." Yet this theory suffered from the lack of ancient clues to the actual diffusion of influences across cultures and geographies. Cross-cultural interactions and "old world encounters," especially at a height in the twelfth-century period, however, have been documented.[2] Scholars now know the specific details and importance not only of spectacular, violent encounters, highly transformative in their own way, but also trade, philosophical and scientific borrowings.

The Almohads and the Second Axial Age

As a major stabilizing bookend on the far west of the world, a unifying force that had never before or since been built in North Africa, the Almohads, although they eventually abandoned their political doctrine of unity, were far from peripheral to this world-historical transformation. They were a major source, not only of brief-but-important political unity during the Twelfth-Century Cultural and Commercial Renaissance in the Mediterranean, but the Almohad Empire also became a well of philosophical, rationalist, and later spiritualist, Sufi influences. At the height of the Empire, trade was encouraged from vibrant ports all across the North African coast and, even as their power waned, Christians, Jews and Muslims traveled into and out of North Africa, bringing with them the philosophical ideas of rationalists such as Averroes and great Sufi masters such as Ibn 'Arabi. From a city exclusive to Islam and symbol of political *tawhid*, Marrakech, the heart of Almohad ambitions, was abandoned to the machinations of mercenaries and rival Berber shaykhs. At the same time, however, it also became Mediterraneanized, a world-city where friars reassigned from Tartary, such as Lorenzo of Portugal, mercenaries, and Jews, restored to their position in the vibrant mellah or Jewish quarter under the Marinids, lived in a city that would soon be called the city of the "Seven Sufi Saints."[3]

Yet there were far more than the semi-legendary seven saints crowding the streets of Marrakech. Sufi shrines in Marrakech seemed as prominent as the churches of Rome. And, often, Muslim saints arbitrated disputes between prominent tribes, just as clerics in the Church arbitrated for nobles and kings.[4] Saintly culture in the far west of Islam spread throughout the region and made connection as far away as India. In this way, North Africans, during and after the decline of the Almohads, emerged with a global influence that the original apocalyptic and political ambitions of the Almohads could never achieve. They were joined by their Christian and even Jewish adversaries who had also created their own spiritual reactions to the one common challenge that caused angst among followers of all faiths: the wealth and temptations of a world-wide commercial revolution that often happened outside the margins of control exerted by central religious and political authorities.

The Mongols unleashed themselves on the Middle East taking Baghdad in 1258 and, later, Timur took Damascus (1400–1), a conquest witnessed by Ibn Khaldun himself. Yet North Africa, as well as Western Europe, was left unharmed by both invasions. In the thirteenth century, Hafsid power radiated from Tunis and increased relative to the East as much as European power. Both North Africa and Europe, almost simultaneously, developed spiritual movements of voluntary poverty, reacting to economic plenty, that spread across the world. For Christian Europe the spread would happen by ship, on a new generation of Genoese and, later, Portuguese and Spanish vessels. The spread of Sufism from North Africa south and east would happen by land and by ship as well. Sufis such as Ibn 'Arabi spread their message to the ends of the known world and travelers such as Ibn Battuta followed the waves of great masters.

Despite a common fear of the Mongols as the presumed pagan forces Juj and Majuj, Gog and Magog, the Western Mediterranean was able to benefit from the silk roads opened up by Mongol Khans without facing the destructiveness of their initial wrath. North Africans (Maghribis) with their heterogeneous Arabo-Berber, Andalusi, Mediterranean populations were recognized as the Hijaz and as respected leaders of an Islamic world that was, along with the West, in the throes of spiritual transformation. The reasons for this simultaneous transformation can be found in the cultural unity of the Western Mediterranean.

Western Mediterranean Cultural Unity

As mentioned earlier, Henri Pirenne, the Belgian historian, argued that the Germanic peoples largely inherited the legacy of Rome and Christendom, and the Arab invasions caused the most serious facture in Western history,

A tear was ripped [through the sea] that remains to this day. On the shores of the Mediterranean there remain today two different and hostile civilizations. The sea that was once the center of Christendom had become the frontier. The unity of the Mediterranean was broken [*L'unité méditerranéenne est brisée . . .*].[5]

He went further in *Medieval Cities,* appealing to the notion of the Mediterranean as a "family" that had been wrested apart by Islam:

> The world-order which had survived the Germanic invasions was not able to survive the invasion of Islam. It is thrown across the path of history with the elemental force of a cosmic cataclysm . . . Its sudden thrust had destroyed ancient Europe. It had put an end to the Mediterranean commonwealth in which it had gathered its strength. The familiar and almost "family" sea which once united all the parts of this commonwealth was to become a barrier between them. On all its shores, for centuries, social life, in its fundamental characteristics, had been the same, religion, the same; customs and ideas, the same or very nearly so . . . But now, all of a sudden, the very lands where civilization had been born were torn away; the Cult of the Prophet was substituted for the Christian Faith. Moslem law for Roman law, the Arab tongue for the Greek and the Latin tongue.[6]

As in every "family," however, differences, political, religious or otherwise, were not uncommon. In some ways, differences in language, law and faith, although mitigated by the divisions within both Europe and North Africa of the Great Sea and the northern shore, only increased. Yet with new differences and influences from Arabia, acculturated into a pre-existing Berber culture, came commercial and intellectual exchange. By the twelfth century, there were certain commonalities in the religious, commercial and political life of the medieval Mediterranean. This similarity of approach, if not of identity, was not only seen amongst the elite in port cities. Instead, they were similarities endemic to the very ideological and religious systems that seemed, to Pirenne, so different. Although he may have been correct to emphasize a dominant element of "hostility," such hostility need not necessarily indicate the source of difference. Hostility can be greatest where intrinsic differences are least. Even when little was understood of an adversary, however, there were sometimes benefits to the existence of a new outsider: it promoted unity among one's own divergent flock.

The medieval Western Mediterranean from the eleventh to the end of the fifteenth century was not, on the whole, a peaceful world system. Neither the Christian north nor the Muslim south gained a complete upper hand through this period. Yet such an upper hand was not always the main objective of warfare. Most common, instead, were struggles within Christendom or among the many dynasties that emerged after the collapse of the Almohad Empire. Also, the rise of European commerce was not a zero-sum game. Despite some geographic disadvantages, North Africa flourished along with the Commercial Revolution, not in spite of it.

Even the Age of Discovery, routes around Africa, and conquest of the New World, was not the definitive end of the importance of the North Africa and the Mediterranean. The Ottoman Empire was a serious, expanding force and independent Morocco had its own imperial ambitions. Morocco under the Sharifian dynasty of Ahmad Al-Mansur would spread to the south, capturing the rich gold of Songhai Africa and becoming a formidable rival to Spain and ally of England. Al-Mansur's secretary, whose name was spelled 'Abd el Ouahed ben Messaoud by English writers, was sent to the court of Elizabeth I.[7]

Conflict, the source of Pirenne's pessimism, was not the end of contact – far from it. Although important, geography was not the most influential factor. Rather than seeing only a long term of common geography and custom that survived Islam and created common Mediterranean culture in spite of cultural and religious conflict, in conflict there was evidence of commonality in the tools of encounter, and in reactions to the commercial growth we see parallels and exchanges between North Africa and Europe. Along with communities of exchange and cultural borrowing there were communities of violence and hostility. Both, however, were communities of contact, a contact fostered as much by difference and conflict as prevented by it. The more North African Muslims and European Christians resisted one another, the more they also learned about the nature of their respective faiths and used similar methods of reason inherited from the classical past, reviving part of a common social, economic, intellectual and spiritual system that Pirenne so lamented with the fall of Rome. Despite being challenged repeatedly and nearly abandoned in the 1980s, Pirenne's argument has remained a frame of reference.[8] Beyond arguments that assume the damaging nature of "Arab" invasions, and later Arab migrations, however, we need a better grasp of the internal dynamics of early and medieval Islamic North Africa.

North African Diversity as Mediterranean Diversity

Returning to the beginning of the history of Islam in the Western Mediterranean, the so-called Arab conquests of North Africa and Al-Andalus were never really "Arab" nor were they ever simply "conquests." As mentioned earlier, scholars such as C. Fenwick and Jonathan Conant have recently questioned the extent that the Arab Muslim conquests impacted the economy of North Africa and its trade with Europe. "A majority of Byzantine towns were not abandoned but remained significant centers."[9] Beyond the specific level of urbanization, a question about the uniformity of conquest itself needs to be asked. At almost no point were the Arabs fully in control of the North African shore, so it seemed impossible that they would actually be able to turn the Mediterranean into a Muslim lake in a unified fashion. Arabs and Arabic speakers were almost certainly the minority over much of North Africa up until recent centuries. Berbers, a people with their own identities, divisions and histories, dominated the populations of North Africa, and later came in great numbers northwards to Iberia settling in Al-Andalus.[10] Although long under the titular control of the Umayyad Arab aristocracy in Iberia, Berbers ruled highly advanced and cultured cities throughout the Peninsula as *ta'ifa* (from "faction") kings or governors. There were Arab commanders but many of the troops during the conquest were non-Arab, Berbers who had been a part of the Mediterranean dynamic for millennia. North Africa was never a monolith of one form of Islam. Almost immediately after the conquest there were Berber revolts, independent Arab governors in Ifriqiya, the Aghlabids of Tunisia, the rise of Berber, Rustamid Ibadi Islam in mountainous Tahert (Algeria), and a constellation of semi-independent reinterpretations and variations of Berber Islam, asserting a very real independence from Baghdad, and Arab governors in major cities arose. Berber revolts spread like fire through Muslim Spain and North Africa. This dissolution of any sort of central control started soon after the Arab commander 'Uqba bin Nafi' had famously ridden his stallion out into the Atlantic, claiming North Africa for Islam proclaiming, "O God, if the sea had not prevented me, I would have galloped on for ever like Alexander the Great, upholding your faith and fighting the unbelievers!"[11] Kusaila, the leader of a Berber revolt, killed 'Uqba Ibn Nafi' in 683 at an oasis near the Algerian town of Biskra.[12]

The coming of Islam to North Africa and the growth of independent Berber and Arab cities and dynasties promoted commerce. Gold seemed to increase in circulation. Coins show evidence of the infusion of currency into the early medieval Mediterranean economy. Land routes into Africa through the founding desert port cities such as Kairouan helped spark commerce in gold, salt and other goods even as raiding by North African ships may have frightened many in coastal European cities. There were also opportunities for profit or ransom. Even as Pope Leo IV riled against the North African threat in 849, Rome itself was engaged in trade with these "barbarians." It was the Christian ruler in Benevento who invited the raiders in to attack his rivals. Later, the revival of Western Mediterranean commerce, diplomacy and intellectual fervor in the eleventh, twelfth and even the thirteenth and fourteenth centuries must be tied not only to the Crusades, but to relations with Egypt and the East. In fact, great Italian cities such as Genoa and Pisa, as well as other growing centers such as Barcelona and Marseille, had their fortunes tied to cities on the North African coast as much as those farther east. The rise of the great Berber Empires, the Almoravids and the Almohads, along with their less impressive, but still influential and powerful successor states, stimulated minds and pocket books from Fibonacci's Bèjaïa to Pisa. In addition to mathematicians, Bèjaïa was full of intellectual luminaries such as the great astronomer Abu Al-Salt, who died in the city in 1134. His works on astronomy were well known in France and Spain and included a description of various important astronomical instruments.[13] In the far west, Ibn Sab'in's letters from Ceuta, near Tangier, answered questions about the nature of the universe of that *Stupor Mundi*, King of Jerusalem Frederick II of Palermo. From Marrakech to Seville to Toledo to Paris came the rational methods of Averroes. Iberian students knew Arabic so well that Roger Bacon, the great Oxford scholar, was embarrassed by his students' superior Arabic skills at the University of Paris.[14]

The cities, merchants, scholars and saints of North Africa were all a part of the twelfth-century revival. By uniting diverse lands and ports, the Almoravid and Almohad Berber Islamic Empires, far from isolating North Africa from Europe, ultimately led to the revival of cosmopolitan commerce, spiritual revival responding to that commerce, and the "Mediterranization" of cities from Tunis to Seville to Marrakech. North Africa was intimately involved in the growth and prosperity of the twelfth century and, from plague to seemingly endless wars of disunity and social disruption, shared in the calamities that would come to all parts of the Western Mediterranean in the fourteenth century. Just before the fourteenth century there were several major threats on the horizon. One calamity that both Western Europe and North Africa narrowly avoided together was Mongol invasion.

Christians and Muslims among Mongols

The manuscript library of Corpus Christi College, Cambridge contains the travels of William of Rubruck (d. 1293), a Franciscan friar sent on a mission to the Mongol ruler. The testimony of this "minor friar" came from France. This was the France of St. Louis, great crusader king, who went on the Eighth Crusade to Ifriqiya in 1267. The Almohads were blamed for the killing of Franciscan friars who were sent to Marrakech to evangelize. They were martyred in 1220 and became a major part of the saintly literature of the Franciscans.[15] The Almohad Caliph was the fearful "Miramolin" (Latin for Prince of Believers or *Amir al Mu'min*). Yet, on a far side of the world where William of Rubruck ventured, Islam was not the frightening enemy. Rather, Muslims became an ally against Mongol paganism. Despite instances of violence, a debate against the Mongols where William allied with the Muslims, revealed a common intellectual culture between Muslims and Christians in the Western Mediterranean. This common, nuanced understanding was brought about through intellectual dispute as well as exchange.

The famed English scholar Roger Bacon (d. 1292) discussed William's mission while trying to equip his readers with the skills needed to convert other sects to Christianity. He was particularly struck by "Tartars, whose emperor says that there should be only one ruler on earth just as there is only one God in heaven, at that he himself ought to be constituted that ruler, as we see in the letter he sent to the Lord Louis, King of France, in which he demands tribute from him. . ."[16] He explained, the Tartars were "inflamed by the lust for dominion" and unable to live "according to laws based on reason." He classed them, following Aristotle's somewhat arbitrary number, as one of only five sects, "Saracens, Tartars, Idolaters [Buddhists], Jews and Christians," the number of which could not change "until the sect of the Antichrist appears." The "Saracens" were, for Bacon, driven by bodily pleasure since he wrongly believed they could take "as many wives as they wish."[17] Even Bacon, however, displayed a hint of understanding and perspective when he said "if Christians deny the histories of Muslims and Jews, they, by the same right, will deny the history of the Christians."[18]

In contrast, Joachim of Fiore (d. 1202), founder of the Joachimite Mystics in southern Italy, wrote in the *Liber Figurarum*, categorizing different faiths and peoples into an apocalyptic geography. Yet, his vision was far gloomier for the future of Christendom. He believed these groups would play an active part in the coming of the apocalypse as Moors from the West (North Africa and Al-Andalus), Saracens from the South (Tunisia and Egypt), Turks from the East, Ethiopians from the South and Teutonic pagans from the North would form a pact and together overrun Christian Europe. All forms of military response were doomed to fail. Evangelism, preaching and conversion were the only answers. In one manuscript at Corpus Christi there is depicted a seven-headed beast of the end times with heads representing Muhammad, Saladin of Egypt and a head named Mesemothus, a figure who probably represented the Caliph of the Almohad Empire.[19] The body of the beast was labeled Gog and Magog, those monstrous races who were held back from spilling over into the world by the mythical walls built somewhere in obscure depths of Central Asia by Alexander the Great, a unifying hero in the literature of Muslims and Christians.[20] Alexander was the subject of the Alexandrian Romances, stories that told of a unified world under one empire, one king.[21] He was also mentioned frequently in Muslim literature. The *Rreck*, an Aragonese-Spanish Alexander Romance written in Arabic letters (*aljamiado*), referred to North African traditions about Alexander as the "Dhul Qarnain" in the Qur'an: a man who, after purification, unified spirit and power over the world. These North African sources dated to the eighth century.[22]

Historians of Europe have recently argued that apocalypse was a far more powerful part of European history than most historians have assumed, providing an opportunity to reform society.[23] Yet North Africa was similarly experiencing real apocalyptic fervor. In fact, the Almohads were among the most successful apocalyptic movements of history. The Almohads had their own apocalyptic literature. The mysterious *Book of Jafr*, a "second Qur'an" allegedly revealed to Muhammad the entire political future of the human race as was handed down to all future rightly-guided rulers of Islam. The *Book of Jafr* was found in the "treasuries and libraries of great kings and caliphs" since the beginning of Islam.[24] It was a source of exclusive information for just rulers, a type of guidebook written by the Prophet that bestowed the ruling elite with special powers of prediction. Just as the Qur'an is window to the divine and a handbook for life written for the *umma*, the common community of Muslims, the alleged *Book of Jafr* was a window to God's will, a handbook for rule passed from the Prophet to future generations of rightly-guided leaders.

Encountering peoples mostly unknown to either Western Islam or Christianity, however, William of Rubruck could not rely on apocalyptic literature alone. Although not the most sophisticated of Franciscans and mostly a failure at converting those he met on his path to the court of the Mongols, William of Rubruck had to ally with the Muslims against the "pagan" shamans of the Mongols. He used a more nuanced and pragmatic view of the "Saracens" than Bacon in his "conversion" section of his *Opus Majus*. He was able to recognize the similarities between Islam and Christianity. He may have known the work of Robert Ketton, who had been working in Iberia to translate the Qur'an into Latin. Although William agreed with Bacon that the world was divided between major sects, he also formed intellectual alliances with Muslim scholars. He formed this alliance to give himself an advantage in one of the greatest, high-stakes disputations of his era: convincing the great Khan of the Mongols, Mongke Khan, to convert from paganism. The conversion of this leader of much of Asia and the largest land empire in history to Christianity or to Islam would have immense consequences: the greatest missionary victory of all time. When the Khan called for a great debate between Christians, pagans (he called them *tuin*) and Muslims, William first attempted to find common ground with the eastern Nestorian Christians who wanted to "debate the [Muslim] Saracens first." William, however, suggested that, "this would not be a good method since the Saracens agree with us in saying there is one God and therefore provide allies for us against the *tuins* [pagans]."[25] The debate ended in a drunken draw as more and more

Mongols, led by the Great Khan, imbibed in more and more fermented milk and theological arguments over the unity of God grew as convoluted and hazy as the inebriated brains of the drinkers.

Nonetheless, William's brisk, intellectual alliance with Muslims thousands of miles away from his sponsor King Louis of France, who was making inroads into Muslim North Africa, was an acknowledgement of something real – a common cultural and religious tradition. He would have been wholly willing to debate the Saracens on their own – many of his Franciscan brothers were sent to North Africa around the same time, becoming martyrs in Marrakech, and the great St. Francis of Assisi, the founder of his order, was famous for his debate with the Sultan of Egypt during the Fifth Crusade.[26] He also wanted desperately to face martyrdom in the hands of the Muslims, going first to North Africa, the realm of the dreaded "Miramolin," and only turning back in Spain after an illness.[27] Yet here at the court of the Mongols, far from home with the sky fearfully open in all directions and his life held on a fraying thread by the fickle Khan, William the Franciscan friar recognized the Muslims as allies, as friends of convenience.

As the Franciscan William of Rubruck's remarkable debate and other disputations mentioned in this book have shown, disputation and even combat between groups forged connections between those groups and spurred changes within each group in reaction to the other. This was true not only for conflict between religious groups but within them as well, as was so prominently shown by the back and forth between Berber and Arab Muslims or between the Genoese and the Venetians. Far from splitting the sea in two, interactions between Christians, Jews and Muslims created a common cultural zone that existed between the North African Maghrib and Europe. Social and religious conflict between representatives of different faiths, especially within the intellectual and spiritual realm, was part of a larger social ecology of interaction. At times conflict actually helped develop a common culture, one based on the rise and reaction to commerce in the popular realm, and the use and integration of reason and argument to support spiritual beliefs in the intellectual realm. Finally, even as dialogue and disputation based on reason and philosophy was spurred on by the dream of conversion, as with R. Lull, or the dream of unity, as with the Almohads, another movement was developing in all three faiths: a spiritual or mystical understanding of the limits of reason that provided solace to believers of Islam, Christianity and Judaism. This mysticism was spurred forward by a more mundane interaction: the Commercial Revolution, an economic boom and prosperity that grew from the interlinking of the Mediterranean world but one that also left many spiritually challenged for something beyond the new promise of wealth.

Rational, military and political attempts to unite the Western Mediterranean under one faith failed. Frustrated as much by their similarities as by the differences between faiths, the narrative arch of almost all the great thinkers and theologians during this period was roughly parallel. From Aquinas to Al-Ghazali to Averroes and Roger Bacon, the story, on a biographical level, was remarkably similar. After being called to defend their faith early in their lives, they used reasoned arguments often influenced by the classical writers. Yet these reasoned arguments by these highly trained theologians not only failed to convince the "other" – they may have failed to convince themselves. Spiritual crisis defined the career of many a monotheistic intellectual. It was beyond coincidence that most of the rationalists of the medieval Western Mediterranean died as mystics, having given up on the world as a place to find God's unity. These were far more than "mid life crises." Rather, they reveal an inner angst common to all three faiths as the world was opening up before them. The arguments Muslims, Christians and Jews used against one another, along with interactions with one another for profit or for convenience, led to a deeper unity of culture in the Western Mediterranean than most members of any one of these faiths would have ever been able to acknowledge.

Beyond Dichotomies of Tolerance and Violence

Using the medieval Western Mediterranean as its frame of reference, this book appeals for a broader understanding of the medieval period as a whole, beyond the dichotomy of tolerance and violence that are the twin peaks of historiography on the region.[28] The history of the medieval Western Mediterranean was not simply a litany of intolerance or a shining example of cosmopolitanism. It was about how those struggles and interactions, some violent, some based on mutual interests, were used or not used to create different social groups with different dreams of unity. Conversion, after all, was only secondary to the universal dream of uniting humanity, whether through natural social bonding, Ibn Khaldun's 'asabiyya, or through religious inspiration or both. Competing dreams of unity, mixing together in the Western Mediterranean, helped set the stage for the Second Axial Age.

Rather than ignoring or downplaying conflict in favor of showing the cosmopolitan, we need to examine what sociologists have called the "functions of social conflict." The medieval Western Mediterranean could be compared, cautiously, with ecological systems found in nature. Losses against a Muslim "Saracen," a Christian crusader or the superior learning of a skilled Jewish debater such as Nahmanides, created an external "enemy." At the same time, debating these "others" required conceding one's own cultural comfort zone and learning the weaknesses of the opponent. These concessions to know the other were not necessarily losses. Even outright defeats inflicted by the infidel were chances for a greater spirit of unity when transformed by the individual charisma of leaders.

There was a great, growing exchange of merchandise up to the fourteenth century between North Africa and Europe. Even more so, however, there was an economy of miracles, an exchange of opportunities to create unity out of those moments of conflict against the other. The Muslim presence was useful to Christians wishing to claim power or religious and intellectual authority. The Christian challenge was similarly useful to those Muslim leaders who attempted to forge unity over a society that was at least as fractured and divided as Christendom. Ultimately, religious and racial categories were cultural constructions built on the conveniently different, but never wholly alien, outsider.

In the midst of leveraged moments of conflict, a wider ecosystem of peoples divided, and even invigorated, by their own similarities would thrive. This ecosystem of conflict, contact and exchange was a web built on trade, intellectual disputation and accidental, miraculous interventions. It prevailed over the attempts by religious preachers to create a single, monolithic Mediterranean even as it supported dreams of one day achieving that unity. As David Cannadine indicated in his book *The Undivided Past, Humanity Beyond our Differences*, so much of this wider web of human interactions has been lost to scholars focused on dichotomies of division or unity, violence or tolerance.[29]

Unlike natural ecology, where the fates of individuals in nature are determined by instinct and predicted by science, humanity is not beholden only to predetermined systems but also to forces located in religion and ideas of the soul. Beyond the categories of linguistic, ethnic or religious background, individuals throughout the medieval Western Mediterranean displayed agency and unpredictable behavior, voluntary poverty, self-doubt and blatant betrayal of self-interest and utility. Debates, as with other competitive encounters, could be a learning experience, victory could mean adopting much of the culture of the conquered, accidents could become miracles; fortune could lead to angst and death to eternal life. The people of the medieval Western Mediterranean, whether from Tunis or Toledo, Marrakech or Marseille, were no less capable of transforming their world than we are today. They shaped a human web of geography and economy and faith as much as that web shaped them.

NOTES

Introduction

1. Kenan Malik, "The Failure of Multiculturalism: Community verses Society in Europe", *Foreign Affairs*, March/April (2015).
2. Oleg Grabar, "Two Paradoxes in the Islamic Art of the Spanish Peninsula," in S. K. Jayyusi (ed.), *The Legacy of Muslim Spain* (Brill, 1992), 583–91.
3. Maria Judith Feliciano and Leyla Rouhi, "Interrogating Iberian Frontiers," *Medieval Encounters*, 12/3 (2006), 317–328, 318.
4. I thank Amira Bennsion for reminding me of Al-Idrisi's Hammudid ancestry. On the Hammudids and their activities in Al-Andalus, see Peter Scales, *The Fall of the Caliphate of Cordoba: Berbers and Arabs in Conflict* (Brill, 1994), 95.
5. Brian Catlos explores these contradictions within kings and soliders in his accessible book, *Infidel Kings and Unholy Warriors, Faith, Power and Violence in the Age of Crusade and Jihad* (FSG, 2014).
6. My graduate student John Sullivan is currently writing his dissertation on this topic. I thank him for his new approaches to thinking about Seville and the Alcazar. Also, see D. F. Ruggles' excellent article, "The Alcazar of Seville in Mudejar Architecture," *Gesta*, 43/2, 2004, 87–98.
7. G. W. R. Hegel, *The Philosophy of History* (Dover, 1956), 103–4.
8. Just as Islam is a "problem" or outlier for Hegel's dilatectical thinking, as it came after Christianity, so too, I believe, is North Africa. Sai Bhatawadekar, "Islam in Hegel's Triatic Philosophy of Religion", *Journal of World History*, 25/2–3

(2014), 397–424. Also see Ian Almond, *History of Islam in German Thought: From Leibniz to Nietzche* (Routledge, 2010).

9. Before being saved by King William, the Almohad pilgrim Ibn Jubayr feared being turned forever into a "slave" by the rabble "Rumi" of Sicily: Ibn Jubayr, *The Travels of Ibn Jubayr*, trans. R. C. Broadhurst (Jonathan Cape, 1952), 338.

10. Hegel, *The Philosophy of History*, 99.

11. The full list of works on the stream of East to West cultural influences would be too long to include here: Deborah Howard, *Venice and the East, The Impact of the Islamic World on Venetian Architecture* (Yale University Press, 2000); Hans Belting, *Florence and Baghdad: Renaissance Art and Arab Science* (Harvard University Press, 2011); Franz Rosenthal, *The Classical Heritage in Islam* (Routledge Reprint, 1994); Dimitri Gutas, *Greek Thought, Arabic Culture: The Greco-Arabic Translation Movement in Baghdad and Early 'Abbasid Society* (Routledge, 1998).

12. Maria R. Menocal, *The Ornament of the World: How Muslims, Jews and Christians Created a Culture of Tolerance in Muslim Spain* (Back Bay Books, 2003), is in all other ways an excellent and beautifully-written introduction to Al-Andalus, except that North Africa is not as well contextualized.

13. Robert Kaplan, *The Revenge of Geography* (Random House, 2012), 143.

14. Robert Bartlett argued in *The Making of Europe* (Princeton University Press, 1994) that it was this interaction with the East that, in part, created what it meant to be European.

15. Several works and special issues have come out in the *Journal of North African Studies*. For instance, Adam Gaiser with Miriam Ali de Unzaga, "Facets of Exchange between North Africa and the Iberian Peninsula," *The Journal of North African Studies* (Spain-North African Project Special Issue), 19/1 (2014). Also, see Alexander Metcalfe and Mariam Rosser-Owen, "Forgotten Connections? Medieval Material Culture and Exchange in the Central and Western Mediterranean," *Al-Masaq*, 25/1 (2013).

16. Richard Hodges and David Whitehouse in *Mohammad, Charlemagne and the Origins of Europe, Archaeology and the Pirenne Thesis* (Cornell University Press, 1983) discussed extensive archaeological evidence against the Pirenne thesis. Emmet Scott writes an inflamatory review of the debate in *Mohammed and Charlemagne Revisted: The History of a Controversy* (New English Review Press, 2012), that is largely in defense of the Pirenne thesis but has its own highly charged political overtones.

17. Patrick Geary, *The Myth of Nations: The Medieval Origins of Europe* (Princeton University Press, 2003).

18. David Abulafia, *The Great Sea: A Human History of the Mediterranean* (Oxford University Press, 2013).

Chapter 1

1. Janet Abu-Lughod, *Before European Hegemony: the World System 1250–1350* (Oxford University Press, 1991).

2. Vincent Cornell, *The Way of Abu Madyan: Doctrinal and Poetic Works* (Cambridge: Islamic Texts Society, 1996).

3. Claude Addas, *The Quest for the Red Sulphur: the Life of Ibn 'Arabi*, trans. Peter Kingsly (Islamic Texts Society, 1993), 165.

4. Addas, *Quest for the Red Sulfur*, 23.

5. The name Ibn Mashish probably meant son of the "small cat" in Berber. Al-Shadhili, his disciple, did not limit his understanding of asceticism to outward displays of poverty. He often dressed in elegant garments. One time a man came to his assembly dressed in worn-out garments and challenged the sheikh. Al-Shadhili responded, "your garments are the garments of worldy desire that bespeak the pursuit of poverty [as an acquisition], our garments bespeak self-restraint and sufficiency." *The Mystical Teachings of Al-Shadhili*, trans. Elmer Douglas (SUNY Press, 1993), 38.

6. For studies of medieval European characterizations of Muslims see Norman Daniel, *Islam and the West, The Making of an Image* (Oneworld Publications, 2009); John Tolan, *Saracens* (Columbia University Press, 2002); and, recently, David Nirenberg, *Neighboring Faiths: Christianity, Islam and Judaism in the Middle Ages and Today* (University of Chicago Press, 2014).

7. Joseph Gies and Francis Gies, *Merchants and Moneymen: The Commercial Revolution, 1000–1500* (Thomas Crowell, 1972). Despite the occasional mistake of identifying all North Africans as "Arabs," this is still, in my mind, an excellent and accessible text, especially for the undergraduate classroom

8. V. V. Bartold, *Mussulman Culture*, trans. Shahid Suhrawardy (Oxford University Press, 2009), 35.

9. Allen Fromherz, *The Almohads: The Rise of an Islamic Empire* (I. B. Tauris, 2010).

10. Charles Haskins, *The Renaissance of the Twelfth Century* (Harvard University Press, 1971); Robert Lopez, *The Commercial Revolution of the Middle Ages, 950–1350* (Cambridge University Press, 2005); Stephen Epstein, *An Economic and Social History of Late Medieval Europe* (Cambridge University Press, 2009).

11. For an excellent overview of Ibn Tumart's journey and its significance see Vincent Cornell, "Understanding is the mother of ability: responsibility and action in the doctrine of Ibn Tûmart", *Studia Islamica*, 66 (1987), 71–103.

12. Mas Latrie, *Traités de paix et de commerce avec les Arabes de l'Afrique septentrionale au Moyen Âge* (Paris, 1866), 22–3.

13. Quoted and translated in Daniel, *Islam and the West*, 279. Daniel proposed the idea that the papal letter deliberately echoed the Qur'an.

14. Ambrosio Huici Miranda, *Historia Política del Imperio Almohade*, vol. 1 (Tetuan, 1956), 40–1. Ibn Tumart spent much of his time at the mosque of Rayhana.

15. For a discussion of the possible reasons for the Almohad directive to convert see Maribel Fierro, *The Almohad Revolution: Politics and Religion in the Islamic West During the Twelfth–Thirteenth Centuries* (Ashgate Variorum, 2012).

16. Bèjaïa was not on the periphery but at the center of the sea. For a recent study of medieval Bèjaïa and its "reorientation" towards the Mediterranean Sea through the period, see D. Valérian, *Bougie: port Maghrébin: 1067–1510* (École française de Rome, 2006).

17. G. Marçais, "Bidjaya," *Encyclopaedia of Islam*, 2nd edn.

18. On the importance of alum, see C. Singer, *The Earliest Chemical Industry: An Essay in the Historical Relations of Economics and Technology Illustrated from the Alum Trade* (The Folio Society, 1948).

19. R. Brunschvig, *La Berbérie Orientale Sous les Hafsides*, vol. 1 (Paris, 1982), 378.

20. Ibid. vol. 1, 411.

21. Peregrine Horden and Nicholas Purcell, *The Corrupting Sea: A Study of Mediterranean History* (Wiley-Blackwell, 2000).

22. Some scholars, including Richard Grimm in "The Autobiography of Leonardo Pisano" question the extent to which Fibonacci was actually influenced by "Moorish," or North African mathematicians. However, it seems clear that Fibonacci found something unique to the superb instruction he did receive in Bèjaïa – whether it be from a native of Bèjaïa, many of the merchants, teachers and traders in the city were part of a dynamic of diverse influences on the port as well as the art and practice of "disputation". *Fibonacci Quarterly*, 11/1 (February 1973), 99–104. On the influence of Fibonacci on accounting, see John Durham, "The Introduction of 'Arabic' Numerals in European Accounting", *Accounting Historians Journal*, 19 (1992), 42–9.

23. According to Ramzi Rouighi's careful study of Bèjaïa, the Almohads were highly supportive of merchants: *The Making of a Mediterranean Emirate* (University of Pennsylvania Press, 2011), 77, n. 6.

24. The idea of the "Twelfth Century Renaissance" comes from the work of Haskins, *The Renaissance of the Twelfth Century*.

25. Lopez, *The Commerical Revolution*, 106.

26. Djamal Aïssani, "Le mathématicien Eugène Dewulf (1831–1896) et les manuscrits médiévaux du Maghreb," *Historica Mathematica*, 23 (1996), 257–68, 262. Also, see D. Aïssani, *Bèjaïa à l'époque médiévale: Les Mathématiques au sein du mouvement intellectuel* (IREM, 1993).

27. *An-Nubda al-Muhtaja Akhbar Sanhaja bi Ifrikiya wa Bèjaïa* in François Woepcke, "Recherches sur les sciences mathématiques chez les orientaux," *Journal Asiatique*, 24 (1854), 348–84. Ibn Hammad was used by Ibn Khaldun (d. 1406) in his account on mathematics in the *Muqaddimah*.

28. François Woepcke , "The Autobiography of Leonardo Pisano", *Journal Asiatique*, 24 (1854),101.

29. The late medieval period saw the fruition of these dialogues, especially between Christians and Muslims with the extraordinary work of Nicholas of Cusa, the humanist and papal legate. For more on dialogues and encounters from the twelfth to the fourteenth century, see David Thomas *et al.* (eds.), *Christian-Muslim Relations: A Bibliographical History*, vols. III–IV (Brill, 2012); I. C. Levy, *et al.* (eds.), *Nicholas of Cusa and Islam: Polemic and Dialogue in the Late Middle Ages* (Brill, 2014). There was ample disputation in the Eastern Mediterranean as well. See Diego Cucarella, *Muslim-Christian Polemics across the Mediterranean* (Brill, 2015).

30. Brian Catlos, *Muslims of Medieval Latin Christendom c. 1050–1614* (Cambridge University Press, 2014).

31. Maribel Fierro, "Alfonso X the Wise: The Last Almohad Caliph?", *Medieval Encounters*, 15/2–4 (2009), 175–98.

32. At the same time, Christians who convert to Islam, "shall be put to death" for apostasy, although this rule could be relaxed for those who did something of "substantial benefit to the country." Samuel P. Scott (trans.), *Las Siete Partidas*, 5 vols., ed. Robert Burns (University of Pennsylvania Press, 2001), 1438–41.

33. Ibn Jubayr, *The Travels of Ibn Jubayr*, trans. R. C. Broadhurst (Jonathan Cape, 1952), 359.

34. Daniel, *Islam and the West*, 139.

35. Abraham ben Daud (c. 1110–80) described the Almohad period as featuring, ". . . the sword of Ibn Tumart, which came into the world when he decreed apostasy on the Jews, saying: 'Come, and let us cut them off from being a nation: that the name of Israel may be no more in remembrance.' Thus, he wiped out

every last 'name and remnant' of them from all of his empire, from the city of Silves at the end of the world until the city of al-Mahdiyya." Quoted in Amira Bennsion and María Gallego, "Jewish Trading in Fes on the Eve of the Almohad Conquest", *MEAH Hebreo*, 56 (2007), 33–51, 38.

36. On this highly controversial topic, some scholars, such as Amira Bennison and María Gallego, have recently suggested, "the assumption that Almohad persecution of non-Muslim religious minorities was a systematic or official policy throughout their rule is more problematic." See "Jewish Trading in Fes", 34.

37. Anselme Tourmede, *Pourquoi J'ai Embrassé L'Islam* (Éditions de la Merci, 2009), 33.

38. Jewish doctors often served as translators and diplomats. Ibid. 36.

39. For a brief life of Anselm, see the introduction to Tourmede, *Pourquoi J'ai Embrassé L'Islam*. Also, see Lluis Deztany (ed.), *Libre de disputacio de l'ase* (Barcelona, 1922). Interestingly, Anselm continues to hold currency: he has become a minor youtube sensation, and major focus of some European Muslim-convert preachers wishing to show a historic basis for Christian conversion to Islam, including the youtube preacher Abdur Raheem Green.

40. Quoted in Michael Ryan, *A Kingdom of Stargazers: Astrology and Authority in the Late Medieval Crown of Aragon* (Cornell University Press, 2011), 86. Also, see Sa'id Al-Andalusi, *Science in the Medieval World: Book of the Categories of Nations*, ed. and trans. Sema'an I. Salem and Alok Kumar (University of Texas Press, 1991).

41. Quoted in William Chittick, *Imaginal Worlds: Ibn al-'Arabi and the Problem of Religious Diversity* (SUNY Press, 1994), 125.

42. *Futuhat al Makkiyya*, II: 616. Quoted in S. Hirtenstein, *The Unlimited Mercifier* (Anqa Publishing, 1999), 97.

43. Addas, *Quest for the Red Sulfur*, 100.

44. Maribel Fierro, "Christian Success and Muslim Fear in Andalusi Writings during the Almoravid and Almohad Periods," in Uri Rubin and D. Wasserstein (eds.), *Dhimmis and Others, Jews and Christians in the Worlds of Classical Islam* (Tel Aviv, 1997), 155–78, 162.

45. Although H. A. R. Gibb's translation remains an important source, here I use Tim MacKintosh Smith's *The Travels of Ibn Battuta* (Picador, 2002), 39.

46. Indeed, the tradition continues to this day. When visiting the holy city of Ouezzane, south of Tangier, in 2002, I went to the shrine of Rabbi Amran ben Diwane, an eighteenth-century Jewish saint. There were Muslims who visited the shrine well into the twentieth century. *Baraka*, or blessing, could come from saintly men or women, regardless of background.

47. For original text in Arabic with translation and commentary see H. R. Idris, "Fêtes chrétiennes célébrées en Ifrîqiya à l'époque zîrîde," *Revue Africaine*, 440–1 (1954), 261–76.

48. Ibid. 273.

49. Ifriqiyan poets such as Al-Mithaq were far from alone in the praise of the beauty of young men in Arabic. He was following a long tradition reminiscent of the tenth-century poet Al-Mutanabbi. See J. Wright and E. Rowson, *Homoeroticism in Classical Arabic Literature* (Columbia University Press, 1997).

50. Full name was 'Abd Al-Wahhab bin Muhammad Al-Azdi. His work is found in al-Kutubi, *Fawat al Wafayat*, after the writings of Ibn Rashiq. See Idris, "Fêtes chrétiennes," 271.

51. Quoted in M. Mansouri, "Cynophagy, Homosexuality and Anthropology in Medieval Islamic North Africa as Signs of Hospitality," *The Journal of North African Studies*, 20/2 (March 2015), 128–43, 138.

52. The phenomenon of cultural exchange in Al-Andalus (Muslim Spain) and Sicily, although itself still full of open avenues for research, remains far better studied and understood than the interactions between Muslim, Jews and Christians in North Africa. On Al-Andalus, see J. Dodds, M. Menocal, A. Balbale, *The Arts of Intimacy* (Yale University Press, 2008). Long out of fashion and possibly associated with French colonial claims of a "proto-Christian" identity for North Africa, the histories of Christianity, Christians and other non-Jewish minorities in the Islamic world have primarily focused on the Islamic East and Baghdad. See Sidney Griffith, *The Church in the Shadow of the Mosque, Christians and Muslims in the World of Islam* (Princeton University Press, 2010) and Gerard Russell, *Heirs to Forgotten Kingdoms* (Basic Books, 2014). Yet there has been some recent scholarship in French adding to what we know on Christian communities in North Africa: Virginie Prevost, "Les derniéres communatés chrétiennes autochones d'Afrique du Nord," *Revue de l'histoire des religions*, 4 (2007), 461–83.

53. Idris, "Fêtes chrétiennes," 266.

54. Quoted in Ibn Jubayr, *The Travels of Ibn Jubayr*, 331. Perhaps a poet from the port of Tunis would have written an opposite sentiment in favor of the sea. On Saharan trade in this period, see Michael Brett, "Ifriqiya as a market for Saharan trade from the tenth to the twelfth century AD," in *Ibn Khaldun and the Medieval Maghrib*, chapter 2 (Ashgate, 1999).

55. Even though the Ma'rib dam was thousands of miles away in Yemen, it was common for Arabic speaking religiously minded Muslims such as Ibn Jubayr to

refer as much to the Arabian geography. The Ma'rib dam in Yemen is referred to as a great catastrophe in the Qur'an, Sura 34: 16.

56. Ibn Jubayr, *The Travels of Ibn Jubayr*, 336.

57. Ibid. 337–8.

58. Ibid. 341.

59. Ibid. 341.

60. Ibid. 350.

61. Ibid. 357–8.

62. P. S. van Koningsveld, "Muslim Slaves and Captives in Western Europe during the Late Middle Ages", *Islam and Christian-Muslim Relations*, 6/1 (1995), 5–23.

63. Brett Whalen, "Corresponding with Infidels: Rome, the Almohads and the Christians of Thirteenth Century Morocco," *Journal of Medieval and Early Modern Studies*, 41/3 (Fall 2011), 487–513.

64. On the idea and implications of the "dream of conversion," see Robert Burns' article, "Christian-Islamic Confrontation in the West: The Thirteenth Century Dream of Conversion," *The American Historical Review*, 76/5 (1971), 1386–434.

65. Although Ibn 'Arabi never actually used the term "Oneness of Being" or *Wahdat al Wujud*, it was a description of his work that other authors around the period, including Ibn Taymiyya, used. Addas, *Quest for the Red Sulfur*, 208, note 87. Also, he was often called Shaykh Wahdat Al-Wujud as well as Sahib Al-Fusus ("Author of the Fusus", his most important work), 278.

66. Quoted in Hirtenstein, *The Unlimited Mercifier*, 25. See Ibn 'Arabi, "Kitaab al-Alif," trans. A. Abadi, *Journal of Muhyiddin Ibn 'Arabi Society*, 111 (1984), 15–40.

67. Quoted in Debra Strickland, *Saracens, Demons and Jews* (Princeton University Press, 2003), 222

68. Maribel Fierro makes this convincing argument in her book of collected articles *The Almohad Revolution*.

69. The Moroccan scholar Halima Ferhat discussed this burst of mysticism in *Le Maghrib aux XII et XIII siècles, les siècles de foi* (Casablanca, 1993). Also, on the relationship between Almohadism and the subsequent rise of Sufism see the work of Vincent Cornell, *Realm of the Saint: Power and Authority in Moroccan Sufism* (University of Texas Press, 1998).

70. Incidentally, the Wahhabis of Saudi Arabia also call themselves "al-Muwah-hidin" or "Almohads" as it would be in Hispanicized form. That said, their doctrine has fundamental differences.

71. Hirtenstein, *The Unlimited Mercifier*.

72. Fabio López Lázaro, "The Rise and Global Significance of the First 'West': The Medieval Islamic Maghrib," *Journal of World History*, 24/2 (June 2013), 259–307.

73. Trans. Peter Lewis (Harvard University Press, 2015).

74. Robert Bartlett, *Trial by Fire and Water: The Medieval Judicial Ordeal* (Oxford University Press, 1989).

75. Hyam Maccoby, *Judaism on Trial, Jewish Christian Disputations in the Middle Ages* (including text of disputation) (Littman, 1993); Nina Caputo, *Nahmanides in Medieval Catalonia, History, Community and Messianism* (University of Notre Dame Press, 2007).

76. James Waltz, "Muhammad and the Muslims in St. Thomas Aquinas," *The Muslim World*, 66/2 (April 1976), 81–95.

77. Saint Thomas Aquinas, "Reasons for the Faith Against Muslim Objections to the Cantor of Antioch," trans. Joseph Kenney, *Islamochristiana*, 22 (1996), 31–52.

78. This is mentioned in the poems of Ibn Ezra's lament at the Almohad conquest in Al-Andalus and in other sources: H. Schirmann, *New Hebrew Poems from the Genizah* (Jerusalem, 1965); J. M. Toledano, "Documents from manuscripts," *Hebrew Union College Annual*, 4 (1927), 449–58.

79. Ramon Lulle, *Disputatio Raymundi christiani et Hamar saraceni* (Pisa, 1308).

80. Daniel, *Islam and the West*, 141.

81. Ibid. 143.

82. *Risala fi Fadl al-Andalus (Elogio del Islam Español)*, trans. Emilio García Gómez (Madrid, 1934).

83. The anonymous *Mafakhir al Barbar*, ed. Lévi-Provençal (Rabat, 1934).

84. Anthony Bonner (trans. and ed.), *Ramon Lull: A Contemporary Life*, (Tamesis Books, 2010).

85. Statue of the Council of Vienne in "Chartulary of the University of Paris," trans. L. Thorndike, *University Records and Life in the Middle Ages* (Columbia University Press, 1975), 149–50.

86. Olivia R. Constable, "Regulating Religious Noise: The Council of Vienne, the Mosque Call and Muslim Pilgrimage in the Late Medieval Mediterranean World," *Medieval Encounters*, 16/1 (2010), 64–95.

87. Fernand Braudel, *The Mediterranean World in the Age of Philip II*, vol. II (University of California Press, 1995), 1244.

88. Sahih Muslim, 33, 6426. The next hadith in the collecton (34) smiliarly says, "It is reported on the authority of Abu Mu'awiya that (the Holy Prophet)

said: Every new-born babe is born on the millat (of Islam and he) remains on this until his tongue is enabled to express himself." See http://www.iupui. edu/~msaiupui/033.smt.html.

89. Infant baptism was practiced as early as the writing of the letters of the Corinthians when whole households were baptised despite the infant not being aware of the meaning or content of the faith. 1 Corinthians 1: 16.

90. Peter Brown, *The Cult of the Saints* (University of Chicago Press, 1982).

91. Mas Latrie, *Relations et Commerce de l'Afrique Septentrionale avec les Nations Chrétiennes* (Paris, 1886).

92. Ibid. ii.

93. Ibid. v.

94. Gian Novati, *L'Africa d'Italia* (Carrocci, 2011).

95. Abdullah Laroui, *L'Histoire du Maghreb: un Essai de Synthèse* (Casablanca, 1995).

96. Edward Said, *Orientalism* (Pantheon Books, 1978), 40.

97. William H. Sewell, *Logics of History: Social Theory and Social Transformation* (University of Chicago Press, 1995), 125.

98. Abu-Lughod, *Before European Hegemony*, 216.

99. Mike Carr, "Crossing Boundaries in the Mediterranean: Papal Trade Licences form the Registra supplicationum of Pope Clement VI (1342–52)," *Journal of Medieval History*, 41/1 (2015), 107–29. On the papal embargo more generally, see Stefan Stantchev, *Spiritual Rationality: Papal Embargo as Cultural Practice* (Oxford University Press, 2014).

100. Charles-Emmanuel Dufourcq, *L'Espagne catalane et le Maghrib aux XII et XIV siècles* (Paris, 1966), 475.

101. Bernard Doumerc, *Venise et l'émirat hafside de Tunis (1231–1535)* (Paris, 1999), 21.

102. Quoted in Gies and Gies, *Merchants and Moneymen*, 36.

103. Adam Sabra, *Poverty and Charity in Medieval Islam* (Cambridge University Press, 2006).

104. Quoted in Daniel, *Islam and the West*, 140.

105. Reginald of Durham, "Life of St. Godric," trans. and ed. G. C. Coulton, *Social Life in Britain* (Cambridge University Press, 1918), 415–20.

Chapter 2

1. Ramon Davis (trans.), *The Lives of the Ninth-Century Popes (Liber Pontificalis)* (Liverpool University Press, 1995), 119.

2. Barbara Kreutz, *Before the Normans: Southern Italy in the Ninth and Tenth Centuries* (University of Pennsylvania Press, 2011).

3. Giousè Musca, *L'emirato di Bari, 847–871* (Dedalo, 1967).

4. Al-Bakri, *Description de l'Afrique septentrionale*, 2nd edn, trans. William MacGuckin de Slane (Algiers, 1913), 84. Scholars are uncertain how long this Coptic community lasted although there have been suggestions it remained for several centuries. On the question of the Christian community and its make up, see C. Courtois, "Grégoire VII et l'Afrique du Nord," *Revue Historique* (1945), 97–122, 193–226; H. H. Abdul Wahab, "Coup d'oeil général sur les apports ethniques étrangers en Tunisie," *Revue Tunisienne* (1917), 305–16.

5. Christian Capelli, *et al.* "Moors and Saracens in Europe: estimating the medieval North African male legacy in southern Europe," *European Journal of Human Genetics*, 17 (2009), 848–52.

6. Fred Donner, *Muhammad and the Believers* (Harvard University Press, 2012).

7. Robert Lopez, "East and West in the Early Middle Ages," in Alfred Havighurst (ed.), *The Pirenne Thesis, Analysis, Critcism and Revision* (DC Heath and Company, 1958), 75.

8. John Tolan, G. Veinstein and H. Laurens, *Europe and the Islamic World: A History* (Princeton University Press, 2013), 35.

9. Lopez, "East and West," 75.

10. Michele Amari, *I Diplomi Arabi del R. Archivio Fiorentino* (Florence, 1867), xiii.

11. Ferdinand Gregorovius, *History of the City of Rome in the Middle Ages*, vol. III, trans. A. Hamilton (G. Bell & Sons, 1903), 79.

12. Ibid. 87.

13. Ibid. 75.

14. Ibid. 87.

15. Edward Gibbon, *History of the Decline and Fall of the Roman Empire*, vol. 6 (London, 1902), 40.

16. The description of the chronicler as a "higher up" in the curia was according to Ramon Davis who translated *Liber Pontificalis*, 99.

17. *Liber Pontificalis*, 113.

18. John Osborne, "The Portrait of Pope Leo IV in San Clemente, Rome: A Re-Examination of the So-Called 'Square' Nimbus, in Medieval Art," *Papers of the British School at Rome*, 47 (1979), 58–65, 58.

19. Ibid. 64.

20. *Liber Pontificalis*, 124.

21. Edward Gibbon, *Decline and Fall of the Roman Empire*, vol. IX (Defau & Co., 1907).

22. Gregorovius, *History of the City of Rome*, vol. III, 92.

23. Interesting to note here a reference to "pagans" not, Muslim Saracens. *Liber Pontificalis*, 132.

24. The "worthless people," condemned for sexual depravity in the Old Testament. 1 Samuel 1: 16, 2 Corinthians 6: 15.

25. *Liber Pontificalis*, 132–3.

26. Ibid. 133.

27. Ibid. 133; Psalm 134: 7.

28. *Liber Pontificalis*, 134.

29. Gregorovius, *History of the City of Rome*, vol. III, 94–5.

30. Amari, *I Diplomi Arabi*, xiii.

31. Michele Amari's reading of Muratori's history of Italy rated this slave market in Rome as "speculation." However, there was evidence for trade in slaves carried out by Naples, Venice and Amalfi with North Africa. *I Diplomi Arabi*, xiv.

32. For more on the legacy of Leo, see Klaus Herbers, *Leo IV und das Papsttum in der Mitte des 9 Jahrhunderts* (Anton Hiersemann, 1996).

33. The North African-influenced mosaic design on the cover dates from the medieval period in the Amalfi Cathedral. W. Heyd, *Geschitchte des Levantehandels im Mittelalter*, vol. I (Stuttgart, 1879), 104.

34. *Liber Pontificalis*, 114

35. *Liber Pontificalis*, 117.

36. S. D. Goitein, *Letters of Medieval Jewish Traders* (Princeton University Press, 1973), 10.

37. See, for instance, their "Coptic" Egyptian "Clavus" dated to the eighth century. http://www.museuepiscopalvic.com/coleccions_more.asp?id=163&s=7&r= (accessed March 17, 2015).

38. This is found in the National Library of France. Amari, *I Diplomi Arabi*, xiii.

39. G. A. Knott, "The Historical Sources of Fierabras", *The Modern Language Review*, 52/4 (1957), 504–9.

40. Probably painted by his assistant Guilo Romano in the Palazzo Pontifici (Papal Palace), in the "Room of the Great Fire of the Borgo."

41. *Essai sur le Moeurs*, vol. 1, chapter XVIII. Quoted in J. Darras, *A General History of the Catholic Church*, vol. II (New York, 1866), 477.

42. Quoted in Lewis Coser, *The Functions of Social Conflict* (The Free Press, 1956), 87.

43. On the role and impact of Byzantine and Greek learning in the writing of Mediterranean history see the work of Maria Mavroudi, including her article, "Translations from Greek into Arabic and Latin during the Middle Ages: Searching for the Classical Tradition," *Speculum*, 90/1 (January 2015).

44. Michael Brett, "Muslim justice under infidel rule: The Normans in Ifriqiya," in *Ibn Khaldun and the Medieval Maghrib*, chap. XIII (Ashgate, 1999).

45. Al-Nuwayri's biography of George of Antioch has been a fruitful source for the period. See *Nihayat al-Arab fi funun al-Adab*, vols. I–XXXI, ed. S. 'Abd Al-Wahhab (Cairo, 1923–92), vol. XIII starting p. 319. Joshua Birk, "From Borderlands to Borderlines: Narrating the Past of Twelfth Century Sicily," in James P. Heifers (ed.), *Multicultural Europe and Cultural Exchange in the Middle Ages and Renaissance* (Brepols Press, 2005), 9–31; Jeremy Johns, *Arabic Administration in Norman Sicily, The Royal Diwan* (Cambridge University Press, 2002).

46. Michael Brett, "Muslim Justice".

47. Edrisi (Al-Idrisi), *Description de l'Afrique et de l'Espagne*, ed. and trans. R. Dozy and M. J. de Goeje (Leiden, 1866), 136.

48. Passage translated in Karla Mallette, *The Kingdom of Sicily, 1100–1250: A Literary History* (University of Pennsylvania Press, 2005), 147–8. See Edrisi, *Description*.

49. Edgar Laird, "Robert Grosseteste, Albumasar, and Medieval Tidal Theory," *Isis*, 81/4 (1990), 684–94.

50. Jeremy Johns, *Arabic Administration in Norman Sicily, The Royal Diwan* (Cambridge University Press, 2002).

51. Norman Daniel, *Islam and the West, The Making of an Image* (Oneworld Publications, 2009), 139.

52. Brett Whalen, "Corresponding with Infidels: Rome, the Almohads and the Christians of Thirteenth Century Morocco," *Journal of Medieval and Early Modern Studies*, 41/3 (Fall 2011), 487–513.

53. There is a great deal of controversy about the authenticity of Constantine's biography and the originality of his writings. See Charles Burnett and Danielle Jacquart (eds.), *Constantine the African and 'Ali ibn al Abbas al Magusi* (Brill, 1994).

54. For the biography by Petrus Diaconus and a list of the works of Constantine the African, see Herbert Bloch, *Monte Cassino in the Middle Ages,* vol. 1 (Harvard University Press, 1986), 127–34.

55. T. Lewicki, "Une Langue Romane oubliée de l'Afrique du Nord", *Rocznik orientalistyczny*, 17 (1951–2), 415–80.

56. There have been many recent advances in the study of the life of Constantine; see Francis Newton, "Constantine the African and Montecassino: New Elements and the Text of the Isagoge," in Burnett and Jacquart (eds.), *Constantine the African*, 16–47.

57. Patricia Skinner, "Amalfitans in the Caliphate of Cordoba – Or Not?," *Al-Masaq*, 24/2 (2012), 125–38.

58. It is intriguing that the first biographical reference to Al-Majusi came from a Western Mediterranean source, the biographer Sa'id Al-Andalusi who wrote about him from Toledo in 1068. Francoise Micheau, "Ali ibn Abbas Al-Magusi et son Milieu", in Burnett and Jacquart (eds.), *Constantine the African*, 1.

59. G. Bos, *Ibn al-Jazzar on Fevers, a Critical edition of 'Zad al-musafir wa-qut al hadir*, book 7 (Wellcome Asian Series, 2000).

Chapter 3

1. G. Regn and B. Huss, "Petrarch's Rome: The History of the *Africa* and the Renaissance Project," *Modern Language Notes (Italian Edition)*, 124/1 (January 2009), 86–102.

2. Nicola Festa's edition (Italian trans. *L'Africa* (Florence, 1926)). See Thomas Bergin and Alice Wilson (trans.), *Petrarch's Africa* (Yale University Press, 1977), xiv.

3. Edrisi (Al-Idrisi), *Description de l'Afrique et de l'Espagne*, ed. and trans. R. Dozy and M. J. de Goeje (Leiden, 1866), 131–2. Al-Bakri, *Description de l'Afrique septentrionale*, 2nd edn, trans. William MacGuckin de Slane (Algiers, 1913), 93.

4. On the validity of the legend that Romans ploughed salt into the fields around Carthage, see R. T. Ridley, "To be taken with a pinch of salt: the destruction of Carthage," *Classical Philology*, 81 (1986), 140–6 and P. J. Visonà, "Passing the salt. On the destruction of Carthage again," *Classical Philology*, 83 (1988), 41–2.

5. On Genseric, the Vandals and the late Roman Empire, see Walter Goffart, *Barbarians and Romans A.D. 418–584: The Techniques of Accommodation* (Princeton University Press, 1980).

6. Ibn abi Dinar, *Kitab al-Mu'nis fi akhbar ifriqiya wa Tunis* [1869, p. 13], trans. J. Magnin, *Revue de l'Institut des Belles Lettres Arabes*, 2 (1952), 166.

7. Al-Bakri, *Description*, 83–4.

8. Ibn Khaldun, *(Muqaddimah) Le Livre des Exemples*, trans. A. Cheddadi (Paris, 2002), 286–7.

9. C. Fenwick, "From Africa to Ifriqiya: Settlement and Society in Early Medieval North Africa (650–800)," *Al-Masaq*, 25/1 (2013), 9–33.

10. Henri Pirenne, *Mohammed and Charlemagne* (Routledge, 2008 [originally published 1939]), 152.

11. Philip Hitti (trans.), *(Al-Baladhuri) The Origins of the Islamic State, Kitab Futuh al Buldan*, vol. 1 (Columbia University, 1916), 371.

12. For more on Berber reaction to conquest, see Elizabeth Savage, *A Gateway to Hell, A Gateway to Paradise: The North African Response to the Arab Conquest* (Darwin Press, 1997).

13. On Tahert and Ibadis in North Africa, see the excellent work of Adam Gaiser, *Muslims, Scholars and Soldiers: the Origins and Elaborations of Ibadi Imamate Traditions* (Oxford University Press, 2010). For the quote on Carthage-Tunis, see E. F. Gautier, *Genseric, roi des Vandales* (Paris, 1935), 215. Quoted in Paul Sebag, *Tunis: histoire d'une Ville* (Paris, 1998), 76.

14. Al-Bakri, *Description*, 80.

15. Ibid. 84.

16. Ibid. 84.

17. Hitti (trans.), *The Origins of the Islamic State.*

18. Ibn Khaldun, *(Muqaddimah) Le Livre des Exemples*, 563.

19. Ibid. 564.

29. Ibid. 563.

21. For a fairly thorough list of these raids, see Paul Sebag, "Les Expéditions Maritimes arabes du VIII siècle," *Les Cahiers de Tunisie*, 8/31 (1960), 73–82.

22. The history of these expeditions comes from several Arab historians including Al-Maqrizi, Ibn Tagribardi, Al-Nuwaryi, Ibn Al-'Idari, Ibn 'Abd Al-Hakam, Ibn Khaldun and Ibn Al-Athir. M. Amari compiled mentions of raids on Siciliy and the Western Mediterranean found in the writings of these historians in his monumental *Storia des Musulmani di Sicilia*, 3 vols. (Italy, 1854).

23. Sebag, "Les Expéditions," 74–6.

24. Al-Bakri, *Description*, 85.

25. For an overview of the Muslim conquest of Sicily, see Alex Metcalfe, *A History of Muslim Sicily* (Edinburgh University Press, 2009).

26. Al-Ya'qubi, *Les pays*, trans. G. Wiet (Cairo, 1937), 210.

27. Sebag, *Tunis: Historie d'une Ville*, 87.

28. Shafique Virani, *The Ismailis in the Middle Ages: A History of Survival, a Search for Salvation* (Oxford University Press, 2007), 47.

29. Al-Bakri, *Description*, 87.

30. Edrisi (Al-Idrisi), *Description*, 130.

31. S. D. Goitein, *Letters of Medieval Jewish Traders* (Princeton University Press, 1973), 18.

32. Ibid., 45. Goitein believed that John may have originated from Tunisia and that he was an Arabic-speaking Christian.

33. On Arabic or Berber speaking Christians, see H. R. Idris, *La Berberie orientale sous les Zirides* (Paris, 1962), 757–64.

34. H. R. Idris, "Fêtes chrétiennes célébrées en Ifrîqiya à l'époque zîrîde", *Revue Africaine*, 440–1 (1954), 261–76, 269.

35. J. Berque, "Du nouveau sur les Banu Hilal," *Studia Islamica*, 36 (1972), 99–111.

36. Marianne Barrucand and M. Rammah (eds. A. Shalem and J. Van-Stäevel), "Sabra al Mansuriyya and her Neighbors during the First half of the Eleventh Century", *Muqarnas*, 26 (2009), 349–76.

37. G. Marçais, *Les Arabes en Berbérie* (Paris, 1913). His worked has been critiqued by J. Poncet, "Le mythe de la catastrophe hilalienne", *Annales ESC*, 22 (1967), 1099–120.

38. It remains a major oral tradition in Egypt to this day. Dwight Reynolds at the University of Santa Barbara set up a digital archive: see http://www.siratbanihilal.ucsb.edu/start-0.

39. L. Saada, *La Geste hilalienne* (Gallimard, 1985).

40. Michael Brett, "The military interest of the battle of Haydaran," in V. J. Parry and M. E. Yapp (eds.), *War, Technology and Society in the Middle East* (Oxford University Press, 1975).

41. Sebag, *Tunis: Historie d'une Ville*, 90.

42. H. E. J. Cowdrey, "The Mahdia Campaign of 1087," *English Historical Review*, 92 (1977), 1–30, 14.

43. Ibid. 29, footnote 67.

44. Edrisi, *Description*, 126–8.

45. Karen Matthews, "Other People's Dishes: Islamic Bacini on Eleventh-Century Churches in Pisa," *Gesta*, 53/1 (2014), 5–23.

46. The National Museum of San Matteo in Pisa has preserved many of these magnicificent Bacini and there remain some disputes about the precise origins of some. There remains some debate about the full meaning of these plates in the context of Pisan culture and politics. Were they triumphalist or a sign of commercial wealth? Or both? See Matthews, "Other People's Dishes," 5–23.

47. Cowdrey, "The Mahdia Campaign of 1087," contains the original Latin poem, 24.

48. M. Amari, *I Diplomi Arabi del R. Archivio Fiorentino* (Florence, 1867), xxvi.

49. Edrisi (Al-Idrisi), *Description*, 149.

50. Max Weber, *On Charisma and Institution Building*, ed. S. Eisenstadt (University of Chicago Press, 1968).

51. R. Brunschvig, *La Berbérie Orientale Sous les Hafsides*, vol. 1 (Paris, 1982), 338.

52. Quoted in Brunschvig, *La Berbérie Orientale*, vol. 2, 412.

53. Brunschvig, *La Berbérie orientale*, vol. 1, 342.

54. Ibid. vol. 1, 343, 344.

55. Ibid. vol. 1, 46–7. Louis Massignon, "'Ibn Sab'in et la conspiration anti-hallegienne' en Andalousie et en Orient au XIIIe s.," in *Études d'orientalisme dédiées à la mémoire de Lévi-Provençal*, vol. II (Paris, 1962), 661–81.

56. D. M. Dunlop, "Relations between Norway and the Maghrib in the 7th/13th Century," Bravmann Memorial Volume, *Journal of the Ancient Near Eastern Society*, 11 (1979), 41–4.

57. Steven Runciman, *The Sicilian Vespers: A History of the Mediterranean World in the Later Thirteenth Century* (Cambridge University Press, 1992).

58. Norman Daniel, *Islam and the West, The Making of an Image* (Oneworld Publications, 2009),142.

59. On Al-'Abdary's description of Tunis, see M. Cherbonneau (trans.), "La Ville de Tunis à la Fin du XIIe S.," *Revue Tunisienne* (1905), 365–8.

60. Brunschvig, *La Berbérie Orientale*, vol. 1, 354.

61. Cherbonneau (trans.), "La Ville de Tunis, 365–8.

62. Michael Lower, "Ibn al-Lihyani: Sultan of Tunis and Would-be Christian Convert (1311–18)," *Mediterranean Historical Review*, 24/1 (2009), 17–27.

63. On the Jewish minority under the Hafsids, see Brunschvig, *La Berbérie Orientale*, vol. 1, 402–14.

64. Ibid. vol. 1, 353–6.

Chapter 4

1. Cola Franzen (trans.), *Poems of Arab Andalusia* (City Lights Books, 2001), 90–1.

2. On the topic of inter-faith brides and concubines in Al-Andalus, see Simon Barton, *Conquerors, Brides and Concubines* (University of Pennsylvania Press, 2015).

3. Quoted in R. Brunschvig, *La Tunisie dans Le Haut Moyen Âge* (Cairo, 1948), 22.

4. Al-Makkari [Al-Maqqari], *The History of the Mohammedan Dynasties in Spain*, vol. 1, trans. P. de Gayangos (Routledge, 2002), 58.

5. Quoted in Louis Crompton, *Homosexuality and Civilization* (Harvard University Press, 2003), 187.

6. "Many common people avoided growing orange trees around their house on account of this ominous statement." But this was not the meaning intended, according to Ibn Khaldun. Rather, gardens and irrigation, such as would soon appear in Marrakech, would lead to the luxuries of a sendentary lifestyle. *Muqaddimah*, trans. F. Rosenthal (Princeton University Press, 1967), 287.

7. *Hulal al Mawshiyya*. There has been some speculation that the author was Ibn Zamrak. With slight modifications, I use the translation of this text by J. F. P. Hopkins: *Corpus of Early Arabic Sources for West African History*, ed. N. Levtzion (Markus Wiener, 2000), 311.

8. P. Hitti (trans.), *(Al-Baladhuri) The Origins of the Islamic State, Kitab Futuh al Buldan*, vol. 1 (Columbia University, 1916), 360–1.

9. The geographer Al-Bakri (d. 1074) described Tadmakka as "Mecca-like." He did not, however, identify the Lamtuna so explicitly as a lost Arab tribe. Hopkins (trans.), *Corpus of Early Arabic Sources*, 85.

10. Ibn Tumart, *Le Livre de Mohammed Ibn Toumert*, ed. I. Goldziher (Algiers, 1903), 390–1.

11. Ibn Tumart's successor, the Caliph 'Abd Al-Mu'min would eventually conquer Marrakech, capital of the Almoravids, in 1147, securing most of North Africa and Al-Andalus by AD 1160. Later, Arab opponents of the Almohads such as Ibn Al-Athir and the writer of the *Hulal al Mawshiyya* rejected Ibn Tumart's propaganda, reifying the Lamtuna as a lost Arab tribe. In an interesting contrast to both the account of Ibn Tumart and the accounts of sources sympathetic to the Almoravids, Ibn Hawqal, providing one of earliest accounts of the mouth veil in the tenth century, described a much more mundane and summary explantion: they wore the mouth veil because they found the mouth shameful.

12. A Bourgeot, "Le Costume Masculin des Kel Ahaggar," *Lybica*, 17 (1968), 355–76, 355.

13. Hopkins (trans.), *Corpus of Early Arabic Sources*, 75–6.

14. Ibid. 75–6.

15. Other geographers hostile toward the Saharans went further. The *Kitab al-Istibsar*, an update of Al-Bakri's geography written in AD 1190 by an anonymous author who was almost certainly sympathetic to the Almohad cause, described the allegedly loose women of the Saharan town of Awdagust.

16. Ibn Tumart, *Le Livre*, 258–66.

17. Ibid. 259.

18. *Histoire des Berbères*, vol. 2, 162.

19. Gaston Deverdun, *Marrakech: Des Origines a 1912*, vol. 1 (Rabat, 1959), 52.

20. *Bayan Almoravide*, f. 8, quoted in Deverdun, *Marrakech*, 52. Rivers, especially rivers in the desert of the nomads, could easily becoming flooded torrents and wash away any standing structure.

21. For a discussion of the vital importance of the gold trade in North African history, see Yves Lacoste, "General Characteristics and Fundamental Structures of Mediaeval North African Society," *Economy and Society*, 3 (1974), 1–17. Ibn Hawqal (10th century) provided the account of the shift in gold trade in *Surat al-Ard*, ed. J. H. Kramers (Brill, 1967).

22. A survey of early Almoravid history is found in Bosch Vilá, *Los Almorávides* (Universidad de Granada, 1990). Also, see Vincent Lagardère, *Les Almoravides Jusqu'au règne de Yusuf B. Tasfin (1039–1106)* (L'Harmattan, 1989).

23. Paul Wheatly defined the *ribat* as "a fortified barracks where tribesmen in the holy war kept post for the defense of Islam and often occupied themselves with religious devotions between campaigns." This adequately described the Almoravid *ribat* system, especially the *ribat* at Tidra. Sfax and Tripoli were famous cities founded as *ribatat*: Paul Wheatly, *The Places Where Men Pray Together* (University of Chicago Press, 2001) 53. See also, Georges Marçais, "Note sur les ribats en Berbèrie," in *Mélanges René Basset*, vol. 2 (Leoux, 1925), 395–430.

24. In the *Muqaddimah*, Ibn Khaldun suggested that "there are few cities and towns in the Maghrib" and that the reason for this was the Berbers were "firmly rooted" in nomadic and tribal life: vol. 2 (1967), 267.

25. For more on Sijilmasa and Almoravid trade during this period, see Ronald Messier and James Miller, *The Last Civilized Place: Sijilmasa and its Saharan Destiny* (University of Texas Press, 2015).

26. Edrisi (Al-Idrisi), *Description*, 66 in text, 76 in French.

27. Ibid. 66 in text, 76 in French.

28. *Bayan Almoravide*, f. 8, quoted in Deverdun, *Marrakech*.

29. For a complete account of the astonishing rise of the Almoravids from the desert, see Muhammad Hajji, "La salida de los Almoravides del desierto," in M. L. Cavero (trans) *Mauritania y España: Una Historia Común* (El Legardo Andalusi, 2003), 17–37. Also, the first chapters of Lagardère, *Les Almoravides* and Ron Messier, *The Almoravids and the Meanings of Jihad* (Praeger, 2010).

30. I. S. Allouche (ed.), *Chronique Anonyme* (Arabic text) (Rabat, 1939).

31. Deverdun speculated that it may have been inspired by the palace mosque built at Sijilmasa: *Marrakech*, 56–9. Recent research, however, has shown that the

palace and the mosque were probably separate. See P. Buresi and M. Ghouirgate, *Histore du Maghreb Médiéval* (Armand Colin, 2013).

32. Ibn 'Abdun, in his book written for an Almoravid prince, wrote with a combination of panegyric and subtle instruction, "the prince constitutes the axis of the social group, the center of a circumfrence around which is formed a harmonious line, perfect and without default . . ." The *qasr al-hajar* would represent the sultan's role as the axis of society. See Évariste Lévi-Provençal, *Séville Musulmane au Début du XII Siècle: Le Traité d'Ibn 'Abdun* (Librairie Orientale et Américaine, 1947), 5.

33. Probably in a bid for more power as a founding Almoravid tribe.

34. *Bayan Almoravide*, quoted in Deverdun, *Marrakech*, 56.

35. Several agree to the date 1070, although there is some wide variation.

36. Edrisi (Al-Idrisi), *Description de l'Afrique et de l'Espagne*, ed. and trans. R. Dozy and M. J. de Goeje (Leiden, 1866), 63.

37. He was also concerned with commercial development, building a bridge over the wadi Tansift, and allowing constant contact with the North during the winter months.

38. Yasser Tabbaa, "Andalusian Roots and Abbasid Homage in the Qubbat al-Barudiyyin in Marrkech," *Muqarnas*, 25 (2008), 133–46.

39. Despite being a legal expert himself, Ibn Khaldun believed too much dependency on a class of complicated legal manuals could sap a system of its power. Commenting on the rise and fall of dynasties like the Almoravids, Ibn Khaldun wrote an intriguing chapter: "the reliance of sedentary people upon laws destroys their fortitude and power of resistance." This does not apply, of course to following religious laws and the Qur'an, which were followed by "self-restraint." It was only after the "religious law became a branch of learning and a craft to be acquired through instruction and learning" that the law caused people to become dependent and to loose the vigor of their own faith. Ibn Khaldun seemed to criticize those Maliki jurists who had expanded the law to include almost every aspect of daily life, creating "dependency" and a "lack of fortitude." The laws compromised the fighting spirit of the people, disarming them and weakening them. The semi-nomadic or nomadic tribes outside of the governmental legal system, in contrast, remained armed, more free and self-sufficient. They were on a plane roughly equal (at least hypothetically) to their chiefs and rulers. *Muqaddimah*, vol. 1 (1967), 258–61.

40. Edrisi, *Description*, 70 in text, 80 in French. Writing in the context of Almoravid Seville, Ibn 'Abdun similarly complained about the unjust and illicit tax

collectors of the markets. "They have neither fear, nor religion, nor piety. They are concerned with nothing but the search for worldly advantage." A similarly abusive tax collecting system probably prevailed in Marrakech as well. See Lévi-Provençal, *Séville Musulmane*, 10.

41. There are several indications that women had a high status in Almoravid religion; they maintained a certain status in Lamtuna tribal society and went unveiled.

42. Oleg Grabar, "The Architecture of the Middle Eastern City from Past to Present: The Case of the Mosque," in Ira Lapidus (ed.), *Middle Eastern Cities*, (University of California Press, 1969), 26–46.

43. Sura 72: 17.

44. Georges Marçais, "Considerations sur les Villes Musulmanes et Notamment sur le Role du Mohtasib," *Recueils de la Société Jean Bodin* (1954), 249–62.

45. Ibn Khaldun, *Muqqadimah*, vol. 1, 449–50.

46. Grabar, "The Architecture", 42. Also, see von Grunebaum, *Medieval Islam: A Study in Cultural Orientation* (University of Chicago Press, 1953) for a discussion of what von Grunebaum considered the intellectual decline in the medieval period with the development of the *'ulama* as defensive preservers of Islamic doctrine. Certainly von Grunebaum goes too far in attributing a "decline" in Islamic cities solely to the jurists.

47. Robert Brunschvig's article, "Urbanisme Médiéval et Droit Musulman" in *Revue des Études Islamiques*, XV (1947), 127–55, explained the important influence of Islamic jurists on urban life. For an account of the wide-ranging laws, the influence of Maliki jurists in the 10th and 11th centuries and their involvement in the administration of the city in the Islamic Occident, see Maribel Fierro, "El derecho maliki en al-Andalus: siglos VIII–XI," *Al-Qantara*, XII (1991), 119–32, and Jean-Pierre van Staevel, "Prévoir, Juguler, Batir," *Cuadernos de Madinat al-Zahra'*, 5 (2004), 31–52. See his explication of Ibn Sahl (d. 1093) who wrote a compendium of Maliki law called the *Ahkam al-Kubra*. For a translation of the jurist Al-Wansharisi's work on magisterial law, see H. Bruno and M. Gaudefroy-Demombynes, *Le Livre des Magistratures d'el-Wancherisi* (Rabat, 1937).

48. Hugh Kennedy, *The Prophet and the Age of the Caliphs* (Longman, 2004), provided a good summary of these developments. It is worth quoting Fazlur Rahman's masterful discussion of the rise of legal commentaries in the medieval period. Rahman was himself a highly respected and learned Islamic scholar in modern Pakistan before his exile to the United States. "The custom of writing systematic commentaries was, in the beginning, combined with original works

... But, later, the habit developed of writing commentaries upon commentaries until the original works, the subjects of commentaries, were almost completely forgotten. Certain works of dogmatic theology found more than half a dozen layers of commentaries. Still later commentary degenerated into mere marginal notes, usually devoted to supergicial quibbles and verbal disputes," Rahman, *Islam* (University of Chicago Press, 1979), 189.

49. Unlike the major urban centers of the East like Baghdad or Aleppo, Marrakech was not divided into communities according to legal school, as described by Ira Lapidus, *Muslim Cities in the Later Middle Ages* (Harvard University Press, 1967). The one and only school was the Almoravid Maliki school.

50. Deverdun provided examples of this narrow legalism practiced by the Almoravid Maliki jurists. He wrote, "The history of the Almoravids began with the rigid discipline of the military convent (*ribat*) but ended with the general corruption of Marrakech . . . they [the Maliki jurists] had fallen into a formalism without heart or spirit . . ." *Marrakech*, 129.

51. Clifford Geertz, *Islam Observed* (University of Chicago Press, 1968), 7–8.

52. Deverdun believed the walls represented the beginning of a permanent separation between city and countryside in North African history. I believe that the walls only represented a momentary gap between the city and its surroundings, a gap that would be remedied with each successive dynasty. It is worth quoting Deverdun directly, "The walls of Marrakech played a symbolic role, faced with the increasingly aggressive Almohads, they concentrated their riches and arts in this immense polygon of dried mud. This was a decisive step: the ancient camp open to all had become a closed city of Islam." *Marrakech*, 117.

53. I want to thank Amira Bennison for encouraging me to think differently about this point. Also, see Camilo Gómes-Rivas, *Law and the Islamization of Morocco under the Almoravids* (Brill, 2015), for the point of view that Marrakech was not so isolated from the countryside. In fact, this may have simply been Almohad doctrine. Nonetheless, Marrakech was, quite certainly, isolating the Atlas Mountain tribes from their traditional sources of revenue by building fortresses and imposing new taxation regimes.

54. For more on the mellah, or Jewish community, in Marrakech, see Emily Gottreich's fascinating book *The Mellah of Marrakech: Jewish and Muslim Space in Morocco's Red City* (Indiana University Press, 2006).

55. Edrisi (Al-Idrisi), *Description*, 70 in text, 80 in French.

56. Emily Gottreich, "On the Origins of the Mellah of Marrakesh," *International Journal of Middle Eastern Studies*, 35/2 (2003), 287–305.

57. See Jane S. Gerber, *Jewish Society in Fez, 1450–1700: Studies in Communal and Economic Life* (Brill, 1980), 14. Also, L. Massignon, "L'Interdit Corporatif à l'encontre des Juifs islamisés à Fés," *Révue du Monde Musulman*, 58 (1924), 221–4.

58. 'Abd Al-Wahid Al-Merrakechi, *Histoire des Almohades*, trans. E. Fagnan (Algiers, 1893), 264.

59. Ibid. 264.

60. Al-Baidhaq, in Lévi-Provençal, *Documents Inédits*, 109.

61. Deverdun, *Marrakech*, 109.

62. See Sura 3: 120. The battle of Uhud was in 625 (3 H), the Banu Salamah and Banu Haarithah almost lost heart: Sura 3: 122. Al-Baidhaq certainly knew of this battle when he described the battle of Al-Buhayra: Lévi-Provençal, *Documents Inédits*, 109.

63. "Dynasties have a natural life span like individuals," *Muqaddimah*, vol. 1 (1967), 343–7.

64. Jared Diamond, *Collapse: How Societies Choose to Fail or Succeed* (Viking Penguin, 2005). Felipe Fernández-Armesto made a similar argument in *Civilizations: Culture, Ambition and the Transformation of Nature* (Touchstone, 2001). See especially his chapter on the highland civilizations of the world, 230–71. The problem with these environmental theses is that they seem to completely ignore human will and the non-determinism of culture.

65. *A'azz ma Yutlab*, Ibn Tumart, *Le Livre*, 260.

66. Ibid. 259.

67. Ibn Khaldun, *Muqaddimah*, vol. 1 (1967), 257.

68. Ibid. vol. 1, 345.

69. "Among the things that corrupt sedentary culture, there is the disposition toward pleasures and indulgence in them, because of the great luxury that prevails. It leads to diversification of the desires of the belly for pleasureable food and drink. This is followed by diversification of the pleasures of sex through the various ways of sexual intercourse such as adultery and homosexuality. It may come about indirectly, through the confusion concerning one's descent caused by adultery. Nobody knows his own son, since he is illegitimate . . . The natural compassion a man feels for his children and his feeling of responsibility for them is lost. Or, the destruction of the human race [in the city] may come about directly, as is the case with homosexuality." Ibn Khaldun, *Muqadddimah*, trans. Rosenthal, vol. 2, 296.

70. Ibn Khaldun described how Ibn Tumart reprimanded Sura, the sister of 'Ali bin Yusuf. *Histoire des Berbères*, vol. 1, 325. "One day he encountered Sura, sister

of this prince, who was going out in public uncovered, as did all the Almoravid women, and, scandalized by this spectacle, he gave her a vigorous reprimand."

71. For further discussions of the role of gender in Islam political thought, see Therese Saliba, Carolyn Allen and Judith A. Howard (eds.), *Gender, Politics and Islam* (University of Chicago Press, 2002).

72. According to Ibn Khaldun, Ibn Tumart's preaching against supposedly non-Islamic taxation was one of the major reasons why the Almohads were successful against the Almoravids. *Histoire des Berbères*, vol. 1, p. 330.

73. Al-Baidhaq, in Lévi-Provençal, *Documents Inédits*.

74. For more on how the Almohads used such as Marrakech and its doors as a monumental statement of their ambitions, see Patrice Cressier's article "Les portes monumentales urbaines almohades: symboles et fonctions," in P. Cressier, M. Fierro and L. Molina (eds.), *Los Almohades Problemas y Perspectivas* (CSIC, 2005),

75. Ibn Khaldun, *Muqaddimah* (1967), 211. Perhaps Ibn Khaldun exaggerated: there was, for example, the famous conquest of the Byzantine fleet by Muslim forces during the Battle of the Masts (655).

Chapter 5

1. Alexander Metcalfe and Mariam Rosser-Owen, "Forgotten Connections? Medieval Material Culture and Exchange in the Central and Western Mediterranean," *Al-Masaq*, 25/1 (2013), 1–8, 5.

2. Madeleine Fletcher, "The anthropological context of Almohad history," *Hespéris-Tamuda* (1988–9), 25–51, 26.

3. The so-called traditionalist view of Andalusi history used is one example of this characteristic rejection of the significance of Islamic empires in Mediterranean history. According to Pierre Guichard's re-reading of Andalusian social history, R. M. Pidal and C. S. Albornoz believed, "the process of Islamisation or Arabisation is to be seen as a superficial phenomenon, affecting only the 'superstructure' of Muslim Spain, whose 'underlying structures' remained fundamentally indigenous." "The Social History of Muslim Spain from the Conquest to the End of the Almohad Régime," in S. K. Jayyusi (ed.), *The Legacy of Muslim Spain* (Brill, 1992), 679–708.

4. Even popular, cinematic representations of the Berbers such as the famous 1961 *El Cid* starring Charlton Heston and Sofia Loren have shown the Berbers as a mass of black-veiled, superstitious fanatics, alien to the urbane and refined Muslims and Christians of Andalusia.

5. I want to thank Amira Bennison for pointing out that Ibn Al-Qitt claimed Arab ancestry, as did Shayqa. Also, see Hugh Kennedy, *Muslim Spain and Portugal: A Political History of Al-Andalus* (Routledge, 2014), 36.

6. See Pierre Guichard, "The Social History of Muslim Spain," in Jayyusi, *The Legacy of Muslim Spain*, 685.

7. María J. Viguera-Molins, "Al-Andalus and the Maghrib (From the fifth/eleventh century to the fall of the Almoravids)," in M. Fierro (ed.), *The New Cambridge History of Islam*, vol. 2 (Cambridge University Press, 2010), 21–47, 30–3.

8. A. Huici Miranda, *Historia Política del Imperio Almohade* (Editora Marroquí, 1957), 156–8.

9. The author visited the Tamegroute madrasa in November 2006.

10. The translation of Ibn Tumart's work by Marc of Toledo is detailed by Madeleine Fletcher in her English translation of the *'aqida* of Ibn Tumart. See O. R. Constable (ed.) *Medieval Iberia: Readings from Christian, Muslim and Jewish Sources* (University of Pennsylvania Press, 1997), 190–7.

11. Ibn abi Zar', trans. A. Huici Miranda, *Rawd al-Qirtas* (J. Nacher, 1964), 118–19.

12. Vincent Cornell, *Realm of the Saint: Power and Authority in Moroccan Sufism* (University of Texas Press, 1998), 97.

13. Georges Marcy, "Les Phrases berberes des documents almohades," *Hespéris*, 14/1 (1932), 61–78.

14. Peter Brown, *The Cult of the Saints* (University of Chicago Press, 1981), 10.

15. Probably because of some confusion over the extent of his sickness, and his being hidden away in his house for up to three years, there are several different dates for his death. Ibn Khaldun, perhaps calculating the time the Mahdi may have been left in the house, claimed the Mahdi died in AH 522 (Hijri date), an early date for his death. Al-Marrakushi, *al-Mu'jib*, claimed that he died in AH 524. Ibn Zar' in *Rawd al-Qirtas* said it was 25 Ramadan AH 524. All the other significant sources and historians, including Ibn Khallikan, give some day in AH 524, usually Ramadan, as the date. For more on these different dates, see note 1 on p. 134 in Lévi-Provençal, *Documents Inédits* (Paris, 1928).

16. Maribel Fierro, "The Almohads and the Hafsids," in M. Fierro (ed.), *The New Cambridge History of Islam*, vol. 2 (Cambridge University Press, 2010), 66–105, 73.

17. Edrisi (Al-Idrisi), *Description de l'Afrique et de l'Espagne*, ed. and trans. R. Dozy and M. J. de Goeje (Leiden, 1866), 74.

18. Ibn Khaldun, *Histoire des Berbères*, vol. 2, trans. William MacGuckin de Slane (Paris, 1925), 53.

19. Cornell, *Realm of the Saint*, 193, a specialist in the history of Sufism in North Africa, discussed the cult of Ibn Tumart upheld by the Saksayuwa Berbers. As he put it, there were "tribally based movements that espoused mahdist beliefs and relied for legitimacy on inspirational or 'revealed' texts . . . [they] regarded Maliki ulama as unbelievers."

20. Indeed, it is fascinating how many remnants of the Almoravid dynasty were left intact after 'Abd Al-Mu'min conquered Marrakech in 1147: the Almoravid Minbar in the Kutubiyya, the Almoravid walls, even the Almoravid Qubba near the Madrasa 'Ali bin Yusuf in Marrakech still survive. Despite this, 'Abd Al-Mu'min refused to enter the city of Marrakech until it was properly "purified" and re-sanctified by Almohad clerics. Several Almoravid mosques were destroyed. Gaston Deverdun, *Marrakech: Des Origines à 1912*, vol. 1 (Rabat, 1959).

21. Amira Bennison and María Gallego, "Jewish Trading in Fes on the Eve of the Almohad Conquest", *MEAH Hebreo*, 56 (2007), 33–51

22. Michael Brett and Elizabeth Fentress, *The Berbers* (Wiley-Blackwell, 1997), 116. The chronicle was *Roger Wendover's Flowers of History*, vol. 2 (London, 1849), 283–7. Brett found this reference in P. G. Rogers, *A History of Anglo-Moroccan Relations to 1900* (Foreign and Commonwealth Office, 1972), 1–5.

23. Deborah Howard, *Venice and the East* (Yale University Press, 2000). Deborah Howard also discusses the need for more studies of other Italian cities, especially on the Western side. In truth, Genoa and Pisa were probably influenced as much by North African as by Eastern ideas. Also see, E. Ashtor, *Levant Trade in the Later Middle Ages* (Princeton University Press, 1983).

24. Jerrilynn Dodds (ed.), *Al-Andalus: The Art of Islamic Spain* (Metropolitan Museum of Art, 1992), p. 385. For a highly detailed study of Almohad numismatic history, see A. Bel, "Contribution à l'étude des dirhems de l'époque almohade," *Hespéris*, 16 (1933), 1–68.

25. Graziella Berti, *I Bacini Ceramici delle Chiese di Pisa* (L'Erma di Bretschneider, 1981).

26. Guillermo R. Bordoy, "The Ceramics of al-Andalus," in J. Dodds (ed.), *Al-Andalus: The Art of Islamic Spain* (Metropolitan Museum of Art, 1992), 100.

27. See Levi Della Vida, "Dante et l'Islam d'après de nouveaux documents," *Revue de la Méditerranée*, 60 (1954). Also, P. F. Kennedy, "The Muslim sources of Dante?" in D. A. Agius and R. Hitchcock (eds.), *The Arab influence in Medieval Europe*, (Ithaca Press, 1994), 63–82.

28. See M. Nakosteen: *History of Islamic Origins of Western Education: 800–1350* (University of Colorado Press, 1964).

29. Isabelle Dolezalek, "Textile Connections? Two Ifriqiyan Church Treasuries in Norman Sicily and the Problem of Continuity across Political Change," *Al Masaq*, 25/1 (2013), 92–112.

30. Hasan Ali Hasan refers to this date in his book in Arabic, *Islamic Civilization in Andalusia and the Maghrib* (Maktabat Al-Khanji, 1980), 287.

31. C. Foucard, *Relazioni dei Duchi di Ferrara e di Modena coi Re di Tunisi* (Modena, 1881).

32. And possibly their desire to thwart the overwhelming Almohad presence by allying with their rebellious rivals. The treaty called for the establishment of a *funduq* (guest house) and a church for the Genoese. For a collection of treaties between Europe and North Africa in the medieval period, see Mas Latrie, *Traités de paix et de commerce avec les Arabes de l'Afrique septentrionale au Moyen Âge* (Didot, 1866), 109–13.

33. A. Huici Miranda, *La cocina hispano-magrebí durante la época almohade*, ed. Manuela Marín (Ediciones Trea, 2005).

34. Ibid. 60.

35. Ibid. 70.

36. Quoted in J. T. Monroe, "Zajal and Muwashshaha: Hispano-Arabic Poetry and the Romance Tradition," in S. K. Jayyusi (ed.), *The Legacy of Muslim Spain*, 412.

37. It was common for fathers to be named after their sons in Arabic, yet only in rare instances was one called after the grandson; that Ibn Rushd was often called "the Grandfather" in the sources indicated the prestige of his grandson.

38. D. M. Dunlop, "Ibn Bajjah's Tadbiru 'l-mutwahhid," in *Journal of the Royal Asiatic Society* (1945), 61–81.

39. This was part of his "Book on the Spirit". Ibn Bajja, *Kitab al Nafs*, ed. M. Saghir Hasan Al-Ma'sumi (Damascus, 1960).

40. Leo Strauss, *Persecution and the Art of Writing* (University of Chicago Press, 1988).

41. Steven Harvey, "The Place of the Philosopher in the City according to Ibn Bajja," in C. E. Butterworth (ed.), *The Political Aspects of Islamic Philosophy. Essays in Honor of M. S. Mahdi* (Harvard University Press, 1992), 199–233.

42. Ibn Bajja, *Tadbir al Mutawahhid*, ed. M. Asín Palacios, *El régimen del solitario* (CSIC, 1946).

43. *Futuhat al Makkiyya*, II: 616. Quoted in Stephen Hirtenstein, *The Unlimited Mercifier: The Spiritual life and thought of Ibn 'Arabi* (Anqa Press, 1990), 97.

44. *Futuhat al Makkiyya*, I: 35. Ibid. 97.

45. The letter was found in the Vatican archives in a collection of unedited Mongol letters. It was first published in 1903 by P. Rabbath in the journal *Mashriq*, vol. VI, 1109–14. Another, more extensive article was published in 1926 by Eugène Tisserant and Gaston Wiet, "Une Lettre de l'almohade Murtada au pape Innocent IV," *Hespéris*, 6, 27–54.

46. Cynthia Robinson, "The Aljafería in Saragossa and Taifa Spaces," in M. Menocal *et al.* (eds.), *The Literature of al Andalus* (Cambridge University Press, 2012), 233–4.

47. See A. Lopes, "Los obispos de Marruecos desde el siglo XIII," *Archivo Ibero-Americano*, 14 (1920), 409–27.

48. F. M. Salgado, "Precisiones para la historia de un grupo éthnico-religioso: Los Farfanes," *Al-Qantara*, 4 (1983), 265–81.

49. Ibid. 268.

50. Ibn Abi Zar', *Rawd al Qirtas*, 491.

51. On Lope d'Ayn, see Padre Atanasio Lopez, *Memoria Histórica de Los Obispos de Marruecos Desde el Sigle XIII* (Madrid, 1920).

52. Ibid. 14.

53. Ibid. 31, 39–40, 102.

54. See Anonymous, trans. A. Huici Miranda, *al-Hulal al-mawshiyya* (Valencia, 1952), 192. Also Le Tourneau, *The Almohad Movement in North Africa* (Princeton University Press, 1969), 95.

55. Tisserant and Wiet, "Une lettre," 44, footnote 2.

56. For the connection between these Marrakech martyrs and St. Francis' evangelism, see P. Cenival, "L'Église Chrétienne de Marrakech au XIIe s," *Hespéris*, 7 (1927), 69–83, and John Tolan, *St. Francis and the Sultan: The Curious History of a Christian-Muslim Encounter* (Oxford University Press, 2009).

57. Norman Daniel, *Islam and the West, The Making of an Image* (Oneworld Publications, 2009), 144.

58. Many of these late events are recorded in the somewhat unreliable text by Ibn Abi Zar', *Rawd al Qirtas*.

59. Huici Miranda, *Historia Política*, vol. 2.

60. See Le Tourneau, *The Almohad Movement*, 95 and Anonymous, trans. Huici Miranda, *Al-Hulal al-Maushiyya*, 192.

61. Fierro, "The Almohads and the Hafsids," 66–105, 78.

62. Huici Miranda, *Historia Política*, vol. 2, 472.

63. Ibn Khaldun, *Le Livre des Exemples*, trans. A. Cheddadi (Paris, 2002), 227.

64. John Adams, *A Defense of the Constitutions of Government of the United States of America*, 1787–8, 1786. See unabridged original edition: http://www.constitution.org/jadams/ja1_00.htm.

65. Fierro, "The Almohads and the Hafsids," 66–105, 78.

66. Patrick Lantschner, "Fragmented Cities in the later Middle Ages: Italy and the Near East Compared," *English Historical Review*, 130/544 (2015), 546–58. I want to thank Amira Bennison for this reference.

67. George Greenaway, *Arnold of Brescia* (Cambridge University Press, 1931). Later, in the mid fourteenth century, Cola de Rienzo rose up also against papal power.

68. On the intellectul activity sparked by the Almohads, see Dominique Urvoy, *Pensers d'al-Andalus: La vie intellectuelle à Cordue et Seville au temps des empires berbères* (Presses Universitaires du Mirail, 1990).

69. Jerrilynn Dodds (ed.), *Al-Andalus: The Art of Islamic Spain* (Metropolitan Museum of Art, 1992), 307.

70. See Cynthia Robinson, *Medieval Andalusian Courtly Culture in the Mediterranean: Hadith Bayad wa Riyad* (Routledge, 2010); Dodds, *Al-Andalus*, 312. Although, some speculate this book may have been produced in Islamic Spain, it was written with Maghribi script.

71. Dodds, *Al-Andalus*, 265.

72. Ibid. 270.

73. Fierro, "The Almohads and the Hafsids," 66–105, 72.

74. Christian Ewert, "The Architectural Heritage of Islamic Spain and North Africa," in Dodds, *Al-Andalus*, 86.

75. Urvoy, *Pensers d'Al-Andalus*.

76. Bennsion and Gallego, "Jewish Trading in Fes," 33–51. Maimonides was able to complete a founding corpus of Jewish intellectual life, the *Guide for the Perplexed*. It was Jews who first translated the philosophy of Ibn Rushd; many of the earliest manuscripts of his writings are in Hebrew. Urvoy, *Pensers d' Al-Andalus*, 190–2.

77. Léon Gauthier (ed.), *Ibn Rochd (Averroès), Traité Décisif (Fasl al-Maqal)* . . ., 3rd edn, Arabic text with French translation, (Éditions Carbonel, 1948), 1. Also see G. Hourani (ed.), *Ibn Rushd Kitab Fasl al-Maqal* . . . (Brill, 1959), and *Averroes' On the Harmony of Religion and Philosophy* (London, 1961). A fairly complete bibliography of manuscripts is S. G. Nogales, "Bibliographfia Sobre las Obras de Averroes," in J. Jolivet (ed.), *Multiple Averroés. Acts du colloque international organisé à l'occasion du 850e anniversaire de la naissance d'Averroes* (Paris, 1978), 351–87. A good, recent analysis of Ibn Rushd, including the important influence

of Almohad doctrine, is Dominique Urvoy, *Ibn Rushd (Averroes)* (Routledge, 1991). In 1996, *Alif: Journal of Comparative Poetics*, produced a special volume of articles on Ibn Rushd called "Averroes and the Rational Legacy in East and West," no. 16.

78. First published in 1861, this was Renan's doctoral thesis. Read extensively, it soon established his reputation as one of the foremost intellectuals of the period. A recent edition was published by Maisonneuve of Paris in 2002.

79. Ibid. 39.

80. Marcia Cosh, *The Medieval Foundations of the Western Intellectual Tradition* (Yale University Press, 1997), 148.

81. Unfortunately, this work, *Sharh 'Aqidat al-Imam al-Mahdi*, may not have survived. See Urvoy, *Ibn Rushd*, 71.

82. Erwin Rosenthal, *Political Thought in Medieval Islam* (Cambridge University Press, 1958), 190.

83. M. Fletcher, "Al-Andalus and North Africa in the Almohad Ideology," in Jayyusi (ed.), *The Legacy of Muslim Spain*, 253.

84. Erwin Rosenthal, *Averroes' Commentary on Plato's "Republic"* (Cambridge University Press, 1956), 166.

85. Quoted in Fierro, "The Almohads and the Hafsids," 66–105, 83. Also, see Émile Fricaud, "Le probleme de la disgrace d'Averroès," in A. Bazzana *et al.* (eds.), *Averroès et l'averroïsme* (Lyons, 2005), 155–89.

87. See L. Gauthier's biography of Ibn Rushd, *Ibn Rochd (Averroès)*.

87. For more on European views of the Saracen, see John Tolan, *Saracens* (Columbia University Press, 2002).

88. Roger le Tourneau, *The Almohad Movement in North Africa in the Twelfth and Thirteenth Centuries* (Princeton University Press, 1969), 107–8.

89. David Abulafia, "Christian Merchants in the Almohad Cities," *Journal of Medieval Iberian Studies*, 2/2 (2010), 251–7, 251.

90. M. Amari, *I Diplomi Arabi del R. Archivio Fiorentino* (Florence, 1867).

91. Archive of the Crown of Aragon, Arabic Documents Collection, no. 158.

92. Antonio de Capmany, *Antiguos tratodes de paces y alianzas entre algunos reyes de Aragon y differentes principes infieles de Asia y África desde el siglo XIII hasta el XV* (Madrid, 1786).

93. Brian Catlos, "To Catch a Spy: The Case of Zayn al Din and Ibn Dukhan," *Medieval Encounters*, 2 (1996), 99–114, 110.

94. John Pryor, "The Origins of the Commenda Contract," *Speculum*, 52/1 (1977), 5–37.

95. Fabio L. Lázaro, "The Rise and Global Significance of the First 'West': The Medieval Islamic Maghreb," *Journal of World History*, 24/2 (2013), 259–307.

96. Muhammad Shahrastani, *Muslim Sects and Divisions*, trans. A. K. Kazi (Routledge, 2014), 9–10.

97. For a critical Arabic edition, see Ibn Hazm, *Al-Fasl fi al-Milal wa al Ahwa wa al Nihal* (Dar al Jalil, 1985). See also the French translation, Ibn Hazm, *Livre des religions et des sects*, trans. D. Gimaret, G. Monnot and J. Jolivet (Peeters, 1993).

98. *Taqrib lil hudud al muntiq*, ed. Ihsan 'Abbas (Beirut, 1959).

99. *Encyclopaedia of Islam*, vol. 2, 2nd edn (Leiden, 1965).

100. On Ibn Hazm's fascinating approach towards reason and its employment in convincing non-believers, see J. P. Montada, "Reason and Reasoning in Ibn Hazm of Cordoba," *Studia Islamica*, 92 (2001), 165–85.

101. Fiero, "Proto-Malikis, Malikis and reformed Malikis," in P. Bearman, R. Peters and F. E. Vogel (eds.), *The Islamic School of Law: Evolution, devolution and progress* (Harvard University Press, 2005), 57–76.

102. Fierro, "The Almohads and the Hafsids," 66–105, 84. On the intellectul activity sparked by the Almohads, see Urvoy, *Pensers d'al-Andalus*.

103. Fierro, "The Almohads and the Hafsids," 84.

104. For more on Marc of Toledo as well as translations of the Qur'an, see M.-T. d'Alverny, "Deux tradutions latines du Coran au Moyen Âge," in Charles Burnett (ed.), *La Connaisance de l'Islam dans l'Occident medieval* (Variorum, 1994), 125–7 and her articles in the same book, "Marc de Tolède", 43–8 and "Marc de Tolède traducteur d'Ibn Tumart."

105. The Latin manuscript ended up in an Italian library. Charles Tieszen, *Christian Identity amid Islam in Medieval Spain* (Brill, 2013), 173.

106. John Tolan, *Petrus Alfonsi and his Medieval Readers* (University Press of Florida, 1993).

107. *Dialogus*, 5:146. Quoted in Tieszen, *Christian Identity*, 191.

108. Tieszen, *Christian Identity*, 204.

109. The number 3 is often used in popular movie titles and other pronoucements that transliterate the Arabic *'ayn* into Latin characters.

110. See Philip Naylor, *North Africa: A History from Antiquity to Present* (University of Texas Press, 2009) and Sebastain Walsh, "Killing Post-Almohad Man: Malek Bennabi, Algerian Islamism and the Search for Liberal Governance," *Journal of North African History*, 12/2 (2007), 235–54.

Chapter 6

1. Robert Lopez, *Genova marinara nel duecento: Benedetto Zaccaria, ammiraglio e mercante* (Milan, 1932).

2. Ibn Khaldun, *Muqaddimah*, vol. 2, trans. F. Rosenthal (Princeton University Press, 1967), 46.

3. Ibid. vol. 3, 117–18.

4. Although modified, portions of this chapter have been published as the third chapter in Amira Bennison (ed.), *The Articulation of Power in the Medieval Maghrib* (Oxford University Press and the British Academy, 2014).

5. There were also dynasties without religious prophecy that could prosper simply with the support of "group feeling." Ibn Khaldun, *(Muqaddimah) Le Livre des Exemples*, trans. A. Cheddadi (Gallimard, 2002), 424.

6. These concepts are the very terms in the title of Ibn Khaldun's masterwork, *Kitab al-'Ibar wa diwan al-mubtada' wa'l-khabar fi ayyam al-'arab wa'l-barbar* of which the famed *Muqaddima* is only the introduction. As several scholars have noted, there are different versions of this title used in the three main manuscripts: the earliest version is found in the national library of Cairo but called the "Tunis manuscript" as it is dedicated to the library of the Hafsid Sultan Abu Al-'Abbas, the patron Ibn Khaldun was both keen to please and convince of his thinking. In this so-called "primitive" version the title starts not with *Kitab* but with *Turjuman* or "interpretation." See Nathaniel Schmidt, "The Manuscripts of Ibn Khaldun," *Journal of the American Oriental Society*, 46 (1926), 171–6. See also, Abdessalam Cheddadi's careful notes in his translation of Ibn Khaldun, *Le Livre des Exemples*, 1292–304.

7. Ronald Messier, "Rethinking the Almoravids, rethinking Ibn Khaldun," in Julia Clancy-Smith (ed.), *North Africa, Islam and the Mediterranean World* (Routledge, 2001), 58–80.

8. Yvon Thébert and Jean-Louis Biget, "L'Afrique après la disparition de la cité classique: Cohérence et ruptures dans l'histoire maghrébine," *L'Afrique dans L'Occident romain, Collection de l'école française de Rome* 134 (École Français de Rome, 1990), 575–602, 576. James Boone and Nancy Benco, "Islamic Settlement in North Africa and the Iberian Peninsula," *Annual Review of Anthropology*, 28 (1999), 51–78, 58.

9. Ibn Khaldun, *al-Ta'rif bi Ibn Khaldun rihlatuhu gharban wa sharqan*, ed. Muhammad Tawit Al-Tanji (Cairo, 1951), 28–9; *Le Livre des Exemples*, 93–4.

10. Ibn Khaldun, *al-Ta'rif*, 28; *Le Livre des Exemples*, 93.

11. The tenuous political power of the Hafsids and Ibn Khaldun's own political motivations is discussed in Ramzi Rouighi, *The Making of A Mediterranean Emirate* (University of Pennsylvania Press, 2011), 18–20.

12. Ibn Khaldun, *Le Livre des Exemples*, 156.

13. Ibid. 157; for the entire poem, see Ibn Khaldun, *al-Ta'rif*, 233–44.

14. Ibn Khaldun, *al-Ta'rif*, 103; *Le Livre des Exemples*, 110.

15. Ibn Khaldun, *al-Ta'rif*, 259–60; *Le Livre des Exemples*, 171.

16. Ibid. 259–60; 171.

17. Ibid. 258–60; 171.

18. On Al-Ghazali's spiritual autobiography, see Montgomery Watt, *The Faith and Practice of Al-Ghazali* (Allen and Unwin, 1953).

19. The title of Ibn Khaldun's autobiography in short is *Al-Ta'rif bi-Ibn Khaldun wa rinlatahu gharban wa sharqan*.

20. See Franz Rosenthal's introduction in his three-volume translation of the *Muqaddimah*, 2nd edn (Princeton University Press, 1967).

21. Maya Shatzmiller, *The Berbers and the Islamic State: The Marinid Experience in Pre-Protectorate Morocco* (Markus Weiner, 2000), xiv.

22. On comparisons between Ibn Khaldun and Machiavelli, see Barbara Stowasser, *Religion and Political Development: Some Comparative Ideas on Ibn Khaldun and Machiavelli* (Georgetown University Press, 1983).

23. Marshall Hodgson, *The Venture of Islam*, vol. 2 (University of Chicago Press, 1974), 371.

24. Passages translated and quoted in Vincent Cornell, *Realm of the Saint* (University of Texas Press, 1998), 144.

25. Ibid. 144.

26. She also notes the importance of warrior virtues and other characteristics that allowed tribal warriors to enter into politics. Amira K. Bennison, "Liminal States: Morocco and the Iberian Frontier between the Twelfth and Nineteenth Centuries," *Journal of North African Studies*, 6/1 (2001), 11–28.

Chapter 7

1. Larry Siedentop, *Inventing the Individual, The Origins of Western Liberalism* (Harvard University (Belknap) Press, 2014).

2. Jerry Bentley, *Old World Encounters: Cross-Cultural Contacts and Exchanges in the Pre-Modern Period* (Oxford University Press, 1993).

3. This designation of the "Seven Men of Marrakech" may have beeen a later legend but it illustrates the point that Marrakech was highly esteeemed for its

spiritual history. On the Mellah, see Emily Gottreich, "Rethinking the Islamic City from the Perspective of Jewish Space," *Jewish Social Sciences*, 11/1 (2004), 118–46.

4. On the famous role of the Ashraf and saints, see E. Gellner, *Muslim Society* (Cambridge University Press, 1981). On women saints in Marrakech, see Elizabeth Fernea's engaging ethnography, *A Street in Marrakech* (Waveland Press, 1988).

5. Henri Pirenne, *Mahomet et Charlemagne* (Paris, 1992), 111.

6. Henri Pirenne, *Medieval Cities, Their Origins and the Revival of Trade* (Princeton University Press, 1969), 23–5.

7. Stephen Cory, *Reviving the Islamic Caliphate in Early Modern Morocco* (Ashgate, 2013).

8. Richard Hodges and David Whitehouse, *Mohammad, Charlemagne and the Origins of Europe, Archaeology and the Pirenne Thesis* (Cornell University Press, 1983).

9. C. Fenwick, "From Africa to Ifriqiya: Settlement and Society in Early Medieval North Africa (650–800)," *Al-Masaq*, 25/1 (2013), 9–33, 9.

10. On the general history of Berbers, see Michael Brett and Elizabeth Fentress, *The Berbers* (Wiley-Blackwell, 1997).

11. Ibn Idhari, *Al Bayan al Mughrib fi Akhbar al Andalus*, vol. 1, eds. G. S. Colin and E. Lévi-Provençal (Brill, 1949), 27.

12. The Sidi Oqba Oasis has since become a major religious shrine and center of the Zab; the mosque, possibly the oldest in Algeria, is said to hold the remains of 'Uqba or "Oqba."

13. Mercè Comes, *Ecuatorios andalusíes: Ibn al-Samh, al-Zarqalluh y Abu-l-Salt* (Universidad de Barcelona, 1991).

14. Madeleine Fletcher, "Almohadism: An Islamic Context for the Work of St. Thomas Aquinas," in P. Cressier, M. Fierro and L. Molina (eds.), *Los Almohades, Problemas y Perspectivas* (CSIC, 2005), 1170.

15. P. Cenival, "L'Église Chrétienne de Marrakech au XIIe s.," *Hespéris*, 7 (1927), 69–83.

16. Bacon, *Opus Majus*, vol. 2, trans. Robert Burke (University of Pennsylvania Press, 1923), 788–9.

17. Ibid. 788. To some extent this may be unfair to Roger Bacon and English knowledge of the "Saracens." The English interest in Islam was extensive.

18. Quoted in Norman Daniel, *Islam and the West, The Making of an Image* (Oneworld Publications, 2009), 291.

19. For more on Joachim of Fiore, see Kenneth Emmerson, *Antichrist in the Middle Ages: A Study of Medieval Apocalypticism, Art and Literature* (University of Washington Press, 1981).

20. Debra Strickland, *Saracens, Demons and Jews* (Princeton University Press, 2003), 225–6.

21. The Pseudo-Methodius account was a popular source in the Latin West. See Benjamin Garstad (trans.), *Apocalypse: An Alexandrian World Chronicle* (Harvard University Press, 2012). The Qur'an was full of possible references to Alexander as Dhul Qarnain.

22. Z. D. Zuwiyya (ed.), *Islamic Legends Concerning Alexander the Great* (SUNY Press, 2001), 62.

23. James Palmer, *The Apocalypse in the Early Middle Ages* (Cambridge University Press, 2014).

24. The book *al-Jafr* is in the Add 9574 British Museum manuscript of the *Muqaddimah* by Ibn Khaldun and an account is in the standard *Muqaddimah* manuscript, which are both translated by A. Cheddadi in Ibn Khaldun, *(Muqaddimah) Le Livre des Exemples* (Paris, 2002), 681 and 1247.

25. Peter Jackson (trans.), *The Mission of Friar William of Rubruck* (Hackett, 2009), 231. In fact, the Muslim reluctance to drink may have done more to damage their cause, at least temporarily, than anything said during that debate.

26. John Tolan, *St. Francis and the Sultan: The Curious History of a Christian-Muslim Encounter* (Oxford University Press, 2009).

27. Thomas of Celano's *First and Second Lives of St. Francis* have been translated by David Burr and made freely available at Fordham University Medieval Sourcebook: see http://legacy.fordham.edu/halsall/source/stfran-lives.html.

28. On the uses of violence and conflict in the context of medieval Aragon, see David Nirenberg, *Communities of Violence* (Princeton University Press, 1998).

29. David Cannadine, *The Undivided Past, Humanity Beyond our Differences* (Knopf, 2013).

BIBLIOGRAPHY

Abulafia, David, "Christian Merchants in the Almohad Cities," *Journal of Medieval Iberian Studies*, 2/2 (2010), 251–7.

—— *The Great Sea: A Human History of the Mediterranean* (Oxford: Oxford University Press, 2013).

Abu-Lughod, Janet, *Before European Hegemony: The World System AD 1250–1350* (Oxford: Oxford University Press, 1989).

Abun-Nasr, J. M., *A History of the Maghrib in the Islamic Period* (Cambridge: Cambridge University Press, 1987).

Adams, John, *A Defense of the Constitutions of Government of the United States of America*, 1787–8, 1786. See http://www.constitution.org/jadams/ja1_00.htm.

Addas, Claude, *The Quest for the Red Sulphur: the Life of Ibn Arabi*, trans. Peter Kingsley (Cambridge: The Islamic Texts Society, 1993).

Aïssani, Djamal, *Bèjaïa à l'époque médiévale: Les Mathématiques au sein du mouvement intellectuel* (Rouen: IREM, 1993).

—— "Le mathématicien Eugène Dewulf (1831–1896) et les manuscrits médiévaux du Maghreb," *Historica Mathematica*, 23 (1996), 257–68.

Allaoua, A., "Retour à la Problématique du Déclin Économique du Monde Musulman Médiéval: La Cas du Maghreb Hammadide (XI–XIIe Siècles)," *Maghreb Review*, 28/1 (2003), 2–26.

Allouche, I. S. (ed.), *Chronique Anonyme* [Arabic text] (Rabat, 1939).

Almond, Ian, *History of Islam in German Thought: From Leibniz to Nietzche* (New York: Routledge, 2010).

d'Alverny, M.-T., "Deux tradutions latines du Coran au Moyen Âge," in Charles Burnett (ed.), *La Connaisance de l'Islam dans l'Occident médiéval* (Aldershot: Variorum, 1994), 125–7.

—— "Marc de Tolède," in Charles Burnett (ed.), *La Connaisance de l'Islam dans l'Occident medieval* (Aldershot: Variorum, 1994), 43–8.

Amari, M., *Storia des Musulmani di Sicilia*, 3 vols. (Florence, 1854).

—— *I Diplomi Arabi del R. Archivio Fiorentino* (Florence, 1867).

—— "Nuovi ricordi arabici sulla storia di Genova," *Atti Soc. Ligure Storia patria*, 5/4 (1873), 561–635.

Al-Andalusi, Sa'id, *Science in the Medieval World: Book of the Categories of Nations*, ed. and trans. Sema'an I. Salem and Alok Kumar (Austin: University of Texas Press, 1991).

Aquinas, Thomas, *De rationibus fidei*, trans. J. Kenney as "Saint Thomas Aquinas: Reasons for the Faith against Muslim Objectives," *Islamochristiana*, 22 (1996).

Ibn 'Arabi, "Kitaab al-Alif," trans. A. Abadi, *Journal of Muhyiddin Ibn 'Arabi Society*, 111 (1984).

Archivo General de la Corona de Aragón, *Los documentos árabes diplomáticos del Archivo de la corona de Aragón* (Madrid, 1940).

Ashtor, E., *Levant Trade in the Later Middle Ages* (Princeton: Princeton University Press, 1983).

Azaykou, Ali Sidqi, *Histoire du Maroc et ses possibles interprétations: Recueil d'articles* (Rabat: Centre Tarik Ibn Zyad, 2000).

Bacon, Roger, *Opus Majus*, vol. 2, trans. Robert Burke (Philadelphia: University of Pennsylvania Press, 1923).

Ibn Bajja, *Tadbir al Mutawahhid* ed. M. Asín Palacios (Madrid: CSIC, 1946).

—— *Kitab al Nafs*, ed. M. Saghir Hasan Al-Ma'sumi (Damascus, 1960).

Al-Bakri, *Description de l'Afrique septentrionale*, 2nd edn, trans. William MacGuckin de Slane (Algiers, 1913).

Balard, Michel, and Christophe Picard, *La Méditerranée au Moyen Âge* (Paris: Hachette Education, 2014).

Bartlett, Robert, *Trial by Fire and Water: The Medieval Judicial Ordeal* (Oxford: Oxford University Press, 1989).

—— *The Making of Europe* (Princeton: Princeton University Press, 1994).

Bartold, V. V., *Mussulman Culture*, trans. Shahid Suhrawardy (Oxford University Press, 2009).

Barton, Simon, *Conquerors, Brides and Concubines* (Philadelphia: University of Pennsylvania Press, 2015).

Ibn Batuta, *Ibn Battuta: travels in Asia and Africa: 1325–1354*, trans. H. A. R. Gibb (London: Broadway, 1929).

Bel, Alfred, *Les Benou Ghanya, derniers representants de l'empire almoravide et leur lute contre l'empire almohade* (Paris: E. Leroux, 1903).

—— *La religion musulmane en Berbérie* (Paris: Geuthner, 1938).

—— "Contribution à l'étude des dirhems de l'époque almohade," *Hespéris*, 16 (1933), 1–68.

Belting, Hans, *Florence and Baghdad: Renaissance Art and Arab Science* (Cambridge, MA: Harvard University Press, 2011).

Bennison, Amira, "Liminal States: Morocco and the Iberian Frontier between the Twelfth and Nineteenth Centuries," *Journal of North African Studies*, 6/1 (2001), 11–28.

—— "The Almohads and the Qur'an of Uthman: The Legacy of the Umayyads of Cordoba in the Twelfth Century Maghrib," *Al-Masaq*, 19/2 (2007), 131–54.

—— *The Articulation of Power in the Medieval Maghrib* (Oxford: Oxford University Press and the British Academy, 2014).

Bennison, Amira, and María Gallego, "Jewish Trading in Fes on the Eve of the Almohad Conquest," *MEAH Hebreo*, 56 (2007), 33–51.

Bentley, Jerry, *Old World Encounters: Cross-Cultural Contacts and Exchanges in the Pre-Modern Period* (Oxford: Oxford University Press, 1993).

Bergin, Thomas, and Alice Wilson (trans.), *Petrarch's Africa* (Yale University Press, 1977).

Berque, Jacques, "Du nouveau sur les Bani Hilâl?" *Studia Islamica*, 36 (1972), 99–111.

—— *L'intérieur du Maghreb: XVe–XIXe siècle* (Paris: Gallimard, 1978).

Berti, Graziella, *I Bacini Ceramici delle Chiese di Pisa* (Rome: L'Erma di Bretschneider, 1981).

Bhatawadekar, Sai, "Islam in Hegel's Triatic Philosophy of Religion", *Journal of World History*, 25/2–3 (2014), 397–424.

Birk, Joshua, "From Borderlands to Borderlines: Narrating the Past of Twelfth Century Sicily," in James P. Heifers (ed.), *Multicultural Europe and Cultural Exchange in the Middle Ages and Renaissance* (Arizona: Brepols Press, 2005), 9–31.

Blancard, Louis, *Documents Inédits sur le commerce de Marseille au moyen-âge*, vol. 2 (Marseille, 1884–5).

Bloch, Herbert, *Monte Cassino in the Middle Ages*, vol. 1 (Cambridge, MA: Harvard University Press, 1986).

Boissonnade, P., "Les Relations commerciales de la France méridionale avec l'Afrique du Nord au Maghreb du XII au XV s.," *Bulletin Section Géographie Paris* (1929), 1–37.

Bonet, Honoré, *Medieval Muslims, Christians, and Jews in dialogue: the apparicion Maistre Jehan de Meun of Honoret Bovat* (Tempe: Arizona Center for Medieval and Renaissance Studies, 2005).

Bonner, Anthony (trans. and ed.), *Ramon Lull: A Contemporary Life*, (Martlesham: Tamesis Books, 2010).

Boone, James, and Nancy Benco, "Islamic Settlement in North Africa and the Iberian Peninsula," *Annual Review of Anthropology*, 28 (1999), 51–78.

Bordoy, Guillermo R., "The Ceramics of al-Andalus," in Jerrilynn Dodds (ed.), *Al-Andalus: The Art of Islamic Spain* (New York: Metropolitan Museum of Art, 1992), 100.

Borruso, Andrea, "Una Poesia di Ibn Hamdis ad al-Mu'tamid," *Quaderni di Studi Arabi*, 9 (1991), 177–82.

Bos, G., *Ibn al-Jazzar on Fevers, a Critical edition of 'Zad al-musafir wa-qut al hadir*, book 7 (London: Wellcome Asian Series, 2000).

Bourgeot, A., "Le Costume Masculin des Kel Ahaggar," *Lybica*, 17 (1968), 355–76.

Braudel, Fernand, "À propos de l'histoire de l'Afrique du Nord de Ch. Andre Julien," *Revue Africaine*, 74/1 (1933), 37–53.

—— *The Mediterranean World in the Age of Philip II*, vol. 2 (Oakland: University of California Press, 1995).

Brett, Michael, "The military interest of the battle of Haydaran," in V. J. Parry and M. E. Yapp (eds.), *War, Technology and Society in the Middle East* (London: Oxford University Press, 1975), 77–88.

—— "The Islamisation of Morocco: From the Arabs to the Almoravids," *Morocco*, 2 (1992), 57–71.

—— *Ibn Khaldun and the Medieval Maghrib* (Aldershot: Ashgate, 1999).

—— *The Rise of the Fatimids: The World of the Mediterranean and the Middle East in the Tenth Century CE* (Leiden: Brill, 2001).

Brett, Michael, and Elizabeth Fentress, *The Berbers* (Oxford: Wiley-Blackwell, 1997).

Brown, Peter, *The Cult of the Saints* (Chicago: University of Chicago Press, 1982).

Bruno, H., and M. Gaudefroy-Demombynes, *Le Livre des Magistratures d'el-Wancherisi* (Rabat, 1937).

Brunschvig, Robert, "Un Calife hafside méconnu," *Revue Tunisienne* (1930), 38–48.

—— "Quelques remarques historiques sur les Médersas de Tunisie," *Revue Tunisienne* (1931), 261–85.

—— *La Berbérie orientale sous les Hafsides: Des origines à la fin du XVe siècle*, vol. 2 (Paris: Maisonneuve, 1947).

—— "Urbanisme Médiéval et Droit Musulman," *Revue des Études Islamiques*, 15 (1947), 127–55.

—— *La Tunisie dans le Haut Moyen Âge: sa place dans l'histoire* (Cairo: Institut français d'archéologie orientale, 1948).

Burnett, Charles, and Danielle Jacquart (eds.), *Constantine the African and Ali ibn al 'Abbas al Magusi* (Leiden: Brill, 1994).

Burns, Robert, "Christian-Islamic Confrontation in the West: The Thirteenth Century Dream of Conversion," *The American Historical Review*, 76/5 (1971), 1386–434.

Cannadine, David, *The Undivided Past, Humanity Beyond our Differences* (New York: Knopf, 2013).

Capelli, Christian, *et al.*, "Moors and Saracens in Europe: estimating the medieval North African male legacy in southern Europe," *European Journal of Human Genetics*, 17 (2009), 848–52.

de Capmany, Antonio, *Antiguos tratodes de paces y alianzas entre algunos reyes de Aragon y differentes principes infieles de Asia y África desde el siglo XIII hasta el XV* (Madrid, 1786).

Caputo, Nina, *Nahmanides in Medieval Catalonia, History, Community and Messianism* (Notre Dame: University of Notre Dame Press, 2007).

Catlos, Brian, "To Catch a Spy: The Case of Zayn al Din and Ibn Dukhan," *Medieval Encounters*, 2 (1996), 99–114.

—— *Infidel Kings and Unholy Warriors, Faith, Power and Violence in the Age of Crusade and Jihad* (New York: FSG, 2014).

—— *Muslims of Medieval Latin Christendom c. 1050–1614* (Cambridge: Cambridge University Press, 2014).

Cenival, P., "L'Église Chrétienne de Marrakech au XIIe s.," *Hespéris*, 7 (1927), 69–83.

Chittick, William, *Imaginal Worlds: Ibn al-'Arabi and the Problem of Religious Diversity* (Albany: SUNY Press, 1994).

Clancy-Smith, Julia, *Mediterraneans: North Africa and Europe in the Age of Migrations, 1800–1900* (Oakland: University of California Press, 2011).

Clancy-Smith, J. (ed.), *North Africa, Islam and the Mediterranean World: From the Almoravids to the Algerian War* (New York: Routledge, 2001).

Comes, Mercè, *Ecuatorios andalusíes: Ibn al-Samh, al-Zarqalluh y Abu-l-Salt* (Barcelona: Universidad de Barcelona, 1991).

Constable, O. R. (ed.), *Medieval Iberia: Readings from Christian, Muslim and Jewish Sources* (Philadelphia: University of Pennsylvania Press, 1997).

Constable, Olivia R., "Regulating Religious Noise: The Council of Vienne, the Mosque Call and Muslim Pilgrimage in the Late Medieval Mediterranean World," *Medieval Encounters*, 16/1 (2010), 64–95.

Contamine, Geneviève, "Traduction et traducteurs au Moyen Âge: actes du colloque international due CNRS organisé à Paris, Institut de recherche et d'histoire des texts, les 26–28 mai 1986," *Bibliotheque d'Humanisme et Renaissance*, 54/2 (1992).

Cornell, Vincent, "Understanding is the mother of ability: responsibility and action in the doctrine of Ibn Tûmart," *Studia Islamica*, 66 (1987), 71–103.

—— *The Way of Abu Madyan: Doctrinal and Poetic Works* (Cambridge: Islamic Texts Society, 1996).

—— *The Realm of the Saint: Power and Authority in Moroccan Sufism* (Austin: University of Texas Press, 1998).

Cory, Stephen, "Breaking the Khaldunian Cycle? The Rise of Sharifianism as the Basis for Political Legitimacy in Early Modern Morocco," *Journal of North African Studies*, 13/3 (2008), 377–94.

—— *Reviving the Islamic Caliphate in Early Modern Morocco* (Aldershot: Ashgate, 2013).

Coser, Lewis, *The Functions of Social Conflict* (New York: The Free Press, 1956).

Cosh, Marcia, *The Medieval Foundations of the Western Intellectual Tradition* (New Haven: Yale University Press, 1997).

Courtois, C., "Grégoire VII et l'Afrique du Nord," *Revue Historique* (1945), 97–122, 193–226.

Cowdrey, H. E. J., "The Mahdia Campaign of 1087," *English Historical Review*, 92 (1977), 1–30.

Cressier, Patrice, "Les portes monumentales urbaines almohades: symboles et fonctions," in P. Cressier, M. Fierro and L. Molina (eds.), *Los Almohades Problemas y Perspectivas* (Madrid: CSIC, 2005), 149–87.

Crompton, Louis, *Homosexuality and Civilization* (Cambridge, MA: Harvard University Press, 2003).

Cucarella, Diego, *Muslim-Christian Polemics across the Mediterranean* (Leiden: Brill, 2015).

Daniel, Norman, *Islam and the West, The Making of an Image* (London: Oneworld Publications, 2009).

Darras, J., *A General History of the Catholic Church*, vol. II (New York, 1866).

Davis, Raymond (trans.), *The Lives of the Ninth-Century Popes (Liber Pontificalis)* (Liverpool: Liverpool University Press, 1995).

Deverdun, Gaston, *Marrakech: Des Origines à 1912*, vols. 1–2 (Rabat, 1959).

Deztany, Lluis (ed.), *Libre de disputacío de l'ase* (Barcelona, 1922).

Diamond, Jared, *Collapse: How Societies Choose to Fail or Succeed* (New York: Viking Penguin, 2005).

Ibn abi Dinar, *Kitab al-Mu'nis fi akhbar ifriqiya wa Tunis* [1869], trans. J. Magnin, *Revue de l'Institut des Belles Lettres Arabes*, 2 (1952).

Dodds, Jerrilynn (ed.), *Al-Andalus: The Art of Islamic Spain* (New York: Metropolitan Museum of Art, 1992).

Dodds, J., A. Balbale and M. Menocal, *The Arts of Intimacy* (New Haven: Yale University Press, 2008).

Dolezalek, Isabelle, "Textile Connections? Two Ifriqiyan Church Treasuries in Norman Sicily and the Problem of Continuity across Political Change," *Al Masaq*, 25/1 (2013), 92–112.

Donner, Fred, *Muhammad and the Believers* (Cambridge, MA: Harvard University Press, 2012).

Doumerc, Bernard, *Venise et l'émirat hafside de Tunis (1231–1535)* (Paris, 1999).

Dufourcq, Charles-Emmanuel, *L'Espagne catalane et le Maghreb aux XIIIe et XIVe siècles* (Presses Universitaires de France, 1966).

Dunlop, D. M., "Ibn Bajjah's Tadbiru 'l-mutwahhid," *Journal of the Royal Asiatic Society* (1945), 61–81.

—— "Relations between Norway and the Maghrib in the 7th/13th Century," Bravmann Memorial Volume, *Journal of the Ancient Near Eastern Society*, 11 (1979), 41–4.

Durham, John, "The Introduction of 'Arabic' Numerals in European Accounting," *Accounting Historians Journal*, 19 (1992), 42–9.

Echevarria, Ana, *Caballeros en la frontera: la guardia morisca de los reyes de Castilla (1410–1467)* (Madrid, 2006).

Edrisi (Al-Idrisi), *Description de l'Afrique et de l'Espagne*, ed. and trans. R. Dozy and M. J. de Goeje (Leiden: Brill, 1866).

Emmerson, Kenneth, *Antichrist in the Middle Ages: A Study of Medieval Apocalypticism, Art and Literature* (Seattle: University of Washington Press, 1981).

Epstein, Stephen, *An Economic and Social History of Late Medieval Europe* (Cambridge: Cambridge University Press, 2009).

Feliciano, Maria Judith, and Leyla Rouhi, "Interrogating Iberian Frontiers," *Medieval Encounters*, 12/3 (2006), 317–28.

Fenwick, C., "From Africa to Ifriqiya: Settlement and Society in Early Medieval North Africa (650–800)," *Al-Masaq*, 25/1 (2013), 9–33.

Ferhat, Halima, *Le Maghreb aux XIIème et XIIIème siècles: Les siècles de la foi* (Casablanca: Wallada, 1993).

Fernández-Armesto, Felipe, *Civilizations: Culture, Ambition and the Transformation of Nature* (New York: Touchstone, 2001).

Fernea, Elizabeth, *A Street in Marrakech* (Long Grove: Waveland Press, 1988).

Fierro, Maribel, "El derecho maliki en al-Andalus: siglos VIII–XI," *Al-Qantara*, 12 (1991), 119–32.

—— "Christian Success and Muslim Fear in Andalusi Writings During the Almoravid and Almohad Periods," in Uri Rubin and D. Wasserstein (eds.), *Dhimmis and Others, Jews and Christians in the Worlds of Classical Islam* (Tel Aviv, 1997), 155–78.

—— "Proto-Malikis, Malikis and reformed Malikis," in P. Bearman, R. Peters and F. E. Vogel (eds.), *The Islamic School of Law: Evolution, devolution and progress* (Cambridge, MA: Harvard University Press, 2005), 57–76.

—— "Alfonso X the Wise: The Last Almohad Caliph?" *Medieval Encounters*, 15/2–4 (2009), 175–98.

—— "The Almohads and the Hafsids," in M. Fierro (ed.), *The New Cambridge History of Islam*, vol. 2 (Cambridge: Cambridge University Press, 2010), 66–105.

—— *The Almohad Revolution: Politics and Religion in the Islamic West during the Twelfth–Thirteenth Centuries* (Aldershot: Ashgate Variorum, 2012).

Al-Fishtali, Abd Al-'Aziz Ibn Muhammad, *Manahil al-safa fi ma'athir mawalina al-shurafa*, ed. Abd Al-Karim Kurayyim (Rabat, 1900).

Fletcher, Madeleine, "The anthropological context of Almohad history," *Hespéris-Tamuda* (1988–9), 25–51.

—— "Al-Andalus and North Africa in the Almohad Ideology," in S. K. Jayyusi (ed.), *The Legacy of Muslim Spain* (Leiden: Brill, 1992), 253.

—— "Almohadism: An Islamic Context for the Work of St. Thomas Aquinas," in P. Cressier, M. Fierro and L. Molina (eds.), *Los Almohades, Problemas y Perspectivas* (Madrid: CSIC, 2005), 1170.

Foucard, C., *Relazioni dei Duchi di Ferrara e di Modena coi Re di Tunisi* (Modena, 1881).

Franzen, Cola (trans.), *Poems of Arab Andalusia* (San Francisco: City Lights Books, 2001), 90–1.

Fricaud, Émile, "Le problème de la disgrace d'Averroes," in A. Bazzana *et al.* (eds.), *Averroès et l'averroïsme* (Lyon: Presse Universitaires de Lyon, 2005), 155–89.

Fromherz, Allen, *Ibn Khaldun, Life and Times* (Edinburgh: Edinburgh University Press, 2011).

—— *The Almohads: The Rise of an Islamic Empire* (London: I. B. Tauris, 2012).

Fuentes, Alvaro Campanery, *Cronicon Mayoricense* (Palma de Majorca, 1881).

Fried, Johannes, *The Middle Ages*, trans. P. Lewis (Cambridge, MA: Harvard University Press, 2015).

Gaiser, Adam, *Muslims, Scholars and Soldiers: the Origins and Elaborations of Ibadi Imamate Traditions* (Oxford: Oxford University Press, 2010).

Gaiser, Adam, with Miriam Ali de Unzaga, "Facets of Exchange between North Africa and the Iberian Peninsula," *The Journal of North African Studies* (Spain–North African Project Special Issue), 19/1 (2014).

Galley, Micheline, and Jennifer Curtiss Gage, "Following the Traces of the Sons of Hilal," *Diogenes*, 56/4 (2009).

Garstad, Benjamin (trans.), *Apocalypse: An Alexandrian World Chronicle* (Cambridge, MA: Harvard University Press, 2012).

Gauthier, Léon (ed.), *Ibn Rochd (Avveroès), Traité Décisif (Fasl al-Maqal)*, 3rd edn, Arabic text with French trans. (Algiers: Éditions Carbonel, 1948).

Gautier, E. F., *Genséric, roi des Vandales* (Paris, 1935).

Geary, Patrick, *The Myth of Nations: The Medieval Origins of Europe* (Princeton: Princeton University Press, 2003).

Geertz, Clifford, *Islam Observed* (Chicago, University of Chicago Press, 1968).

Gellner, Ernest, *Muslim Society* (Cambridge: Cambridge University Press, 1981).

Gerber, Jane S., *Jewish Society in Fez, 1450–1700: Studies in Communal and Economic Life* (Leiden: Brill, 1980).

Gibbon, Edward, *Decline and Fall of the Roman Empire*, vol. IX (New York: Defau & Co., 1907).

Gies, Joseph, and Francis Gies, *Merchants and Moneymen: The Commercial Revolution, 1000–1500* (London: Thomas Crowell, 1972).

Gilchrist, John, "The Papacy and the War against the 'Saracens', 795–1216," *The International History Review*, 10/2 (1988), 174–97.

Goffart, Walter, *Barbarians and Romans A.D. 418–584: The Techniques of Accommodation* (Princeton: Princeton University Press, 1980).

Gómes-Rivas, Camilo, *Law and the Islamization of Morocco under the Almoravids* (Leiden: Brill, 2015).

Goitein, Shlomo D., *Studies in Islamic History and Institutions* (Leiden: Brill, 1966).

——— *Letters of Medieval Jewish Traders* (Princeton: Princeton University Press, 1973).

Gottreich, Emily, "On the Origins of the Mellah of Marrakesh," *International Journal of Middle Eastern Studies*, 35/2 (2003), 287–305.

——— "Rethinking the Islamic City from the Perspective of Jewish Space," *Jewish Social Sciences*, 11/1 (2004), 118–46.

——— *The Mellah of Marrakech: Jewish and Muslim Space in Morocco's Red City* (Bloomington: Indiana University Press, 2006).

Grabar, Oleg, "The Architecture of the Middle Eastern City from Past to Present: The Case of the Mosque," in Ira Lapidus (ed.), *Middle Eastern Cities* (Oakland: University of California Press, 1969), 26–46.

——— "Two Paradoxes in the Islamic Art of the Spanish Peninsula," in S. K. Jayyusi (ed.), *The Legacy of Muslim Spain* (Leiden: Brill, 1992), 583–91.

Greenaway, George, *Arnold of Brescia* (Cambridge: Cambridge University Press, 1931).

Gregorovius, Ferdinand, *History of the City of Rome in the Middle Ages*, vol. III, trans. A. Hamilton (London: G. Bell & Sons, 1903).

Griffith, Sidney, *The Church in the Shadow of the Mosque, Christians and Muslims in the World of Islam* (Princeton: Princeton University Press, 2010).

von Grunebaum, G. E., *Medieval Islam: A Study in Cultural Orientation* (Chicago: University of Chicago Press, 1953).

Guichard, Pierre, "The Social History of Muslim Spain from the Conquest to the End of the Almohad Régime," in S. K. Jayyusi (ed.), *The Legacy of Muslim Spain* (Leiden: Brill, 1992), 679–708.

Gutas, Dimitri, *Greek Thought, Arabic Culture: The Greco-Arabic Translation Movement in Baghdad and Early 'Abbasid Society* (New York: Routledge, 1998).

Gutierrez, Eva Lapiedra, "Christian Participation in Almohad Armies and Personal Guards," *Journal of Medieval Iberian Studies*, 2/2 (2010), 235–50.

Hajji, Muhammad, "La salida de los Almoravides del desierto," in M. L. Cavero (trans.) *Mauritania y España: Una Historia Común* (El Legardo Andalusi, 2003), 17–37.

Halm, Heinz, *The Empire of the Mahdi: The Rise of the Fatimids*, trans. Michael Bonner (Leiden: Brill, 1996).

Hannoum, Abdelmajid, "The Historiographic State: How Algeria Once Became French," *History and Anthropology*, 19/2 (2008), 91–114.

Harvey, Steven, "The Place of the Philosopher in the City according to Ibn Bajja," in C. E. Butterworth (ed.), *The Political Aspects of Islamic Philosophy: Essays in Honor of M. S. Mahdi* (Cambridge, MA: Harvard University Press, 1992), 199–233.

Haskins, Charles, *The Renaissance of the Twelfth Century* (Cambridge, MA: Harvard University Press, 1971).

Hasan, Hasan Ali, *Islamic Civilization in Andalusia and the Maghrib* (Cairo: Maktabat Al-Khanji, 1980).

Ibn Hawqal, *Surat al-Ard*, ed. J. H. Kramers (Leiden: Brill, 1967).

Ibn Hazm, *Taqrib lil hudud al mantiq*, ed. Ihsan Abbas (Beirut, 1959).

—— *Al-Fasl fi al-Milal wa al Ahwa wa al Nihal* (Beirut: Dar al Jalil, 1985).

—— *Livre des religions et des sects*, trans. D. Gimaret, G. Monnot and J. Jolivet (Louvain: Peeters, 1993).

Healey, John F., "The Christians of Qatar in the 7th Century," in I. R. Netton (ed.), *Studies in Honor of Clifford Edmund Bosworth, Vol. 1: Hunter of the East: Arabic and Semitic Studies* (Leiden: Brill, 2000), 222–37.

Heffernan, Thomas J., and Thomas E. Burman (eds.), *Scripture and Pluralism: Reading the Bible in the Religiously Plural Worlds of the Middle Ages and Renaissance* (Leiden: Brill, 2005).

Hegel, G. W. R., *The Philosophy of History* (Mineola: Dover, 1956).

Herbers, Klaus, *Leo IV und das Papsttum in der Mitte des 9 Jahrhunderts* (Stuttgart: Anton Hiersemann, 1996).

Heyd, W., *Geschitchte des Levantehandels im Mittelalter* (Stuttgart, 1879).

Hirschberg, Haim, *A History of the Jews in North Africa: From Antiquity to the Sixteenth Century*, 2nd edn, trans. M. W. Eichelberg (Leiden: Brill, 1974).

Hirtenstein, Stephen, *The Unlimited Mercifier: The Spiritual Life and Thought of Ibn 'Arabi* (Oxford: Anqa Press, 1990).

Hitti, Philip (trans.), *(Al-Baladhuri) The Origins of the Islamic State, Kitab Futuh al Buldan*, vol. 1 (New York: Columbia University, 1916).

Hodges, Richard, and David Whitehouse, *Mohammad, Charlemagne and the Origins of Europe, Archaeology and the Pirenne Thesis* (Cornell: Cornell University Press, 1983).

Hodgson, Marshall, *The Venture of Islam*, 3 vols. (Chicago: University of Chicago Press, 1974).

Hopkins, J. F. P. (trans.), *Corpus of Early Arabic Sources for West African History*, ed. N. Levtzion (Princeton: Markus Wiener, 2000).

Horden, Peregrine, and Nicholas Purcell, *The Corrupting Sea: A Study of Mediterranean History* (Oxford: Wiley-Blackwell, 2000).

Houben, Hubert, "Religious Toleration in the South Italian Peninsula During the Norma and Staufen Periods," in G. A. Loud and A. Metcalfe (eds.), *The Society of Norman Italy* (Leiden: Brill, 2002), 319–40.

Hourani, G. (ed.), *Ibn Rushd Kitab Fasl al-Maqal . . .* (Leiden: Brill, 1959).

—— *Averroes' On the Harmony of Religion and Philosophy* (London: Luzac, 1961).

Howard, Deborah, *Venice and the East: The Impact of the Islamic World on Venetian Architecture* (New Haven: Yale University Press, 2000).

Huici Miranda, Ambrosio, *Historia política del Imperio Almohade*, vol. 1 and 2 (Tetuán: Editora Marroquí, 1956–7).

—— *La cocina hispano-magrebí durante la época almohade*, ed. Manuela Marín (Gijón: Ediciones Trea, 2005).

Ibn 'Abd Al-Hakam, *Futuh misr wa-a-Maghrib* (Al-Qahirah: Maktabat al-Thaqafah al-Diniyah, 1995).

Ibn Idhari, *Al Bayan al Mughrib fi Akhbar al Andalus*, 2 vols., eds. G. S. Colin and E. Lévi-Provençal (Leiden: Brill, 1949).

—— *Al-Bayan al-Mugrib: Nuevos fragmentos almorávides y almohades*, trans. Ambrosio Huici Miranda (Valencia: Anubar Ediciones, 1963).

Idris, Hady Roger, "Fêtes chrétiennes célébrées en Ifrîqiya à l'époque zîrîde," *Revue Africaine*, 440–1 (1954), 261–76.

—— *La Berberie Orientale sous les Zirides: Xe–XIIe Siecles, vol. 1–2* (Paris: Librairie d'Amerique et d'Orient, 1962).

Jackson, Peter (trans.), *The Mission of Friar William of Rubruck* (Indianapolis: Hackett, 2009).

Jacquart, Danielle, and Francoise Micheau, *La médecine arabe et l'Occident médiéval* (Paris: Maisonneuve & Larose, 1996).

Al-Jazni, Abu al-Hasan Ali, *La fleur du myrte: Traitant de la fondation de la ville de Fès*, Arabic text with annotated French trans. by Alfred Bel (Algiers: Jules Carbonel, 1923).

Johns, Jeremy, *Arabic Administration in Norman Sicily, The Royal Diwan* (Cambridge: Cambridge University Press, 2002).

Ibn Jubayr, *The Travels of Ibn Jubayr*, trans. R. C. Broadhurst (London: Jonathan Cape, 1952).

Julien, Charles André, *History of North Africa, Tunisia, Algeria, Morocco*, ed. R. Le Tourneau (New York: Praeger, 1970).

Kalby, Mohammed, *Société, pouvoir et religion au Maroc à la fin du Moyen Âge* (Paris: Maisonneuve & Larose, 1968).

Kaplan, Robert, *The Revenge of Geography* (New York: Random House, 2012).

Kennedy, Hugh, *The Prophet and the Age of the Caliphs* (London: Longman, 2004).

—— *Muslim Spain and Portugal: A Political History of Al-Andalus* (New York: Routledge, 2014).

Kennedy, P. F., "The Muslim sources of Dante?" in D. A. Agius and R. Hitchcock (eds.), *The Arab influence in Medieval Europe* (New York: Ithaca Press, 1994), 63–82.

Ibn Khaldun, *Histoire des Berbères*, 2 vols., trans. William MacGuckin de Slane (Paris, 1925).

—— *Al-Taʿrif bi Ibn Khaldun rihlatuhu gharban wa sharqan*, ed. Muhammad Tawit al-Tanji (Cairo, 1951).

—— *The Muqaddimah*, 3 vols., trans. Franz Rosenthal, 2nd edn (Princeton: Princeton University Press, 1967).

—— *(Muqaddimah) Le Livre des Exemples*, trans. A. Cheddadi (Paris: Gallimard, 2002).

Ibn Khurradadhbih, Ibn Al-Faqih Al-Hamadhani and Ibn Rustih, *Description du Maghreb et de l'Europe*, Arabic text with French trans. by Muhammad Hadj-Sadok (Algiers: Éditions Carbonel, 1949).

Knott, G. A., "The Historical Sources of Fierabras," *The Modern Language Review*, 52/4 (1957), 504–9.

van Koningsveld, P. S., "Muslim Slaves and Captives in Western Europe During the Late Middle Ages," *Islam and Christian-Muslim Relations*, 6/1 (1995), 5–23.

Kreutz, Barbara, *Before the Normans: Southern Italy in the Ninth and Tenth Centuries* (Philadelphia: University of Pennsylvania Press, 2011).

Lacoste, Yves, "General Characteristics and Fundamental Structures of Mediaeval North African Society," *Economy and Society*, 3 (1974), 1–17.

Lagardère, Vincent, *Les Almoravides Jusqu'au règne de Yusuf b. Tasfin (1039–1106)* (Paris: L'Harmattan, 1989).

Laird, Edgar, "Robert Grosseteste, Albumasar, and Medieval Tidal Theory," *Isis*, 81/4 (1990), 684–94.

Lantschner, Patrick, "Fragmented Cities in the Later Middle Ages: Italy and the Near East Compared," *English Historical Review*, 130/544 (2015), 546–58.

Lapidus, Ira, *Muslim Cities in the Later Middle Ages* (Cambridge, MA: Harvard University Press, 1967).

Laroui, Abdullah, *The History of the Maghreb: An Interpretive Essay*, trans. Ralph Manheim (Princeton: Princeton University Press, 1977).

—— *L'Histoire du Maghreb: un Essai de Synthèse* (Casablanca: Centre Culturel Arabe, 1995).

Lázaro, Fabio L., "The Rise and Global Significance of the First 'West': The Medieval Islamic Maghrib," *Journal of World History*, 24/2 (2013), 259–307.

Le Gall, Michel, and Kenneth J. Perkins (eds.), *The Maghrib in Question: Essays in History and Historiography* (Austin, University of Texas Press, 1997).

Levi Della Vida, G., "Dante et l'Islam d'apres de nouveaux documents," *Revue de la Méditerranée*, 60 (1954).

Lévi-Provençal, Évariste, *Les historiens des Chorfa: Essai sur la littérature historique et biographique au Maroc, du XVIe au XXe siècle* (Paris: Larose, 1922).

—— *Documents inédits d'histoire almohade* (Paris: P. Geuthner, 1928).

—— *Séville Musulmane au Début du XII Siècle: Le Traité d'Ibn 'Abdun* (Paris: Librairie Orientale et Américaine, 1947).

Levy, I. C., *et al.* (eds.), *Nicholas of Cusa and Islam: Polemic and Dialogue in the Late Middle Ages* (Leiden: Brill, 2014).

Lewicki, T., "Une Langue Romane oubliée de l'Afrique du Nord," *Rocznik orientalistyczny*, 17 (1951–2), 415–80.

Lopez, Atanasio, *Memoria Historica de los Obispos de Marruecos desde el siglo XIII* (Madrid, 1920).

Lopez, Molina, "Dos importantes privilegios a los emigrados," *Cuadernos de historia del Islam*, 9 (1979), 5–28.

—— "El globiemo independiente de Menorca," *Revista de Menorca: publicacion del Ateneo Cientifico, Literario y Artistico de Mahon*, LXXIII (1982), 5–88.

Lopez, Robert, "East and West in the Early Middle Ages," in Alfred Havighurst (ed.), *The Pirenne Thesis, Analysis, Critcism and Revision* (Boston: D. C. Heath & Co., 1958), 75.

—— *The Commercial Revolution of the Middle Ages, 950–1350* (Cambridge: Cambridge University Press, 2005).

Lopez, Robert S., *Genova marinara nel duecento: Benedetto Zaccaria, ammiraglio e mercante* (Milan, 1932).

Lower, Michael, "Ibn al-Lihyani: Sultan of Tunis and Would-be Christian Convert (1311–18)," *Mediterranean Historical Review*, 24/1 (2009), 17–27.

Love Jr., Paul M., "The Sufris of Sijilmasa: Toward a History of the Midrarids," *Journal of North African Studies*, 15/2 (2010), 173–88.

Lulle, Ramon, *Disputatio Raymundi christiani et Hamar saraceni* (Pisa, 1308).

Maccoby, Hyam, *Judaism on Trial, Jewish Christian Disputations in the Middle Ages* (including text of disputation) (Oxford: Littman, 1993).

Makhzumi, Ahmad Ibn 'Abd Allah, *Kitab Tahri Mayurqa: cronica arabe de la conquista de Mallorca* (Palma de Mallorca: Universitat de les Illes Balears, 2009).

Al-Makkari [Al-Maqqari], *The History of the Mohammedan Dynasties in Spain*, 2 vols., trans. P. de Gayangos (New York: Routledge, 2002).

Malik, Kenan, "The Failure of Multiculturalism: Community versus Society in Europe," *Foreign Affairs*, March/April (2015).

Mallette, Karla (trans.), *The Kingdom of Sicily, 1100–1250: A Literary History* (Philadelphia: University of Pennsylvania Press, 2005).

Mansouri, M., "Cynophagy, Homosexuality and Anthropology in Medieval Islamic North Africa as Signs of Hospitality," *The Journal of North African Studies*, 20/2 (2015), 128–43, 138.

Marçais, George, "Bidjaya," in *Encyclopedia of Islam*, 2nd edn, eds. P. J. Bearman, *et al.* (Leiden: Brill, 2010), 1204–6.

—— *Les Arabes en Berbérie* (Paris, 1913).

—— "Note sur les ribats en Berbérie," in *Mélanges René Basset*, vol. 2 (Paris: Leroux, 1925), 395–430.

—— "Considerations sur les Villes Musulmanes et Notamment sur le Role du Mohtasib," *Recueils de la Société Jean Bodin* (1954), 249–62.

Marcy, Georges, "Les Phrases berbères des documents inédits almohade d'histoire," *Hespéris*, XII (1932), 61–78.

Al-Marrakushi, 'Abd al-Wahid, *The History of the Almohades: Preceded by a Sketch of the History of Spain from the Time of the Conquest till the Reign of Yúsof ibn-Téshúfín, and of the History of the Almoravides*, 2nd edn, ed. R. P. A. Dozy (Amsterdam: Oriental, 1968).

Mas Latrie, M. L., *Traités de paix et de commerce: Les relations des Chrétiens avec les Arabes de l'Afrique septentrionale*, 2 vols. (Paris, 1886).

Massignon, Louis, "L'Interdit Corporatif à l'encontre des Juifs islamisés à Fés," *Révue du Monde Musulman*, 58 (1924), 221–4.

—— "'Ibn Sab'in et la conspiration anti-hallegienne' en Andalousie et en Orient au XIIIe s.," *Études d'orientalisme dédiées à la mémoire de Lévi-Provençal*, vol. 2 (Paris, 1962), 661–81.

Matthews, Karen, "Other People's Dishes: Islamic Bacini on Eleventh-Century Churches in Pisa," *Gesta*, 53/1 (2014), 5–23.

Mavroudi, Maria, "Translations from Greek into Arabic and Latin during the Middle Ages: Searching for the Classical Tradition," *Speculum*, 90/1 (January 2015).

Menocal, Maria R., *The Ornament of the World: How Muslims, Jews, and Christians Created a Culture of Tolerance in Medieval Spain* (New York: Back Bay Books, 2003).

Messier, Ronald A., "Rethinking the Almoravids, rethinking Ibn Khaldun," in Julia Clancy-Smith (ed.), *North Africa, Islam and the Mediterranean World* (New York: Routledge, 2001), 58–80.

—— *The Almoravids and the Meanings of Jihad* (Santa Barbara: Praeger, 2010).

Metcalfe, Alex, *A History of Muslim Sicily* (Edinburgh: Edinburgh University Press, 2009).

Metcalfe, Alex, and Mariam Rosser-Owen, "Forgotten Connections? Medieval Material Culture and Exchange in the Central and Western Mediterranean," *Al-Masaq*, 25/1 (2013), 1–8.

Monroe, J. T., "Zajal and Muwashshaha: Hispano-Arabic Poetry and the Romance Tradition," in S. K. Jayyusi (ed.), *The Legacy of Muslim Spain* (Leiden: Brill, 1992), 412.

Montada, J. P., "Reason and Reasoning in Ibn Hazm of Cordoba," *Studia Islamica*, 92 (2001), 165–85.

de Montêquin, François-Auguste, "Pérsistance et diffusion de l'esthétique de l'Espagne musulmane en Afrique du Nord," *Maghreb Review*, 10/4–6 (1985), 88–100.

Montgomery, James E., "The Lamp and the Wine Flask," in Anna Akasoy, James Montgomery and Peter E. Pormann (eds.), *Islamic Crosspolinations: Interactions in the Medieval Middle East* (Cambridge: Gibb Memorial Trust, 2007), 149–74.

Musca, Giousè, *L'emirato di Bari, 847–871* (Bari: Dedalo, 1967).

Nakosteen, M., *History of Islamic Origins of Western Education: 800–1350* (Boulder: University of Colorado Press, 1964).

Naylor, Phillip C., *North Africa: A History from Antiquity to the Present* (Austin: University of Texas Press, 2009).

Newton, Francis, "Constantine the African and Montecassino: New Elements and the Text of the Isagoge," in Charles Burnett and Danielle Jacquart (eds.), *Constantine the African and 'Ali ibn al 'Abbas al-Magusi: The Pantegni and Related Texts* (Leiden: Brill, 1994), 16–47.

Nicolaisen, Johannes, *Ecology and Culture of the Pastoral Twareg* (Copenhagen: National Museum of Copenhagen, 1963).

Nirenberg, David, *Communities of Violence* (Princeton: Princeton University Press, 1998).

—— *Neighboring Faiths: Christianity, Islam and Judaism in the Middle Ages and Today* (Chicago: University of Chicago Press, 2014).

Nogales, S. G., "Bibliographfia Sobre las Obras de Averroes," in J. Jolivet (ed.), *Multiple Averroés. Actes du colloque international organisé à l'occasion du 850e anniversaire de la naissance d'Averroes* (Paris: Belles Lettres, 1978), 351–87.

Norris, H. T., *Saharan Myth and Saga* (Oxford: Oxford University Press, 1972).

—— *The Berbers in Arabic Literature* (London: Longman, 1982).

Novati, Gian, *L'Africa d'Italia* (Rome: Carrocci, 2011).

Al-Nu'man, Al-Qadi, *Founding the Fatimid State: The Rise of an Early Islamic Empire*, trans. and annotated Hamid Hajj (London: I. B. Tauris, 2006).

Osborne, John, "The Portrait of Pope Leo IV in San Clemente, Rome: A Re-Examination of the So-Called 'Square' Nimbus, in Medieval Art," *Papers of the British School at Rome*, 47 (1979), 58–65.

Palmer, James, *The Apocalypse in the Early Middle Ages* (Cambridge: Cambridge University Press, 2014).

Penda, Salvador, and Miguel Vega, "The Qu'anic symbol of fish on Hammudid coins: Al-Khidr and the holy geography of the Straits of Gibraltar," *Al-Andalus Magreb*, 13 (2006), 269–84.

Pirenne, Henri, *Medieval Cities, Their Origins and the Revival of Trade* (Princeton: Princeton University Press, 1969).

—— *Mahomet et Charlemagne* (Paris: Presses Universitaires de France, 1992).

—— *Mohammed and Charlemagne* (New York: Routledge, 2008 [originally published 1939]).

de Planhol, Xavier, *L'Islam et la Mer: La Mosquee et le Matelot (VIIe–XXe siècle)* (Paris: Perrin, 2000).

Poncet, J., "Le mythe de la catastrophe hilalienne," *Annales ESC*, 22 (1967), 1099–120.

Powers, David S., *Law, Society, and Culture in the Maghrib, 1300–1500* (Cambridge: Cambridge University Press, 2002).

Prevost, Virginie, "Les derniéres communatés chrétiennes autochones d'Afrique du Nord," *Revue de l'histoire des religions*, 4 (2007), 461–83.

Pryor, John, "The Origins of the Commenda Contract," *Speculum*, 52/1 (1977), 5–37.

Rahman, Fazlur, *Islam* (Chicago: University of Chicago Press, 1979).

Reginald of Durham, "Life of St. Godric," trans. and ed. G. C. Coulton, *Social Life in Britain* (Cambridge University Press, 1918), 415–20.

Regn, G., and B. Huss, "Petrarch's Rome: The History of the *Africa* and the Renaissance Project," *Modern Language Notes Italian Edition*, 124/1 (2009), 86–102.

Renan, Ernest, *Averroés et l'Averroisme* (Paris: Maisonneuve, 2002).

Ridley, R. T., "To be taken with a pinch of salt: the destruction of Carthage," *Classical Philology*, 81 (1986), 140–6.

Robinson, Cynthia, *Medieval Andalusian Courtly Culture in the Mediterranean: Hadith Bayad wa Riyad* (New York: Routledge, 2010).

—— "The Aljafería in Saragossa and Taifa Spaces," in M. Menocal *et al.* (eds.), *The Literature of al Andalus* (Cambridge: Cambridge University Press, 2012), 233–4.

Rogers, P. G., *A History of Anglo-Moroccan Relations to 1900* (London: Foreign and Commonwealth Office, 1972).

Rosenthal, Erwin, *Averroes' Commentary on Plato's "Republic"* (Cambridge: Cambridge University Press, 1956).

—— *Political Thought in Medieval Islam* (Cambridge: Cambridge University Press, 1958).

Rosenthal, Franz, *The Classical Heritage in Islam* (New York: Routledge Reprint, 1994).

Rosser-Owen, Mariam, "Andalusi Spolia in Medieval Morocco: Architectural Politics, Political Architecture," *Medieval Encounters*, 20/1 (2014), 152–98.

Roth, Norman, "The Kahina: Legendary Material in the Accounts of the 'Jewish Berber Queen,'" *Maghreb Review*, 7/5–6 (1982), 122–5.

Rouighi, Ramzi, *The Making of a Mediterranean Emirate: Ifriqiya and Its Andalusis, 1200–1400* (Philadelphia: University of Pennsylvania Press, 2011).

Ruggles, D. F., "The Alcazar of Seville in Mudejar Architecture," *Gesta*, 43/2 (2004), 87–98.

Runciman, Steven, *The Sicilian Vespers: A History of the Mediterranean World in the Later Thirteenth Century* (Cambridge: Cambridge University Press, 1992).

Russell, Gerard, *Heirs to Forgotten Kingdoms* (New York: Basic Books, 2014).

Ryan, Michael, *A Kingdom of Stargazers: Astrology and Authority in the Late Medieval Crown of Aragon* (Ithaca: Cornell University Press, 2011).

Saada, L., *La Geste hilalienne* (Paris: Gallimard, 1985).

Sabra, Adam, *Poverty and Charity in Medieval Islam* (Cambridge: Cambridge University Press, 2006).

Salgado, Felipe Maillo, "Precisiones para la historia de un grupo éthnico-religioso: Los Farfanes," *Al Qantara*, 4 (1983), 265–81.

Saliba, Therese, Carolyn Allen and Judith A. Howard (eds.), *Gender, Politics and Islam* (University of Chicago Press, 2002).

Savage, Elizabeth, *A Gateway to Hell, A Gateway to Paradise: The North African Response to the Arab Conquest* (Princeton: Darwin Press, 1997).

Scales, Peter, *The Fall of the Caliphate of Cordoba: Berbers and Arabs in Conflict* (Leiden: Brill, 1994).

Schirmann, H., *New Hebrew Poems from the Genizah* (Jerusalem, 1965).

Schmidt, Nathaniel, "The Manuscripts of Ibn Khaldun," *Journal of the American Oriental Society*, 46 (1926), 171–6.

Scott, Emmet, *Mohammed and Charlemagne Revisted: The History of a Controversy* (London: New English Review Press, 2012).

Scott, Samuel P. (trans.), *Las Siete Partidas*, 5 vols., ed. Robert Burns (Philadelphia: University of Pennsylvania Press, 2001).

Sebag, Paul, "Les Expéditions Maritimes arabes du VIII siècle," *Les Cahiers de Tunisie*, 8/31 (1960), 73–82.

—— *Tunis: Historie d'une Ville* (Paris: L'Harmattan, 1998).

—— *Histoire des Juifs de Tunisie* (Paris: L'Harmattan, 2000).

Sewell, William H., *Logics of History: Social Theory and Social Transformation* (Chicago, University of Chicago Press, 1995).

Sezgin, Fuat (ed.), *Constantinus Africanus (11th century) and his Arabic sources: texts and studies* (Frankfurt am Main: Institute for the History of Arabic-Islamic Science at the Johann Wolfgang Goethe University, 1996).

Al-Shadhili, *The Mystical Teachings of Al-Shadhili*, trans. Elmer Douglas (Albany: SUNY Press, 1993).

Shahrastani, Muhammad, *Muslim Sects and Divisions*, trans. A. K. Kazi (New York: Routledge, 2014).

Shatzmiller, Maya, *The Berbers and the Islamic State: The Marinid Experience in Pre-Protectorate Morocco* (Princeton: Marcus Weiner, 2000).

Siedentop, Larry, *Inventing the Individual: The Origins of Western Liberalism* (Cambridge, MA: Harvard University (Belknap) Press, 2014).

Singer, C., *The Earliest Chemical Industry: An Essay in the Historical Relations of Economics and Technology Illustrated from the Alum Trade* (London: The Folio Society, 1948).

Skinner, Patricia, "Amalfitans in the Caliphate of Cordoba – Or Not?" *Al-Masaq*, 24/2 (2012), 125–38.

Slaughter, Jane, *et al.*, *Sharing the Stage: biography and gender in Western civilization*, vol. 1 (Independence: Cengage Learning, 2008).

Soler, G., "Caballeros españoles en Africa y Africanos en España," *Revue Hispanique*, 12 (1905), 299–372.

van Staevel, Jean-Pierre, "Prévoir, Juguler, Bâtir," *Cuadernos de Madinat al-Zahra*, 5 (2004), 31–52.

Stantchev, Stefan, *Spiritual Rationality: Papal Embargo as Cultural Practice* (Oxford: Oxford University Press, 2014).

Stowasser, Barbara, *Religion and Political Development: Some Comparative Ideas on Ibn Khaldun and Machiavelli* (Washington, DC: Georgetown University Press, 1983).

Strauss, Leo, *Persecution and the Art of Writing* (Chicago: University of Chicago Press, 1988).

Strickland, Debra, *Saracens, Demons and Jews* (Princeton: Princeton University Press, 2003).

Tabbaa, Yasser, "Andalusian Roots and Abbasid Homage in the Qubbat al-Barudiyyin in Marrkech," *Muqarnas*, 25 (2008), 133–46.

Talbi, Mohamed, *L'emirat aglabide* (Paris: Librairie d'Amérique et d'Orient, 1966).

—— "Al-Kahina," in *The Encyclopedia of Islam*, 2nd edn, eds. P. J. Bearman, *et al.* (Leiden: Brill, 2010), 422–3.

Terrasse, H., *Villes Impériales du Maroc* (Grenoble: Arthaud, 1937).

Thébert, Yvon, and Jean-Louis Biget, "L'Afrique après la disparition de la cité classique: Cohérence et ruptures dans l'histoire maghrébine," in *L'Afrique dans L'Occident romain, Collection de l'école française de Rome 134* (Rome: École Français de Rome, 1990), 575–602.

Thomas, David *et al.* (eds.), *Christian-Muslim Relations: A Bibliographical History*, vols. I–V (Leiden: Brill, 2012).

Tieszen, Charles L., *Christian Identity Amid Islam in Medieval Spain* (Leiden: Brill, 2013).

Tisserant, Eugène, and Gaston Wiet, "Une Lettre de l'almohade Murtada au pape Innocent IV," *Hespéris*, 6 (1926), 27–54.

Tolan, John, *Petrus Alfonsi and his Medieval Readers* (Gainesville: University Press of Florida, 1993).

—— *Saracens* (Columbia: Columbia University Press, 2002).

—— *St. Francis and the Sultan: The Curious History of a Christian-Muslim Encounter* (Oxford: Oxford University Press, 2009).

Tolan, John, G. Veinstein and H. Laurens, *Europe and the Islamic World: A History* (Princeton: Princeton University Press, 2013).

Toledano, J. M., "Documents from manuscripts," *Hebrew Union College Annual*, 4 (1927), 449–58.

Tourmede, Anselme, *Pourquoi J'ai Embrassé L'Islam* (Perpignan: Éditions de la Merci, 2009).

Le Tourneau, Roger, *The Almohad Movement in North Africa in the Twelfth and Thirteenth Centuries* (Princeton: Princeton University Press, 1969).

Ibn Tumart, *Le Livre de Mohammed Ibn Toumert*, ed. I. Goldziher (Algiers, 1903).

Al-Umari, Ibn Fadl Allah, *Masalik al-Absar fi mamalik al amsar*, ed. Abdulwahab, partial trans. M. Gaudefroy-Demombynes (Paris: Geuthner, 1927).

Urvoy, Dominique, *Pensers d'Al-Andalus: La Vie Intellectuelle à Cordue et Seville au Temps des Empires Berbères* (Toulouse: Presses Universitaires du Mirail, 1990).

—— *Ibn Rushd (Averroes)* (London: Routledge, 1991).

Vajda, G., and M. T. D'Alveny, "Marc de Tolede, traducteur d'Ibn Tumart," *Al-Andalus*, 16 (1951), 259–307.

Valérian, Dominique, "Ifriqiyan Muslim Merchants in the Mediterranean at the End of the Middle Ages," *Mediterranean Historical Review*, 14/2 (1999), 47–66.

—— *Bougie, Port Maghribin, 1067–1510* (Rome: Publications de l'École française de Rome, 2006).

Viguera-Molins, María J., "Al-Andalus and the Maghrib (From the fifth/eleventh century to the fall of the Almoravids)," in M. Fierro (ed.), *The New Cambridge History of Islam*, vol. 2 (Cambridge: Cambridge University Press, 2010), 21–47.

Vilá, Bosch, *Los Almorávides* (Granada: Universidad de Granada, 1990).

Virani, Shafique, *The Ismailis in the Middle Ages: A History of Survival, a Search for Salvation* (Oxford: Oxford University Press, 2007).

Visonà, P. J., "Passing the salt. On the destruction of Carthage again," *Classical Philology*, 83 (1988), 41–2.

Wahab, H. H. Abdul, "Coup d'oeil général sur les apports ethniques étrangers en Tunisie," *Revue Tunisienne* (1917), 305–16.

Walsh, Sebastain, "Killing Post-Almohad Man: Malek Bennabi, Algerian Islamism and the Search for Liberal Governance," *Journal of North African History*, 12/2 (2007), 235–54.

Waltz, James, "Muhammad and the Muslims in St. Thomas Aquinas," *The Muslim World*, 66/2 (1976), 81–95.

Watt, Montgomery, *The Faith and Practice of Al-Ghazali* (Crows Nest: Allen and Unwin, 1953).

Weber, Max, *On Charisma and Institution Building*, ed. S. Eisenstadt (Chicago, University of Chicago Press, 1968).

Wendover, Roger, *Roger Wendover's Flowers of History*, vol. 2 (London: H. G. Bohn, 1849).

Whalen, Brett, "Corresponding with Infidels: Rome, the Almohads and the Christians of Thirteenth Century Morocco," *Journal of Medieval and Early Modern Studies*, 41/3 (2011), 487–513.

Wheatly, Paul, *The Places Where Men Pray Together* (Chicago, University of Chicago Press, 2001).

Woepcke, François, "Recherches sur les sciences mathématiques chez les orientaux," *Journal Asiatique*, 24 (1854), 348–84.

—— "The Autobiography of Leonardo Pisano," *Journal Asiatique*, 24 (1854), 101.

Wright, J., and E. Rowson, *Homoeroticism in Classical Arabic Literature* (New York: Columbia University Press, 1997).

Al-Ya'qubi, *Les pays*, trans. G. Wiét (Cairo, 1937).

Yayha, Al-Shadhili Bu, *La vie littéraire en Ifriqiya sous les Zirides (362–555 de l'H./ 972–1160 de J.-C.)* (Tunis: STD, 1972).

Zar', Ali Ibn Abd Allah Ibn Abi, *Rawd Al-Qirtas*, 2nd edn (Valencia: Anubar Ediciones, 1964).

Zuwiyya, D., *Islamic Legends Concerning Alexander the Great* (Albany: SUNY Press, 2001).

INDEX